CHILDREN'S READING IN THE HOME

MAY HILL ARBUTHNOT

SCOTT, FORESMAN AND COMPANY

PREFACE

Parents, grandparents, uncles, aunts, teachers, librarians, and all who are interested in children's reading in the home, this book is especially for you.

It is planned to guide you through the morass of today's books for children to a small choice selection of many sorts of books, both old and recent, books too good to miss.

As the selection of books was made, the child himself kept determining choices and rejections. What was he like at two or six or ten? What were his varying problems and interests and needs at different ages? Obviously, there is no such thing as *the* perfect book for the ten-year-old. But then there is also no such thing as *the* ten-year-old. There are ten-year-olds and ten-year-olds, and they differ as widely as forty-year-olds. For your special ten-year-old, though, there are many wonderful books at his particular level of maturity and reading skills and for his particular interests. This book has been planned to help you find such books. Also, it is to be hoped that this selection of books and the criteria developed in the chapters will help you choose among the hundreds of new children's books coming out each year.

Some six hundred books for children are discussed, and still one or more of your favorites will be missing—some by chance but others because for one reason or another they have been rejected by today's children. And you will find a few books that are useful but not great by literary standards—the easy-to-read books, for example, in Chapter 5. Again the child himself determined the choices—in this instance, his need for books high in interest but written simply enough for his uncertain reading skills.

Part One, the first three chapters of this book, describes good home environment for reading and ways to promote lasting interest in books. Part Two, the next seven chapters, discusses books

Library of Congress Catalog Card Number 68-31567

according to very general age ranges—for example, books for the prereader (two to six) in Chapter 4; books for children beginning to read (six, seven, and eight) in Chapter 5. Every chapter has a brief introductory discussion of the variations to be expected of children in that age bracket—their uneven growth, physically and socially, and their extreme differences in reading skills and interests. These discussions should give some general clues to possible book interests. Within each of these chapters, annotations are grouped according to broad types of books—folk tales, modern fantasy, historical fiction, and so on. Part Three, the last four chapters, discusses books according to children's special reading interests—poetry, biography, informational books, and books on religion and the arts. Throughout, the annotations for most books are fairly detailed to help you gauge more surely whether or not the content will intrigue your young readers, hold their attention, and keep them reading with enjoyment.

Even though the books so annotated are selective rather than inclusive, your children will reject some of them, and that is to be expected. But the books children really love, they will cherish and reread many times. As children grow and change, try to expose them to a healthy variety of books. They are sure they know what they like, but they don't know all the kinds of books they might like if they encountered them. So as has been indicated, the lists include books about today's world, historical fiction, biography, pure fantasy, poetry, animal stories, and informational books—those listed, by the way, are only a trickle from the great flood of informational books that threatens to overwhelm us these days.

Limited as the lists are, the offering is rich and impressive. And don't hesitate to skip around in this book to find what you want. For instance, do not observe the suggested age ranges rigidly. After you have read the descriptions of children at certain age ranges, you may decide that your child or children are more mature or less so. If your children seem more advanced dip into the chapter at the next level; or if your children need to proceed at an easier pace, turn back to the preceding chapter. No need to worry either, for after all, some of the masterly books written for the youngest children are enjoyed, as one man said about *Ferdinand* and *Charlotte's Web*, "from the nursery to the night club."

The illustrations have been chosen not only to introduce you and your children to some distinguished artists but to give you lively clues to the content, manner, and mood of the books. Your child may look at one of these pictures and say, "I want that story." It sometimes happens.

It is hoped that the book lists will meet your children's changing needs, and so make them converts to reading forevermore. Where else can they so readily find comfort or inspiration, laughter or tears, insight, knowledge, and dreams? May you and your children grow joyfully with books.

Acknowledgments

No author ever felt more grateful to children's librarians than the author of this book. In Cleveland, Margaret Clark, Ruth Hadlow, Adeline Corrigan, and Winifred Macham have unfailingly supplied me with the needed book at the crucial moment. In the Pasadena Public Library, Mildred Phipps and her staff have done the same, and all these librarians have shared with me their experiences in bringing children and books together. The editorial staff of Scott, Foresman acknowledges the same indebtedness to the children's librarians of Oak Park, Glenview, Evanston, and the Center for Children's Books, University of Chicago. Where would authors and editors be without dedicated librarians?

My special indebtedness is to Frances Ekins of Scott, Foresman, who has worked with me since 1945 with unfailing patience and perspicacity; to B. Kathleen Shamp of the Cleveland Public Library, who prepared the annotations for "Books on Music and Musicians" in Chapter 14; and to Margaret Clark, Head of the Lewis Carroll Room, Cleveland Public Library, who has read galleys with her usual thoroughness and so made the completion of this book easier for my faulty vision.

To all these and more my heartfelt thanks.

Cleveland   May Hill Arbuthnot
1968

CONTENTS

3

READING IN SPECIAL AREAS

PART ONE
ENJOYING BOOKS IN THE FAMILY

WHO READS BOOKS?

❖❧❦❖

1

A father, finding a book among his birthday presents, held it up with mock surprise and exclaimed, "Look, it's a book! Does anybody read books anymore?" Considering all the pressures of modern life, to say nothing of the ubiquitous television, it was a fair question.

People *are* busy these days. The average mother is doing her own housework and running a taxi service for the family, and she is probably also helping with various school, church, and civic activities or may even be holding down a full-time outside job. Fathers, too, regardless of their regular work, are usually also doing their stints in Scouting, 4-H, and Little League activities, and in assorted church and civic associations. The children in their hours after school have assignments to prepare or errands to run for mother, or they are busy pursuing their current hobbies or taking music, dancing, or skating lessons. In the evening, if the parents and children are home, both entertainment and information are available on radio and television. Moreover, some of these programs bring the family together as a contented unit. Why, then, make the effort to read books? As a matter of fact, *do* people read books anymore?

Happily, librarians, backed by circulation statistics, reply, "Yes, people do read, both children and adults, more books than ever before." Furthermore, their reports are confirmed by the astonishing publication figures for paperback as well as hardback books. And teachers tell of their children's intense delight in each bright new allotment of books for the school library or in a fresh selection of books for the classroom.

The formats of books today are alluring, with gay, handsome jackets—the publishers' enticing leads into the books just inside the front flaps. And don't think the canny children have not learned to use those summaries in selecting their books. The paper and print of books are better than ever, and the illustrations are so beautiful they should break down the resistance of the most determined nonreader. Finally, the content of the new books is so varied, from accurate information to beguiling fantasy, that there is a book to meet almost any interest at any stage of life. In spite of these encouraging facts, a question remains: Why are some children eager readers while others—both children and adults—never voluntarily touch a book? Environment undoubtedly is a first clue.

HOME ENVIRONMENT FOR READING

When parents say, "My children just don't seem to have time for reading—they aren't much interested in books," it usually means that the parents "aren't much interested in books" either. Generally, children who like to read come from families where reading is taken for granted and books are all about the house, not according to an interior decorator's plan, but according to use and convenience. There are overflowing bookshelves with some of them set aside for the children's books, and there are also books in every room. In addition to cookbooks, the kitchen may have the novel mother is currently reading and a book or two of poetry for those odd moments when she must wait for the pot to boil. In the living room, beside father's easy chair, there is a table for his newspaper, trade magazines, and the books he wants. Books are found on bedside tables, on window sills, and even occasionally on chairs where the interrupted reader has left his book hoping for a speedy return. A dictionary and an atlas lie open near the television set. In short, this is the bookish house of a reading family. Eleanor Farjeon describes such a home:

> In the home of my childhood there was a room we called "The Little Bookroom." True, every room in the house could have been called a bookroom. Our nurseries upstairs were full of books. Downstairs my father's study was full of them. They lined the diningroom walls, and overflowed into my mother's sitting room, and up into the bedrooms. It would have been more natural to live without clothes than without books. As unnatural not to read as not to eat.[1]

Nowadays, with space at a premium, a home like Eleanor Farjeon's would be difficult to duplicate. Even children living in luxury apartments or expensive new suburban houses may not know such homes. They may be familiar with built-in ovens, built-in bars, and built-in television sets but not with a shelf for books, built in or not. And hundreds of thousands of children growing up in overcrowded city dwellings not only have never seen a bookshelf in a home but have never known an adult who ever owned a book. For those children there may never be any examples of reading adults in their environment. Teachers and librarians, then, must furnish books and the incentives to reading. A bookless environment is something to be coped with in one way or another. Bookshelves, for instance, may be made of the ever handy orange crate, painted and tucked into one small space or another. Books, at first, may be temporary loans from the public library, housed carefully on shelves prepared for them. And somehow from this beginning, the image of book ownership may grow. Books may suddenly seem precious, even essential.

THE PUBLIC LIBRARY

This suggests the need for all children to be introduced to our public libraries, because whether a home is spacious and supplied with many books, or small and cramped with no books at all, chil-

---

[1]Eleanor Farjeon, *The Little Bookroom*, Walck, 1956, p. vii.

dren should discover early the resources of public libraries. It is a tremendous experience for a small child to walk into a large library and see stacks and stacks of books. Do you remember in William Saroyan's *The Human Comedy*, Lionel and Ulysses, neither of whom could read, exploring the public library?

> . . . they entered an area of profound and almost frightening silence. . . . Lionel not only whispered, he moved on tiptoe. Lionel whispered because he was under the impression that it was out of respect for books, not consideration for readers. . . . "These," he said, "And those over there. And these. All books, Ulysses." He stopped a moment to think. "I wonder what they say in all these books. . . ."
>
> A little frightened at what he was doing, Lionel lifted the book out of the shelf, held it in his hands a moment and then opened it. "There, Ulysses!" he said. "A book! There it is! See?" . . . He looked at the print of the book with a kind of reverence, whispering to himself as if he were trying to read. Then he shook his head. "You can't know what a book says, Ulysses, unless you can read, and I can't read," he said.[2]

But wouldn't you wager that Lionel was eager and ready when the time came for him to learn to read?

Now that the dark fortress-type of library architecture is giving way to sunny daylight or brightly illuminated buildings gay with color, the public library has become one of the most inviting spots in our towns and cities. Even in old buildings, the children's rooms are invariably warm and appealing places, thanks to imaginative librarians. Sometimes there are fireplaces with real fires to add glamor to the story hour. Often there are plants, pictures, little storybook figurines, easy chairs, even rocking chairs, and everywhere enticing displays of books for all ages. What a pity Lionel and Ulysses did not discover such a room, with a friendly librarian ready to steer them over to the picture books, just right for them to "read."

Public libraries are also full of invitations to adults to look at, read, or take home to read all sorts of intriguing books. There are small open shelves with the latest fiction on display, even stands

[2]William Saroyan, *The Human Comedy*, Harcourt, 1944, pp. 200-203.

with whodunits, paperback and hardback, right up to the minute. For more serious readers there are groups of substantial books on world affairs to catch the eye and hold the interest. There are innumerable books in the fields of the sciences, and of child care and homemaking books there is no end. Mothers soon learn to find and use these compendiums of recent information from child psychology to gourmet cooking or plumbing repairs. There are even "Reading Counselors" in our large city libraries to advise adults who may wish to begin a systematic reading program in one field or another. In short, the modern public library sets up book displays and irresistible invitations to reading for all ages and interests. So parents who begin taking their children to the public library for story hours or for looking with the children's librarian through an enticing table full of picture stories, may find plenty to do with their spare time, browsing profitably through the adult book displays.

In the young child's first visits to the library, his mother or father must stay with him, of course, until he is familiar with the place and the librarians, and feels secure. In the beginning, parents will also select books for this youngest literary explorer to take home. Such aid will lessen as the child grows older but should not entirely cease, because children are likely to fall into reading ruts—all horse stories or fairy tales or exceedingly easy, oversimplified books. Keeping an eye on a child's choice of books should continue without becoming too intrusive or compulsive. After all, adults do not read at a Shakespeare level continuously. To be sure, there are some books the child wants and needs again and again. In Julia Sauer's book *Mike's House*, the little boy called the library "Mike's House," because that was where he found his favorite book—*Mike Mulligan and His Steam Shovel*,[3] by Virginia Burton. That child really should have owned the book, but if ownership was impossible, what a blessing that he discovered "Mike's House." On the other hand, adolescent girls may not need to own a book like Maureen Daly's *Seventeenth Summer*, but they will certainly enjoy it when the problems common to teen-age girls begin to bother them. So there are many books that command a temporary but, while it lasts, strong interest, and these interests may be as well satisfied by library withdrawal as by ownership.

Another tremendous service a library can render both homes and

[3]Most of the children's books mentioned in this chapter are discussed elsewhere in this book. To locate these discussions, check the index.

schools is to supply quantities of those books which bridge the gap between inefficient, slow reading and skilled reading. By third and fourth grade that gap can assume discouraging proportions for some ' children. For instance, a child may have only first- or second-grade reading ability, but he may be capable of comprehending and enjoying the content of fifth-, sixth-, or seventh-grade-level books which he cannot possibly read for himself. Then teachers of reading usually suggest that the child be provided with easy-to-read books for his own age level so that he can acquire the confidence that comes from a sense of comfortable fluency. These are not always books parents wish to buy, but the library can supply them and can also provide lists which help parents and teachers locate more such books if a child needs them.

From *Mike Mulligan and His Steam Shovel* by Virginia Burton. Copyright 1939 by Houghton Mifflin Company. Reprinted by permission of the publishers.

THE READING FAMILY

In homes where books are prized both by children and grown-ups, birthdays and Christmas are made doubly important by book acquisitions. For instance, in one home a child gradually acquired a complete set of Laura Ingalls Wilder's *Little House* books for her very own. One boy collected a good basic group of science books. In another home, where family councils were the rule, the members chose an encyclopedia rather than barbecue equipment, on the somewhat utilitarian grounds that the barbecue could only be used part of the year, while the encyclopedia was practically a necessity the year round. Even the die-hard holdouts for the barbecue rejoiced when the encyclopedia in all its glory was unpacked and placed on a shelf. Everyone had something to look up, and mother had the inspiration to look up *cats* with the four-year-old cat-lover. They looked at the pictures together, and mother read enough to satisfy him of the worth of this imposing set of books. This is a good way to help prereaders and reluctant readers form the reference habit. Use the reference books with them, read the information to them if necessary, and explain how you found the information, so that they will know how to use such books when they are on their own in reading. And what better investment for a growing family than a fine encyclopedia?

These examples are typical of the fact that in bringing children and books happily together, the family group has certain advantages over schoolrooms and libraries. And by the way, "family group" may be mother, father, and children, or it may vary greatly and still be a stable family—it may be a close group deprived of one parent or it may include a stepfather or stepmother, or there may be a trusted maid or housekeeper or (and this is less frequent today) there may be one or both grandparents in the group. But whatever the group, if the adults give the children a feeling of love, understanding, and stability, then it is a "family" in the best sense of the word.

In the everyday framework of a home, reading adults encounter the child on an informal, intimate basis that no institution can fully simulate. Mother chants *Mother Goose* jingles while she irons, or she reads some of her favorite poems aloud or tells a story while she makes applesauce, and the youngest child is entranced. Father shares his *National Geographic* with his six-year-old, explaining and interpreting at six-year-old level as the two of them pore over the pictures. One adult recalls happily the hair-raising ghost and banshee stories with which a beloved Irish maid used to regale him and his brothers and sisters. A young woman cherishes the memories of a great aunt who read aloud to the whole family, and from the oldest to the youngest held them spellbound. And a boy developed a lifelong interest in history from his grandfather's tales of long ago. Such informal experiences introduce children painlessly to literature of many kinds enhanced by the prestige of adult enthusiasm. These are experiences long remembered and they send a child off to school with a vocabulary and a literary appreciation well above the average.

TELEVISION, RADIO, AND BOOKS

To all of this, the objection may still be raised that so much emphasis on books and reading is unrealistic today, when television and radio supply the family with admirable and effortless entertainment and information. This is partially true. Actually, some of the programs send children and adults to the very books we would like them to read. Furthermore, in radio and television programs great conductors lead orchestras and distinguished actors present whole plays that many of us cannot hope to hear and see first hand. Notable experts in many fields discuss their areas of specialization or exploration, and such programs may well touch off new interests in the viewers and lead to completely new reading interests.

Such radio and television programs are good, but their availability should not obscure the fact that children's passive viewing may steadily increase to include a lot of trivialities which crowd out reading, school work, and out-of-door play. Television viewing can become, both for children and adults, a lazy evasion of work and responsibility. Worse still, if the youngsters are not supervised, their selection of programs may include much that is decidedly unwholesome. In any media, the trivial, trashy, or predominantly violent and sensational is poor fare for children.

It is also well to recognize the fact that the offerings on television and radio often have a curious evanescence which is not conducive either to concentration or to a thoughtful response. The programs come and go with such rapidity and are immediately replaced by something unrelated and equally evanescent, that there is no time to think about them or, of course, to turn back and listen again. Commercials with their infectious ditties or loud-voiced insistence are another distraction. They break the continuity of programs and lessen their chance of making much of an impression. No one wants to remember the tooth paste, chewing gum, and cigarette commercials, but their repetitious slogans and catchy tunes compel memorization while serious documentaries may be forgotten. Children sing the commercials and forget the words of the national anthem! Compared with the viewing of a brief and frequently interrupted television story, reading a book is a slower and more challenging process. There is time to go back and reread what is memorable or to stop and think over or check or verify something that seems doubtful or that calls for more information. The continuity of a book makes for concentration, an ever increasing attention span, and the likelihood that what is read understandingly will be remembered. These are the values—concentration, attention span, and recall—that are dissipated by television breaks and by long periods of viewing brief unrelated programs. All these points are true for adults as well as children.

Not that these flaws mean that television and radio should be banished from the home. Far from it. There are too many significant programs which the whole family can enjoy together—national and international events, for example, that we could neither see nor hear in person. But here are some questions grownups in the family might well ask themselves to determine whether or not a program is suitable for home viewing: (1) Are the subjects of the program and the children's interest compatible? (2) Is the emotional tone of the program wholesome and at the child's level? or (3) Is there a preponderance of brutality and violence? (4) Is the humor really gay and amusing? (5) Are the characters stereotypes (monsters, outlaws, lazy Jacks or Janes) or convincing, real people? (6) Is the theme basic to children's better understanding of life and social relationships? (7) Does the action of the plot develop logically and reasonably? (8) Is the news objectively reported? (9) Is the advertising decently honest? (10) Does it interrupt too frequently and insistently? Some of these questions are bound to be answered negatively, and are then worth discussing frankly in the family group. In fact, family discussions of programs are the best way of developing critical judgment and also appreciation. At the present time, some of our finest programs suffer from the most repulsive and repetitious advertising, and apparently all the public can do is to grin and bear it. But a critical family approach to these problems may help today's children do something about them tomorrow. And meanwhile, let's encourage with praise and attention some of the marvelous programs our mass media provide today.

PROGRESS IN THE QUALITY OF READING

Of course, people are still reading despite the lure of radio and television. And through the guidance of librarians, teachers, and parents, children progress from the easy reading of comics and second-rate books to better written books with more significant content at each age level. At this point, it might be well to ask ourselves if the grownups in the family make comparable progress. Or have they, for instance, settled down to endless mystery tales or slick romances, about as challenging as a tranquilizer? Or are newspapers and pictorial magazines their sole or chief reading material? How about a substantial biography for a change or one of the Great Books series or a timely and authoritative book on some phase of our muddled world affairs? Then, having checked our own reading habits, we may be more aware of our children's progress or lack of progress in reading maturity. For after all, parents have a better opportunity than either teachers or librarians for a closeup of children's overall book consumption. It may be either mother or father who notices that John has taken off on space fiction to the exclusion of any other kind of reading, or that Nancy reads nothing but horse stories. Instead of disapproving of these obsessions, which are probably only temporary, the wise parent simply provides a related book with a lead in another direction. For the boy, perhaps a biography of Jules Verne, "father of modern inventions," based on science. For the girl, perhaps Archie Binns' *Sea Pup*, centered on the boy rather than on the animal. What you offer as a substitute will depend, of course, on the age of the child. In one family, the boy was so fact minded that he was in danger of settling into a tight literalness, and so his father started reading aloud Keith Robertson's *Henry Reed, Inc.*, hoping the boy would see the joke of scientific, humorless Henry, and he did. Later, the boy was so captivated by the archaeological background of Harry Behn's *The Faraway Lurs* that he read and reread the book and commented to his mother, "Well, maybe it didn't happen that way, but the author makes it seem so. Wow, what an ending!" Perhaps father or mother watches the volumes of fiction building up on the children's bookshelves to see that if horse stories predominate for a spell, historical fiction and biography make their appearance. Fantasy is kept in balance. There are a few "funny books" and a few classics such as *The Wind in the Willows, Adventures of Tom Sawyer, The Odyssey,* and *Robin Hood,* and in each category there are choice selections. As parents look at their children's bookshelves, it is to be hoped that they can smile to themselves at the special interests and maturity levels the books represent, and that they can take pride in what the

Illustration by Robert McCloskey. From *Henry Reed, Inc.* by Keith Robertson. Copyright © 1958 by Keith Robertson. Reprinted by permission of The Viking Press, Inc.

range of books means. When readers, for example, have grown from Wanda Gág's *Millions of Cats* to Rosemary Sutcliff's *Warrior Scarlet,* they have grown and grown well.

When the children go off to college, an amusing thing may happen. They may take along a dog-eared book or two from their childhood collections. They think they are going to reread them. Usually they don't, but that favorite book sitting on the bookshelf of a strange room in a faraway college dormitory speaks to them warmly of home. "Mother read that book aloud." Or "Father and I picked out that book." Or "Pete and I read and reread that book I don't know how many times." The book is their symbol of home, family, and good times together. They'll keep that book for their own children. It is part of their sense of family, which they in turn mean to create. This is one of the many rewards for family reading, for buying books and sharing them in read-aloud sessions. Families that send their children out of the home knowing good books of many kinds—honest, dependable books, sensibly written and absorbing, written with imagination and beauty or fun—have given their children a lifelong source of strength and enjoyment.

CHOOSING
BOOKS
FOR
CHILDREN

2

First Aids to Book Selection
Children's Needs
Literary Yardsticks for Children's Books
Criteria for Books Other Than Fiction
Bibliography

If the grownups in a family are bookish individuals, they generally hope that their children will be too. But how can they bring this about? They realize that hundreds and hundreds of books for children have been published since Louisa May Alcott's *Little Women*, Mark Twain's *Adventures of Tom Sawyer*, Kate Seredy's *The Good Master*, Carol Ryrie Brink's *Caddie Woodlawn*, and Esther Forbes' *Johnny Tremain*, or any of the other books they read and loved as children. Among these hundreds and hundreds of books both old and new, how can they find the best for their children?

FIRST AIDS TO BOOK SELECTION

The quickest and the easiest way to discover the best children's books is to consult a children's librarian, who will not only be glad to advise you but will probably provide you with lists of books grouped by age or grade levels or sometimes by special subjects—science books, animal stories, fairy tales, picture stories, biography, and the like. If your community lacks a public library, consult the librarians of the county or state libraries. Those in charge of either one of these agencies will undoubtedly supply you with lists of books or the books themselves. The various library services in the United States are astonishingly active and useful and nearly always include one specialist in children's literature.

From one source or another, you can always obtain good general lists of children's books. A selection of such lists has been included in the bibliography following this chapter. This entire book is actually another such list, because each chapter provides discussions of many of the best books in the different areas. This chapter is designed to give parents a running start on sources of books so that they can stay a couple of jumps ahead of the children whose book needs they are trying to supply.

But far better than choosing books from a list is reading children's books or at least skimming them, and then deciding for yourself what books are for your child at each age and what few special books you simply can't bear to have him miss. *Children's Books Too Good to Miss*, by the way, is the title of a list of some two hundred and sixty books. Among these choice books there will probably be some of your own favorites remembered from childhood. But be warned—some old books have stood the test of time with undiminished popularity, while others have been replaced by books that are far better written and have greater child appeal. Antiquity is no guarantee of excellence any more than recency is an indication of triviality or mediocrity. Be alert, also, to the fact that your child may be entirely different from the child you were at his age, and so be flexible with remembered books. Some of these favorites your child will love, but others he will reject with disconcerting finality. These you must resignedly save for him for later or just save for yourself because of your own nostalgic memories.

To choose books for children, you need to know your children and you need standards for evaluating books. First of all, a book must satisfy the child at his particular age. If he is reading for himself, you may ask, Can he read this book with comfortable fluency? No matter how appealing the content, if the child finds the book heavy going, he may drop it and return to the easy comics or to undemanding television programs. If the child is a prereader, you will read aloud to him and notice whether he asks for the book again. His wanting it again is a good sign. If he never asks for it again, put it away, even though it is a choice book. Rejection means that the book is too hard for his present reading skill or that its content is over his head or that it lacks child appeal. The crux of the problem is, What constitutes child appeal? What are some of children's basic needs which books can satisfy vicariously and in so doing give them insight into their own problems and expand their social understanding and their reading enjoyment?

Of course, children's books should measure up to most of the standards for good writing that we demand of adult books. Mediocrity is easily come by these days, and is to be found in abundance on the shelves of our supermarkets and drugstores, and even in our bookstores. Children's immaturity can be prolonged by an overdose of poorly written, inconsequential books, with stereotypes for characters; so we do need literary yardsticks by which to scrutinize children's reading. But let's look first at the children themselves and their basic needs.

CHILDREN'S NEEDS

Security—material, intellectual, emotional

Even if physical or *material security* looks like a mirage in this troubled age of ours, the human race is going to keep on struggling for it in one form or another. Like adults, children yearn to be safe, warm, well fed, and comfortable. So the reader of the fairy tales feels a glow of satisfaction when the hero or heroine after frightful perils and suffering comes upon a brightly lighted castle, with the hospitably open door leading to a warm fire burning on the hearth and a table spread with every good thing to eat. When Cinderella wins a prince all equipped with a palace, or Boots wins the princess and half the kingdom into the bargain, young readers enjoy a vicarious satisfaction in such security. These satisfying conclusions have kept the old tales in circulation for hundreds of years. They supply readers with a wish-fulfilling dream of security that will probably always haunt the human race. Incidentally, many adults never outgrow the need for a happy ending, an ending that makes them feel safe and snug. The Cinderella or Cinderlad theme of rags to riches motivates literally thousands of short stories and novels written for adults hungry for material security.

Intellectual security sounds like an adult need, but it is a need of children as well. The very fact that a child is small and inexperienced means that he is continually in an inferior position and often in the wrong. No one listens to him with respect. That is the theme of Elizabeth Guilfoile's amusing story *Nobody Listens to Andrew*.[1] Children's longing for intellectual security also accounts for the fact that they pester adults with questions, try all sorts of explorations, and eventually may turn to books for the answers. Fortunately, there are fine factual books in many fields, with simple texts and clear illustrations to answer the questions of even the youngest children. For older children, informational books answer questions with more thoroughness and with scientific detail. Some fiction also vicariously satisfies children's hunger to be right, to know and to do the right thing. So children rejoice when the fairy-tale hero Boots triumphs over his scoffing brothers who made fun of his "wondering." And they are thrilled when the little mute boy in Marguerite Henry's *King of the Wind* lives to see his faith in his neglected horse justified and to have that horse honored above all others. To know accurately or to be proved right in judgment is satisfying to children as well as to adults, and stories that deal with such themes are popular with all ages.

Emotional security, or the need to be loved, is undoubtedly the most important motivating force in life and in fiction, from picture stories for the youngest to the latest novel for the grownups. The prereader's heart goes out to the lonely, homely little cat who in Wanda Gág's *Millions of Cats* wins love and a snug home for herself. So the older children rejoice when David in Ester Wier's *The Loner* finally wins back the respect and the home he so nearly forfeited. Such books give children deep vicarious satisfaction. But more than this, these books also help them realize that limitations, failures, and mistakes are not necessarily forever, but may be righted. This is an indirect kind of guidance that young things— and adolescents also—need, because they *are* young and unsure of themselves, and every mistake or failure seems monumental. They

---

[1]Most of the books mentioned in this chapter are discussed elsewhere in this book. To locate such discussions, check the index.

also need the experience of bestowing love, and that is one reason why stories about animals are so important. They make a child aware of an animal's helplessness and of its need to be cherished and protected. A child's care of his own beloved dog or cat satisfies this need, but apartment-dwelling children are usually denied even this solace. For them, the stories about pets misunderstood, lost, sold, or cruelly treated or about wild animals trapped or shot call out their protective, cherishing feelings vicariously, and the happy endings, with the animal safe and secure, give them enormous relief and satisfaction.

Competence—achievement

Next to a human being's need for love is his never ending struggle to achieve competence in one way or another. Competence bestows a certain status in the eyes of one's peers, but unfortunately, children (and also adults) can be satisfied to shine because of undesirable types of behavior, as every teacher and youth counselor knows all too well. Here is an area where the child's reading can give him indirect, wholesome guidance through an absorbing story. One research report pointed out that the most admired book heroes of children are generally the doers. Certainly the fairy-tale and epic heroes, such as Hansel and Gretel or Odysseus, rank high in this respect. And among the heroes of realistic stories, Tom in *Adventures of Tom Sawyer*, Henry in *Henry Huggins*, Janey in *The Middle Moffat*, Kate in *The Good Master*, and Tim in the *Little Tim* stories are also tops, because they are all up-and-at-'em doers in a big way. In the beginning of *The Good Master*, Kate tries to get attention by undesirable behavior. Her outrageous antics and subsequent reform always provoke lively discussions. So getting things done, achieving independently without benefit of adults, is a prime need of children and is an unfailingly satisfying theme in their books. Incidentally, in the course of their reading, children unconsciously form ideals of behavior. To achieve with selfless courage, to acquire competence instead of bluffing, to endure deprivation and self-discipline in order to attain a desirable goal, to persist in the face of obstacles or failures or humiliation or injustice, and to succeed with quiet simplicity is to possess the characteristics of heroes who command admiration and emulation. These characteristics stand out brightly in the biographies of famous men and women (see Chapter 12).

Acceptance

To be an accepted person in a group one admires is a wholesome motive—if the group is a desirable one. If the group is made up of wild, rebellious, intractable individuals, then there is danger. The yearning for acceptance seems to be another facet of the need to be loved and the need to achieve. When a child is continually rejected by his peers or feels unloved by his parents, he may develop a withdrawal type of behavior or become extra aggressive to attract attention, and to prove his dominance, or he may satisfy his need to be liked by giving all his affection to a responsive pet which becomes a substitute for people. If a child can be helped to discover why he is unacceptable to the people whose liking he craves or can learn to distinguish between likable and unlikable behavior, he can perhaps win over the people who have rejected him or can achieve competence in a field the group respects. Here, again, books often furnish insight and guidance that is so indirect it does not offend. Reading Ester Wier's *The Loner,* a child has no difficulty in understanding why the Boss lost her respect for David and withdrew her favor. David's mistakes, due to his self-centered irresponsibility, endangered a flock of 900 sheep, and so he had to undergo grueling self-discipline and achieve the skills of a dedicated shepherd before Boss could finally give him once more her trust and affection. A city child may find that this book throws light on his problems, too, though his difficulties may be completely unrelated to sheep herding. A daughter in the house who lets the stew boil dry while she sits glued to the television set, or a son whose vegetable garden withers for lack of attention may be enlightened by David's sheep-herding failures.

Play, or the need for change

By comparison with the need for love, competence, and acceptance, the need for play or for a change seems fairly trivial, but it is not. It is a craving that depends on certain rhythms in life's activities. For instance, after prolonged exertion or strain, we need rest and relaxation; after dull routines or drudgery, we yearn for gaiety or sheer hilarity, and if our need for change is satisfied, we can go back to our work or routines or problems refreshed and with new insight. Books that present nonsense or fantasy help satisfy this need for change, provide a healthy, imaginative kind of play after grim realities! The wild nonsense verses of Edward Lear and

Ogden Nash[2] tickle both adults and children, and the daft episodes of *Alice's Adventures in Wonderland* combine nonsense and fantasy that defy reason and show us a topsy-turvy world in which one must keep running to stay where he is. Such a world is a happy change after the painful realities of the family budget or of a political convention or of an arithmetic test. So Alice has survived the years, while many a moralistic tract has died a-borning. That lovely fantasy by Kenneth Grahame, *The Wind in the Willows*, has long been a sanctuary for troubled souls when the realities of life have grown too insistent or too cruel to be endured. Then, to float vicariously down the sunny river with Ratty and Mole is to participate in marvelously refreshing and restorative imaginative play. Youngsters who love this book generally keep it, as I suspect children also keep and cherish E. B. White's *Charlotte's Web*, to resort to when things go wrong.

Aesthetic need for order and beauty

Finally, there is that nebulous, hard-to-define hunger for order, beauty, and harmony, which often begins primitively with the crudest sort of self-adornment but may eventually develop into ideals of moral order and behavior. For many people, the aesthetic sense remains on a fairly simple level, but it can develop amazingly through experiences with the arts—music, dancing, drama, story, poetry, painting, sculpture, architecture. Indeed, one little slum-dwelling girl came home from an art museum weeping, so moved by beauty that she was almost incoherent. "But I never knew there were such things," she cried. "I never knew!" The great artist in any one of these media seizes upon some aspect of life and shows it complete and understandable. His work may be gay or tragic, but if it presents a harmonious whole, it possesses a beauty that satisfies. Of course, children under six generally reject a sad ending. It violates their code of the hero, the doer who must triumph in the end. Older children, though, accept and are often comforted by the fact that the hero makes mistakes, tastes the bitterness of failure, but they still want him to learn by his mistakes and to succeed in the end. Still older children and adults do not demand a happy ending, but they usually want a sense of completion. Life is episodic and generally an enigma. We seldom know how things

[2]The poems of Lear and Nash are included in the nonsense sections of most poetry anthologies for children.

turn out in real life, but in our stories we want an ending. A book can take the reader behind the scenes and show him the reason for the events and for the tragedy. The sense of wholeness that the reader receives can make even failure endurable. James Ramsey Ullman's *Banner in the Sky,* for example, is a satisfying story even though Rudi, the hero, does not succeed in his struggle to climb the mountain peak he had set his heart on reaching. Others succeed instead. But Rudi scores a moral victory over himself which is so completely right that the conclusion has a satisfying quality young readers accept. Even Shakespeare's tragic story of *Romeo and Juliet* is satisfying to youth as well as to adults because its conclusion is logical and inevitable. From the beginning of the play, the audience is prepared for a sorrowful ending. The bitter feud between the two families can end only in tragedy; so when the youthful lovers die, our tears are not bitter or angry, but gentle or, to use Aristotle's term, provides us with *catharsis.* We understand everything, and for us the play is a harmonious whole.

In children's books these needs—for security, for love, for competence, for belonging, for change, and for beauty and harmony— supply the motivating forces that spark the action of the characters. From strong stories so motivated, young readers gain insight into their own difficulties—not through moralizing but through innumerable examples of good and bad social relationships. In short, from *truly good literature,* children and adults may derive insight into the causes and results of human behavior. This last statement inevitably brings up the question: What is good literature? And to this question this next section is devoted.

LITERARY YARDSTICKS
FOR CHILDREN'S BOOKS

As we suggested in the beginning of this chapter, children's books should measure up to two sets of criteria: (1) Do they meet the child's needs and interests at a particular age level? (2) Do they fulfill standards essential for good writing for any age group?

Characters
Of course, not all adult standards for good writing are applicable to children's books. It has been said, for instance, that a novel

stands or falls on the author's ability to create convincing, flesh-and-blood characters. Yet children start with stereotypes—the third little pig, ever wise, ever smart, ever resourceful; or Cinderella, unfailingly humble, kindly, and forgiving; and the ugly sisters, relentlessly mean, suspicious, and deceitful. Such stereotypes have their place as clearly defined patterns of good and bad behavior. Yet the child, even while he accepts these traditional stereotypes along with some recent ones like Hans A. Rey's *Curious George*, is beginning to chuckle over Ludwig Bemelmans' *Madeline*, a rugged individualist if ever there was one, and Louise Fatio's *The Happy Lion*,[3] who has ideas of his own which he carries out indomitably. So even in the picture-book stage, the young child is beginning to encounter book characters who are real individuals, not stereotypes. By the time he is enjoying Marjorie Flack's *The Story About Ping* or A. A. Milne's *Winnie-the-Pooh* or is old enough to read for himself Carolyn Haywood's *Little Eddie* or Beverly Cleary's *Henry Huggins*, he has begun to know book characters so convincing that he remembers them long after he has forgotten the action of the story. Nor does it matter whether the story is realistic or fantastic. The crotchety, airborne nurse in P. L. Travers' *Mary Poppins* is every bit as real to young readers as that red-headed tomboy in Carol Ryrie Brink's *Caddie Woodlawn*. And Pod, Homily, and Arrietty in Mary Norton's *The Borrowers* seem as homey and real as *Henry Huggins* or the neighbor next door. In books for the pre-adolescents, the well-drawn characters grow and change as people do. For example, Johnny in Esther Forbes' *Johnny Tremain* changed from self-centered bitterness to complete self-forgetfulness, and Kate in *The Good Master* grew from a rebellious hoyden into a sensible, competent member of the family group. So when you are appraising books for children who are past the age for stereotypes, virtues personified, look for characters that have a salty uniqueness which makes them real and memorable individuals, and that are so well drawn the reader feels he knows them.

Theme

Another important factor in a well-told story is its theme—what the story is about. A well-defined theme supports the action or plot of the story and gives it unity. Themes are sometimes implied in

---

[3]Each of these three books is one of a series of delightful books about the same character.

the titles. Edward Ardizzonne's *Tim All Alone* wrings the hearts of the four- and five-year-olds, because as the title suggests, Tim *is* alone. He has mislaid his parents, he is shipwrecked, far from home; in fact, he could hardly be more alone! So of course, the action and happy conclusion evolve around and out of this theme. For the twelve-year-olds, Ester Wier's *The Loner* has the same theme. In Armstrong Sperry's *Call It Courage*, a frightened boy's struggle to conquer his fears and develop courage motivates the whole development of the story. A lively plot that keeps young readers racing along from page to page requires a suitable and substantial theme to give body and unity to the development of the story. And the action which begins with a conflict or obstacles or problems that grow more and more acute will involve rising suspense before the satisfying conclusion.

Illustration from *Tim All Alone* by Edward Ardizzone. Used by permission of Henry Z. Walck, Inc.

he found they were short of crew and he was signed on at once as a cabin boy.

Once at sea Tim was kept so busy painting, scrubbing, running errands and helping the steward serve the officers' meals that he had little time to fret.

Plot

Plot is the action of a story, what happens to and because of the theme. *Johnny Tremain* gets caught up in the teeming action of such pre-Revolutionary heroes as Paul Revere before he loses completely his bitter self-centered desire for revenge on his fellow apprentices. Even at the picture-book level, there are plenty of action and some narrow escapes for Peter in *The Tale of Peter Rabbit* before he gets back to his own snug home. Because all children yearn for competence and independent achievement, their favorite heroes are generally doers and their favorite books are full of suspenseful action. Even that Newbery Medal book *It's Like This, Cat*, by Emily Neville, which seems at first to be merely episodic, actually has a good plot. The theme is Dave's growing up and his reflections on and reactions to the curious things and people he encounters in the big city. This theme is implied in the title—a boy explaining to his cat, a nonargumentative audience! But there are action and unity in the development of this remarkable big-city story about a boy's slow maturing and the conclusion of his conflict with his father.

Style

Finally, there is style, difficult to define, a quality of which children are unconscious but to which they respond with delight. In all too many books for children, style is conspicuous by its absence, and this accounts for their depressing mediocrity and flatness. By style we mean, in part, that the words, fraught with meaning, should fall felicitously on the ear and read aloud comfortably and pleasantly. Try these excerpts, the first from the folk tale, the second from Wanda Gág's small classic, *Millions of Cats:*

"Little pig, little pig, let me come in."
"No, not by the hair on my chinny-chin-chin."
"Then, I'll huff and I'll puff and I'll blow your house in."

"Hundreds of cats, thousands of cats, millions and billions and trillions of cats."

There are, of course, many styles. As Thrall, Hibbard, and Holman say in their *A Handbook to Literature,* "The best style, for any given purpose, is that which most nearly approximates a perfect adaptation of one's language to one's ideas."[4] In other words, there must be perfect compatibility of form and content. The predatory cat in *The Two Reds*, by Will and Nicolas, observes Polly the parrot and remarks, "All feathers and beak, nothing to eat." A remark obviously in character! Ezra Jack Keats, in his picture story *Whistle for Willie* for the prereaders, states the whole theme and problem of the story with minimum words, "Oh, how Peter wished he could whistle!" For older children, Laura Ingalls Wilder in *Little House in the Big Woods* writes with disarming simplicity:

She looked at Ma, gently rocking and knitting.
    She thought to herself, "This is now."
    She was glad that the cozy house, and Pa and Ma and the

[4]William Flint Thrall and Addison Hibbard, *A Handbook to Literature*, revised and enlarged by C. Hugh Holman. Odyssey Press, 1960, p. 474.

And over the cat he tumbled.
The fishman went tumbling over Red.

From *The Two Reds* by Will and Nicolas, copyright 1950 by William Lipkind and Nicolas Mordvinoff. Reproduced by permission of Harcourt, Brace & World, Inc.

firelight and the music, were now. They could not be forgotten, she thought, because now is now. It can never be a long time ago.

In sharp contrast to the peaceful mood of *The Little House* books, consider this excerpt from *It's Like This, Cat* by Emily Neville. In spite of the fact that this book won the 1964 Newbery Medal, it was criticized for its lack of literary distinction. But where could you find a closer synchronization of content, meaning, and style than in the breezy, colloquial reflections of this teen-age boy, fighting for the right to be himself and going through a stage of being intensely critical of his parents?

> My father is always talking about how a dog can be very educational for a boy. This is one reason I got a cat.
> My father talks a lot anyway. Maybe being a lawyer he gets in the habit. Also, he's a small guy with very little gray curly hair, so maybe he thinks he's got to roar a lot to make up for not being a big hairy tough guy. Mom is thin and quiet, and when anything upsets her, she gets asthma. In the apartment—we live right in the middle of New York City—we don't have any heavy drapes or rugs, and Mom never fries any food because the doctors figure dust and smoke make her asthma worse. I don't think it's dust; I think it's Pop's roaring.
> The big hassle that led to me getting Cat came when I earned some extra money baby-sitting for a little boy around the corner on Gramercy Park. I spent the money on a Belafonte record. This record had one piece about a father telling his son about the birds and the bees. I think it's funny. Pop blows his stack.

Here is a modern, adolescent boy to perfection. The book may not have the lyric beauty of *The Wind in the Willows*, but after all, a family conflict is not lyrical, and the fact that the author can maintain this laconic, first-person style together with a high degree of interest throughout the story is evidence of skillful writing. Styles do and should differ if they are valid for the subjects they describe. Incidentally, notice, too, how in those brief paragraphs from *It's Like This, Cat*, the author suggests the theme, the problems, and the conflict of the entire story, and makes the reader want to go right on reading.

Elizabeth Enright surprises and delights her young readers with pat, amusing use of words. In *Gone-Away Lake,* when Portia appears at the farm with braces on her teeth, her boy cousin comments, "When you smile, it looks just like the front of a Buick." This rings true today, and children laugh. Good writing has integrity which children may not be able to identify but to which they respond with unfeigned pleasure.

So then, in searching for children's stories that are most worth while, look for a substantial *theme,* robust enough to give rise to a lively *plot* with action, conflict, suspense, and a satisfying, if not always completely happy, ending. Look, too, for *characters* that are well drawn, unique, and memorable, and for *style* that is appealing, forthright, with humor or beauty or those elements of the dramatic appropriate to the story. A book may not have all of these qualities in equal balance and yet be a good book for children. But there are so many books available today for children that adults can unhesitatingly dismiss those that are conspicuously lacking in these qualities.

CRITERIA FOR BOOKS
OTHER THAN FICTION

Special criteria will be given in later chapters dealing with poetry, biography, and informational books. Biography, for instance, can be evaluated in part by the same standards as those for fiction—theme, action, convincing characterization, and good style—but it requires special criteria as well. These standards for fiction apply also to the picture books for the youngest and to the folk tales, with certain limitations which will be discussed in later chapters. Informational books should be judged first of all by the criterion of accuracy, but they are also in special need of good style in order to maintain reader interest. Furthermore, to judge picture books and picture stories, one needs a critical eye to appraise color, design, format, and the pictures themselves. There is considerable gaudy mediocrity in this field, and some say, "Well, what of it? What difference does it make with children as young as three or four?" A tremendous difference! These years may minister to a child's sensitivity to color and line as well as to his intellectual curiosities that prompt all the "whys" of this period. So look to the special criteria for illustration in children's books because these are important in the child's prereading years as well as later.

There are also special criteria for poetry. Style in poetry, for example, is a composite of line scheme, rhyme, rhythm, and the musical sound of the words themselves. These qualities catch the ear like a tune, and because of them children learn a poem by heart as easily as they learn a song. In both arts—poetry and music—the child's taste will grow with what it feeds on, and so we may expect strikingly different levels of taste among adults. One man may never go beyond the Tin Pan Alley level of musical enjoyment, while another man may find his greatest pleasure in listening to Brahms or Mahler. But that first man might have grown to like symphonies had he been exposed to them. So it is with poetry. When a child chuckles over the little tumpity-tump jingles of *Mother Goose,* he is getting ready to enjoy Robert Louis Stevenson's *A Child's Garden of Verses,* and then he will be able to take the next step toward appreciation of the subtler music and content of Harry Behn's poetry or Walter de la Mare's or Robert Frost's. In short, good taste in any of the arts can be cultivated. Vigorous style in either poetry or prose satisfies the longing for beauty, order, and harmony—a longing to be carefully nurtured in every child.

Here, then, are some first aids to parents, grandparents, uncles, aunts, teachers, camp counselors, and all other baffled adults trying to find suitable books for children. These broad generalizations are not guaranteed to be one hundred per cent successful, but they should help. After all, it takes omnipotence to always find the right book for the right child at the right moment. However, if we know the child and his particular interests and needs, and also know many fine books for different ages, we have a fair chance of guiding that child to reading that will capture his interest, widen his horizons, and improve his reading taste.

BIBLIOGRAPHY

Arbuthnot, May Hill. *Children and Books,* Third Edition. Scott, 1964.
    Most of the areas of children's reading discussed in *Children's Reading in the Home* are here developed more fully and provided with more extensive bibliographies.

Arbuthnot, May Hill, Margaret Mary Clark, and Harriet Geneva Long. *Children's Books Too Good to Miss*, Fifth Edition. Western Reserve University Press, 1966.
A basic list of some 260 children's books "too good to miss," for either a home or a school library. Chosen by three specialists in the field, grouped for age levels, this is a carefully selected list, and not too voluminous.

Best Books for Children: A Catalog of 4000 titles. Ninth Edition. R. R. Bowker Company, 1967. Compiled in the offices of *School Library Journal* by Ann M. Currah.
This list is issued annually. It is well annotated and organized both by age levels and by subject matter.

Child Study Association of America. *The Children's Bookshelf:* A Guide to Books for and About Children. Bantam Books, 1962, 1965.
An annotated list of 2000 juvenile and 300 adult books with brief authoritative articles in between.

Eakin, Mary K. *Good Books for Children:* A Selection of Outstanding Children's Books Published 1950-65. Third Edition. Phoenix Books. The University of Chicago Press, 1966.
Here are 1400 carefully selected books ranging "from pre-school through high school, with a majority of the books falling within grades four through nine [ages 9-14]."

Fenner, Phyllis. *The Proof of the Pudding:* What Children Read. Day, 1957.
A thoroughly entertaining discussion of many books children enjoy and an explanation of the reasons why they enjoy the books.

Hazard, Paul. *Books, Children and Men*, tr. from the French by Marguerite Mitchell. Horn Book, 1944, 1947, 1960.
For adults sufficiently interested in children's literature and children to look for a thoroughly engaging book about them from the French standpoint, this is the book. Written by a member of the French Academy, it is a small, choice discussion.

Larrick, Nancy. *A Parent's Guide to Children's Reading*. Revised Edition. Hardback: Doubleday, 1964. Paperback: Pocket Books, 1964.

A sound and stimulating guide for adults, with well-annotated bibliographies.

Townsend, John Rowe. *Written for Children:* An Outline of English Children's Literature. First American Edition. Lothrop, 1967.
From the early English juveniles to the outstanding books of the twentieth century, this is a good summary of the British contribution.

READING ALOUD AND TELLING STORIES

❖❧❧❖

3

Shared Enjoyment
The Prereaders' Needs
The Rewards of Reading Aloud
Sharing Adult Books
The Values of Storytelling
Read or Tell?
Essentials for Storytelling and Reading Aloud
Bibliography

To suggest to many modern families that reading aloud and telling stories are desirable and possible home activities is to meet with considerable skepticism. There are abundant reasons for this reaction, the omnipresent television being only one reason. A major reason is the enormous increase in reading matter. Father has to keep up with his trade journals and mother with at least one woman's magazine full of household hints, articles on child care, and endless recipes in full color. And everyone in the family, old or young, must keep up with the pictorial magazines. These, by the way, are for viewing not reading. Today, even for children, there is so much emphasis on rapid silent reading that there seems to be no time for leisurely reading aloud and, in the process, savoring good writing. Gone forever apparently are the days when a family listened to one of its members read aloud slowly, night after night, week after week, a whole novel by Charles Dickens. There just doesn't seem to be that much time any more or any such lure as a new Dickens' book. Why, then, suggest that the well-nigh lost arts of telling stories and reading aloud in the home should be revived, that they are still worth while and have something precious to offer the family even in the days of television, radio, moving pictures, multiple automobiles, and all the other frenzied distractions of our modern world?

SHARED ENJOYMENT

Actually, there are signs that the pleasant practice of reading aloud is staging a modest comeback. Mothers, fathers, grandparents, uncles, and aunts are discovering that when they read a picture story to a prereader, the child is likely to demand, "Read it again!" Very flattering to the adult and a sure sign that he has joined the illustrious company of approved readers-aloud. A mother could not bear to have her little boy miss Rudyard Kipling's *The Jungle Books*, which he was not getting in school and could not read for himself. So she read the books aloud, and later, when the child's reading skills had matured, he read them over and over for himself. Orville Prescott, critic, editor, lecturer, and author, has compiled an anthology with this significant title: *A Father Reads to His Children*. In his Introduction, he says he hopes his selection of prose and poetry "will help spread the noble art of fathers' reading aloud to their children." And it certainly should, for it is a splendid selection of twenty-four stories and twenty-four poems which Mr. Prescott has enjoyed sharing with his children.

Indeed, good, television programs are not the only means of bringing the family together for shared enjoyment. Lucky is the family with the accepted habit of reading aloud now and then. Not every night, perhaps not even every week, because avid readers like to fly over the pages of a chosen book with the speed that only silent reading permits. But when the outstanding book comes along —so well written, so exciting, so humorous, or so compelling that the entranced reader can't bear to have the other members of the family miss it—then, that is the book to read aloud. It doesn't matter whether the content is for the oldest or the youngest, just so the book provides first-rate reading with depth and significance. Thor Heyerdahl's *Kon-Tiki* surely has held many a family enthralled, and young children who listened to it read aloud when it was first published must have been eager to read *Aku-Aku* for themselves when that book appeared several years later. Ruth Gagliardo, in her delightful introduction to *Let's Read Aloud,* writes that

> When *Mr. Popper's Penguins* first appeared the children's father missed not a word. "Don't read *Mr. Popper* without me," he would warn as he set off in the morning for The Hill."[1]

And surely other fathers said the same about E. B. White's *Charlotte's Web,* if that was being read aloud in the family.

[1]Ruth Gagliardo, *Let's Read Aloud,* J. B. Lippincott Company, 1962, p. 9.

From *Mr. Popper's Penguins* by Richard and Florence Atwater. Illustrated by Robert Lawson. Copyright 1938 by Richard and Florence Atwater. By permission of Little, Brown and Company.

Mr. Popper hesitated. "Well, I call it Captain Cook."

"That makes it a he," said the reporter, writing rapidly in his notebook.

Still curious, Captain Cook started walking round and round the tripod, till the clothesline, the penguin, Mr. Popper and the tripod were all tangled up. At the advice

55

A child came home from the public library with *Island of the Blue Dolphins* by Scott O'Dell and announced, "I won't even start this because the librarian said it is a wonderful read-aloud book." Then she added the librarian's bait to reading, a briefing of the book: "It's the true story of an Indian girl who got left behind on a barren island with a pack of ferocious wild dogs, and she lived there all alone for eighteen years before she was rescued!" That sold the book, and the expectant family audience was not disappointed. Sheila Burnford's *The Incredible Journey* holds all ages, with the younger ones begging each night for just one more chapter or else the promise that nothing more will be read after they go to bed.

THE PREREADERS' NEEDS

Of course, the prereaders in the family should have special privileges beyond the communal reading-aloud sessions. Going to bed is made bearable by the stories that accompany it. In one family, Great-Aunt Mary always told her stories, mother read hers, and father sometimes intoned made-up stories about a little girl called Melissa Melinda, who was remarkably like the recumbent child. There were other times with father that were special for the youngest. After supper, while mother and the girls were still polishing off the dishes, father would settle in his easy chair with the smallest child on his lap, and together they would look at the latest favorite in the picture-story group, stopping now and then to study the illustrations appreciatively. Father liked books about dinosaurs or rockets which made a pleasant variation from mother's daytime choices of Charlotte Zolotow's *The Storm Book* or perhaps A. A. Milne's *Winnie-the-Pooh. Winnie-the-Pooh* was for the private hearing of the youngest, because the older children had already heard it many times. Even so, they occasionally dropped in to listen when a favorite section was under way.

This induction of the prereading child into the magical variety of books should, of course, continue after he is six. For such a child, who has already known the heady delights of books, that first year of learning to read may come as something of a shock. He generally thinks he will be reading by the end of the first day, and great is his amazement at the slowness of the process. Here the home can help the school by providing the child with book experiences which keep him wanting to read for himself and which keep reminding him that something the adults and the older children do so easily he too will be able to do if he continues to try.

THE REWARDS OF READING ALOUD

If more parents realized the power of reading aloud in the home, more would try it. Consider for a moment some excerpts from *That Eager Zest*, an anthology of "First Discoveries in the Magic World of Books," compiled by Frances Walsh.[2] Here, men and women, writers themselves, describe some of their childhood experiences with books. First, read the poet Robert P. Tristram Coffin's comment:

> Peter's father had said Shakespeare to him long before he knew what half the words were about. Peter knew from the first, though, that they were about something fine. . . . They came up from something deep. (p. 99)

That is an arresting idea—"They came up from something deep." Children do sense this, and it is a prime reason for sharing with them the books they cannot read for themselves, books that stretch their minds and imaginations.

In praising *The Jungle Books*, Lionel Trilling also praised reading aloud:

> . . . it was not until I read the stories aloud that I fully understood how wonderful they are. (p. 60)

Robert Lawson praised the skill of a teacher who used to read aloud to her children:

> . . . although I have not the faintest recollection of what she looked like, I can still remember her low, mellow voice as she read to us. (p. 61)

[2]J. B. Lippincott Company, 1961.

And Elizabeth Enright, describing the good, stout fare read aloud to the children in her family by their cook, quotes these excerpts:

> "Gretel gave a push which sent the wicked witch right in, and then she banged the oven door and bolted it. The witch howled horribly, but Gretel ran away and left her to perish in misery."
>
> . . . I often think of that rich bedtime fare when I am reading to my youngest son. Opening whatever book he chooses, I find myself declaring something like this: "Jimmy had a red express wagon. His little sister Janie had one, too." (p. 155)

Don't these few excerpts suggest what listening to good reading aloud from good books can do for children? And Miss Enright's selections of contrasting styles should remind adults *not to read aloud what is not worth reading in the first place.* When a child listens to an adult read aloud, the selection takes on the prestige of adult approval, and the story or the poems may be enhanced for him by the reader's interpretation and enjoyment. Later, as an adult, he remembers such selections vividly, and the whole occasion of the reading—the room, the family circle, the light falling on loved faces—becomes a cherished memory for life. Isn't such companionship with a child worth cultivating?

Certainly reading aloud is the way of ways to introduce children to exceptional books that they might not choose for themselves or might not enjoy without this added lift of family enjoyment and the reader's enthusiasm. *The Wind in the Willows,* by Kenneth Grahame; *The Children of Green Knowe* and *A Stranger at Green Knowe,* both by Lucy M. Boston; *The Gammage Cup* and *The Whisper of Glocken,* by Carol Kendall; *Rifles for Watie,* by Harold Keith; . . . *And Now Miguel,* by Joseph Krumgold; and Will James' *Smoky,* which is difficult because of the vernacular—these are just a sampling of choice books that may need such a lift. Besides, to read any one of these aloud is to discover inestimable values, both literary and social, that neither the adult reader nor the juvenile listeners would have felt so strongly from silent reading.

How wonderful to have someone in the family read aloud with gusto such old favorites as Mark Twain's *Tom Sawyer* and *Huckleberry Finn.* These are generally the choices of the man in the house, and there is many an adult today who cannot read either one of these books without recalling the father's voice as he read aloud, and remembering how he stopped now and then, his eyes crinkled up with laughter over some favorite episode. To hear Elizabeth Janet Gray's *Penn* or Esther Forbes' *Johnny Tremain*, which are beautifully written, beautifully read is a literary treat. To read *Winnie-the-Pooh* silently, in solitude, isn't half as much fun as to read it aloud or to listen to it read aloud. And by the way, every family needs an excursion into sheer hilarity now and then, whether by way of Astrid Lindgren's *Pippi Longstocking* or Keith Robertson's *Henry Reed, Inc.* To laugh together is to relax and to blow away not only the cobwebs, but anxieties and doldrums as well.

More will be said later about the necessity of reading poetry aloud for its own sake as well as for the children's (see Chapter 11). This admittedly is a field where there are few volunteers for reading aloud. In fact, most adults probably are self-conscious about reading poetry aloud. Most mothers, though, manage to read their children *Mother Goose* and the verse of Robert Louis Stevenson and A. A. Milne, but rarely tackle any other poetry. However, one young mother, who was born in a foreign country and spoke English with a heavy accent, fell in love with the poetry in this country available for children in an anthology. She began to read it aloud when her children were mere toddlers. She and her brood literally wore out that anthology, replaced it, and bought other anthologies as well as books of poetry by single authors. Those children are going to remember their poetry with an accent, but by the time they reach high school, they are going to know a range of fine lyric poetry such as few children of the United States know. If that young woman can so love and so read our poetry, other parents who are not handicapped by a strange language can do so, too. Children may start with an ear for only doggerel or nonsense verse, but by hearing good poetry intelligently read, they will gradually develop an ear for words and an enjoyment of verse richer both in content and lyric quality.

SHARING ADULT BOOKS

For the most part, the books suggested so far for reading aloud have been for children. They are choice books a child might not

discover or take the time to read on his own. They are books which
need the lift of adult prestige and the adult's casual explanations.
They are books that adults can enjoy reading and discussing in the
family. However, some adult books are choice for reading aloud and
may well attract the interest of the younger members of the family.
Almost anything by E. B. White is excellent for family reading—
for example, *The Points of My Compass*.[3] In a dog-loving family, the
chapter on "Bedfellows" delighted both children and adults. And
the adolescent in the family paused in full flight when he heard his
father chuckling over "The Motor Car" and later "The Railroad."
Even if the youngster made only a brief pause, perhaps the apparently effortless perfection of that prose style of E. B. White had
time to register. Two history-loving parents were reading aloud,
after the small fry were in bed, Catharine Drinker Bowen's *John
Adams and the American Revolution*.[4] To their surprise, one of
their older children joined them now and then. One poetry-loving
mother, completely baffled by the verse of a modern poet, read her
husband a particularly enigmatic example, only to discover that
their teen-ager "loved it," though she couldn't quite explain why.
But that is all right. Can most of us explain the reasons for our
symphonic tastes? When a famous Shakespearean company came
to town for one performance, the adults in the family read the play
aloud before seeing it. The children listened, too, apparently caught
by the sound of the words, beautifully spoken. Hopefully also, they
carried away something of the meaning. This indeed is stretching
minds and emotions, and is an important reason why family reading aloud should include adult as well as children's books.

THE VALUES OF STORYTELLING

If there is skepticism at the suggestion of reading aloud to the
entire family, there is downright consternation at the idea of storytelling. "Whoever heard of such nonsense?" is the reaction. Yet
there is quite a bit of it going on. No mother or teacher can read
"The Three Little Pigs" or "The Brementown Musicians" or
"Sleeping Beauty" some five or six times without knowing the

[3]Harper & Row, Publishers, 1962.
[4]Little, Brown and Company, 1950.

stories by heart. Mothers with prereading children in the family often acquire a considerable repertoire of favorite nursery tales which they can tell, using the books merely for pictorial commentaries. Fathers frequently regale their offspring with chosen bits from the newspaper which gradually grow fuller and more story-like with each retelling. For example, a newspaper picture launched one father on the story of a cat which adopted an orphaned pup to bring up along with her kittens. From this simple beginning, "Mrs. Tabby" grew into quite a saga under the insistent demands of the children. Father may not have realized it, but he had herewith embarked on the practice of the ancient and honorable art of storytelling. Undoubtedly, each generation of little girls has said, "Mother, tell me about when you were a little girl." And each generation of boys has asked, "Dad, what did you do when you were a boy?" When parents respond with their most vivid or amusing memories, this, too, is storytelling.

It is to be hoped that most children will have these happy experiences with storytelling. But no child need miss completely that homeliest, warmest, and most intimate of the arts. Not if there is a public library with a children's librarian within reach and you are able to convey your child to her story hours. All over the country, dedicated librarians have made story hours for children little centers of culture and delight. In these hours, the traditional tales are told—"Snow White," "Rumpelstiltskin," and all the other folk tales with their ancient wit and wisdom. For the older children, there are the myths and epics, without which how would they know that the adventures of Odysseus gave rise to the familiar use of "an Odyssey" for an interminable journey? How else would they know the meaning of Mercury's winged sandals as an emblem for airborne flights? How else could they recognize dozens of other mythical and epical persons, places, and things which have become symbols in modern literature and advertisements. Traditional literature —the folk tales, the fables, the myths, the epics—was created orally, for the most part, and comes to life more vividly when told rather than read. Blessings on children's librarians who keep these traditional tales and the art of storytelling alive.

And what if there is no library story hour available for your children? Then why not develop the art for yourself? Believe it or not, it is actually easier than reading aloud, though of course good reading is always preferable to halting, uncertain telling.

Directness of storytelling

One virtue of storytelling is that it is more direct than reading from a book. With no book between you and your audience, you will discover that your facial expressions, your occasional gestures, your emphases will come spontaneously in response to your listeners. If a youngster looks baffled, you drop in a casual word of explanation. If he yawns or begins to fidget, you may speed up your narrative or make it a shade more dramatic. You may make your villain a bit oilier and the lassie more guileless. All these are natural responses to what you see in the faces of your listeners, because you can look at them directly and not at the page. This is why storytelling is especially beloved by the youngest children in the family. The threes, fours, and fives feel the closeness, the warmth, and the intimacy of the storyteller, and it is a homelike and comforting feeling. For these reasons, kindergarten teachers usually tell stories on the first days of school and, in so doing, help the children forget their fears and give the big group the warm, personal feeling of home.

Flexibility and informality of storytelling

Another virtue of storytelling is that you can practice the art under the most diverse circumstances. When you are ironing or sewing or preparing dinner—in short, whenever your hands are occupied but the children are not—storytelling is a life saver. It is wonderful for picnics or long automobile trips or camping, when books have of necessity been left at home. And once you have acquired the storytelling habit and a small repertoire, you will be astonished to discover how much more you are carrying along in your memory than you ever realized. Stories from the Old Testament come back to you—"David and Goliath," for example, or "Joseph and His Brethren." Perhaps your unrehearsed narrative is somewhat in the rough, but if you command spellbound attention, that is the test. You can polish the story later. Or you can relate, on the spur of the moment, some historical episode to match a roadside marker or a famous monument or building. You may even remember a whole episode from Robin Hood or the Trojan Horse strategy, which launched Odysseus. Once you give yourself just a little experience with storytelling, you will find all sorts of storylike episodes or excerpts from famous tales coming back to you at need.

Listening training

Another reason for telling stories is that it provides excellent listening training. Because of the prevalence and the beauty of picture stories, young children have sometimes come to use the pictures as a crutch to understanding. Without illustrations, some children just do not comprehend a story. They have not learned to attend to and follow word meanings. Both stories on television and picture-story books *show* the meaning; words are secondary. Story-telling is a helpful antidote. Children who listen to a story told without pictures will learn to attend to words, to understand and to follow the continuity of the plot to its logical conclusion. For example, a four-year-old, perched on a kitchen stool listening to his mother tell the story of "Budulinek,"[5] soon caught on to the disastrous action sequence that followed the warning, "And mind you don't open the door." "Uh huh, but he's going to," muttered the absorbed listener, and of course Budulinek did. That child was not only comprehending the spoken words, but he was anticipating a very human reaction to a taboo.

READ OR TELL?

The younger the child, the more he needs the close, intimate experience of storytelling—perhaps sitting in someone's lap or lying in bed, all warm and comfortable, while he is told a favorite story. It may be an old fairy tale, "Sleeping Beauty" or "The Three Little Pigs," or it may be one of father's famous made-up stories.

Fireside, campfire side—these, too, are places and times when storytelling can capture hearts and emotions as reading aloud can rarely do. Over and over, it has been said that the folk tales, myths, and epics are far more dramatic and convincing when told rather than read—and the reason is that they grew out of the oral tradition and were told for centuries before the printed word imprisoned them in a fixed form.

It is true that artists like Marcia Brown, Adrienne Adams, and Erik Blegvad, to name only three, have made picture-story editions

[5]From *The Shepherd's Nosegay;* Stories from Finland and Czechoslovakia; retold by Parker Fillmore, ed. by Katherine Love; ill. by Enrico Arno. Harcourt, Brace & World, Inc., 1958.

of single tales that are entrancing. But a good storyteller who already knows these tales finds it well-nigh impossible to read these versions verbatim. Many a skilled teller of tales either disregards the texts and tells the story, showing the pictures as she proceeds, or she tells the story first and then puts the glorious picture-book edition out for the children to look at on their own. However, the moment children can read for themselves, you have to stick to the text or some precocious child will pipe up with, "But that isn't what it says!" Use the pictures somehow, of course, but remember that the traditional tales are more alive when they are told. Try it and see!

On the other hand, it is only natural and honest to read verbatim, tales whose charm depends in large part upon the exact words of the author. For example, chapter by chapter, the episodes in E. B. White's *Charlotte's Web* are readily recalled and could be related, but what a waste. Half the fun of the book lies in the matchless dialogue, the increasing befuddlement of the grownups in the story, and the characterizations of every one of the barnyard animals, from Templeton the Rat to Wilbur the "terrific" Pig. There isn't a wasted paragraph or superfluous word in the whole book. To tell *Charlotte's Web* would be desecration. It might be memorized and recited, but this is not storytelling and robs the book of its unique value. The same is true of A. A. Milne's *Winnie-the-Pooh*, Kipling's *Just So Stories* and *The Jungle Books*, and dozens of other little masterpieces. In short, when the charm and force of a story require the precise words and style of the author, the story should be read with appreciation and gratitude for so much good writing in the juvenile field. Perfect phrases may well be reread and savored.

This means that the best of the picture stories should be read rather than told. In such books as *Millions of Cats, The Story About Ping, Make Way for Ducklings, Madeline,* and *The Happy Lion,* pictures and text are so skillfully synchronized that one reinforces the other. So with the children, you read and look, reread and look again, and, finally, leave the book around for them to pore over and to reconstruct the story from the pictures. This they do and you hear them muttering phrases they remember because you have respected the author's words, and they have caught the children's attention and are recalled.

Do these distinctions between stories to tell and stories to read seem reasonable? Such old tales as "Hansel and Gretel," "Puss in

Boots," and "East o' the Sun" grew and changed with each telling just because they were passed on by word of mouth. As a matter of fact, the same story told today differs somewhat with each story-teller. It is said that there are over three hundred variants of the familiar "Cinderella" story in different countries, and, now, in different printed versions. Folk tales are flexible indeed. But when a writer creates for print a precise art form like Beatrix Potter's *The Tale of Peter Rabbit,* which has been beloved for over half a century, no one should take liberties with the text. The form of the story is fixed in print and the author's words should be respected in the reading. So, we tell "The Three Bears," but we read *The Tale of Jemima Puddle-Duck.*

From *The Tale of Jemina Puddle-Duck* written and illustrated by Beatrix Potter. Copyright 1908. Reprinted by permission of Frederick Warne & Co., Ltd.

27

ESSENTIALS FOR STORYTELLING
AND READING ALOUD

Sincerity and enjoyment

One of the first principles of good storytelling or reading aloud is sincerity, or you may prefer to call it naturalness. For storytelling and reading aloud are not the arts of the stage but of small, intimate groups by fireside, cribside, or campfire. Children are peculiarly sensitive to insincerity. A patronizing tone of voice, a sugary over-sweetness, or a heavy pomposity—any of these will set children to squirming. For that matter, they are enough to set anyone's teeth on edge. Use your normal, everyday voice; read or tell directly, honestly, and unaffectedly; but let your enjoyment shine through the words.

This enjoyment of the story you are telling is another essential to success. Never try to read or tell a story you dislike or find boring. Indifference is just as infectious as enjoyment. So when you find a story that delights you, share it with the children, and your obvious relish for what lies ahead will lend added luster to the story and to your telling of it. It tickles children when an adult shows genuine liking for their books and, of course, heightens their pleasure in the books.

Voice and diction

A good speaking voice is an unmitigated blessing not only for storytelling and reading aloud but for peaceful coexistence with family and friends. A small boy who was asked why he was standing outside his classroom replied wearily, "I'm so tired of her voice." And that is precisely how some voices affect us. Everyone has encountered the harsh, flat voice that can take the joy or the beauty or the fun out of any situation, or the whining, complaining voice, or, worst of all, the nagging voice. None of us can afford to have any one of these voices, and so we need to listen to our own voices and to good voices on stage and screen. Take courage! A voice that is used continually in the service of beauty will grow in richness and depth. All by yourself, practice reading fine literature, especially poetry. Habituate yourself to speaking with some buoyancy, gaily or gravely, but never despairingly or complainingly. A voice with a lift helps everyone. Just try saying "Good morning" in character: as a *complainer* with a grievance; as a *nagger*, lying in wait to drive someone to something unpleasant; as a *cynic*, who is sure there is nothing much to hope for; and, finally, as a healthy, decent human being, confronted with a rainy day and suddenly aware that it is going to be just dandy for finishing off some long overdue chores. She would say "Good morning" with a lift. Nor does this mean any obnoxious oversweetness, overcheerfulness—just an honest-to-goodness "morning gladness," as Robert Frost called it; that is, gladness to be breathing and with something to do.

Part of good speech is, of course, good diction—clear, conventional pronunciation and clear, crisp enunciation that can be readily followed by the listeners. Some singers of English songs might as well be singing in Greek for all the listeners can understand of the words, while others sing so that every word comes through clearly and intelligibly. The same is true of speaking. Vigorous enunciation, with crisp consonants and pure vowel sounds, and conventional pronunciation are components of good diction. Without these, the most mellifluous voice is wasted. One benefit of having to read *Mother Goose* aloud is that the verses bounce and trip along so gaily and the sounds are so tuneful, they improve adults' as well as children's speech. In fact, teachers use these jingles with foreign-speaking children to help them with word sounds, to enable them to attain pure vowels and clear consonants. For example, the long *o*'s in "Blow, wind, blow," the explosive *g*'s and *d*'s in "Higgledy, piggledy, my black hen," and the sounds in dozens of other jingles will do much to liven up sluggish, slovenly speech. And so will telling the huffing, puffing dialogue in "The Three Little Pigs" or reading "Hundreds of cats, thousands of cats, millions and billions and trillions of cats." Words come clearer, voices become more musical in reading and telling good stories.

Appearance

Sometimes mothers and fathers become such skillful story-tellers that they are in demand for occasions outside the home. If your audience is a sizable group of children in a class or camp or on a picnic or party, you will, for example, avoid clanking jewelry and jingling keys. Both are distracting, but your costume may be anything from shorts by the campfire to formal attire at a party. It is not your clothes but you that counts. If you look easy but alert, quiet but alive, the children will give you their attention and be ready to listen to your stories. To be sure, mousey girls often come vividly alive in the course of a dramatic story, and quite a few young men reveal in their storytelling or reading aloud, a subtle or even hilarious sense of humor. A good story is as good for the teller as for the audience. For the most part, forget how you look, just so you are alert and erect, never slouched or draped over a table or chair as if you needed a prop. Enjoy your story and show it.

Preparation

A lively, pleasant voice; clear, crisp articulation; and an alert, unself-conscious appearance are all essential to storytelling and reading aloud. But there are certain special requirements for story-telling, particularly if you expect to hold the attention of a whole group of children. For such occasions, a story should be learned to the point where you can relate it as easily as you can tell about something funny that happened that day in the supermarket. Don't let this learning requirement frighten you. Because we tell stories chiefly to young children—the threes to the sevens or eights—the stories are fairly short. Even stories for the eights, which have more plot and more elaborations, are still comparatively short. Further-more, because folk tales were composed orally, certain words and phrases are repeated and even the pattern of the episodes is often in a repetitive form that helps recall. This is why these old tales were remembered and passed on by word of mouth for centuries. And this is why you will be able to learn them readily. If you like, use one of the handsomely illustrated editions of a single tale with your children; you will find that you know it by heart after two or three readings. However, if you discover a folk tale that fascinates you but has no illustrations, don't be dismayed. Before you tell your tale to an audience of Cub Scouts or a Saturday-morning group at your children's school, sit down with the story of your choice and after you have read it silently a couple of times, begin to tell it to yourself aloud. If you stumble, go back and reread, and then start telling it from that point on. Repeat this until you have told the whole story. Then, still with your book on your lap to look at now and then, retell the story, not silently but always aloud. A few such trials and you will have it.

By this time, you are doubtless saying to yourself, "Does anyone expect a mother to do all this for a bedtime story for her child?" Probably not, but for the Sunday School class or for picnic or camp or other group outings, yes! And it is not half so hard as it sounds.

Old Testament stories are magnificent to tell, but they must be learned. Tall tales are hilarious to tell, but they must be learned, and what is more, you must listen to yourself tell them—must listen to your voice, your articulation, your vocabulary, and, above all, your own interest in the story that makes it come alive for your listeners.

Language. It must be admitted that language is one stumbling block to the easy learning of a story. An Irish tale has a different vocabulary and cadence from a good English translation of a Norwegian or German story, and part of the tang and flavor of a tale lies in its unique cadence and language patterns. If you are sensitive to words, your eyes and ears soon catch this, and you could not possibly interject into a traditional tale some of our modern expressions: "Cinderella looked real cute" or "OK," said the prince. Before you learn a story, read it aloud until you have caught its peculiar folk flavor—"lassie" in one story, "maiden" in another, sometimes "goody" for an old woman, generally "king" for royalty, but not in Russian tales or in some others that require "czar" or "emperor." An Irish tale generally has a peculiar cadence due to repetition or to inverted speech forms—"It was himself, it was," or "So it came about, as I'm telling ye," or "And to herself, she said." One other problem is that old tales, for the most part, speak of a rural world, whereas over half of our modern children are urban. To say to an urban child, "The mare foaled in the market place" is to leave him completely baffled, but you say it nevertheless and add casually, "The mare gave birth to a little colt right there in the market place." After the story is over, you may explain "mare" and "foal" further, but when you retell the story, you tell it in the old form. At least you do, if you like words and are glad to add words to a child's vocabulary, after making sure that their meanings are clear. Such little parenthetical explanations are essential with many new words in many different sorts of reading and they need not disturb the flow of the story in the least.

Adapting a story. If you enjoy storytelling so much that you tell stories to sizable groups of children—in Sunday School or in camp or in Cub dens—then you must know how to adapt stories. Myths, epics, and Old Testament tales generally require considerable adaptation. A few mothers and fathers are using storytelling on a fairly large scale and doing it most effectively. But these comments are addressed primarily to home situations—informal, often spontaneous, and not overly rehearsed. For home telling, adaptation is on a simpler scale. Besides providing casual explanations of unfamiliar words or phrases, adaptation may take the form of cutting an overlong story. Perhaps Boots will ride up the Glass Hill only once instead of three times, or the prince will perform only one of three prodigious tasks. But don't delete all the violence from these old tales, not only because children are seeing much worse in their daily TV fare but also because the violence is not without purpose. When the bad wolf falls down the chimney into Little Pig's kettle of boiling water, or when the wicked queen comes to a bad end, the listening child is reassured. Such conclusions provide a good riddance and spell security. Once and for all, the world is cleared of ravening wolves and witchlike queens and is a much safer place for pigs and Snow Whites. To tone down these endings is to rob the tales of the sense of justice and reassurance they were meant to carry.

Occasionally, an adult overtone in some of the tales may need a bit of doctoring. In "East o' the Sun," the unseen creature gets into bed with the lassie each night. That is easily changed to "Each night, she heard someone enter the next room and she wondered who it could be." On the whole, there are few such episodes, and they are not difficult to take care of.

For descriptions of more ambitious adaptations, read Ruth Sawyer's delightful book *The Way of the Storyteller* (see bibliography) or read Chapter 13 in May Hill Arbuthnot's *Children and Books*, 1964 edition. Telling stories to large groups of children requires detailed preparation and painstaking practice before storytelling becomes the fine art described in those two books.

Beginnings and endings of stories. The beginnings and endings of stories, whether of folk or of modern tales, are fascinating and worth study. Apparently, good storytellers of every generation have known the importance of these parts of a story and have taken pains with them. Children like brisk beginnings that get them into the tales with an irresistible come-on. And they like conclusions that are conclusive, with all their hopes and fears properly settled. If a story satisfies on both counts, it means that the author, whether ancient and anonymous or modern and well known, has polished these parts of his tale to perfection and that we who tell the story or read it aloud should do the same. Polish the beginning and ending of a story, and the middle part of the tale will almost take care of itself. To launch a story, see that it catches the children's attention and focuses attention on what lies ahead, a sort of "Here we go, what do you suppose will happen next?" kind of atmosphere. Then, with the conflict increasing, suspense building up, a lively climax imminent, see that you make a really strong conclusion. No weakening on the "happily ever after," but a vigorous picking up of the threads of the story with the villain properly punished and out of the way and the heroine free of witchlike queens and properly safe and rewarded. The beginnings must come off with vigor and the endings with a flourish.

Except for learning a story and perhaps making some adaptations in it, everything that has been said about storytelling applies to successful reading aloud in the family. You do have a book between you and your audience, but you learn to read with your eyes alternately on the text and on the children. Watching your audience is important not merely to keep attention but also to watch for children's blank looks, when they do not understand or are no longer interested, and also to get the feel of mounting excitement and enjoyment. Using the marvelous picture stories for the youngest children, you soon get the knack of holding the book sidewise so the children can see the pictures or you even hold the book so that the children see the pictures and you must read the print upside down. Once in a while you encounter a book in which the text and illustrations are not synchronized. Then there is a to-do. You are reading one thing, and the illustration shows something else. Every child rises to protest and to attempt to find the right picture. When you have untangled heads, hands, and book, you say firmly that you are going to read the story first and show the pictures afterwards. Many people always prefer to follow this pattern of reading first and showing the pictures afterwards. This procedure works well in a classroom but not always so well at home. As children grow older, their books have fewer illustrations. For these older children, of course, you always read first and show the illustrations afterwards, leaving the book around for them to reread on their own if they choose or, as so often happens with the best readers in the family, to race ahead to finish the story. This is fine, if the eager story-devourer honorably refrains from giving away the solution or conclusion of the tale. A fast reader around ten or twelve years old has real need for racing ahead with a book, but he may still come back to the family reading-aloud sessions. Whether he does or not, be thankful that you have such a reader in the family. For of course, you use reading aloud first for the joy of sharing a choice book in the warm intimacy of the family group, but also as a bait to more and richer reading on the part of the children themselves. When you have accomplished these goals, the children are happily on their reading way and a lot of pleasant memories will go with them.

BIBLIOGRAPHY

Arbuthnot, May Hill. *Children and Books*, Third Edition. Scott, 1964.
    See Chapter 13, Storytelling and Reading Aloud, for a full discussion of these arts, including an account of four master storytellers with contrasting styles.

New York Library Association. Children's and Young People's Section. *Once Upon a Time*. Revised Edition, 1964.
    This pamphlet is a help for librarians with preschool hours, picture-book hours, and story hours. Suggested programs and bibliographies are included.

Prescott, Orville. *A Father Reads to His Children*. Dutton, 1965.
    An anthology of prose and poetry with an introduction by Orville Prescott. Here are twenty-four poems and twenty-four stories that this father has enjoyed sharing with his children. They include old, familiar, and recent selections along with some little-known selections. All are of high literary quality. This book will enrich any children and adults who share it together.

Sawyer, Ruth. *The Way of the Storyteller*. Viking, 1942, 1962.
    Informally written in Ruth Sawyer's fine style, this is a contribution both to the art of storytelling and to the history of the old tales. It also contains eleven unusual stories, including a favorite, "The Princess and the Vagabone."

Shedlock, Marie L. *The Art of the Story-Teller*, Third Edition, bibliography by Eulalie Steinmetz. Dover, 1951.

Guidance in selection of material, techniques of storytelling, and useful bibliographies.

Stories to Tell to Children. Carnegie Library of Pittsburgh, Boys and
   Girls Department.
   Frequent revisions. One of the outstanding bibliographies of literature available for the storyteller. The seventh edition (1960) is "for use by libraries, schools, clubs, and by radio and television storytellers, with a special listing of stories for holiday programs."

Tooze, Ruth. *Storytelling.* Prentice, 1959.
   Extensive bibliographies add to the value of this helpful guide for storytellers.

PART TWO
GROWING INTO BOOKS AND READING

BOOKS BEGIN

FOR AGES TWO-SIX

4

Mother Goose
Picture Books
Picture Stories
Folk-Tale Anthologies
The Art of Picture Stories
Poetry
Format of Children's Books
Book Care

For the fortunate child, books begin long before reading does, and grownups who are privileged to give young children their first experiences with books are indeed blessed. To chant and act out nursery rhymes with a bright new baby, to watch a slow smile gather, and then, after a few repetitions, to hear a crow of laughter—there's a triumph a prima donna might envy.

MOTHER GOOSE

Of course, before books begin, there are lullabies and finger plays that come chiefly from and lead directly into *Mother Goose.* A mother plays "Pat-a-cake" with her baby's hands or counts his toes with "This little pig went to market," giving a special tweak to his *little* toe when the last pig cries, " 'Wee, wee, wee,' all the way home." Then the baby waves his feet in the air to see that the toes are all there. Or the mother winds up the dramatic "Sing a song of sixpence" with her thumb pressed between her first and second fingers as she says, "Along came a blackbird/ And snipped off his nose." And her thumb, as she quickly withdraws her hand from his nose, looks so noselike the baby squeals, and feels to see that his is still with him. *The Oxford Nursery Rhyme Book*, assembled by Iona and Peter Opie[1] has a lot of these "Baby Games and Lullabies" grouped together, so that you can readily give yourself a refresher course in these first games and chants that begin even before books begin.

Someone has said that when a child is at this age, somewhere under a year old, you could treat him to a cadenced reading of the telephone book and he would be charmed, but this is not quite true. It is, to be sure, the mother's loving attention to him that he likes: the play that goes on between the two of them, her smiles and pats, and above all, the sound of her voice directed just to him. But one day a word here and there gets through with meaning, and so communication by words begins. This process is long and involved, and both the beginnings and the development are sporadic, but when the baby responds to words, there *is* a beginning.

After these games and chants, the next step is a book, and generally the first is *Mother Goose* in one edition or another. There are so many attractive editions that it is hard to choose among them.

The Real Mother Goose, ill. by Blanche Fisher Wright. Fiftieth Anniversary Edition. Introduction by May Hill Arbuthnot. Rand McNally, 1965.

For over fifty years, *The Real Mother Goose* has been a favorite edition of *Mother Goose*, both in homes and in schoolrooms. It is a big, handsome book, with over 400 verses, copiously illustrated. The large pictures, all in color, are sparing of details and are easy to see, and the book is easy to hold for a whole group of children to look at or for the one special child sitting on your lap.

The Tall Book of Mother Goose, ill. by Feodor Rojankovsky. Harper, 1942.

[1]Oxford University Press, 1955.

As the title implies, this is a tall, narrow book approximately 5 x 12 inches, but surprisingly easy to hold. The humorous pictures are in bold, rich colors, with some delightful double-page spreads like the panoramic landscape of "one misty, moisty morning."

Mother Goose and Nursery Rhymes, ill. by Philip Reed. Atheneum, 1966.

There are only sixty-six of the old jingles in this edition; but the whole design of the book—the typography, margins, and arrangement of verses and pictures—and the illustrations themselves are a treat for the eyes. Philip Reed's beautiful wood engravings have humor, lively action, and complete compatibility with the verses.

A Family Book of Nursery Rhymes, collected by Iona and Peter Opie, ill. by Pauline Baynes. Oxford, 1964.

There was an old woman who lived in a shoe,
She had so many children she didn't know what to do;
She gave them some broth, without any bread;
She whipped them all soundly and sent them to bed.

Originally published in 1963 as *The Puffin Book of Nursery Rhymes*, this collection has 358 memorable rhymes, a number of which have "hitherto been known only locally or in individual families."

The Mother Goose Treasury, comp. and ill. by Raymond Briggs. Coward-McCann, 1966.

Here is a big, handsome book with 408 rhymes and 897 illustrations. With warm, earthy colors, lusty action, and humor, this is an all-
round gay collection.

Book of Nursery and Mother Goose Rhymes, ill. by Marguerite de
Angeli. Doubleday, 1954.

Over 370 of the verses, with 260 pictures and innumerable decorations. This was a labor of love for the artist's own grandchildren and
is a big book for lap, table, or floor enjoyment.

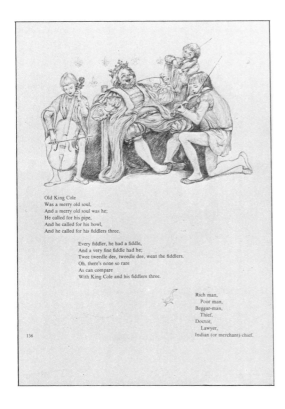

From *Book of Nursery and Mother Goose Rhymes*, by Marguerite de Angeli. Copyright 1954 by Marguerite de Angeli. Reprinted by permission of Doubleday & Company, Inc.

Old King Cole
Was a merry old soul,
And a merry old soul was he;
He called for his pipe,
And he called for his bowl,
And he called for his fiddlers three.

Every fiddler, he had a fiddle,
And a very fine fiddle had he;
Twee tweedle dee, tweedle dee, went the fiddlers.
Oh, there's none so rare
As can compare
With King Cole and his fiddlers three.

Rich man,
Poor man,
Beggar-man,
Thief,
Doctor,
Lawyer,
Indian (or merchant) chief.

136

Ring o' Roses, ill. by L. Leslie Brooke. Warne, n.d.

It seems a pity for any child to miss Leslie Brooke's pictures for a handful of the *Mother Goose* rhymes. His lovely, colorful landscapes, his funniest pigs that ever cried "Wee, wee," and his droll people are not merely interpretations but the very embodiment of the words.

There are many other delightful editions of *Mother Goose*, so be sure to examine them in bookstores or libraries before you buy. Tastes differ, and your favorite *Mother Goose* will be a book to smile over and cherish forever and a day.

It may be well to warn parents that their first uses of *Mother Goose* may be disconcerting. Mother gets baby and book comfortably propped on her lap and begins to read a jingle that matches a bold, bright picture. But the child interrupts with a firm "Wha'zat?" pointing to an object in the illustration. This means that the child is still in the Adam-and-Eve stage of getting names for things, and this activity may go on for days, with mother employed merely as identifier of objects in the pictures. But one day when she starts out half-heartedly with "Little Miss Muffet," there is a pause in his page-turning search for new objects, and so she finishes up hastily with the verse story of Miss Muffet's frightened retreat from the spider. Of course, she puts a jump in "frightened," and the child commands, "Say it again!" Another triumph, and this one marks a genuine attention to word meanings—the book is suddenly a new thing to the child who has taken this step. Sometimes we wonder if any other book will ever be as important as the one that suddenly opens up this association of word sounds and sentence sounds with meaning. It is not always *Mother Goose* that achieves this miracle, but with English-speaking children it frequently is. And don't let anyone talk down the values of this ancient soother of crying bairns. Some of these persistent belittlers of good Dame Goose insist, "It is all nonsense, all doggerel, with no improving morals and, worse still, both the language and content are so old they carry no meaning for the modern child, accustomed as he is to elevators, escalators, automobiles, and gas stations." The best answer to these detractors is a question: "Why, then, has this book lasted so many years? Why—to the delight of artists, who never stop illustrating the verses—does it continue to be loved by generation after generation of children, parents, and teachers?"

Perhaps one of the greatest charms of these old verses for chil-

dren is their hypnotic sound—their rhyme, cadence, and spellbinding use of words. There are lullabies, but there are also gallops,
skips, runs—all easily identified when you read the verses aloud.
The hissing s's of "Sing a song of sixpence," the m's of "One misty,
moisty morning" or the b's of "Baa, baa, black sheep"—these and
dozens of other delightful uses of alliteration charm young listeners.
In the following poem, listen to the two subtly contrasted sound
patterns:

> Blow, wind, blow!
> And go, mill, go!
> That the miller may grind his corn;
>
> That the baker may take it,
> And into bread bake it,
> And bring us a loaf in the morn.

These contrasts come alive when you give full sound values to
the long o's in *blow* and *go* and speak briskly and crisply the staccato consonants of the first two lines of the second stanza. Very
likely, babies love the sounds of words and cadenced lines spoken
by a comforting voice, long before they single out all the words and
meanings. And then, as well as later when they *do* understand
meaning, children get from these verses training in the sound and
the beauty of the English language.

These amusing verses also introduce children to story form. Even
"Miss Muffet" is a pint-sized story with a serene beginning, a violent climax, and the sudden departure of Miss Muffet, whey, and
serenity. "I had a little pony," "The Queen of Hearts," "Pussy
Cat, Pussy Cat," and the sad, tender ballad of "The Babes in the
Wood" are all narrative poems; and once a child has learned to
attend to the continuity of these small tales, he is ready for the
longer folk tales and picture stories that not only follow hard upon
Mother Goose but are enjoyed while he is still enthralled with
these melodious jingles.

Finally, the variety and humor of the *Mother Goose* verses are
never ending sources of wonder and enjoyment. There are poems
about people, animals, birds, and weather; there are stories, lullabies, proverbs, songs, tongue twisters, games, riddles, alphabet
and counting out rhymes, and so on. Moreover, many of these

seem hilarious to children. Anything grotesque, out of the usual run, is funny to them; and so the crooked man with his crooked house is very funny, as are the pranks in "Georgie Porgie" or "The Little Woman and the Pedlar," and the sounds of "Intery, mintery, cutery-corn" and the tongue twisters. Somehow, to adults brought up on these ditties and with a chance to try them with their favorite child or children, the richness and gaiety of *Mother Goose* are inexhaustible. Make the most of these delectable collections of old rhymes, for they will send a child into school with an ear and a tongue for the sounds and forms of words, a greatly enriched vocabulary, and a language flexibility that takes "does" and "doth" in stride and catches the import of words from context as well as from literal meaning.

PICTURE BOOKS

When children are still in the labeling stage, their book experiences may begin with picture books devoid of any verbal content. Some of these are cloth books. Fortunately, since many people heartily dislike the floppy, unbooklike feel of these cloth creations and will have none of them, picture books also come in hard covers and begin where children's interests and language are—with familiar objects. There are picture books of pets, wild animals, boats, airplanes, farms, stores, and assorted subjects. Regrettably, the art work in many of these picture books is either crude or simpering; in others—most notably some of the ABC books—it is distinguished by wit and beauty. Indeed, many of the recently published ABC books are the work of well-known artists, as, for example, the following four books:

Bruno Munari's ABC, ill. by author. World, 1960.
This is a treat for the eyes, with clear, pure color and beautiful line. Children are delighted with the interesting associations built around each letter—"A Fly/ a Flower/ a Feather/ and a Fish," with "more Flies" at the top of the page to go buzzing on through the book.

The Big Golden Animal ABC, ill. by Garth Williams. Golden Press, 1957.

Garth Williams makes use of amusing contrasts. For the letter *A*, for example, he has drawn a huge alligator, with jaws agape, and near the bottom of the page, a small, scared rabbit, racing madly away on his bicycle.

Animals in the Zoo, by Feodor Rojankovsky. Knopf, 1962.
A handsome zoo alphabet book, with an animal for each letter.

Brian Wildsmith's ABC, ill. by author. Watts, 1963.
This book is a veritable bath in colors. A fuchsia page says, "cat, CAT," with letters in three colors, and the opposite page, in muted blue, pictures a green-eyed black cat.

Such picture alphabets call for and reward close observation. Some of the ABC books gradually grow more complex and develop themes around which the pictures are grouped, or they may even have a small storylike continuity, as in Wanda Gág's *The ABC Bunny* (Coward-McCann, 1933). They are useful, too, because they make children letter conscious and are an invitation to symbol recognition. But children soon demand more from looking at pictures than they themselves can supply, and this is a sign that they are ready for stories.

PICTURE STORIES

By the time children can listen attentively to "Little Miss Muffet" or "Jack and Jill," they are ready for the longer continuity of the picture stories. In picture stories, the pictures are so completely integrated with the text that a child, after several hearings, will often take the book and volunteer to "read it," and this he can do from the pictures alone. Incidentally, teachers and parents soon master this same technique, showing the pictures to the children with the print upside down for themselves and "reading" from the illustrations.

Favorite fanciful tales
The Tale of Peter Rabbit and *Millions of Cats*, both picture stories, are landmarks in the field of children's literature which no child should miss. *The Tomten*, too, is well loved.

The Tale of Peter Rabbit, by Beatrix Potter, ill. by author. Warne, 1903.
    The Tale of Peter Rabbit was written in 1893 to amuse a little in-
valid boy, but it was not officially published until several years later.
This small, beautiful book is a gem of good writing and exquisite illustrations. It is also a perfect example of the synchronization of pictures
with text. The delicate water colors show Peter in his little shoes and
blue coat, setting off to do precisely what his mother told him not to do,
go into Mr. McGregor's garden. There he gets into real trouble, makes a
perilous escape, but reaches home safely minus his shoes and blue coat.
He is punished for his sins, but he is safely home, and there are warmth
and reassurance in that firelit interior with Peter in his own little bed.
The Tale of Jemima Puddle-Duck and many of the other *Tale* books are
equally beloved.

Millions of Cats, by Wanda Gág, ill. by author. Coward-McCann, 1928.
    The publication of this highly original story marked the beginning
of a spectacular development of picture stories. *Millions of Cats* is
written in folk-tale style and has wood-block illustrations of great distinction; their flowing, rhythmic lines are in complete harmony with the
cadenced text. "Hundreds of cats, thousands of cats, millions and billions and trillions of cats," the children chant with you, after a couple
of readings. No picture story in full color is more popular than this one
in its striking blacks and whites. Wanda Gág's other picture stories and
her fine *The ABC Bunny* are also popular with children.

The Tomten, adapted by Astrid Lindgren from a poem by Viktor Ryd-
    berg, ill. by Harald Wiberg. Coward-McCann, 1961. Also *The Tom-
    ten and the Fox* (1966).
    American children have taken to their hearts the kindly Swedish
Tomten, who protects the home and farm while people sleep. The first
book follows his nightly guardianship. The second book shows how he
diverts a fox from raiding the hennery. Both books are quietly reassuring, and the winter pictures have a breath-taking beauty.

The next three picture stories are about inanimate objects, and
all three are exceptionally popular.

Little Toot, by Hardie Gramatky, ill. by author. Putnam, 1939. Reissued,
    1964.
    Little Toot is about an irresponsible young tugboat who gets into

serious trouble and then reforms once and for all. The gay, bright water colors add much to the charm of the story and its hero. A sequel, *Little Toot on the Thames*, was published in 1964. See also *Hercules* (1940) and *Loopy* (1941).

Mike Mulligan and His Steam Shovel, by Virginia L. Burton, ill. by author. Houghton, 1939.
Mike Mulligan is devoted to his steam shovel, Mary Ann, and bad times do not diminish his faith in her powers. Sure enough, given a chance, she performs a prodigious feat, and the two of them are snug and secure for the rest of their lives.

The Little House, by Virginia L. Burton, ill. by author. Houghton, 1942. Caldecott Medal.
This is really a story of the evolution of a rural area into a city, told through the eyes of a little house. That sounds dull, but the story is so

beautifully told and illustrated that it is enjoyed by children as young as four and as old as eight. Virginia Burton's ballet of swirling lines and solid verticals makes every picture worth studying, and children pore over the details.

The next two titles stand for popular series that the preschool and even the primary children pursue avidly to the last book.

Curious George, by Hans A. Rey, ill. by author. Houghton, 1941.
    Curious George is a mischievous monkey, who gets into all sorts of scrapes and messes, but who somehow or other manages always to extricate himself neatly. This is very reassuring to the young child, who does not come off so successfully in most cases.

The Happy Lion, by Louise Fatio, ill. by Roger Duvoisin. McGraw, 1954.
    The Happy Lion stories have fascinating illustrations with details that make the French town where the stories take place just as familiar as the child's own home town. The lion, like the child, is cribbed and confined, but he has his own ideas. These he carries out gently but firmly, whether his project is going for a walk in the village or winning himself a beautiful lioness. With these *Happy Lion* stories, the husband-and-wife team of illustrator and author has made a real and lasting contribution to books for young children.

The everyday world of small children
Children identify themselves with the successful heroines and heroes of their stories, even though the characters may be tugboats, steam shovels, or a Happy Lion. Still, children are also continuously interested in other children like themselves and in the real world that surrounds them. And fortunately, there are many picture stories about the child's everyday world to meet this interest.

Play with Me, by Marie Hall Ets, ill. by author. Viking, 1955.
    One of the most sensitive and charming books for children as young as three or four is this story about a child who wanted the little animals of the meadow to play with her. But not until she learned to be quiet would they come to her. Illustrated in delicate springtime colors. *Nine Days to Christmas,* written by Marie Hall Ets and Aurora Labastida,

and illustrated by Miss Ets, won the Caldecott Medal in 1960. It tells of a little Mexican girl and her first *posada*.

Umbrella, by Taro Yashima, ill. by author. Viking, 1958.
   Also for the very young is this story of a little Japanese girl living in a big city. What is the use of owning a beautiful blue umbrella and red boots if it doesn't rain? When rain finally comes, the pictures of the child's triumphant walk are a joy to behold.

The Snowy Day, by Ezra Jack Keats, ill. by author. Viking, 1962. Caldecott Medal. Also *Whistle for Willie* (1964).

From *Play with Me* by Marie Hall Ets. Copyright 1955 by Marie Hall Ets. Reprinted by permission of The Viking Press, Inc.

"Grasshopper," I said, "will you play with me?"
And I tried to catch him, but he leaped away.

7

Before he got into bed he looked in his pocket.
His pocket was empty. The snowball wasn't there.
He felt very sad.

The illustrations for these books are beautiful examples of collage.
The plots are of the simplest and relate the everyday activities of Peter,
an appealing little Negro child, enjoying a snowy day and learning to
whistle for his dog Willie.

Moy Moy, by Leo Politi, ill. by author. Scribner, 1960. Also *Little Leo*
(1951).

Leo Politi has a wonderful way of tying old-world customs into the
new-world customs of the United States. *Moy Moy* is about an enchanting little girl from Chanking Street in Los Angeles. She and her two
brothers make ready for the Chinese New Year's Festival in one of the
gayest, most colorful of all of Leo Politi's picture stories. *Little Leo* is
the story of Mr. Politi as a child, journeying back to Italy with his family
to visit his grandparents. Mr. Politi's *Song of the Swallows* won the
Caldecott Medal in 1950.

Henry the Explorer, by Mark Taylor, ill. by Graham Booth. Atheneum,
1966.

When Henry decided to go exploring, he made proper preparations such as a lot of flags for claiming what he discovered, and, of course, plenty of food, because exploring is hungry business. Well, Henry discovered quite a lot of things, so that it was dark by the time he and his dog, Angus, returned home—just ahead of the searching party sent out to discover Henry. This droll story has delightful illustrations, and with the text, they make an entertaining and beautiful book.

Where the Wild Things Are, by Maurice Sendak, ill. by author. Harper, 1963. Caldecott Medal.

Here is a touch of wildness that might be classified with the fanciful stories, but since it begins and ends in the real boy's bedroom and the fantasy is only a dream, it has been classified with the realistic tales. This extremely funny story is about a small boy who puts on wolflike pajamas complete with tail, and then becomes outrageously naughty. After he is put to bed, he falls asleep and dreams of horrible monsters, but *he* becomes king of them all. The drawings are hilarious, and children thoroughly enjoy both them and the text.

From *Where the Wild Things Are* written and illustrated by Maurice Sendak. Copyright © 1963 by Maurice Sendak. Reprinted by permission of Harper & Row, Publishers.

Little Tim and the Brave Sea Captain, by Edward Ardizzone, ill. by author, Walck, 1955.

This adventurous tale, which appeared in 1936, was followed by a whole series of books about Tim's daring deeds, generally involving a sea voyage and shipwreck. *Tim All Alone* is one of the most popular. Mr. Ardizzone's superb seascapes add to the excitement of the hero's activities. Only a man could have spun these convincing tales, and small girls enjoy them as much as the boys do.

Madeline, by Ludwig Bemelmans, ill. by author. Viking, 1939.

Here is an up-and-doing French heroine to match *Little Tim* in heroics. She lives in Paris, but she is universally admired. The text and the big, splendid pictures that accompany her adventures through a series of books delight grownups as much as children. *Madeline's Rescue* won the Caldecott Medal in 1954.

"B" Is for Betsy, by Carolyn Haywood, ill. by author. Harcourt, 1939.

Generously illustrated but emerging from the picture-book category, this is the first in a long series of books about Betsy's activities in her home, school, and neighborhood. *"B" Is for Betsy* focuses on six-year-old Betsy's experiences in first grade. To read one of these books aloud to children is to give them experience in following a longer continuity than most of the picture stories afford. If, however, this seems too much book for your child's attention span, postpone it until "Reading Begins" (see Chapter 5).

Real animals

Children also enjoy tales about real animals in their everyday world. Indeed, one of the interesting characteristics of children in these prereading days is their casual adjustment to the real and the fanciful. They chant with complete conviction the conversation of the third Little Pig and the Wolf, but they know the farmer's pig won't converse. They accept Peter Rabbit's shoes and little blue coat, but they don't expect the rabbit in their yard to be so dressed. People who think picture stories with talking animals will confuse a child underestimate his capacity to move from playful make-believe to his own equally interesting world of facts. Just as he enjoys tales of fanciful animals, so does he enjoy stories about real animals, living near him or with him but living their own independent lives, true to their species—stories like the following:

Make Way for Ducklings, by Robert McCloskey, ill. by author. Viking, 1941. Caldecott Medal.

Robert McCloskey has won the Caldecott Medal twice, the second time in 1958 for his *Time of Wonder*. All of his books are full of gentle reassurance. Like the ducklings, children sometimes see themselves imperiled by city traffic but brought safely through it by their mothers with the help of a policeman. That is what happened to the ducklings when their mother decided to move them from their nesting place, through busy Boston streets to the public gardens where popcorn was plentiful. With the help of Michael, the policeman who held up all traffic, Mrs. Mallard and her eight ducklings waddled safely through these perils to their destination. Humorous, realistic pictures have made this book a delight to children and their parents.

Time of Wonder, which tells of a threatened hurricane on the Maine Coast, provides reassurance and portrays warm family affections. A most beautiful book.

Angus and the Ducks, by Marjorie Flack, ill. by author. Doubleday, 1930. See also *The Story About Ping*, by Marjorie Flack, ill. by Kurt Wiese. Viking, 1933.

These amusing little animal stories by Marjorie Flack are perennial favorites with very young children. The *Angus* books are about an active little Scotch terrier, whose curiosity is always getting the better of him. *The Story About Ping* tells of the little Chinese duck, who runs away from home but discovers that home is best even with a spanking. Although these are simple plots, each book tells a good story. Miss Flack's pictures lack distinction, but they are as clear and uncomplicated as her plots. Kurt Wiese's illustrations for *Ping* are charming.

Marshmallow, by Clare Turlay Newberry, ill. by author. Harper, 1942.

Most of Mrs. Newberry's picture stories are about cats, but this story is about the white bunny, Marshmallow. Her other stories include a puppy (*Barkis*, 1938) and occasional children. The stories are slight, but children "ooh" and "aah" over the pictures of the little animals, with the texture of their furry bodies so realistic that the children want to touch them. One of the great values of these little books is that they promote even in the timid child a tenderness and love for animals.

Buttons, by Tom Robinson, ill. by Peggy Bacon. Viking, 1938.

This story of the king of alley cats who won his own snug comfort and security is a sternly realistic picture of homeless city cats. Of course, as a result of hearing this story, children may bring home every stray cat they encounter, but that is a risk parents should be willing to take for the superb drawings in this remarkable book and for the likelihood that it will help develop in children compassion for homeless, starving creatures, human as well as four-footed. This book is a fine balance for Mrs. Newberry's stories of fluffy, well-fed pets.

Dash and Dart, by Mary Buff and Conrad Buff. Viking, 1942. See also *Forest Folk* (1962) and *Hurry, Skurry, and Flurry* (1954).

Here are poetic but realistic studies of wild creatures of the forest by an author-artist team who write and illustrate with rare sensitivity and beauty. *Dash and Dart* recounts the first year in the life of twin fauns, and *Forest Folk* continues the story of the life of Dash to the time when he fights his way to be king of the herd of deer. *Hurry, Skurry, and Flurry* are three forest squirrels, who frolic through their first year of life but are always aware of the lurking dangers and enemies that finally trap one squirrel. One of the values of these books is that death is introduced casually and faced realistically. It is part of the cycle of birth, living, and death. The books read aloud beautifully, the pictures are as poetic as the cadenced text, and the stories give children an awareness of the independent life of wild creatures, and prepare them for the more complex animal stories to come.

The Big Snow, by Berta and Elmer Hader, ill. by authors. Macmillan, 1948. Caldecott Medal.

Here are beautiful pictures of birds and small animals preparing for the winter—this particular one so severe that they might never have survived without the help of their human friends.

Picture-book editions of single folk tales

Storytelling (see Chapter 3) is particularly important for the pre-readers, and so it is to be hoped that parents have told their children those classic nursery tales "The Three Little Pigs," "Chicken Little" (or "Henny Penny"), "The Little Red Hen and the Grain of Wheat," "The Three Billy Goats Gruff," "The Pancake" (or "The Gingerbread Boy"), and a few others, most of which can be found in collections of folk tales. But there are also some picture-book editions of single folk tales which parents will enjoy sharing with their children, both because reading aloud is fairly effortless and because the illustrations are entrancing. Some of the following editions will appeal to the older child as well as to the nursery child.

Dick Whittington and His Cat, ill. by Marcia Brown. Scribner, 1950.
The Old Woman and Her Pig, ill. by Paul Galdone. McGraw, 1960.
The Shoemaker and the Elves, ill. by Adrienne Adams. Scribner, 1960.
The Sleeping Beauty, ill. by Felix Hoffmann. Harcourt, 1960.
Snow White and the Seven Dwarfs, freely trans. and ill. by Wanda Gág.
    Coward-McCann, 1938.
The Three Billy Goats Gruff, ill. by Marcia Brown. Harcourt, 1957.
The Traveling Musicians, ill. by Hans Fischer. Harcourt, 1955.

And so the old woman got home that night.

32

From *The Old Woman and Her Pig,* illustrated by
Paul Galdone. Copyright 1960 by McGraw-Hill Book
Company, Inc. Reprinted by permission of the
publishers.

The Wolf and the Seven Little Kids, ill. by Felix Hoffman. Harcourt, 1959.

FOLK-TALE ANTHOLOGIES

Of course, an anthology of folk tales is a useful investment in these prereading years when adults must read aloud or tell the traditional tales. There are many such anthologies available. Here are two useful editions.

Chimney Corner Stories, collected and retold by Veronica S. Hutchinson, ill. by Lois Lenski. Putnam, 1925.
This is a small, early, but very choice collection of folk tales for young children.

Told Under the Green Umbrella, comp. by the Literature Committee of the Association for Childhood Education, ill. by Grace Gilkison. Macmillan, 1930.
This collection has twenty-six fairy tales, "all old favorites with kindergarten children."

You may wonder why traditional literature should have any appeal to or value for young children today. After all, Louise Fatio's *The Happy Lion* may be every bit as fantastic as "The Three Little Pigs," but the Lion's world of streets, stores, parks, and people is all fairly familiar to children. However, once a child takes the plunge into the world of talking wolves, wily foxes, and brave lads who tackle giants and ogres, the old stories have much of value to tell him. They warn him, for example, that in a world where wolves are very wolfish and foxes are very foxy, one had best use his head. The penalties for credulity are severe, as Henny Penny discovered; the penalty for pride and cockiness is sometimes extinction, as the Pancake learned too late. On the other hand, a gentle, kindly girl like Cinderella can always fit her foot neatly into the glass slipper and can instantly win her way into the prince's heart; and courageous, generous lads get their just rewards, but the sneering, mean sisters and brothers, the giants, and the ogres invariably come to bad ends. These are good concepts for a child to grow on. So while most of these old tales are for the next age level, parents may well start their children with a few of the simpler tales in these early years.

THE ART OF PICTURE STORIES

The picture stories are astonishingly versatile in content, as the brief samples make clear; and for this reason they have attracted some of our finest illustrators. By way of these books, children encounter the everyday realism of the here and now. They accept children of different ethnic groups, find them likable, and discover that they encounter difficulties similar to their own. By way of these books, children also enter into the diverse worlds of the fairy tales, into seriousness, nonsense, and subtle humor. And so through these picture stories, young children receive an introduction to different types of art expression and of literature. The best of these books will train their eyes to appreciate various art media, their ears to enjoy the cadence and meaning of words, and their minds to respond to something of the richness of life, real and imagined.

Since books for prereaders are predominantly picture books and picture stories, the illustrations are of major importance. But how can we evaluate this art? We know that young children will accept badly drawn, crudely colored, or simpering pictures if they illustrate a lively story. In the beginning, children will also settle for stereotypes in their stories, but they grow gradually to appreciate vividly created and unique characters. So in the field of illustration, they can be carried from a liking for the lurid or saccharine to an enjoyment of illustrations of considerable subtlety and beauty, providing that they encounter good art in their books.

The children themselves can help us draw up our criteria for illustrations. We know that children begin as stern realists, demanding a *truthful interpretation of the text*. If the hero is redheaded, no child is going to accept a brown topknot without protest. If Ludwig Bemelmans says there are twelve little girls who go walking from Madeline's school, children are strict accountants and check each picture to see that the twelve are all there. And they check all eight ducklings in Robert McCloskey's *Make Way for Ducklings*, taking notice of that last little waddler, who is always

just a bit different from the other seven. But these same children
will accept the undetailed, posterlike effect of Roger Duvoisin's
pictures for Alvin Tresselt's *White Snow, Bright Snow* and *Autumn
Harvest,* and all the others in that series.

Another phase of children's literalness at this stage is their demand that *pictures and text be precisely synchronized.* Neither
Ludwig Bemelmans nor Robert McCloskey ever fails children in
this respect, nor does Leo Politi nor do a dozen other favorite artists. If the text describes "a large tulip petal where Thumbelina
could sit and row herself," children want the picture right beside
the text to verify and amplify the words. Picture placement may
seem of minor importance to adults, but children are puzzled or
irked by illustrations that appear before or after the episodes described in the text.

Illustration from *White
Snow, Bright Snow* by
Alvin Tresselt, illustrated
by Roger Duvoisin, copy-
right 1947 by Lothrop,
Lee & Shepard Co., Inc.
By permission of
Lothrop, Lee & Shepard
Co., Inc.

Of course, children like *action* in pictures as well as in stories, and so they enjoy Ernest Shepard's tiny sketch of Christopher Robin going "Hoppity, hoppity, hop" or Nicolas Mordvinoff's illustration of Red and Russet scrambling madly over the fence with the gang in full pursuit (*Russet and the Two Reds*, Harcourt, 1962). Such action pictures will keep children poring over books long after the read-aloud adult has departed.

Finally, we know that children like bright colors, but this liking does not preclude their enjoyment of muted hues or black-and-whites. A nursery-school staff that tested children's color choices in both clothes and picture books was surprised to find no conclusive preference for primary colors. The children responded happily to the clear reds and blues the Petershams use so often in their pictures, but they also enjoyed Tasha Tudor's and Marguerite de Angeli's illustrations in gentle, pastel colors. On the whole, there is some evidence to show that children prefer colored illustrations to black-and-white illustrations, and yet no book has been more popular with young children than Wanda Gág's *Millions of Cats* or Lynd Ward's *The Biggest Bear*, with their delightful black-and-white illustrations.

Obviously, these likes and dislikes of children afford wide latitude to the adult who is sharing picture books with children. They will accept posterlike simplicity or pore over the finely drawn details of a picture. They move from pen-and-ink sketches to the unadorned beauty of a rose in *Bruno Munari's ABC* or the modern use of collage by Ezra Jack Keats and enjoy them all. In short, a child's taste is only a starting point. Adults must always remember that a child will accept any kind of picture that wraps up a story, and so it is the grownups' responsibility to train his eyes and taste with good art. Today, this training is a delightful task, because the picture story enlists the best efforts of many distinguished artists, and by way of their books a child's eyes and taste may be trained away from acceptance of gaudy saccharine illustrations to a keen enjoyment of good art in all its modern diversity. For a good sampling of the variety of illustrations available in children's books today, glance through the illustrations in this book. And examine as many as possible of the books that have received the Caldecott Medal— the medal awarded for the most distinguished picture book published each year in the United States (see the list at the end of this book). See also the discussion "The Graphic Arts" in Chapter 14.

POETRY

If poetry begins exuberantly with *Mother Goose*, children usually are disposed to continue its exploration.[2] Parents' and teachers'
experiences with reading *Mother Goose* aloud to their children
have probably convinced them that verses, whether mere jingles
or authentic lyrics, are easier to understand and enjoy if they are
heard. Fortunately, children under six must get all of their poems
through their ears, just as early peoples did, and so they speak their
favorites right along with you and have them "by heart" (a lovely
phrase) in no time at all.

Poetry anthologies

In order that children may savor a variety of verse, parents' best
investment for youngsters' early years is a good anthology which
will probably carry them through elementary school. In an anthology you can generally find excellent indexes which will lead you to
poems about the seasons, the weather, pets, people, wild animals,
festivals, and so on. Thus, on the day of the first snow you can come
up with some snow poems that are timely and delightful. Or a new
puppy in the neighborhood can be the occasion for poems about
dogs and pups or maybe for verses about a child's beloved cat,
which is now going to have to coexist with the pup. There are many
fine anthologies from which to choose, but the following three are
all good for young children.

> *Sung Under the Silver Umbrella*, comp. by the Literature Committee
> of the Association for Childhood Education. Macmillan, 1935.
> A discriminating selection of authentic poetry of great variety and
> charm.

> *Time for Poetry*, comp. by May Hill Arbuthnot and Shelton L. Root, Jr.,
> ill. by Arthur Paul. Third General Edition. Scott, 1968.
> Over 770 poems, ranging from nonsense verse to heroic ballads and
> lovely lyrics to grow on. Delightfully illustrated in pen and ink. This
> will carry a child into his high-school years.

---

[2]Poetry will be treated only briefly here, since Chapter 11 is devoted to its presentation and to its continuation with children.

Under the Tent of the Sky, ed. by John E. Brewton, ill. by Robert Lawson. Macmillan, 1937, 1966.

This is one of the best anthologies of poems about pets and wild animals that we have ever had. Although this 1937 publication was out of print for a while, it is once more available.

Books by single poets

Useful as the well-selected anthologies are, they should not be a child's only introduction to poetry. Even in his early years, he should have the experience of knowing thoroughly a single poet and his book of poems. When a child asks for "My Shadow," he should be able to find the book by Robert Louis Stevenson that contains this poem. Or if he wants "Puppy and I" or "The King's Breakfast," he should be able to go to his shelves and unerringly produce A. A. Milne's *When We Were Very Young*. Five- or six-year-olds may also know the names of the poets who wrote their favorite verses.

Perhaps it should be added at this point, by way of warning, that because of the popularity of Milne's poetry with grownups, there is a tendency to neglect those earlier lyrics by Robert Louis Stevenson. Or Stevenson's poems may be passed over for the endless stream of innocuous little rhymes and fetchingly illustrated books of "first poems" for the young that are as trivial as they are numerous. But why this constant search for the voguish and the new? It is the children who are forever new. A book does not have to be. Better a good sixty-year-old poem than some bit of versified fluff just off the press.

But parents and other adults interested in children's literature should watch for volumes of poetry by current poets. There are many charming ones, like those by Aileen Fisher and William Jay Smith, to name but two.

A *Child's Garden of Verses*, by Robert Louis Stevenson. First published in 1885. Ill. by Brian Wildsmith. First American Publication, Watts, 1966. Also ill. by Tasha Tudor (Walck, 1947), and by Jessie Wilcox Smith (Scribner, 1905).

Here are poems of the child's everyday play and his imaginative world, all sincere, forthright expressions of the child's point of view. "Windy Nights" is a fine lyric poem by any standard, and as timely now as when it was first published. Its galloping rhythm heightens the excitement and mystery of the unseen rider. "Where Go the Boats" is set to the melody of a little river, rippling along between its banks—the same water rhythm as Smetana's "The Moldau."

When We Were Very Young, by A. A. Milne, ill. by Ernest Shepard. Dutton, 1924. Also *Now We Are Six* (1927).

The verses of A. A. Milne are such fun to read aloud that mothers, fathers, and teachers enjoy them right along with the children. In spite of their occasional whimsy and their British atmosphere of nurseries, nannies, and Buckingham Palace, there is enough common ground in these verses to make their appeal universal. Milne's use of nonsense words tickles children—"biffalo-buffalo-bisons," a mouse with a "woffelly nose," "wheezles and sneezles," and all the others. "Puppy and I" is a favorite, and so is Mary Jane with her abominable "Rice Pudding." "Sand-Between-the-Toes," every seashore child understands, and in "Happiness," John in his "Great Big Waterproof Mackintosh"

From *A Child's Garden of Verses*
by Robert Louis Stevenson.
Illustrated by Brian Wildsmith.
First American Publication 1966
by Franklin Watts, Inc.

MARCHING SONG

Bring the comb and play upon it!
    Marching, here we come!
Willie cocks his highland bonnet,
    Johnnie beats the drum.

Mary Jane commands the party,
    Peter leads the rear;
Feet in time, alert and hearty,
    Each a Grenadier!

All in the most martial manner
    Marching double-quick;
While the napkin like a banner
    Waves upon the stick!

Here's enough of fame and pillage,
    Great commander Jane!
Now that we've been round the village,
    Let's go home again.

is one with the little Japanese girl and her *Umbrella* (by Taro Yashima).
Children as young as four, five, or six are ready for these verses and
should not miss them.

Going Barefoot, by Aileen Fisher, ill. by Adrienne Adams. Crowell,
  1960.
This is the first and the favorite of the seasonal books in verse that
Aileen Fisher has written. Children and grownups will enjoy the beautiful and colorful illustrations as well as the verse.

Laughing Time, by William Jay Smith, ill. by Juliet Kepes. Little, 1955.
This is clever, light verse with the kind of humor that sets young
children to chuckling. *Boy Blue's Book of Beasts* is good nonsense
poetry about animals wild and tame.

FORMAT OF CHILDREN'S BOOKS

In addition to content and illustrations, the adult, in choosing
books for children, should consider format—the shape, size, binding, paper, margins, and type size of a book. Books for children under six lead a rough life at best and should be put together sturdily.
Even the books of older children suffer more wear and tear than do
the books of adults. A favorite book goes to bed with a small child
or to camp with an older child and is generally lugged around to be
enjoyed at odd moments in odd places.

If a picture story for a young child is to last, it must have substantial paper, firm stitching, and sturdy hard covers. Size is another
consideration. For the child under six, most books should be neither too big nor too heavy for him to handle. But oddly enough,
even the smallest child sometimes enjoys a huge book that he can
stand over at a table or look at on the floor, lying on his stomach,
propped on his elbows, and oblivious to the world.

The type size, spacing, number of words to a page, and margins
are also important in a child's book. Even for the nonreader, adult-
sized type and crowded pages are undesirable. Wide margins and
large, well-spaced, clear, plain type attract a child's eye to those
queer squiggles we call letters. Then one day that child will recognize a letter or, more likely, a whole word, and reading begins.

BOOK CARE

It is never too early to teach children the proper care of the books they look at. Gradually they must understand that books are not to be used as blocks or stepping stones or weapons. Clean hands should be a requisite for the privilege of looking at books, and those hands, however small, should be taught to handle books carefully. A bookcase of a child's own or a space set aside in the family bookcases for his treasures will increase his respect for these possessions. Willful destruction or careless treatment of books should be dealt with promptly but gently. An accident should be treated with sympathy. In Lois Lenski's *Cotton in My Sack,* poor Joanda drops her precious book into the mud and is too frightened by this disaster to go back to school. One book mislaid or accidentally soiled or torn should not be allowed to frighten a child away from books or school or library.

All these admonitions testify to the fact that the baby who squirms in his mother's lap, who endures picture books only because they supply the names of things, gradually learns to follow the continuity of a well-developed story when he hears it, with or without pictures. If he has good early experiences with books, he progresses from jingles of *Mother Goose* to little poems by such poets as Robert Louis Stevenson and A. A. Milne. In some respects he becomes a complete realist, but he can also take nonsense, fairy tales, and fantasy in his stride. He learns to look at representational art and stylized pictures, cartoonlike drawings, poster effects, pictures with intricate details, bright colors, muted tones, and blacks and whites. A good beginning in art appreciation. And finally, with all these entertaining and varied experiences with books, he develops, it is to be hoped, a readiness to read for himself that should carry triumphantly into the next age level when reading begins.

READING BEGINS

FOR AGES SIX-SEVEN-EIGHT

5

If children have happy experiences with books and see their parents reading with enjoyment, they probably will be ready to learn to read when the time comes. With the help of attractive pre-primers, primers, and manuals, their skillful first-grade teachers will see that they get the necessary practice in word recognition, develop confidence that they *are* reading, and grow steadily in reading skills. As teachers know, the point at this stage is to hold children's interest and keep up their sense of achievement so that they will move ahead buoyantly and with anticipatory delight through all the stages in beginning to read.

HOW PARENTS CAN HELP

As a parent, you can help, too. If your child wants to read to you from his new books, encourage him and greet his efforts with interest and proper astonishment at his prowess. Continue to tell him stories or read aloud to him from informational books that meet his particular interests. Temper your zeal if you think that you should lay in a supply of those much advertised "easy-to-read" books that are flooding the market. Let that patient and knowledgeable teacher have your child on her own through those crucial months of the first semester or term of the first grade. But if at the end of that time, the teacher tells you or you discover yourself that your child is showing signs of discouragement or of falling behind, discuss the problem with her. Probably she will encourage you to find for the slow learner some easy books that will provide him with needed independent practice, and for the fast learner, books with substantial content that will keep him reading and improving his skills.

Of course, it is well to remind ourselves that children differ widely in the ages at which they learn to walk or talk or at which they evince readiness to learn to read. Most boys come to the reading readiness stage later than girls do and should therefore be given more latitude in these early months if they are not to be turned against reading. If your child is slow at mastering rudimentary reading skills, be patient. Frequently a Johnny-come-lately turns into a Johnny-goes-further in the end. Keep up his confidence and his interest during the slow periods and provide him with tempting materials and, above all, with an easy, unharassed atmosphere. No prodding and no nagging! Actually, what any child needs at any level of reading difficulty is plenty of practice with reading material so easy that as he tackles it on his own he begins to enjoy a sense of fluency and with it growing confidence. Needless to say, what he reads must interest him. It is for these reasons that both teachers and parents must be on the alert for easy books that will afford this practice and command the child's interest.

HOW TO FIND EASY-TO-READ BOOKS

Teachers can often suggest easy-to-read books for parents to borrow from the public library. These are not always books parents

will want to buy for their child's own library, though some of them
may be. A children's librarian, too, will be an invaluable source,
for she will know the latest books in this field as well as the older
tried-and-true favorites. She will have lists of easy books grouped
according to subject matter and grade levels. Best of all, she will
have the superior books in this field available for parents to look
over and to decide for themselves which books are right for their
child's reading and interest levels. If parents cannot consult a children's librarian, then they must resort to book lists and try from
their annotations to guess which books will do the most for their
child at his particular level of reading difficulty.

To date, the following two lists of easy books are the best available:

Books for Beginning Readers, by Elizabeth Guilfoile. National Council
of Teachers of English, 1962.

The introduction deals with the reading difficulties of beginners and
also discusses in detail some of the most significant books. The list contains more than 320 books from 38 different sources, a list that "tends to
be inclusive rather than selective because the need for these books, so
long apparent, has only begun to be met." See also Elizabeth Guilfoile's "One Hundred More Books for Beginning Readers," *Elementary
English*, April 1963.

I Can Read It Myself! by Frieda M. Heller. Revised Edition. Ohio
State University, 1965.

This is a list of "some books for independent reading in the primary
grades." In supplying children with easy-reading books, the compiler
thinks that it is "best to think of the children not as first graders, second
graders, or third graders, but as children who have just experienced
the thrill of reading by themselves, those who read a little better than
that, and those who (in their own words) read 'real good.'" This list,
with its triumphant title, has been prepared in terms of these three
levels.

CRITERIA FOR EASY-TO-READ BOOKS

As you scan the lists, you will probably be overwhelmed by the
number of titles. What are some criteria by which you can evaluate
these books? The physical aspect of the book is the most obvious.

For the sixes and sevens, large, clear type is essential as is plenty of white space so that there is not a depressing amount of print to a page. Short sentences and short thought units are important. For the eights who are having trouble, sentences should still be short, but the content should be stepped up to the point where they can enjoy and respect what they are able to read. For the youngest children, the pictures should furnish clues to the action and to word meanings. For the eights, the pictures may be fewer and not so literally interpretative, and they may well supply something over and beyond the precise action or the meaning of the words.

Easy books should also measure up to the literary criteria set for any stories (see Chapter 2). After all, a child probably will not know the words *theme, plot, characterization,* and *style*—or their significance—but it is to be hoped that he has been enjoying all four in his prereading years of picture stories, and that he will continue to encounter good examples of theme, plot, characterization, and style in his easy-to-read books.

The easy-to-read books should also be based on or grow out of the child's basic needs for various types of security, for competence or achievement, and especially for loving and being loved. Some of the books will supply him with plain facts, and some may provide him with the therapy of laughter or tears or of sheer nonsense.

It is well to remember, however, that we may find few if any examples of imperishable literature among these easy-to-read books. After all, we are looking for useful and appealing tools to help children toward independent reading. If at a particular time a book helps a child gain reading fluency and if it proves to be a book he likes and can handle alone, then that book is for him a worthwhile reading experience.

EASY BOOKS FOR BEGINNERS, LATE 6's AND EARLY 7's

I Know a Farm, by Ethel Collier, ill. by Honoré Guilbeau. W. R. Scott, 1960.

Ethel Collier has written some charming books for the beginners, the late 6's and early 7's. They are gaily and sensitively illustrated in color. In this book a father drives his little girl to a farm for the day. On the way he sometimes stops for something she wants and sometimes drives past something she wants. At the farm her experiences are also a balance between success and failure, permissions and refusals, always reasonable. Even at the end of the day, when she has discovered baby kittens, she cannot have one to take home until it is older. Ethel Collier's books do not have rousing plots, yet they give young readers an inexplicable amount of satisfaction. This is partly due to the beautiful, uncomplicated, and truly interpretative illustrations, but also to the fact that the grace and simplicity of the texts reflect the child's world of wonder and delight. See also Ethel Collier's *Who Goes There in My Garden?* and *The Birthday Tree.*

Little Bear, by Else Holmelund Minarik, ill. by Maurice Sendak. Harper, 1957. Also *Father Bear Comes Home* (1959), *Little Bear's Friend* (1960), and *Little Bear's Visit* (1961).

These epoch-making, easy-to-read books are just as popular today as they were when they were first published. Stories and illustrations are equally beguiling. Despite their shortness and primerlike quality, the sentences sound natural and have a pleasant flow. The first book, perhaps, is the warmest and the funniest. When Little Bear thinks no one remembers his birthday, Mother Bear appears with a glorious cake complete with candles. When Little Bear returns after taking off for the moon, Mother Bear asks who he is, but this pretending soon goes too far for comfort. Finally, Little Bear says, "Mother Bear, stop fooling,/ You are my Mother Bear/ and I am your Little Bear,/ and we are on Earth and you know it./ Now may I eat my lunch?" Maurice Sendak's drawings are exactly right and enhance the humor and the loving reassurance of the stories.

Are You My Mother? by P. D. Eastman, ill. by author. Random House, 1960.

This humorous and tender fantasy for very young readers is about a baby robin who set out in search of his mother. He asked every animal he met, "Are you my mother?" but not until a steam shovel picked him up and put him down again close to his nesting place, did he find his own true mother. The scientists may not care for this picture of a newly hatched robin off on a pilgrimage, but young readers enjoy the appealing and readable little tale, which is told in only one hundred words.

The Cat in the Hat, by Dr. Seuss (pseud. for Theodore Seuss Geisel), ill. by author. Random House, 1957.

Another favorite with children, *The Cat in the Hat* is one of Dr. Seuss' best. It is a preposterous, nonsensical fantasy about Cat, who takes over a house in the absence of the mother and does all the appalling things the children might *dream* of doing but would never really do. Readers are, of course, horrified at the increasing mess and are also happily titillated that it is so terrific with mother liable to walk in any moment! The serene conclusion is a gem of wishful thinking that brings every young reader back to a rereading of this completely satisfying nightmare. See also *And to Think That I Saw It on Mulberry Street* (1937), *The 500 Hats of Bartholomew Cubbins* (1938), *Horton Hatches the Egg* (1940). These are not so easy to read as *The Cat in the Hat,* but they are enormously popular with children.

Nobody Listens to Andrew, by Elizabeth Guilfoile, ill. by Mary Stevens. Follett, 1957.

This is a masterly story and deservedly popular. The title is the theme of the book and reveals a predicament that every young child suffers from and understands thoroughly. After Andrew has tried vainly to get the attention of his family and a neighbor, he finally screams his information—and then there is a to-do! The hilarious conclusion evokes delighted chuckles from all readers, who return to the book again and again.

Flip, by Wesley Dennis, ill. by author. Viking, 1941. Also *Flip and the Cows* (1942) and *Flip and the Morning* (1951).

The texts for these three books about Flip, a lovable colt, are less simple than those for the books just listed, but Mr. Dennis' pictures almost tell the stories. The first two books, *Flip* and *Flip and the Cows,* are about the colt's fears. In the former, he is afraid to jump a little brook but finally learns in spite of himself. In the latter, he gets into a panic at the approach of the cows, but after their benign interest in him almost scares him out of his wits, he gets over his silly fright. These stories of timidities made to look a bit foolish and then conquered have a strong appeal for young children. The third book, *Flip and the Morning,* is just plain funny. A cross old goat develops a plan for putting a stop to Flip's early rising, but his plan boomerangs hilariously. The humorous and beautiful drawings not only give clues to the text but will make animal lovers of the children who see them.

Other books for these beginning readers may be found among the picture stories listed for the prereaders (Chapter 4) as well as in the bibliography for this chapter. These books, all with strong child appeal, not only provide easy reading practice but introduce children to city and country experiences, to realism, fantasy, and nonsense.

EASY BOOKS FOR 7's AND 8's

If by the beginning or by the second half of the second year in school, your child is markedly falling behind the other children in his ability to read or is showing signs of discouragement or lack of interest in school, then indeed he needs help. Talk over the situation with his teacher and follow through on her suggestions. If she thinks easy books will help, you may start him with some of those listed for the 6's and 7's, but obviously, *Little Bear*, for example, despite its humor, will look and seem too immature for an eight-year-old. On the other hand, any age will chuckle over Dr. Seuss' *The Cat in the Hat* or the absurdities of the Syd Hoff books (see p. 107); or perhaps the easy informational books (see pp. 103-104 and Chapter 13) may catch his interest and start him reading. Then step up the content with other books, like those in the following list:

Emmett's Pig, by Mary Stolz, ill. by Garth Williams. Harper, 1959.
This story seems to be for younger children than the 7's and 8's, but it deals with a problem many city, apartment-dwelling children share—the hopeless desire for a pet. Emmett's heart's desire was for, of all animals, a pig! The solution of his problem makes a good story, and the illustrations add to the fun. Mary Stolz writes well, whether for the 6's or the 16's.

May I Bring a Friend? by Beatrice Schenk de Regniers, ill. by Beni Montresor. Atheneum, 1964. Caldecott Medal.
Despite the picture-book format, this fantasy should tickle any age. A small boy tells how, whenever he was invited to the castle by the king and queen, he asked whether he might bring a friend. The king invariably replied, most politely, "Any friend of our friend is welcome

here." And this politeness never wavered, even when the friends turned out to be such outsize specimens as a giraffe and a hippopotamus. Dramatic and startling pictures by Beni Montresor, a famous designer of stage sets, make reading easy and add to the fun.

The Snow Party, by Beatrice Schenk de Regniers, ill. by Reiner Zimnik. Pantheon, 1959.

The story sounds like a dream, but is based on a real event. An old woman and an old man, living by themselves on a Dakota farm, are lonely, and the old woman wishes she could give a party. Then the blizzards begin, bringing one carload of stranded motorists after another

The King said, "Hello."
He said, "How do you do?"
The Queen said, "Well!
Fancy meeting you!"

Pictures copyright © 1964 by Beni Montresor. From *May I Bring a Friend?* by Beatrice Schenk de Regniers. Used by permission of Atheneum Publishers and William Collins Sons & Co. Ltd.

to seek refuge in the little farmhouse. Finally, when a bakery truck breaks down at their door and the driver brings in all the delectable foods any hostess could hope for, the old woman has a wonderful party. This happy exaggeration of a real experience makes a warm, satisfying story.

The Biggest Bear, by Lynd Ward, ill. by author. Houghton, 1952. Caldecott Medal.

This big picture story may look babyish to the older primary children, but if they look at the pictures, they will be won over—as readers are, of any age. Ashamed that his family did not have a bearskin nailed to the side of the barn as all the neighbors had, Young Johnny was determined to capture a bear all by himself, and he did—a beguiling cub. But the cub didn't stay a cub. It grew, and so did Johnny's problems. The results are funny, but the solution is not easy, nor can it be wholly satisfactory. However, both Johnny and his bear seem fairly well resigned at the end. Even without Mr. Ward's powerful, droll illustrations, this is a good story.

At this point, look at two child-made fantasies because the years from five to eight are periods when the difference between dreams and facts, "moonshine" and the real, can sometimes become seriously confused. In the first book, a busy mother handles the problem matter-of-factly, and in the second, it is an understanding father.

Tigers in the Cellar, by Carol Fenner, ill. by author. Harcourt, 1963.

Even after mother said, "Nonsense!" the small heroine was sure there were tigers in the cellar; so one night she climbed out of bed to investigate. Sure enough, there were two tigers, one a weeping tiger, the other a singing tiger, who invited her to take a ride on his back. Next morning, mother's only response to our heroine's account of the night's excitement was, "What a funny dream! . . . Now go pick up your clothes." And the world was disgustingly everydayish once more. Amusing illustrations add to the fun.

Sam, Bangs, & Moonshine, by Evaline Ness, ill. by author. Holt, 1966. Caldecott Medal.

Evaline Ness, a distinguished artist, has told an unforgettable story. Sam (for Samantha) can dream the doormat into a chariot drawn by dragons, in imagination replace her dead mother with a mermaid, and give herself a baby kangaroo for a pet, and also insist that Bangs, her cat, can talk. This "moonshine," as her father calls it, gets Sam's best friend and poor Bangs into grave peril. Their narrow escape teaches Samantha the danger of "flummadiddle" and the necessity for truth in place of moonshine.

By the second half of the second year of school or by the beginning of the third grade, children should have developed considerable independence in reading and should be able to enjoy stories with a fair amount of content and continuity, like those in the following list:

Billy and Blaze, by C. W. Anderson, ill. by author. Macmillan, 1936, 1962. Also *Blaze and the Forest Fire* (1938, 1962), *Blaze and the Gypsies* (1937), *Blaze Finds the Trail* (1950).

These are exciting boy and pony stories, with splendid drawings by the author-artist, who knows every rippling muscle and every movement of horses.

From *Sam, Bangs & Moonshine* written and illustrated by Evaline Ness. Copyright © 1966 by Evaline Ness. Reprinted by permission of Holt, Rinehart and Winston, Inc.

Little Eddie, by Carolyn Haywood, ill. by author. Morrow, 1947.

This is the first of the books about the amusing adventures of Eddie and his friends, by the author of the *Betsy* books. Little Eddie collects "valuables" from a goat to an old fire engine and has his ups and downs through some eight books—*Eddie and the Fire Engine* (1949), *Eddie and Gardenia* (1951), *Eddie's Pay Dirt* (1953), *Eddie and His Big Deals* (1955), and others.

Did You Carry the Flag Today, Charley? by Rebecca Caudill, ill. by Nancy Grossman. Holt, 1966.

The fact that mountaineer Charley is only "four a goin' on five" will make the sevens and eights feel happily superior, and so will Charley's mistakes. His bump of curiosity and his ignorance of teachers and school lead to some very funny mishaps. But Charley is such a good-natured and happy nonconformist that no one blames him. Only his family worries that unless Charley learns to read and do a few other expected things he may never have the honor of carrying the flag. But thanks to patient and understanding teachers, Charley finally makes peace with education, and comes home in triumph, having carried the flag at last.

John Billington, Friend of Squanto, by Clyde Bulla, ill. by Peter Burchard. Crowell, 1956. Also *Squanto, Friend of the White Men* (1954) and *The Poppy Seeds* (1955).

Now is the time to introduce young readers to the varied and numerous books of Clyde Bulla. They are action stories told with a rare combination of simplicity and charm. Here are three of the simpler tales—Mr. Bulla's subjects and plots will keep pace with the growing child. *John Billington* is the amusing record of a small, obstreperous Pilgrim, who frequently managed to get himself into trouble and who eventually was captured by Indians. Scrappy young John was returned to his home, and peace was established with the Indians through the help of the kindly Indian, Squanto. Squanto's own story—*Squanto, Friend of the White Men*—is a well-told account of an unusual man and makes a good introduction to biography. *The Poppy Seeds* is in an entirely different vein. It is a gentle story of a Mexican boy's dream of bringing beauty to his arid land. How eventually he persuades a miserable hoarder of spring water to share his dream and also the precious treasure of water makes a satisfying story, illustrated by the distinguished Mexican artist Jean Charlot.

The Bears on Hemlock Mountain, by Alice Dalgliesh, ill. by Helen Sewell. Scribner, 1952. Also *The Thanksgiving Story,* ill. by Helen Sewell, 1954; *The Fourth of July Story,* ill. by Marie Nonnast, 1956; and *The Columbus Story,* ill. by Leo Politi, 1955.

Miss Dalgliesh's historical stories are good not only for easy reading at a more advanced content level but also for enrichment. *The Bears on Hemlock Mountain* is the simplest and the most amusing of these books. It is both a thriller and a chiller. Jonathan, who has to go over the mountain to borrow a big kettle for his mother, is assured that there are no bears on Hemlock Mountain, but there are—two big ones. Jonathan's method of saving himself is scary but sensible. *The Columbus Story* is an appealing introduction to the man Columbus, and *The Thanksgiving Story* and *The Fourth of July Story* are beginnings for United States history. These books should not prove too difficult reading, but if they do, put them off for a few months.

BOOKS FOR SLOW OR RELUCTANT READERS, 8's AND 9's

By third grade, children, it is hoped, have attained enough ease and fluency in reading so that they enjoy reading independently. But this does not always happen. If by the second half or the end of the third grade, children still have not mastered the basic reading skills, their troubles will pile up in the fourth grade. Arithmetic, science, and social studies all begin to make heavy demands on their ability to read on their own. The third grade, therefore, is critical in the learning-to-read process, a grade where all too many children bog down into indifference or acquire a deep-seated aversion to books.

Even able readers—those who have mastered the basic skills —may at the eight- to nine-year-old period turn into reluctant readers, averse to spending any time with books outside of school. Children may acquire a lasting impatience with reading if the books they encounter are childish in content compared to, say, the programs they watch on TV. About this time, children become much more social, and their group interests—games, cliques, and clubs —may take over to the point where there is literally no time for reading. Sometimes there are also too many outside pressures—

dancing lessons or music lessons, dentist appointments, and the
like. Time is at a premium for the modern child as well as for his
hard-pressed parents.

For these two different types of nonreading eight- and nine-year-
olds—the poor reader and the reluctant reader—the treatment
differs. In general, the poor readers need expert help which must
be left largely to the school or to the clinic specialists. Often the
classroom teacher or someone from the school reading clinic will
suggest helpful measures to be carried out in the home to reinforce
school aid. By and large, the diagnosis and the remedy are best
left in the hands of such experts.

But the slow reader and the able though reluctant reader share
one need in common—the need for plenty of books, high in interest
for each individual child. For one child, fairy tales, tall tales, and
fantasy may be "high in interest." Another wants only horse or
dog stories. Still another wants books about sports or adventure or
mystery. Others search for informational books about snakes or
rockets, stones or stars, and, of course, space. These are all available
at different levels of reading skill. Many are listed in the succeeding
chapters of this book; most are found in abundance in libraries
and book stores. For the poor or the reluctant reader, look first for
books in his particular field of interest, but don't stop there. Children fall into deplorable reading ruts—all horse stories or fairy tales
or all informational books. These are fine, up to a point, but try
to lure them into other fields by offering some super-duper book
that no child can resist.

The following stories are high in child appeal. Furthermore, they
will provide easy reading for the slow readers and rapid reading for
the able readers. They should also lead children into other books
and perhaps into other reading interests as their reading fluency
improves.

Lentil, by Robert McCloskey, ill. by author. Viking, 1940. Also Homer
Price (1943).

Lentil is pure Americana and tickles grownups as well as children.
Glorious pictures and an easy text relate the adventures of a harmonica-
playing boy. He practiced in the bathtub, he practiced as he sauntered
past the Soldiers and Sailors Monument and the other village landmarks. Finally, his exuberant pipings led to a surprising triumph, a
great satisfaction both to Lentil and to the town.

Homer Price is about another small boy's series of adventures that range from trapping burglars and debunking a Superman to starting and not being able to stop the doughnut machine. Perhaps *Homer* belongs on the list of books for the fluent readers of this age level or older, but it is so hilarious that slow readers have been known to tackle it and come through in spite of themselves.

Betsy and Billy, by Carolyn Haywood, ill. by author. Harcourt, 1941. Also *Betsy and the Boys* (Harcourt, 1945) and *Betsy's Little Star* (Morrow, 1950).
This long series of Betsy stories, beginning with *"B" Is for Betsy,* discussed in Chapter 4, can be started with any one of the books. They give children practice in following a series of related episodes.

Here Comes Kristie, by Emma L. Brock, ill. by author. Knopf, 1942. Also *Kristie and the Colt and the Others* (1949) and *Kristie's Buttercup* (1952).
These are all amusing horse stories, but the first one is tops. The books are often listed for older children, although they are relatively easy reading except for an occasional lapse into dialect—"yust" for "just," for example—but once the children get used to the repetitive patterns of the narratives, they have plain sailing. Two farm boys, Elmer and Einer, have saved $15, with which to buy their heart's desire—a horse of their own. They acquire an ancient, bony specimen named Kristie. She seems amiable, but once they get her home, they discover strange things about her. For instance, she won't go unless she is wearing her straw hat. When she does go, she goes not forward, but in circles. Other bothersome habits turn up, but as the old horse grows fatter, handsomer, and more affectionate, the boys adore her. Finally, just as they have solved all her left-over circus habits and all is going well, the pigs eat Kristie's straw hat. The handling of this emergency makes a hilarious conclusion to a droll tale.

Ponies of Mykillengi, by Lonzo Anderson, ill. by Adrienne Adams. Scribner, 1966.
Told with simplicity and directness, this is a remarkably suspenseful story. Mykillengi is "a lonesome farm in Iceland," and the time is "long ago." The long Iceland winter is moderating at last, and Rauf and his young sister Egli are wild to be outdoors again. The family gives them permission to ride their ponies to the river to see if the salmon

are running. The expedition starts out gaily, but before they reach the river, the south wind has stopped, the cold is creeping up, and there is a strange darkness. With an ominous rumbling and roar, the earth trembles and opens. How the children survive an earthquake, a volcanic eruption, and a blizzard and also see the pony Hekla through her foaling time and carry home the little newborn colt is a thrilling story, well told and beautifully illustrated.

Riding the Pony Express, by Clyde Bulla, ill. by Grace Paull. Crowell, 1948. Also *Down the Mississippi,* ill. by Peter Burchard, 1954; *The Secret Valley,* ill. by Grace Paull, 1949; and *The White Bird,* ill. by Leonard Weisgard, 1966.

Riding the Pony Express tells the exciting story of a boy who traveled alone from New York westward, searching for his father, a rider for the Pony Express. When boy and father finally met, they were separated almost immediately by the father's next assignment. Left behind in the station, the boy hated the place, the people, and the horses, but he learned to put up with all three and to do what needed to be done. Through caring for and riding the horses, he developed a new respect and love for the gallant animals. The climax came when his father was wounded and the boy took his place and carried the mail through triumphantly.

Down the Mississippi pictures an entirely different kind of life. A farm boy, attracted to the great river that flowed by the farm, finally boarded a raft to travel down the full length of the river. He was only an assistant to the cook, a job that did not promise much excitement, but storms and an Indian attack provided more action than the boy ever dreamed of.

Still another environment is provided in *The Secret Valley,* the story of a family's search for gold in California. The gold remained elusive, but the family found other treasures. So each book by Clyde Bulla provides a glimpse of life in a different environment and in a different time. He tells his action stories in an easy, pleasant style.

Less adventurous than the preceding stories, *The White Bird* is a distinguished and deeply moving book, a story of loneliness and a search for love. As a baby, John Thomas was rescued from a flood by Luke Vail, who raised him. Man and boy lived alone in a deserted valley, and stern Luke told the boy that people were bad and that it was better to live alone. The boy found an injured crow, pure white, nursed it back to health, and loved it despite Luke. When the bird was taken away with Luke's knowledge, John Thomas ran away to search for his pet. In the world beyond his valley he met kindness and help. Finally, he came to realize that Luke had loved and cared for him; so John Thomas went back to their valley to help Luke and to bring him out of the valley to people.

THE ADVANCED READER AMONG THE 8's

At last we come to that joy of every teacher and the pride of every parent, the child who learns to read easily and fluently, almost by osmosis it would seem. By the end of the third grade, he can read comfortably books listed for fifth and sixth graders, and parents should be sure to use those lists freely. Anything he can and will read that fits his social needs and interests, the child should be allowed to have. By high-school years, this same child will be able to take on any adult book that interests him. These superior readers may not represent more than a very small per cent of all the children, but they are worth a grownup's best efforts to keep them challenged and excited over their reading. Dull books or books that strike them as babyish can lead to boredom and complete indifference to books. Hence, the need to keep them interested. When such children are not interested, they sometimes begin to read quantities of easy, second-rate books just to fill time. Such books may not do the child any appreciable harm, but they waste his time, leave him intellectually unchallenged, and probably lessen his ability to concentrate on more substantial reading matter. To such a child, it is well to say now and then, "Here is a book I believe you are equal to right now, though it is intended for older children. Try it and see how you like it." Of course, you should not expect every book your child reads to provide intellectual stretching exercises, any more than you demand that all your reading is on a high intellectual plane. Sometimes, we need easy entertainment, sometimes sheer hilarity, and occasionally a little chill up the backbone. And so it is with children.

Books like the following are good to try out with these superior readers among the eights.

Big Tree, by Mary and Conrad Buff, ill. by Conrad Buff. Viking, 1946.
Texts and pictures tell the story of a giant redwood growing in the

forests of California. It began as a tiny seed that was in existence before
the events of recorded history. The seed had grown into a tree almost
eight hundred years old by the time the Egyptians were building the
pyramids. Then the narrative follows the growth of the redwood through
the period when Christ was born and through the succeeding years
until at last the tree has grown to its full majesty. This is a rare book,
which gives children an almost overpowering sense of time and of
nature's impressive achievements. It should also give impetus to our
present-day pleas for conservation.

Blue Willow, by Doris Gates, ill. by Paul Lanz. Viking, 1940.
   There have been several good stories about the families of migrant
workers (Lois Lenski's *Strawberry Girl*, Lippincott, 1945, won the
Newbery Medal), but *Blue Willow* remains one of the tenderest and
most perceptive of all these books. Janey yearned for a permanent home
and for regular school, but she and her parents made the most of their
inadequate housing and pay and were friendly with their more desirable fellow migrants. How Janey's dream came true, only after cruel
vicissitudes, makes a heart-warming story, beautifully written and
illustrated.

   Books like *Blue Willow* confront young readers with definite
social problems and will widen and deepen their sense of social
relationships and responsibilities. Other such books are discussed
in Chapter 6 and listed at the close of this chapter.
   But what about folk tales and modern fantasy? Children, even the
most able readers of the eights, shouldn't be concerned only with
serious tales of problems faced and surmounted. It is said that
around eight and nine years old the interest in make-believe
reaches its peak. Fortunately, the choice of such books for this age
group is almost unlimited. Furthermore, since the folk tales and
fables represent a distillation of the wit and wisdom of the race,
this is the time to give children more of the picture-story editions
of the old tales to read for themselves. The following list, arranged
alphabetically by artist, is just a sampling of the beautiful and sometimes humorous single editions of fables, folk tales, and fanciful
tales available today (see Chapter 4 for collections and other single
tales). Of course, many of these books are read aloud to the younger
children, and so don't be surprised if the eight-year-olds reject
them. But try them and see.

Adams, Adrienne, ill. *Thumbelina*, by Hans Christian Andersen. Scribner, 1961.
Snow White and Rose Red, from the Grimms. Scribner, 1964.
The Ugly Duckling, by Hans Christian Andersen. Scribner, 1965.

Blegvad, Erik, ill. *The Swineherd*, by Hans Christian Andersen. Harcourt, 1958.

Brown, Marcia, ill. *The Flying Carpet*, an adaptation of the Magic Carpet story from *The Arabian Nights*. Scribner, 1956.
Cinderella, a favorite French tale. Scribner, 1954. Caldecott Medal.
Puss in Boots. Scribner, 1952. (See also Hans Fischer's illustrated version of this tale—Harcourt, 1959.)
Stone Soup, based on an old French folk tale. Scribner, 1947.
The Wild Swans, by Hans Christian Andersen. Scribner, 1963.

"I want ten kisses from the Princess," answered the swineherd.
"Saints preserve us!" cried the lady-in-waiting.
"It can't be had for less," said the swineherd.
"Well, what does he say?" asked the Princess.

18

Burkert, Nancy Ekholm, ill. *The Nightingale*, by Hans Christian Andersen, trans. by Eva Le Gallienne. Harper, 1965.

Burton, Virginia, ill. *The Fast Sooner Hound*, by Arna Bontemps and Jack Conroy. Houghton, 1942.
This American tall tale may lead boys to the Paul Bunyan and Pecos Bill stories.

Cooney, Barbara, ill. *Chanticleer and the Fox*, adapted from Geoffrey Chaucer's "The Nun's Priest's Tale." Crowell, 1958. Caldecott Medal.

Ness, Evaline, ill. *Tom Tit Tot*, Joseph Jacobs' tale, adapted by Evaline Ness. Scribner, 1965.

Wildsmith, Brian, ill. *The Lion and the Rat*, from La Fontaine. Watts, 1963.
The North Wind and the Sun, from *Aesop*. Watts, 1964.

As for modern fantasy, it is so varied and entrancing that you can take any one of these books and find something to delight and intrigue children. The books in the following list are ones many children have heard read aloud and may now be ready to try for themselves. For the superior readers, look also to the books listed in Chapters 6 and 7.

Winnie-the-Pooh, by A. A. Milne, ill. by Ernest Shepard. Dutton, 1936. Also *The House at Pooh Corner* (1928, 1961).
These amusing whimsies are about Christopher Robin and his chatty toys—Winnie the Pooh, the Bear of Very Little Brain, Eeyore, Kanga, Roo, and Piglet. If children like these books, they read and reread them for a number of years. If they can't read the books on their own, the stories are delightful to read aloud.

Rabbit Hill, by Robert Lawson, ill. by author. Newbery Medal. Viking, 1944. Also *The Tough Winter* (1954).
Robert Lawson had already won the Caldecott Medal for distinguished illustrations when his delightful fantasy *Rabbit Hill* was given the Newbery Medal. The story begins with the four-footed denizens of Rabbit Hill worrying about what kind of folks are going to move into

the big house. But even pessimistic Uncle Analdos Rabbit is reassured when a sign appears, which says, "Please Drive Carefully on Account of Small Animals." Later, Mother and Father Rabbit, Willie the Field-mouse, and Porky the Woodchuck cannot say enough for the generous "garbidge," no poison, no trap policy of the New Folks. Even so, mishaps do occur, but the year ends on a high note with the appearance of a lovely little sanctuary, complete with pool, a presiding St. Francis, and a sign, "There is enough for all."

Ten years after the publication of *Rabbit Hill*, Robert Lawson continued the adventures of his Rabbit Hill characters in *The Tough Winter*. This story, despite its gentle humor, is a grave picture of what can happen to small animals during long periods of icy, freezing weather. This time there are no kindly human beings on hand to help the animals, and their plight is desperate. If ever there was an effective plea for first aid to winterbound birds and beasts, this book is it. Delightful pen-and-ink sketches illumine both stories.

The Adventures of Pinocchio, by C. Collodi (pseud. for Carlo Lorenzini). (There are many editions of this nineteenth-century Italian classic.)
Pinocchio has proved as popular in this country as abroad. It would be a pity for any child to miss it. The story of the impudent, ungrateful puppet who came to life is almost too well known to need any briefing. The episode that no child ever forgets is that about the outrageous puppet running away from school and subsequently growing long donkey ears. Humorous and disconcerting as the tales of Dr. Seuss, but with a wonderful moral sense permeating the whole, the adventures and eventual reform of the naughty Pinocchio make a spellbinding tale.

Charlotte's Web, by E. B. White, ill. by Garth Williams. Harper, 1952.
It is useless to assign this beloved fantasy to any particular age level. It can be read aloud to the prereaders, read by the good readers of eight, nine, and ten, and thoroughly enjoyed by any age thereafter. The story begins with complete realism—Fern, a farm child, is raising a runt of a pig as a pet. But when the farmer relegates Wilbur the pig to the barnyard and Fern follows her pet as an observer, she discovers that she can understand the language of all the barnyard animals and fowls. Charlotte the spider has befriended Wilbur and promises to save him from the fall butchery. How she manages involves some very funny episodes and a poignant conclusion with the death of Charlotte. Written

by a master of prose style, dialogue and narrative are captivating to children and adults as well.

It must be said that there is no area of children's reading (unless poetry, perhaps) where tastes differ more strongly than in the field of fantasy. Take the folk tales. Some children outgrow them much earlier than others. Little girls are often reading them avidly at twelve years, when boys their same age are reading space fiction, or no fantasy at all. Some children reject *Winnie-the-Pooh* completely. Perhaps it's too British or too whimsical or talking toys seem too babyish. One small boy, however, loved his copy so dearly that every summer, when the family made its annual trek to their island and each of the four children was limited to one favorite book, he chose his battered copy of *Winnie-the-Pooh*. All you can do is expose your children to some of these well-conceived, well-written fantasies, sometimes serious, sometimes hilarious, and see what they like. But don't let a child miss these books entirely. Our age is full of violence, threats, and anxieties which are bound to carry through to the child's world. Fantasies furnish him with a momentary release from the pressure of the factual—an escape, if you will, into a bright world of wish fulfillment and delight. He knows it is make-believe, but that does not make Pinocchio's adventures any less funny or hair raising or the death of wise Charlotte the spider any less poignant—nonsense and self-sacrifice, both savored vicariously by way of enthralling stories!

HOW TO PREVENT READING DIFFICULTIES

If this discussion of beginning reading seems to give undue emphasis to reading difficulties, it is for good reasons. These are crucial years. Parents assume that each child entering first grade is going to learn to read and that he will improve continuously with each succeeding grade. It does happen this way with many children, and some have even learned to read before they go to school. But for others, the process is neither so regular nor so comfortable. Parents do not always sense when their child is developing an increasing feeling of failure because of his reading difficulties. How can reading problems be prevented? What can parents do to help a child if they do develop? And what should parents do for the child who is an eager reader capable of reading way beyond his grade level? Most parents are faced with one or another of these questions. Answers to some of these questions have already been suggested in the preceding pages, but the prevention and cure of reading problems are so important that some of these points will be summarized and expanded in the following paragraphs.

First, to prevent reading difficulties from developing, provide a rich environment of books in the home either by buying choice picture stories or borrowing them regularly from the public library. Perhaps a group of mothers could buy a collection of books and exchange them from time to time. Read aloud to your child often enough so that his vocabulary, comprehension, and attention span all increase naturally. The child who has such a background of seeing books and hearing them read aloud will bring to his first school years a liking for reading, an ear for new words, and an ability to concentrate and to attend to a fairly long story. Incidentally, if a child understands a word from hearing or speaking it, he is more likely to recognize it when he sees it in print.

In addition to a prereading environment of books, a child should have rich all-round experiences, especially sensory. The child who knows the four seasons through satisfying outdoor experiences—flying kites in the winds of spring, skating or coasting in winter, scuffing through fallen leaves in autumn, picking berries in the hot summer sun—will bring a greater depth of comprehension to his reading. So the child who has cherished a pet or cared for farm animals or watched wild animals in woods or meadows or zoo will bring to the reading of animal stories a deeper understanding than will the child who has missed all such experiences. In short, the wider and richer the child's preschool experiences, the keener will be his perceptions and understandings when he begins to read for himself.

Second, if reading difficulties do start or accumulate, look for the easy-to-read books that will interest your particular child. It is well to remember that some children can be more easily lured into reading by informational books than by stories. One boy wants to know about the turtles he has acquired and is surprised to discover that there is a book which tells all about them and their care. A little girl turns into a bird watcher by way of a birds' feeding box and is delighted to find a bird book that she can read for herself. The following list suggests some of the variety of informational books. Turn also to the bibliographies for Chapters 13 and 14, for books in the field of your child's particular interest. Whether it is stones, grasshoppers, stars, space travel, music, art, or what-have-you, there are usually easy-to-read books available, as well as fuller accounts for more competent readers.

Caudill, Rebecca. *A Pocketful of Cricket,* ill. by Evaline Ness. Holt, 1964.

This is not strictly an informational book, yet it has a great deal of information about the capture, care, and charm of crickets for small boys. This particular small boy took his cricket to school, where a sympathetic teacher let him display it for "Show and Tell." Evaline Ness' illustrations made this book a runner-up for the Caldecott Medal.

Goudey, Alice E. *Here Come the Bears!* ill. by Garry MacKenzie. Scribner, 1954. Also *Here Come the Squirrels!* (1962).

These are just two of the series of books which give simple, readable accounts of different animals. See also Alice Goudey's *Houses from the Sea* (1959), ill. by Adrienne Adams, whose exquisite illustrations make seashells fascinating and identifiable for young readers.

Podendorf, Illa. *The True Book of Weeds and Wildflowers,* ill. by Mary Gehr. Children's Press, 1955.

The large print and colorful illustrations make this book and others in the series attractive to young readers. *The True Book of Weeds and Wildflowers* is an interesting introduction to nature study.

Schlein, Miriam. *It's About Time,* ill. by Leonard Kessler. W. R. Scott, 1955.

This useful little book explains, in language understandable to young children, the concept of time and how to tell time.

Selsam, Millicent. *Let's Get Turtles,* ill. by Arnold Lobel. Harper, 1965. Also *Seeds and More Seeds,* ill. by Tomi Ungerer, 1959; and *Tony's Birds,* ill. by Kurt Werth, 1961.

A simple vocabulary is used to provide remarkably good information about turtles, seed development, and bird watching.

Webber, Irma E. *Bits That Grow Big: Where Plants Come From,* ill.

by author. W. R. Scott, 1949. Also *Travelers All: The Story of How Plants Go Places* (1944).

Interesting and well-illustrated explanations of plant propagation and seed development.

Zim, Herbert. *What's Inside of Me?* ill. by Herschel Wartik. Morrow, 1952. Also *What's Inside the Earth?* (1953) and *What's Inside of Engines?* (1953).

This writer of reliable informational books for young children has over forty such books to his credit. Try also his series on animals with young children, and as soon as children can read it, give them his *The Sun* (1953).

All children, slow or fast learners, bookish or nonbookish, need the continual love and protection and the watchful care of their parents, especially in these early years in school. It is often the well-trained teacher who discovers a child squinting at the blackboard or at the big letters on the charts or holding his book too close to his face. She reports to the parents, and a timely visit to the oculist may prevent endless school difficulties now and later. And so it is with hearing deficiencies. But when a young child falls asleep over his desk every morning, the reasons may be more difficult to identify. There may be too many children in a bed or too late hours watching TV or too small quarters with noisy adults who may make sleep impossible. These are matters of parental responsibility, and the facts should be faced and remedied. A sleepy child cannot learn at a normal rate, and chronic fatigue can account for failures now and later, too. Children of six, seven, and eight are also more susceptible to contagious diseases and are therefore likely to be out of school with numerous and long illnesses. When these occur, the teacher generally tells the mother how she can help her child catch up or keep up with his school work, and together they pull him through the work he missed.

The child's emotional disturbances are a different matter. The teacher may report the manifestations as she sees them, but in most cases the causes go back to the home. Quarreling between the parents or the children, broken homes, jealousies, anxieties, shock —any one of these or a dozen different tensions may upset a child to the point where he misbehaves in school or loses interest and ceases to learn. Sometimes it takes the professional help of a psychiatrist to straighten out the tangle, but in the main, parents who love their children can compensate for or allay the anxieties and tensions with which the child is beset. Over and over, it has been observed that a child who is loved and cherished can weather periods of stress and come through remarkably unscathed, even though he is from a disturbed home, whereas a neglected, unloved child may go to pieces. To be loved and to love—these are basic securities that every human being needs and is searching for. These are the indispensable foundations that help a child stand up to life, to change and grow and learn happily in these crucial early years of school.

ADDITIONAL TITLES

Here are more books for the five to ten-year-olds, arranged alphabetically by author. Suggested age ranges are given after the date of publication. For additional easy-to-read books, check titles in Chapter 4.

Aldridge, Josephine Haskell. *A Penny and a Periwinkle*, ill. by Ruth Robbins. Parnassus, 1961. (7-8)
With only a penny and a periwinkle, the old man catches larger bait, snares a flounder for his cat, some lobsters for himself and to sell, and buys milk for a chowder. Then he and his cat sit safe, snug, and well fed, with no rushing around and no struggle. The poetic text is warm and reassuring, and the delicate water colors add greatly to the charm of this little story with its euphonious title. If children have help on a few words, they will have no trouble reading the book for themselves.

Aulaire, Ingri and Edgar Parin d'. *Abraham Lincoln*, ill. by authors. Doubleday, 1939, 1957. Caldecott Medal, 1940. Also *Benjamin Franklin* (1950). (7-10)
These and other picture biographies by this husband and wife author-illustrator team are historically sound and illustrated with remarkably fine pictures.

Beim, Jerrold. *Country School*, ill. by Louis Darling. Morrow, 1955. (6-8)
Jerrold Beim has written a number of easy-to-read books for children. This story tells about young Tony's initial sadness when the coun-

try school is torn down and his later happy adjustment to attending the big consolidated school.

Bishop, Claire. *The Five Chinese Brothers*, ill. by Kurt Wiese. Coward-McCann, 1938. (6-8)
This Chinese version of the three brothers, each with a magical gift, is an unfailing favorite.

Buckley, Helen E. *Grandmother and I*, ill. by Paul Galdone. Lothrop, 1961. (5-7)
This is only one of Helen Buckley's many little stories for children. *Grandmother and I* makes clear the comfort and solace the small girl feels in her grandmother's lap.

Clymer, Eleanor. *Chipmunk in the Forest*, ill. by Ingrid Fetz. Atheneum, 1965. (7-9)
Chipmunk, a little Indian boy, was afraid of the deep forest with its wild animals. But when Little Brother was lost in the woods, Chipmunk knew he must find the boy, and he did.

This illustration is reprinted by permission of Charles Scribner's Sons: Illustration by Leonard Weisgard from *The Courage of Sarah Noble* by Alice Dalgliesh. Copyright 1954 Alice Dalgliesh and Leonard Weisgard.

Dalgliesh, Alice. *The Courage of Sarah Noble*, ill. by Leonard Weisgard. Scribner, 1954. (8-10)
This story of an eight-year-old who went out into the wilderness to cook and care for her father details a rare test of stamina and courage. It is based on a true historical episode.

Daugherty, James. *Andy and the Lion*, ill. by author. Viking, 1938. (6-8)
Andy is a modern version of the old story of "Androcles and the Lion," and is a little masterpiece because of the text and the inimitable drawings. The modern setting makes the tale more incredible and funny.

Flack, Marjorie. *Wait for William*, ill. by the author and Richard A. Holberg. Houghton, 1935. Also *Ask Mr. Bear*, Macmillan, 1932. (5-7)
In the first story, young William, who is left behind by the impatient older children, triumphs gloriously by riding the elephant in the circus parade. In the second story, little Danny, with Mr. Bear's advice, decides upon the best possible birthday present for his mother.

Friskey, Margaret. *Indian Two Feet and His Horse*, ill. by Katherine Evans. Children's Press, 1959. (5-7)
With only 130 words, Margaret Friskey tells a lively story about a small Indian boy who was told to use his two feet. This he does so effectively that he finds himself a horse.

Godden, Rumer. *Impunity Jane*, ill. by Adrienne Adams. Viking, 1954. (7-10)
This unusual doll story by a distinguished novelist tells of Jane's exciting adventures once she is taken over by a small boy. Boys and girls like this story, and it will serve as an introduction to a whole series of doll stories by Rumer Godden, all delightful. (See p. 159 for other doll stories by Rumer Godden.)

Hodges, Margaret. *The Wave*, adapted from Lafcadio Hearn's *Gleanings in Buddha-fields*. Ill. by Blair Lent. Houghton, 1964. (7-9)
This distinguished book, based on an old Japanese legend, is outstanding for the illustrations as well as the story.

Hoff, Syd. *Danny and the Dinosaur*, ill. by author. Harper, 1958. (5-8)
Mr. Hoff can tell a tall tale with plenty of humor, even with a limited

vocabulary. Danny on the loose with his museum dinosaur is genuinely droll.

Leaf, Munro. *The Story of Ferdinand*, ill. by Robert Lawson. Viking, 1936. (5-8)
This droll perfection of pictures and text is about a peaceful bull who is accidentally cast in the role of a killer, but Ferdinand would rather smell flowers than fight.

Lexau, Joan M. *Benjie*, ill. by Don Bolognese. Dial, 1964. (5-8)
Benjie is a timid little Negro boy who thinks he can't talk to people. But when he goes on a search for Granny's lost earring, he finds he can talk.

MacGregor, Ellen. *Miss Pickerell Goes to Mars*, ill. by Paul Galdone. McGraw, 1951. (8-11)
There are other books in the *Miss Pickerell* series, but the story of her flight to and from Mars is the favorite. After her yearly visit with her seven nieces and nephews, Miss Pickerell is on her way home in her eighteen-year-old car, pulling a trailer which holds her ailing cow. Her adventures actually begin when she gives Mr. Haggerty, a pleasant and accommodating stranger, a lift. After she reaches her own home, things really begin to happen—all of them exciting.

Mason, Miriam E. *Caroline and Her Kettle Named Maud*, ill. by Kathleen Voute. Macmillan, 1951. Also see *Susannah, the Pioneer Cow*, ill. by Maud and Miska Petersham. Macmillan, 1941. (7-9)
These stories of pioneer adventures are genuinely easy to read, with good historical details and unusual humor. Caroline wanted a gun for her pioneering but was given a kettle instead. How it proved itself makes a very funny story. The story of Susannah, the cow, is also an appealing addition to the pioneer stories.

Rounds, Glen. *The Blind Colt*, ill. by author. Holiday, 1941, 1960. Also *Stolen Pony* (1948) and *Whitey's First Roundup* (1960). (8-11)
A Dakota Badlands ranch is the background for these Westerns. Whitey falls in love with a blind colt, and through his care and training, gives the colt the right to live. Whitey's adventures continue through several books.

Sauer, Julia L. *Mike's House*, ill. by Don Freeman. Viking, 1954. (5-8)
   To small Robert, the library was "Mike's House," because his favorite
book, *Mike Mulligan and His Steamshovel*, was there. This vague address proved most confusing to the kindly policeman who was attempt-
ing to restore a lost Robert to his mother on a blustery winter day.

Slobodkin, Louis. *Space Ship Under the Apple Tree*, ill. by author.
   Macmillan, 1952. (8-10)
   Eddie's vacation on his grandmother's farm is enlivened by a visitor
from Martinea. Marty proves a mixed blessing, with amusing complications.

Tarry, Ellen, and Marie Hall Ets. *My Dog Rinty*, ill. by Alexander
   and Alexandra Alland. Viking, 1946. (8-10)
   This is a story of a Negro boy faced with the heartbreaking decision
to dispose of a destructive dog. Appealing characters have made this
small book a long-time favorite.

Todd, Ruthven. *Space Cat*, ill. by Paul Galdone. Scribner, 1952. (8-10)
   Flyball, the adventuresome cat, traveled to the moon in a proper
space suit. See also *Space Cat Visits Venus* (1955) and *Space Cat Meets
Mars* (1957).

Tresselt, Alvin. *White Snow, Bright Snow*, ill. by Roger Duvoisin.
   Caldecott Medal. Lothrop, 1947. (5-7)
   The wonder, excitement, and fun of the first snowfall. A companion
book to *Autumn Harvest* (1951), *"Hi, Mister Robin!"* (1950), and *Sun
Up* (1949), all by the same author-artist team.

Will [Lipkind] and Nicolas [Mordvinoff]. *The Two Reds*, ill. by Nicolas.
   Harcourt, 1950. See also *Russet and the Two Reds* (1962). (5-8)
   These are amusing city-life stories for young children. In the first
story, Red a city boy and Red an alley cat successfully outmaneuver the
militant club known as the Seventh Street Signal Senders. In the second
story, the two Reds finally accept Russet, the new girl in the neighborhood, after she dramatically proves herself to be a useful ally.

Yamaguchi, Tohr. *The Golden Crane*, ill. by Marianne Yamaguchi.
   Holt, 1962. (8-12)

Based upon a Japanese folk tale, this beautiful book tells the story of a brave boy who risked his life to save an injured sacred crane.

Zemach, Harve. *Salt*, ill. by Margot Zemach. Follett, 1965. (6-8)
This story from the Russian folk tale by Alexei Afanasev is a choice edition.

Zolotow, Charlotte. *Sleepy Book*, ill. by Vladimir Bobri. Lothrop, 1958. (5-7)
"Against a dream-like blue background, birds and beasts and, finally, a little boy and a little girl, are going to sleep—each in its own way." See also *The Storm Book*, illustrated by Margaret Bloy Graham (Harper, 1952). As one reviewer said, this book captures "the force and power of the story without making it something to fear," as a small boy and his mother share the excitement of watching a storm on a summer's day.

REALISM FOR THE MIDDLE YEARS

FOR AGES NINE-TEN-ELEVEN

6

Stories of Today's World
Stories of Times Past
Animal Stories

Like Janey in Eleanor Estes' *The Middle Moffat,* children in the middle years have their problems. At nine, ten, or eleven, they have generally outgrown the games and literature of the sixes, sevens, and eights, as their remarks indicate. They say scornfully: "Oh, they're just young kids!" or "That's baby stuff!" or "I can remember when I was only six," as if they were now forty. So, of course, when the twelves, thirteens, and fourteens won't let them play in their games, the middles are outraged. Adults watching children in these middle years find them baffling and hard to keep up with. They seem to change overnight. Interests and skills are developing rapidly in many directions. Friendships and closely knit social groups, like clubs or gangs, are formed in these years and command deep loyalties. With these group experiences, children in the middle years should also develop increasing sensitivity to the cause-and-effect of human behavior; that is, they should begin to understand what is acceptable and unacceptable behavior. Here their reading may help them understand themselves in relation to their group.

These middle years also bring unique problems in school work, because these are years of astonishing variation in reading skills. In fourth or fifth grade, some children may be reading with difficulty at third-grade level, while others are reading easily anything that interests them at high-school, or even adult, level. But despite the great variance in reading skills and interests, there are a number of books that will appeal to many of the children in the middle years. They range from stories about today's world—here in the United States and in other countries, historical fiction, and animal stories (all discussed in this chapter) to stories about magic and make-believe—folk tales, fables, myths, epics, and modern fanciful tales (discussed in the following chapter). Supplement these lists by turning back to Chapter 5 for books for your slow or reluctant readers and to Chapters 8 and 9 for books for your advanced readers. Use also the lists in the special fields—Poetry (Chapter 11), Biography (Chapter 12), Informational Books (Chapter 13), and Religion, Ethics, and the Arts (Chapter 14).

STORIES OF TODAY'S WORLD

These United States

Because life is moving so vigorously in these middle years, children can't explore their everyday world fast enough. So this first group of stories is realistic and, in the main, includes familiar, or at least possible, experiences in the here and now.

> *The Moffats*, by Eleanor Estes, ill. by Louis Slobodkin. Harcourt, 1941. Also *The Middle Moffat* (1942) and *Rufus M.* (1943). (8-12)
> The three books about the four Moffat children are enjoyed by children, especially girls, because of Janey, the middle Moffat. This series is not quite modern times, but the seamstress mother and the small town activities are not too remote to prevent them from being

completely understandable. Janey and her small brother, Rufus, are generally trying to achieve some worthy end, but whether it is Janey in the school play getting her bear head on backward, or Rufus trying to obtain a library card and going completely astray in the big building, their paths are strewn with mishaps that make delightful reading.

The Saturdays, by Elizabeth Enright, ill. by author. Holt, 1941. Also *Gone-Away Lake*, ill. by Beth and Joe Krush. Harcourt, 1957. (9-12)
The Saturdays is the first of a series about the Melendy family. In this story, the four children decide to pool their allowances each week, so that one of them can enjoy a tremendous Saturday fling. What each child does with his wealth tells something about his character, his interests, and the vast variety of delights a big city has to offer an intelligent child. Some of their choices are admirable, some a bit startling, as might be expected; and most produce more excitement than the child had counted on.

In *Gone-Away Lake*, Portia and her boy cousin Julian discover a colony of elaborate but mainly empty summer cottages on the edge of a swamp. Only two of the big houses are occupied by a delightful elderly brother and sister, former residents of the "Big House," who tell the children the history of this ghost community, and who help make the summer an eventful and happy one for Portia and Julian. In the sequel, *Return to Gone-Away* (1961), the joy of the children is complete when Portia's family decides to restore one of the houses and live there the year around. No briefing of any one of Elizabeth Enright's books can give any idea of her lively, witty style. Her *Thimble Summer* won the 1939 Newbery Medal.

Henry Huggins, by Beverly Cleary, ill. by Louis Darling. Morrow, 1950. (8-10)
The first in a series of hilarious tales about Henry and his friends, *Henry Huggins* begins with Henry's earnest efforts to get a stray dog, encased in a paper shopping bag, home on a bus. Ribsy, the dog, shares most of Henry's subsequent adventures: his experiences with "Gallons of Guppies," the night crawlers, the school Christmas play, and the dog show. The book closes with the dramatic reappearance of Ribsy's original owner. This poses an ethical problem for conscientious Henry, but the solution is masterly. Ribsy, a favorite character in the Henry books, survives to have a book of his own (*Ribsy*, 1964).

A Dog on Barkham Street, by Mary Stolz, ill. by Leonard Shortall. Harper, 1960. (8-12)

Here is a contemporary neighborhood story to the life, with every character as real as your own next-door neighbors, and with humor and an exciting plot into the bargain. Poor Edward Frost suffered acutely from two sorrows: first, his mother wouldn't let him have a dog; and, second, he lived next door to Martin the bully, both older and larger and dedicated to making Edward's life miserable. His family sympathized but could do nothing. Then along came his Uncle Josh with his collie dog Argess for an extended visit. Edward and his best friend, Rod Graham, were enamored with both Uncle Josh and Argess; in fact, the boys took over the care of the dog so completely it was a question who was happier, dog or boys. Suddenly, Uncle Josh and Argess disappeared as abruptly as they had come. Inconsolable for their loss, the two boys got themselves into a frightening predicament from which they were rescued just in time. When Edward reached home, there were Uncle Josh and Argess waiting for him. Uncle Josh, however, stayed just long enough to explain that Argess refused to leave Edward, and so she was to be Edward's dog forever. The family arguments in this book sparkle with humor and reality. This is one of the best stories in this field for the ten-year-olds.

Harriet the Spy, by Louise Fitzhugh, ill. by author. Harper, 1964. (9-12)

Another completely contemporary story, *Harriet the Spy* is a popular book with children and a controversial one with adults. Harriet is a nonconformist and a rebel with unusual potentials. She is never without her notebook in which she records not only her secret life as a spy, sleuthing around her neighborhood, but also, alas, her personal and caustic comments on her classmates. So when the children find and read the notebook, they are properly indignant and gang up on Harriet. She is definitely out. With ostracism, her behavior goes from bad to outrageous. Harriet's rebellion comes to a hopeful conclusion that is not wholly conclusive. Children find this book convincing, because Harriet is urban, modern, and a very real little girl.

The Long Secret (1965), a sequel to *Harriet the Spy*, is more Beth Ellen's story than Harriet's. It takes place in the summertime at Water Mill. In addition to some of the characters from the earlier book, it introduces new ones, including Beth Ellen's silly, heartless mother and her husband, and the Jenkinses, a most unusual family from Mississippi. One chapter in which Janie, Harriet, and Beth Ellen discuss menstruation strikes some adults as very funny but shocks others. Certainly, the chapter is an improvement on some of the lugubrious attitudes of the past, but it is probably for home rather than school reading. The story has some hilarious episodes as well as some sad ones, especially for Beth Ellen. On the whole, it is not nearly so well knit as *Harriet the Spy*.

Ellen Grae, by Vera and Bill Cleaver, ill. by Ellen Raskin. Lippincott, 1967. (9-11)

Because her parents are divorced, eleven-year-old Ellen Grae Derryberry (who tells the story) is staying in the small town of Thicket with the McGruders. She tolerates her roommate, Rosemary, also the child of divorced parents, but is good friends with twelve-year-old Grover, her fishing companion, and with Ira, a strange, gentle, slow-witted man of indeterminate age, who lives in a two-room shack with his goat Missouri. Ellen, a child of astonishing and precocious imagination, becomes notorious for her wild tall tales, a source of amusement to Mrs. McGruder and her bridge club, as well as to most of the other townspeople. Ellen's ebullience, however, disappears after Ira tells her of an incident of his youth, a dreadful tale of attempted murder and lonely burial. Torn between the belief that she should report the story to the authorities and sorrow at betraying her friend, Ellen becomes so distraught that the bewildered McGruders finally send for her parents. After a great deal of pressure from Jeff and Grace, Ellen reveals Ira's story, and the three Derryberrys go to Sheriff Fudge with the account. Not surprisingly, the sheriff does not believe the story and succeeds in convincing Ellen's indignant parents that this is another of their daughter's tall tales. Again under pressure, Ellen retracts her story. "Well, I *did* try," she thinks. "Nobody can say that I didn't try. Hell's afire." And so back to the city go her parents, and Ellen, in disgrace but at least relieved of her burden, stoically sloughs off their anger and disappointment, and with the help of the kindly and sympathetic McGruders resumes her everyday life in Thicket. Oddly enough, this is an amusing book with excellent dialogue and lively characterizations.

Queenie Peavy, by Robert Burch, ill. by Jerry Lazare. Viking, 1966. (10-12)

Nonconformists and rebels are usually popular in books for children and young people. The year of 1966 produced several powerful books about young delinquents in the making, among them *Queenie Peavy*. Thirteen-year-old Queenie, growing up in Georgia in the depression times of the early thirties, is warm hearted and intelligent, but she is fast becoming the outlaw of the school and community. With her mother away all day working at the canning plant, Queenie is often alone. She gives all her love to Dominick, her old rooster, the children next door, and her absentee father, whom she has idealized out of all reality. So when the school children taunt her about her jailbird father, she goes berserk, and her deadly rock-throwing skill gets her into real trouble. Queenie is saved from the reformatory only by the understanding efforts of the school principal and the wise old judge who tells her she has been "living under the shadow of the jail," and that it is time to come out and be herself. Queenie is intelligent and brave enough to do it. This is a grim story, but it has great sweetness, too. The author has painted convincingly the two faces of Queenie—one hard and defiant, the other loving and vulnerable.

Robert Burch is a writer to watch. His earlier book *Skinny* (1964) is about a delightfully philosophical young orphan who does *not* get adopted, but who meets each situation cheerfully and successfully.

Strawberry Girl, by Lois Lenski, ill. by author. Lippincott, 1945. Newbery Medal. (9-12)

In Lois Lenski's series of regional stories, young readers encounter families of sadly limited resources, economic and otherwise. In *Strawberry Girl*, Birdie Boyer's family belongs to Florida's small crop farmers. The Boyers are hard working, neat, and efficient, but they are pestered by mean, shiftless neighbors, Paul Slater and his slatternly wife. However, Shoestring Slater, their son, is intelligent and quick to learn better ways from the Boyers, even though his loyalty to his family keeps him on the defensive.

In Lois Lenski's *Cotton in My Sack* (1949), everyone in the family works to the point of exhaustion cotton-picking all week, only to go on a Saturday spree of aimless, foolish spending. Other of the Lenski regional stories include *Boom Town Boy* (1948), *Judy's Journey* (1947), *Prairie School* (1951), and *Coal Camp Girl* (1959). These are grim stories, despite occasional flashes of humor. What lifts the characters out of the squalor in which they live is their patient endurance, courage, and a fierce family pride that binds them together with unshakeable loyalty. It is good for children of suburbia to discover that enduring family love at whatever level gives richness to life.

. . . And Now Miguel, by Joseph Krumgold, ill. by Jean Charlot. Crowell, 1953. Newbery Medal. (9-14)

This story, set in the sheepherding country of New Mexico, is one
of the great books for children. But because of its unique style and content, adults may need to read some of it aloud to get young readers into
the swing of the story. Miguel's goal is special—to become an expert
sheepherder like the rest of the men in his family. But his problem is
a universal one for twelve-year-olds. Miguel's wish is to persuade his
father to accept him as a responsible adult like his nineteen-year-old
brother, Gabriel. The boy struggles to fulfill competently all the tasks
of sheepherding that come his way, but he feels that he fails more frequently than he succeeds. He always measures himself by adult
standards, and there is no part of the four-hundred-year-old skills in
sheep care and breeding that Miguel does not love and strive to learn.
This is a remarkable story on many counts—deep family love, pride in
the family skills and work, passionate desire for independent achievement and competence, and a boy's love for his grown-up brother. The
discussion of prayer between the two boys, Gabriel and Miguel, is
unique in children's literature as is the rather subtle style in which
this book is written.

Henry Reed, Inc., by Keith Robertson, ill. by Robert McCloskey.
Viking, 1958. (10-14)

In sharp contrast to the comparatively simple problems and goals
of Miguel is the sophisticated fun of Henry Reed, a humorless, intellectual thirteen-year-old. Since Henry's father is in the diplomatic service in Naples, Italy, Henry is spending the summer with his Uncle Al
and Aunt Mabel in Grover's Corner, near Princeton, New Jersey. Henry
keeps a journal describing his summer activities, which cover the period from Sunday, June 23, until Tuesday, August 27, when Henry is
on his way back to Naples. Intrigued by the numerous research enterprises in the Princeton area and eager to carry out his history and government teacher's advice to do something that could be used to illustrate "free enterprise," Henry takes over an old carriage house in the
vacant lot next to his uncle's property and puts up a sign—"Henry Reed,
Inc.," a sign that gradually evolves into "Pure and Applied Research,
Agricultural and Biological Research Supplies." In all his enterprises
he is aided and abetted by twelve-year-old Margaret (Midge) Glass,
the pushy, adventuresome daughter of a research chemist. Naturally,
she wants her name added to the sign, but Henry insists that she must

first prove herself. The proving involves both children in a series of hilarious situations, which are embellished by some of Robert McCloskey's funniest drawings. Actually, this is a book that adults have been known to enjoy as much as the young readers. See also *Henry Reed's Journey* (1963) and *Henry Reed's Baby-Sitting Service* (1966).

Sea Pup, by Archie Binns, ill. by Robert Candy. Duell, 1954. (9-14)
Here is a story with unusual values. It might be classified with animal stories except that it is boy centered. Clint, the hero, is a lonely boy living with his mother and father in a remote section on Puget Sound. When Clint finds an orphan seal and brings it home to raise as a pet, both parents warn him that he is in for trouble, but certainly there was never a funnier or more appealing pet than Buster. Clint and his pet are inseparable on land and in the ocean. This is all right during summer vacation, but when Clint has to return to school, the lonely seal begins to get into serious mischief. For instance, he milks the neighbors' cows when he is thirsty, he barges into the neighbors' houses when he gets lonesome, and all by himself in the ocean he is shot at and wounded by hunters. This last misadventure involves Clint and his father in a harrowing nighttime search, during which they are surrounded by a school of killer whales. But Clint's more serious problem concerns his own future education. To be the oceanographer he hopes to be, Clint knows he must go to a city high school for adequate science courses and that means deserting Buster for good and all. The family sympathizes but leaves the decision to Clint. Growing up isn't easy. Warm friendly relationships, a unique pet, and an action tale full of adventure compel interest from the first page to the last, and the solution is not too painful.

Dandy's Mountain, by Thomas Fall, ill. by Juan Carlos Barberis. Dial, 1967. (10-14)
The family called Amanda "Dandy," but her hard-as-nails cousin Bruce called her "Crazy Miller, my cousin." That was only after Bruce was on good terms with the girl he started out by hating. For Dandy herself it was a strange summer. She had decided to make it special by going right through the dictionary. She was doing well with the *A*'s when her father took her to New York to pick up her cousin Bruce. His mother was in the hospital, and Bruce was in trouble. Dandy decided then and there to try to help Bruce, never dreaming her efforts would land her in the police court with a gang of housebreaking boys.

How she astounded the police force with her liberal use of *A*'s, all
applied to Bruce—*abandon, abscond, abhorrent, acrimonious*, and
the like—makes a very funny chapter. Once on the farm, Bruce ran
true to form—lying, stealing, being as surly and "abhorrent" as possible.
But when both Bruce and Dandy were lost on the mountain, the boy
proved his courage and broke down sufficiently to admit he liked the
farm, loved the horses, and was afraid to go back to his gang in the city.
The wilderness experience was a narrow escape, and both children
knew it, but it solved a number of problems. Dandy is a completely
off-beat youngster, but endearing and memorable. This is one of the
best girls' stories in a long time.

The next three books have at least one quality in common with
Harriet the Spy. All three deal with the intense, secret play-
enterprises of intelligent children. These activities are sometimes
funny, usually highly imaginative and dramatic, and, in the case
of *The Egypt Game*, have some significant social overtones. But
never has the imaginary play of children been more vividly re-
created.

Jennifer, Hecate, Macbeth, William McKinley, and Me, Elizabeth,
  by E. L. Konigsburg, ill. by author. Atheneum, 1967. Runner-up
  for the Newbery Medal. (8-11)
  Two little girls meet for the first time the day of a school Halloween
party. Elizabeth, who tells the story, is dressed in a hand-me-down
Pilgrim costume, but Jennifer is in authentic Pilgrim attire, complete
with huge shoes, "real Pilgrim shoes made of buckles and cracked old
leather." Jennifer makes it clear that she is a real witch. "Witches convince; they never argue," she says, and from then on she takes Elizabeth
in hand to make her an authentic witch also. Poor Elizabeth! The mysterious notes and incantations are exciting, but some of the witch diets
are pretty terrible. Elizabeth endures a great deal, but dropping a live
toad into boiling water is too much. She balks (Jennifer would never
have gone through with it anyway), the toad escapes, and witchcraft
is over. But not, it turns out, the friendship of the two little girls. That
is casually resumed as if nothing had happened. Only an incidental
reference in the text and the illustrations show that Jennifer is Negro
and Elizabeth white. Their united stand against giggly, beautiful
Cynthia and her friends cements their loyalty to each other, and with
Jennifer's ability to create ceremonies, it is not likely to weaken. The

story ends with Elizabeth's happy comment: "Neither of us pretends to be a witch any more. Now we mostly enjoy being what we really are . . . just Jennifer and just me . . . just good friends."

From the Mixed-Up Files of Mrs. Basil E. Frankweiler, by E. L. Konigsburg, ill. by author. Atheneum, 1967. Newbery Medal. (9-12)
The unusual titles of Mrs. Konigsburg's books are matched only by the droll originality of the contents. The adventures in this book are a little more complex and sophisticated than the Jennifer and Elizabeth antics, but suburban children used to traveling to a big city and knowing something about its institutions will be vastly entertained by this story.

Claudia, just under twelve, is disturbed by "injustice" and plagued by boredom, and so there seems to be nothing to do but run away from home for a while until her family learns a "lesson in Claudia appreciation." For her companion she chooses her nine-year-old brother, Jamie, who is rich from saving his allowance and from his winnings from the card game "War," which he plays with his buddy Bruce. Jamie, reluctant at first, is finally persuaded partly because he likes "complications," with which Claudia's plans are replete. Claudia wisely refrains from telling Jamie their final destination—the Metropolitan Museum of Art—until they are actually on their way. How they manage to reach the Museum and live there for a week despite closing checks, changing of the guards, and other complications is almost unbelievable. They even take a bath in the restaurant fountain, where Jamie discovers enough coins to give their sinking finances quite a boost. The plot turns upon the Museum's recent acquisition of an exquisite Angel, thought to be the work of Michelangelo, although proof is lacking. Claudia falls in love with the statue and, in order to solve the mystery of the statue's origin, promptly puts herself and Jamie to work in the library, boning up on Michelangelo. Their efforts and the end of their money finally bring them to the home of Mrs. Frankweiler, from whom the Museum had acquired the Angel. It is Mrs. Frankweiler, a youthful and perceptive octogenarian, who writes up the children's adventures for her lawyer and, through permitting the children to find the proof in her files, makes it possible for Claudia to go home again "different" and for both children to be reunited with their frantic family. The story within a story adds complication, but the ingenuity of Claudia and Jamie in meeting every emergency makes this an exciting and satisfying adventure story. Says Claudia, "Five minutes of planning are worth fifteen minutes of just looking."

The Egypt Game, by Zilpha Keatley Snyder, ill. by Alton Raible.
Atheneum, 1967. (10-12)

Perhaps this is a book parents should be sure to read before they give it to their child. It is mainly a story about an absorbing group play, but it includes a briefly scary confrontation with a problem children face in our big cities and should know about—the child molester.

The "Egypt Game" takes place in an abandoned storage yard, adjoining a shabby little antique shop, which is run by a mysterious old man, commonly referred to as the "Professor." Next door to the shop and yard is the Casa Rosada, a seedy old California-Spanish apartment house, the home of the main characters and the principal performers in the "Egypt Game": April Hall, who lives with her grandmother; her best friend Melanie Ross and her four-year-old brother, Marshall, who live with their mother, a schoolteacher, and their father, a graduate student at the university; and fourth-grader Elizabeth Chung, who lives with her mother and two small sisters in a semibasement apartment. They are joined in the game by two boys, sixthgraders like April and Melanie. In the course of weeks, the children develop an elaborately imaginative game, complete with a temple, altars, gods, an oracle, costumes, chants, and imposing ceremonies.

For a time, the game is halted because of the unsolved murder of a child from a neighboring area—all the children are kept at home most of the time by their anxious parents. But, finally, tensions ease up, and the game is resumed. The climax comes one night when April is babysitting for Marshall, while the Rosses attend a university concert. April remembers that she has left her math book in "Egypt" and, accompanied by Marshall and his flashlight, goes back to retrieve it. Suddenly, as she is leaving the yard, she is seized from behind. From then on, events happen fast, ending up with the capture of the murderer, the exoneration of the Professor, the lionizing of Marshall, and, finally, "Christmas keys" for all six Egyptians.

The book has more than ordinary significance. Its social implications are numerous but unobtrusively presented, and the story is skillfully told.

Three minority groups

The United States is a vast colorful patchwork of peoples—our native Indians, the Negroes first brought here by force, immigrant Jews, and other immigrants from almost every country of the old world. These diverse peoples have tended to settle together in our cities and in our rural areas. Like Miguel's family of sheepherders who settled in the Southwest and like the Swedes who settled in Minnesota, all these different people with their varying work, religions, customs, and traditions have contributed color and variety to our urban and rural areas. There are so many books about interesting minority groups that it is impossible to list examples of each. However, here are examples of three large groups which have contributed richly to our country and are much in the public eye today: the Negroes, the American Indians, and the Jews.

Bright April, by Marguerite de Angeli, ill. by author. Doubleday, 1946. (8-10)

Books about Negroes have tended to be so rife with problems or propaganda that the stories have a hard time surviving. *Bright April* has its problems, too, but the book has great charm and is popular with young readers. One reason is that April and her family are exceedingly attractive human beings. They live in a good house, pleasant inside and out. They are intelligent people, reasonably tolerant of their racial difficulties even when some of them hurt cruelly. For brave, pretty little April, the problems eventually work out to a happy conclusion. Undoubtedly, Mrs. de Angeli's beautiful and appealing illustrations in full color account in part for the popularity of this book. For refreshing stories of friendships between Negro and white children, free of propaganda, see *The Egypt Game* and *Jennifer, Hecate, Macbeth, William McKinley and Me, Elizabeth.*

Roosevelt Grady, by Louisa R. Shotwell, ill. by Peter Burchard. World, 1963. (9-12)

Roosevelt Grady and his family—mother, father, seven-year-old Sister, five-year-old lame Matthew, and baby Princess Anne—move with the crops. When one crop is picked, they are off to another crop, but not always another school for nine-year-old Roosevelt. Cap Jackson, the crew leader and owner of the truck that transports the Gradys and several other families, is a decent man, but his old truck is always falling apart. And the Grady family is a gentle, loving unit. Roosevelt and his mother share a secret which they talk about only when they are alone. It is their dream of having a permanent home so that the mother can fix it up and Roosevelt can go to the same school every day.

By the time this seemingly impossible dream is close to fulfillment, the Grady family has acquired Manowar, an orphan boy enslaved and brutally treated by the leader of another crew. So the family is larger, the dream is coming true, and the whole Grady family is full of hope. Only the illustrations indicate that the Gradys are Negro.

How Many Miles to Babylon? by Paula Fox, ill. by Paul Giovanopoulos. David White, 1967. (10 up)
> The title of this book comes from the old nursery rhyme:
> > How many miles to Babylon?
> > Three score miles and ten.
> > Can I get there by candle-light?
> > Yes, and back again.

The story is about ten-year-old James Douglas' terrifying adventure one cold November day and night. Because James' father is off somewhere and his mother is in the hospital, James lives in a tenement flat in Brooklyn with three old aunts—Grace, Althea, and Paul. In the course of this one day and night, the reader gets vivid glimpses of slum life, but the emphasis is on James, who knows what is real but who is happy only in his fantasy world, in which he is a prince waiting for his mother's return from Africa and his subsequent recognition as royalty. His dream world comes to a violent end during the course of the nightmare day and night—his capture by three older boys and forced involvement in their dog-stealing racket; his long, cold bicycle ride to Coney Island and back; his escape and his eventual happy reunion with his worried aunts and his mother, just home from the hospital. Like *Dorp Dead* (see p. 175), this story emphasizes the need for a child to use his wits and put up a stiff resistance when he finds he is being victimized.

Zeely, by Virginia Hamilton, ill. by Symeon Shimin. Macmillan, 1967. (9-12)
This haunting story is told half in terms of a little girl's imagination and half in the light of stark reality. At the beginning, eleven-year-old Elizabeth Perry and her young brother John board a train for their Uncle Ross' farm, where they are to spend the summer. Elizabeth wants the summer to be special, and so she starts it out by renaming her brother "Toeboy" and herself "Geeder." Geeder is a great one for making things up, including her name, but when she sees a mysterious figure striding down a dark road at night, she really has something to work on. It is a woman, but taller than any other women she has ever

seen before. Even in broad daylight, herding a drove of hogs, Zeely Tayber walks majestically, tall, black, regal, and beautiful. So Geeder feels sure that she must be a queen from Africa (a belief Geeder thinks is confirmed when she finds a photograph of a Watusi queen that resembles Zeely); and Geeder is proud to belong to such a race, even though her relationship is remote and she is of inferior shortness. All summer, Geeder invents a noble past for her Watusi queen, until Zeely hears about it and calls the little image-maker to learn the harsh facts. This sensitively told story is as important as Geeder's need to have a real live heroine of her own people. And happily, Zeely, who is indeed Watusi, never loses her heroic aura even in a world of harsh reality.

Little Navajo Bluebird, by Ann Nolan Clark, ill. by Paul Lantz. Viking, 1943. (8-12)

This story is a realistic if limited approach to the modern American Indian and his problems. Doli, the heroine, loves the quiet old ways of her people, hates all the noisy white people who want to change everything, and resists in every way she knows how the family plan to send her to the reservation school the coming autumn. But she has a summer with her brother and his wise, gentle young wife, who have returned from the reservation classes. Through them, but especially with the sympathetic understanding and help of the young wife, Doli comes to see that white men and red men may meet and live together, learning new wisdom from each other. Certainly her brother and his wife have learned much without losing their respect for the richness of their Indian heritage. So, when the time comes, Doli, little Navajo Bluebird, sets off for the reservation school convinced that she can cherish the old ways of her people and still learn new, helpful ones that will aid her people today and in the future.

Indian Hill, by Clyde R. Bulla, ill. by James Spanfeller. Crowell, 1963. (8-10)

A young Navajo boy moves from the Indian reservation to the city. The father has work he likes, but the mother and boy hate the noise, the speed, and all the strange new ways involved in apartment living in a big city. The father makes the adjustment easily but grieves because his wife and child are unhappy; so they go back to the reservation, and that does it. The mother suddenly appreciates the conveniences she enjoyed in the city, and the boy realizes that the advantages he enjoyed there are not to be found on the reservation. Strangeness and being a stranger are universal problems for children and families today. This story deals sympathetically with the special difficulties of rural, reservation Indians adjusting to city life.

All-of-a-Kind Family, by Sydney Taylor, ill. by Helen John. Follett, 1951. Also *More All-of-a-Kind Family* (1954) and *All-of-a-Kind Family Uptown* (1958). (9-12)

The books about this delightful Jewish family are models of what good writing about a minority group can and should be. The five little girls, the "all-of-a-kind," living on New York's lower East Side during the early 1900's, might be any little girls growing up in the crowded, poor district of any big city. Their ups and downs, their everyday adventures are sometimes funny, sometimes sad, but always set against the background of a loving, pious Jewish family. They observe reverently all the orthodox feasts and fasts of their religion—of course, preferring the feasts with mama's mouth-watering traditional foods. They are proud of their traditions but not self-conscious about them. And despite their economic limitations, it would be hard to find a more pleasant family group. At the end of the book, baby brother Charlie is born. Mama explains that their family is still all-of-a-kind, because they are "all close and loving and loyal." The stories are entertaining for children of any background.

In other lands

The colorful differences of life in other countries have always attracted young readers. But let's be sure that the stories in this area avoid the old fiesta atmosphere of some of the earlier books and that they give children an honest picture of everyday life, with its struggles as well as its joys. Among the books about children in other lands, *Heidi* is an old favorite and a classic.

Heidi, by Johanna Spyri. First translated and published in 1884. Ill. by Agnes Tait. Lippincott, 1948. Other recommended editions include those published by Grosset, Scribner, and World. (9-12)

Orphaned Swiss Heidi is so full of the joy of life and the love of people that nothing daunts her. Even meager living and the grumpy ways of her old grandfather cannot dim for her the glories of the mountaintops where she and her grandfather live. She loves everything from the stars, which she watches by night from her bed up in the loft, to the frisky little goats, which she helps guard by day. Then she is suddenly taken from her beloved mountain home to a city to be a companion for an invalid child. In this new situation, she gives so much of herself that, though she is perishing for the free life of the mountains, she is able to help poor invalid Clara. Eventually, both Heidi and Clara go back to the mountains and to Grandfather. There to Heidi's joy, Clara's health and happiness bloom, and life is wonderful for both little girls.

The Secret Garden, by Frances Hodgson Burnett, ill. by Tasha Tudor. Lippincott, 1962. (9-12)

This old book, first published in 1909, has become a classic of romantic realism for children, and because of its otherworld flavor remains comparatively undated. At the beginning, Mary Lennox, the heroine, is plain and sour. She lives in India with her parents, but when they die of cholera, she is sent to England to her uncle, a dour man with a crooked back. On her uncle's estate on a Yorkshire moor, she finds a key that unlocks the door to a secret garden. Together with Dickon, a country boy of unusual spirit and tenderness, she restores the beauty of the long-neglected garden. Between the two of them, Mary and Dickon also bring Mary's cousin, the invalid Colin, into the garden to help with its care. Earth, sun, and sky work miracles of healing for Mary's bruised spirit and for Colin's body. Both bloom along with the garden, and happiness takes over the forbidding house and its people. To reread this old book is to discover the compelling charm of good writing. Tasha Tudor's delicate, old-fashioned illustrations are precisely right for this timeless story.

The Good Master, by Kate Seredy, ill. by author. Viking, 1935. (9-12)

The Good Master gives children a glimpse of ranch life in Hungary, with no political overtones, just the problems of taming a spoiled little girl, motherless Kate, who is sent by her father against her will to live with an uncle and his family. There is also a boy, Kate's cousin Jancsi, who makes this story interesting to boys as well as to girls. Kate begins by taking out her anger with her father on her uncle and his family. At the station, she starts a runaway. At the house that night, she climbs up into the rafters and gorges on the delectable sausages she finds there. Eventually her patient uncle, the good master, and also the absorbing activities of life on the ranch, outdoors with Jancsi and indoors with her aunt, tame rebellious Kate and turn her into a decently competent, well-behaved girl, skilled as a horsewoman and a homemaker. This is a continuously popular book.

Call It Courage, by Armstrong Sperry, ill. by author. Macmillan, 1940. Newbery Medal. (10-12)

Call It Courage is a boy's story about the conquest of fear. Mafatu, the son of a Polynesian chief, is rejected by his people because of his cowardice about the sea. But life becomes so unbearable he goes to sea with his dog, Uri, expecting to die. Shipwrecked and marooned on an island, he meets one challenge after another, because he must if he is to survive. He even learns how to make his own weapons and his own canoe. When he finally escapes from man-eaters, he knows his fears are gone and that he can cope with whatever life brings. He returns a hero. Full of suspense, this is a most satisfying adventure story about Polynesian life.

The Family Under the Bridge, by Natalie Savage Carlson, ill. by Garth Williams. Harper, 1958. Also *The Happy Orpheline* (1957), *A Brother for the Orphelines* (1959), *A Pet for the Orphelines* (1962), and *The Orphelines in the Enchanted Castle* (1964). (9-12)

Both *The Family Under the Bridge* and the series of stories about the orphelines take place in modern-day Paris. *The Family Under the Bridge* is about postwar Paris during a bitterly cold winter when there was a terrible housing shortage. Armand, the hero, is an elderly, jaunty hobo, who is completely averse to work, family life, and especially children. Imagine his horror when he returns one night to his home —a snug corner under an old bridge—to find it occupied by three children and their dog. This is intolerable, but little Suzy refuses to leave because "we're a family, and families have to stick together! That's what mama says." The children graciously permit Armand to join them; and their laundress mother, when she returns from work, agrees because Armand, she sees immediately, can look after the children during the day, while she is working at the laundry. How the five of them get through that winter is a gallant story of struggles—sometimes funny, sometimes sad. How the family conquers Armand's aversion both to cleanliness and to work is something of a miracle, and makes most entertaining reading.

Brigitte, in *The Happy Orpheline,* is so contented in the orphanage with Madame Flattot and Genevieve that she resorts to strategy to keep from being adopted. This first book is as lively as the strategy. In the second book, the orphelines find a baby boy on the front steps. The problem is to keep him in an orphanage for girls only. But chiefly through the exploits of Josine, the "stubbornest" orpheline, the story has a happy conclusion, and the girls get to keep their baby brother. So the stories go on. They are slight but well written, thoroughly amusing, and easy to read.

Threat to the Barkers, by Joan Phipson, ill. by Margaret Horder. First American Edition, Harcourt, 1965. (9-12)

The first book about the Australian Barker family was *The Family Conspiracy* (1964). In this sequel, *Threat to the Barkers*, the family is still laboriously wresting a living from sheepherding on their big ranch. The story opens with irascible father Barker reading the riot act to whoever closed a flock of his sheep into a sun-baked area with no water. After poor Belinda confesses and is duly lectured on her irresponsibility, life seems to swing back to normal. However, an enterprising gang of sheep thieves has spotted the prize flock of stud sheep which the eldest boy, Jack, has acquired. Eventually the whole family is mixed up in danger, especially fourteen-year-old Edward, who tries to swing alone a situation that is much too big for him. But he is instrumental in catching the would-be thieves and saving the flock. It is the family life, the characterizations of the six children, and the activities of the entire family that have special charm and humor. In Joan Phipson's first fine story, *The Boundary Riders* (1963), a group of children, with no adults to turn to, survive a dangerous adventure completely on their own. Throughout her books, she stresses independent achievement and competence. Sometimes she emphasizes these qualities drolly, sometimes gravely, but they never override the exciting action of the tale she is telling. *Birkin* (1966) is another appealing story of children's group action to save a steer.

"*What Then, Raman?*" by Shirley L. Arora, ill. by Hans Guggenheim. Follett, 1960. (10-12)

Here is an authentic picture of India today, a place of cruel deprivations for the poor. The book also tells the story of one boy's struggle for learning and of something even harder, his conquest of self-interest. Raman, shy and earnest, is the only person in the village who has learned to read. The other boys in the village taunt him, and he avoids them. His one desire is to own a beautiful copy of the Indian classic, the *Ramayana*. To earn money for the book, he works for an American teacher and is well paid, but she makes Raman understand that learning carries with it responsibility. Has he taught anyone else in the village to read? How is he helping his family? Raman wakes up. He begins with his little sister, eager to learn, and teaches her to read. Then he takes on the boys in the village, who are also hungry for learning. When at last he has enough money to buy the book he has yearned for, what he does is the result of an educated heart. The reader knows, though, that Raman will keep his dreams and that he will someday be a scholar and own the coveted book.

The Bushbabies, by William Stevenson, ill. by Victor Ambrus. Houghton, 1965. (9-12)

Three strange companions—the girl Jackie, her mischievous pet tarsier, called a bushbaby, and their protector, Tembo Murumbi, a faithful old African—made an incredible journey afoot through the jungles and animal lands of Kenya. The child Jackie had forgotten the permit for her bushbaby and knew that without it the tiny creature would be put off the ship taking her family back to England. Impulsively she got off the ship with Kamau. When she met Tembo, who had been her father's first assistant in the animal preserve, she persuaded him to go with her to take Kamau back to his native home. But soon word went out over the radio that Tembo had kidnapped the child and that searchers were to shoot him on sight. This was only one of their worries, which included a prolonged drouth that made the wild animals desperate and unpredictable; devastating fires; and, finally, the most destructive flood in many years. Somehow they got through one peril after another. This is a moving story of animal life in the wilds of Africa, but above all, it is a picture of a man's devotion to a child and of her growing awareness of his self-sacrifice and amazing intelligence. The antics of Kamau, the tiny bushbaby, are amusing, and at the last, the creature plays an unusual role in their rescue.

STORIES OF TIMES PAST

By the middle years, a child's sense of times past is developing. He has encountered the periods of the American Revolution and the Civil War and he may have read stories about knights and far-off battles in other lands. But he is still likely to think of his parents as growing up in pioneer days or "olden times," as he delicately puts it. Thus, the success or the special values of historical fiction lie not only in theme, plot, style, and characterization, but in the author's ability to re-create for the child the details of earlier everyday living. He knows, for example, that Ma's fragrant bread baking in her oven in the *Little House* books belongs to a later period than that of the hard, dry, saltless chunks of corn bread carried by the long hunters of frontier days. For children of the middle years, historical fiction has delightful stories, splendid writing, and lively and authentic details to familiarize them with the earlier periods both in the United States and in other countries. The books listed are outstanding examples of good writing in this field.

Otto of the Silver Hand, by Howard Pyle, ill. by author. Scribner, 1916, 1954. (10-14)
Sometimes this powerful story of the robber barons of Germany (originally published in 1888) is the child's first encounter with realistic cruelty. Certainly no child who reads this book ever forgets it. For revenge, the enemies of one baron strike off the hand of his only son, frail Otto. The mutilation of the boy is gently treated in the story, but there remains the infinite pathos of a child in the hands of ruthless men. The story details two phases of life in that medieval period—the turbulent strife of the barons and the peaceful, scholarly pursuits of the monks within the protective walls of their great monasteries. Howard Pyle's illustrations are as powerful as his stories, and since he was so steeped in the customs of the Middle Ages, his stories and pictures together bring the period vividly to life.

The Door in the Wall, by Marguerite de Angeli, ill. by author. Doubleday, 1949. Newbery Medal. (9-12)
This is a story of thirteenth-century England in the days of knights. At the beginning of the story, Robin, the young hero, has been left alone in his castle home with the servants—his father off to the wars and his mother with the Queen, as a lady in waiting. Then the plague strikes, and Robin not only falls ill but is deserted by the servants. Unable to move his legs, he lies helpless until Brother Luke discovers him and moves him to St. Mark's hospice to care for him. To despairing Robin, he says, "Thou hast only to follow the wall far enough and there will be a door in it." And as soon as Robin is better, Brother Luke and the other monks teach the boy to read, to use his hands, and to get about agilely on crutches—all achievements that are doors in the wall of his

helplessness. Still Robin knows he can never be the knight his father expected him to be, but he does what he can and keeps a stout heart. Finally, when he has played a heroic part in saving the beleaguered town, he is honored by the king and is received with joyful pride by his parents. This is a story of unusual significance, beautifully told and illustrated.

Wind in the Chimney, by Cornelia Meigs, ill. by Louise Mansfield. Macmillan, 1934, 1958. Also *The Covered Bridge,* ill. by Marguerite de Angeli. Macmillan, 1936, 1957. (9-12)

Cornelia Meigs has made a real contribution to historical fiction for children. The following two books are good examples of her work.

Wind in the Chimney is the name the Morelands, newly arrived from England—the widowed mother, fourteen-year-old Richard, "middle-sized" Ann, and eight-year-old Deborah—give to the little deserted house they move into, six miles out of Philadelphia. The story begins in September, about ten years after the Revolutionary War. There are two threads of interest—Dick's adventures helping a wagoner take his Conestoga wagon and line of packhorses across country; and Debbie and her mother and sister's activities at the Cherry Hill home. The most exciting episodes concern Dick's struggles to find the Wheel of Fortune quilt pattern and Debbie and her mother's desperate but successful efforts to finish weaving the quilt just in time to secure for the family their beloved home.

The Covered Bridge takes place in 1788. While her mother and father are away on a West Indies voyage, young Constance Anderson stays on a Green Mountain farm in Vermont with her aunt's housekeeper, Sarah Macomber, and Sarah's twelve-year-old grandson, Peter. It is an eventful winter, including meeting up with Ethan Allen and, most exciting of all, saving the covered bridge which the flooding Hebron Brook threatens to destroy. Whether it is a debt to be paid, a contract to be fulfilled, or a necessary bridge to be saved, the characters in Cornelia Meigs' books see their obligations through with no whining and no heroics, just as a matter of course, because that's the way life is and one does what needs to be done. See also *Master Simon's Garden* (1929), *Swift Rivers* (1932), *The Willow Whistle* (1931), *Fair Wind to Virginia* (1955), and others.

Winter Danger, by William O. Steele, ill. by Paul Galdone. Harcourt, 1954. Also *Wilderness Journey* (1953). (9-12)

In their middle years, boys and girls should encounter the frontier stories of William Steele. One book will generally send them back to the library for another, for Steele not only re-creates movingly the details of wilderness life, but shows his boy heroes changing and growing under the impact of life's hard lessons and challenges. *Winter Danger* is about a father-son conflict. Young Caje yearns for the security of a settlement. He hates with all his heart his life with his woodsy father, hiding out in caves from hostile Indians and from marauding animals. Finally, signs of Indians nearby and the impending bitter winter move his father to leave the boy with farmer kinsfolk. To dirty, half-starved little Caje, the good food, the cleanliness, and the gentle ways are heaven, until winter comes. Through that terrible season of bitter cold and starvation, Caje learns the hard way that the only security one has in this world, one must make for oneself. He comes out of his ordeal with new compassion and respect for his lonely, intrepid father. *Wilderness Journey* tells the story of a sickly, pusillanimous little pioneer who is forced to travel the wilderness under the unwilling escort of a long hunter. This is an exciting study of wilderness ways and skills. See also *The Buffalo Knife* (1952), *Tomahawks and Trouble* (1955), and *The Far Frontier* (1959).

Little House in the Big Woods, by Laura Ingalls Wilder, ill. by Garth Williams. Harper, 1932, 1953. Also *Little House on the Prairie, On the Banks of Plum Creek, By the Shores of Silver Lake, Farmer Boy, The Long Winter, Little Town on the Prairie,* and *These Happy Golden Years.*

No child in the United States should miss the Wilder *Little House* series, splendidly and authentically illustrated by Garth Williams. The eight books carry the Ingalls family from Wisconsin westward into Indian country and beyond. The first book appeals to children of eight and nine; the last is written for the almost grown-up girl, who if she has followed the adventures of the Ingalls family in the earlier books, by this time feels that Laura is her oldest and dearest friend. The girls in the story grow older in each book until in the last book, *These Happy Golden Years*, Laura Ingalls and Almanzo Wilder are married. One book—*Farmer Boy*—is devoted to the Wilder family and especially to Almanzo, who reappears in the lives of the Ingalls family in *The Long Winter*. This pioneer saga is filled with blizzards, drouths, crop failures, Indian perils, and all the other vicissitudes of frontier life, but family courage never fails. Ma's gift for homemaking, Pa's wonderful fiddle music and singing, and warm, cheerful affection and trust keep the Ingalls family hopeful and determined, come what will. Here in these books, children will find security of the heart and of the emotions, the kind of security that weathers every storm. If only one book in the series is read, don't let a child miss *The Long Winter*. It is the summation of the quiet, unsung heroism of thousands of nameless people who ventured into the wilderness and took and held the land.

Caddie Woodlawn, by Carol Ryrie Brink, ill. by Kate Seredy. Macmillan, 1935. Newbery Medal. (9-12)
 Like *The Good Master*, this book is a perennial favorite. Although the story is set in the Civil War period, the menace for the Woodlawn family is not the war but hostile Indians. Caddie, the redheaded tom-

DANCE AT GRANDPA'S

them with the syrup they set out more. They set
the filled ones away, to cool into maple sugar.
 Then Grandma said:
 "Now bring the patty-pans for the children."

From *Little House in the Big Woods* by Laura Ingalls Wilder. Copyright, 1932 by Laura Ingalls Wilder. Illustrations copyright 1953 by Garth Williams. Reprinted by permission of Harper & Row, Publishers.

boy heroine, has two brothers who are her willing followers but who are a little uneasy about her long friendship with the nearby Indians. Nothing, however, can stop the girl's exploration of anything in the vicinity that will yield a little excitement. She sometimes carries her pranks too far as when she perpetrates a rather mean joke on a visiting girl cousin whose ladylike behavior is a reproach to hoydenish Caddie. Lively girls admire her spunk, are thrilled with Caddie's success in averting an imminent uprising of hostile Indians, and sympathize with her voluntary reform at the conclusion of the story. This is less a story of frontier life than it is the story of the gentling of a tomboy by an understanding but firm father.

Chancy and the Grand Rascal, by Sid Fleischman, ill. by Eric von Schmidt. Little, 1966. (9-12)

Somewhere between the everyday realism of *Henry Huggins* and the realistic fantasy of *Half Magic* (see p. 157) lie the hilarious tales of Sid Fleischman. *Chancy and the Grand Rascal* is almost a tall tale, something in the style of Mark Twain's tall tales, yet the characters and action are so possible that the reader goes chuckling and convinced from one wild episode to the next. Orphaned Chancy Dundee is determined to find his two sisters and brother, who were separated from him after the death of their parents during the Civil War. Last he knew about them, his sister Indiana had been apprenticed to a chair bottomer in Paducah, and Mirandy and Jamie had been taken in by Miss Callie Russell, a neighbor lady. Chancy starts out to find them, with his possessions in a wheelbarrow and a gold piece hung around his neck. He soon loses the latter to a swindler, but is joined in the nick of time by his remarkable uncle Will Buckthorn, known as the Grand Rascal. He had earned his title because, as he said himself, he could "out-laugh, out-exaggerate, and out-rascal any man this side of the Big Muddy, and twice as many on the other!" This is glorious nonsense, warmed by family affection and loyalty. It is fun to read aloud in the family or to cheer up a convalescent child or anyone else in need of a real laugh.

The Matchlock Gun, by Walter D. Edmonds, ill. by Paul Lantz. Dodd, 1941. Newbery Medal. (9-12)

Some authors, like James Fenimore Cooper and Henry Wadsworth Longfellow, have idealized the Indian as the "noble savage." Others, like Walter D. Edmonds in this story, have tended to emphasize the scalping, massacring Indian, and to ignore his just grievances and his point of view. However, this Newbery Medal book by the author of the popular adult book *Drums Along the Mohawk* is well written and continues to be popular, especially with boys. The story, according to the author, took place "in 1757, when New York State was still a British Colony, when the French were still leading Indians out of Canada against the settlers," and tells of an incident of "the raid that came all the way to Guilderland, just outside of Albany City." It is about real people, the Van Alstynes, and especially about the brave mother and ten-year-old Edward, who fired the ancient Spanish matchlock gun at his mother's signal, killing three Indians and frightening the other raiders away. When the father, Teunis, and a half-dozen militiamen arrived later, they found the house burned, the mother unconscious from a tomahawk wound, the baby sister asleep, and Edward still awake, holding the huge gun across his lap, "the bell mouth pointing at the three dead Indian bodies." The suspense is harrowing and only slightly ameliorated by a preliminary glimpse of happy family life and by the fact that the whole family was saved. For a more balanced presentation of relations between the Indians and the settlers, children who read this book should also read Cornelia Meigs' *The Willow Whistle*, which is about friendly Indians and settlers, or M. O'Moran's *Trail of the Little Paiute*, which is an important record of the Paiutes' courageous but hopeless last stand against the encroaching white men.

Island of the Blue Dolphins, by Scott O'Dell. Houghton, 1960. Newbery Medal. (10-14)

In the early 1800's, on the rocky island of San Nicholas, off the coast of California, an Indian girl spent eighteen years alone. Hostile Aleuts had almost exterminated her people, and the tribe was being moved to a new and protected site. But as the ship left the island, the girl Karana saw that her six-year-old brother had been accidentally left behind. She jumped off the ship and swam ashore to her brother and home.

This is the story of her struggles for survival. The brother was killed by a ferocious pack of wild dogs that later stalked her. This danger forced her to make weapons, build a house with a strong fence, and secure her food under constant peril. She killed several dogs but only wounded the leader. By the time she had nursed him back to health, they were inseparable companions and he was her protector. Karana hid from the Aleuts when they returned; she battled an octopus and a bull elephant from the sea; but she also tamed birds, otters, and other dogs and found them much like people. What makes the book unique is the girl's patient endurance, her quiet serenity, and her deep love for her island home. She was a gentle, normal young woman when she was finally rescued. This is a true story, stranger than fiction.

ANIMAL STORIES

By the middle years, talking beast stories have with a few exceptions been left behind. However, Felix Salten's *Bambi*, from the time it was first published, has been enjoyed by all ages, from young children who listen to it read aloud, to the adults who read it to them. In *Bambi* the animals talk to each other about their unique animal concerns, but they are never humanized. On the whole, children nine years and over like their animal stories to be true to the life of whatever species is being described. The best of these realistic animal stories have great value in developing in children compassion for the helplessness and suffering of animals at the hands of man and also concern for the health and safety of wild creatures as well as of pets.

Interestingly enough, in this mechanized age, horse stories were for a long time tops in popularity, even though urban children rarely see horses and few children today have any contact with them. Evidently writers have succeeded in building up the image of the noble horse, although sometimes, as in the case of Anna Sewell's *Black Beauty*, oversentimentalizing the animals. Generations of children have wept over the sufferings of that Victorian equine, but *Black Beauty* is an example of what is undesirable in realistic animal stories. The horse is overly humanized; he suffers as a person would, not a horse. Of course, the book was written as propaganda against the checkrein, and as such apparently did some good. But it is a sob story and does not compare with the best of the modern stories about domestic and wild animals, as a little reading in this field will prove. There are so many fine books about animals that it is hard to make a selection, but the following group has variety and distinction. It ranges from stories that are comparatively easy reading to ones that are fairly complex both in form and content. Archie Binns' *Sea Pup*, discussed on page 118, might be included in this list. And for your advanced readers, scan also the reviews of animal stories in Chapter 8.

Salute, by Clarence W. Anderson, ill. by author. Macmillan, 1940. Also *High Courage* (1941). (9-12)

Salute tells the story of the boy Peter's devotion to a broken-down race horse. How Peter nursed his protégé back to health and then began retraining him for the track is a study in patience, persistence, and love. *High Courage* is also about a race horse, this time handled by a girl, Patsy, and a fine Negro trainer. Children who know nothing about these great thoroughbreds still enjoy the fascinating details concerning their care and meticulous training for racing. Mr. Anderson's beautiful pen-and-ink drawings make the horses seem quiveringly alive in every rippling muscle.

Honk: The Moose, by Phil Stong, ill. by Kurt Wiese. Dodd, 1935. (8-10)

Although this book belongs to the middle years, it could be listed for every age group. The sixes, listening to it read aloud, get the joke and enjoy the illustrations. The fourteen-year-olds, who can read it in a matter of minutes, thoroughly enjoy and appreciate the absurd situations and the soulful looking moose Mr. Wiese has pictured so amusingly. The story concerns a dilemma two earnest little boys approached with compassion and understanding. It all begins when they discover an enormous wild moose, who has been driven by the bitter winter weather and lack of food to seek the warm shelter of the town livery stable. When the boys find him, he is busily eating up the hay intended for the horses. The creature seems amiable but firmly attached to his soft bed and plentiful hay. How the boys try to support their moose and finally engage the townsfolk in "Operation Moose" makes good reading for any age, and Mr. Wiese's pictures of the melancholy moose are unforgettable.

King of the Wind, by Marguerite Henry, ill. by Wesley Dennis. Rand McNally, 1948. Newbery Medal. Also *Brighty of the Grand Canyon* (1953). (9-12)

As far as children are concerned, Marguerite Henry is the poet laureate of horses. Her *Justin Morgan Had a Horse* (1954) and *Misty of Chincoteague* (1947) are as popular as her Newbery Medal book, *King of the Wind,* and her *Brighty of the Grand Canyon,* about a legendary burro who is supposed to have pounded out that terrifying path known as Bright Angel Trail. Brighty is a free spirit, but he does make friends with the old prospector, and helps bring to justice the old man's murderer.

King of the Wind relates the misfortunes that befell a great Arabian stallion sent as a gift to the King of France. The trouble started on board the ship that carried and starved these great horses and was increased because the devoted boy who cared for the prize horse was a mute and could not explain things. After rejection by the king and mistreatment from others, boy and horse eventually landed in the English stables of the Earl of Godolphin, who bred race horses. Even then, their troubles were not over. Not until the Arabian horse had sired a great colt was his quality recognized. Then King of the Wind was too old to race, but he sired a glorious line of race horses of which the American Man o' War was a descendant.

The quality of Marguerite Henry's books lies not only in her compelling storytelling power, but in her ability to make her creatures live and act true to their own species with all the helplessness and suffering of animals in the hands of cruel or ignorant men. Another great quality of these books is that they are peopled by admirable human characters who command as much interest as the animal heroes. These books stir deep compassion in young readers and the desire to nurture and protect. One reason that *Brighty* is so popular is that this solitary, courageous little burro triumphs over the men who try to victimize him.

Wesley Dennis, the illustrator, loved horses as much as the author loves them. His identification with and interpretation of these stories are such that children and adults think of illustrations and text as an inseparable whole.

Junket, by Anne H. White, ill. by Robert McCloskey. Viking, 1955. (9-12)

When the tragedies of some of the animal stories become too oppressive, turn to *Junket,* the tale of that hilarious Airedale who took a city family in hand and taught each one of them what a farm should be. This dog does not talk except by a variety of barks, moans, or joyful yelps, but, oh, how he acts! Returning from one of his private journeys, Junket finds a brand new family of human beings on his farm and all the farm animals he has bullied and protected completely vanished. Fortunately, three new children welcome the dog joyfully, and no one tells the gay, affectionate Junket that the man of the house has issued an ultimatum: "positively no animals." While Junket is slowly but surely retrieving every one of the farm animals, he is also educating each member of his family in the joys of farming, assisted to be sure by a former hired man. Eventually, the animal-resistant Mr. McDonegal finds himself the proud owner of a pony, a cow, a pig with a litter, two hens, innumerable cats, and, of course, the ubiquitous Junket. In spite of these machinations, Junket remains strictly a dog, doing what a well-trained farm dog might or could do.

The illustrations, too, are excellent. Certainly no one can draw small boys or an Airedale better or more amusingly than Robert Mc-Closkey.

Rascal: A Memoir of a Better Era, by Sterling North, ill. by John Schoenherr. Dutton, 1963. (11 up)

Sooner or later most farm boys try to make a pet of a wild animal, and sooner or later they learn for one reason or another that the creature must go back to the wilds from which he came. Sterling North has written such a story of his own boyhood. Living alone with his somewhat vague but amiable father (who incidentally lets him build a boat in the middle of the living room), the eleven-year-old boy finds a baby raccoon, Rascal, and discovers an enchanting pet and companion. As in *Sea Pup,* the pet grows and so do the young boy's problems. Rascal merits his name, and after enjoying complete freedom, he is miserable when he is confined to a cage. The end is inevitable, and boy and raccoon face it together. The mating season has come and Rascal is mature; so the boy rows him back to the forest from which he came and watches him depart—handsome, healthy, and eager for the life he was born to. This is more than an animal tale; it is a nostalgic recollection of boyhood that has been enjoyed by as many grownups as children.

Bambi, by Felix Salten, ill. by Kurt Wiese. Grosset, 1931. (10-14)

In contrast to the other books about animals just reviewed, the animals in this story talk. But more than most books, *Bambi* gives children deeper insight and compassion for the wild creatures of the forest. Bambi is a deer, but this sensitively written story includes the other forest creatures, too, from the tiny field mice and the sentry jays to foxes and the huge elk. There is also "He," the enemy of all forest animals. His scent carries terror; his pale hairless face fills them with horror; and worst of all, his terrible "Legs" reach out with a stick that shoots fire and death. The reader follows Bambi from the first day of his life to his maturity and parenthood. There are tragic and unforgettable episodes in this book, notably the hunt, in which the hunters encircle the animals, frightening them out of hiding with terrible noises and constant shooting, a barbarous method of wholesale slaughter. Fortunately, the main part of this book and its sequel, *Bambi's Children*, are chiefly concerned with the development of the young deer, the relationship of males and females, the organization of the herd, and the life of the forest creatures, idyllic or miserable, depending upon the season. *Bambi* is a fine book to read aloud in the family because it is full of suspense and beautifully written.

The Incredible Journey, by Sheila Burnford, ill. by Carl Burger. Little, 1961. (10 up)

No book was ever more truly named. It tells of a journey of 250 miles through Canadian wilderness, made by a Labrador retriever, a bull terrier, and a Siamese cat. The animals were headed back to the place and the people that meant home to them. The retriever led the way, and his sense of direction never failed. The aging bulldog gave out first, but the cat fed him until he regained his strength. Indeed, the cat was the most competent of the trio. Even after a near drowning and a rescue by a little girl who wanted to keep him, he managed to rejoin his dog companions and keep them supplied with food. Their worst encounter, worse even than the encounter with a bear, was the time the retriever tangled with a porcupine and got his face full of barbs which festered and made eating impossible for him. Then the cat and the bulldog brought him the kill first so that he could lap up the blood and keep his strength. Somehow those intrepid animals made the journey, although the last fifty miles, according to the forest rangers, were impossible. The reunion with the people they loved is described with a restraint that makes the meeting even more poignant. Never once in this wonderful book are the animals humanized. Never once are their thoughts interpreted; only their actions are objectively and movingly reported. This is a book for the whole family.

This chapter gives children a glimpse of the real world with struggles and complexities of many kinds. Whether it is a story of modern days in our United States or in some other land, historical fiction, a story about a horse or a dog or a deer or a raccoon, these realistic stories could have happened. They are plausible and possible. There are two exceptions. The first is *Bambi*, in which the animals talk and we know their thoughts. But the author has kept them true to the species; their problems are animal not human; and the resultant picture is true to animal life in the forest. The other exception is the hilarious *Junket,* who never speaks a word nor comes out of dog character, but manages to take over and run a whole family of human beings. These two borderline books are not pure realism, but both reveal much about animals that is strictly true. Both give children a grave or humorous insight into animal nature and animal vulnerability at the hands of man.

In conclusion, remember as always that no single child is going to like or be able to read every book in these lists. Look back or forward in the reading lists if you have some doubts about those in this chapter and always look for books suited to the taste and reading level of the child or children you have in mind. Any of these books that a child thoroughly enjoys is a good book for him.

MAGIC AND MAKE-BELIEVE FOR THE MIDDLE YEARS FOR AGES NINE-TEN-ELEVEN

7

Folk Tales
Fables
Myths
Epics
Modern Fanciful Tales

In an age when the work of computers and the feats of space exploration are dramatically visible on television, in moving pictures, and in pictorial magazines, children still turn to stories of magic and make-believe. Are they trying to escape from the frightening complexities they encounter in the adult world of science and human relations? Are they trying to return to or to remain within that simpler, cozier world of wish-fulfilling magic, with its flying carpets, impudent puppets, humble goose girls, and penguin-loving paper hangers—a happy, anything-can-happen world that never was but ought to be?

Whatever the reasons, children still enjoy tales of fantasy— both the traditional tales (including folk tales, fables, myths, and epics) and the modern fanciful tales. Such labels are of course no concern of children, who are merely looking for satisfying stories, let the categories fall where they may. But for adults, categories are useful as reminders that children need a balanced reading diet during these exploratory years, and that the pic- torially alluring recent books should not crowd out the standard fare which is so valuable a part of our literary heritage. For instance, children should know such folk tales as "The Three Little Pigs," "Cinderella," "The Sleeping Beauty," and "Hansel and Gretel," all of which they call fairy tales; and they should also know the fables, myths, and epics. Librarians say that the nine- and ten- year-olds, given the opportunity, are enthusiastic readers of the traditional tales, but that the eleven-year-olds, probably because of the modern emphasis on science and facts, are less likely to be devotees of the old fairy tales. However, because these old tales embody the wit, the wisdom, and the dreams of the race and have entered into our language and our symbols, children should have them. They dramatize the conflict of good and evil, they show chil- dren heroes who risk their lives to rid the world of ogres, and they demonstrate that in the end, cruelty and meanness are destroyed while the humble but courageous, the obscure but kindly are greatly rewarded. These are concepts worth building early into a child's consciousness.

Children also enjoy the modern fanciful tale—the type of story that Hans Christian Andersen developed to a high level as an art form and created in great variety. Indeed, almost any type of fanciful tale written today is usually to be found in Andersen's stories composed in the nineteenth century. These incomparable tales, no child should miss. From Andersen's time on, fantasy has attracted distinguished writers of every generation. In this generation, authors such as C. S. Lewis, J. R. R. Tolkien, E. B. White, James Thurber, and Rumer Godden have enjoyed excur- sions into this area of writing. The modern fanciful tales are more popular than the folk tales with children today, possibly because they are, on the whole, gayer than the folk tales and also because they are tied into the realistic, everyday world the children know. For instance, E. B. White's *Charlotte's Web* takes off into a whole barnyard of talking animals, but it begins with Fern's temper tantrum. Mary Poppins slides *up* the banister instead of down, and this kind of magic is funnier because it is so firmly rooted in reality. Fanciful tales range from the sheer nonsense of Astrid Lindgren's *Pippi Longstocking*, an outrageous superchild, to the beautiful, allegorical Narnia stories by C. S. Lewis. In between, there are sorrowful tales, drolls, tales of slapstick humor or of subtle irony, and romances. And for these stories there is a wealth of distinguished writing and writers.

FOLK TALES

Most countries have their folk tales—tales passed on from one generation to the next by word of mouth long before they achieved the permanency of print. Because such stories were created and kept alive by storytellers, the best of them have strong themes, vigorous plot development, and compelling style. They had to have or the audience would have walked out on the storyteller, just as children do today when overtaken by dullness. It is to be hoped that by the time the child is seven or eight he knows such nursery classics as "The Story of the Three Bears" (Goldilocks), "The Four Musicians" (The Bremen Town Musicians), "The Three Billy Goats Gruff," and "The Master Cat" (Puss in Boots). It is also to be hoped that he has had an opportunity to pore over the wonderful picture-book editions of single folk tales illustrated by such artists as Marcia Brown, Adrienne Adams, Warren Chappell, and Paul Galdone.

By the time the child is ten or so, he should explore at least one fairly complete edition of a major folk-tale collection, notably the Grimms' from the German, Perrault's from the French, Jacobs' from the English, and Asbjörnsen and Moe's from the Norwegian —this collection is generally called *East o' the Sun and West o' the Moon.* If you wish your child to have the folk tales of some other group as well—Scotch, Italian, Czech, Japanese, and so on —look for Virginia Haviland's splendid collections grouped by countries, or consult a children's librarian or check the bibliographies in May Hill Arbuthnot's *Children and Books.* However, the collections of the Grimms and of Perrault, highly contrasted in mood and style, are basic. They, along with those of Jacobs and of Asbjörnsen and Moe, contain some of the best-known tales in the world. The titles listed below are only a few of the many excellent editions:

Favorite Fairy Tales Told in Germany, retold from the Brothers Grimm, by Virginia Haviland, ill. by Susanne Suba. Little, 1959.
This is only one example of the series of national folk-tale collections prepared by Virginia Haviland. Each book contains five to seven well-known stories, skillfully adapted by a librarian with real feeling for the tales. Parents who are squeamish about the violence in large numbers of the traditional tales may feel safer with these adaptations.

Tales from Grimm, freely tr. and ill. by Wanda Gág. Coward-McCann, 1936.
Here is a popular edition of a fair number of the stories, with real folk flavor.

Household Stories from the Collection of the Brothers Grimm, tr. by Lucy Crane, ill. by Johannes Troyer. Macmillan, 1954.
A standard edition with thirty-two favorite stories.

Grimms' Fairy Tales, tr. by Mrs. E. V. Lucas and others, ill. by Fritz Kredel. Grosset, 1945.
An excellent translation supplemented by bright, appealing pictures.

All the French Fairy Tales, retold by Louis Untermeyer, ill. by Gustave Doré. Didier, 1946.
If this edition is available, it is most worth while for Doré's romantic pictures.

Puss in Boots, The Sleeping Beauty, and Cinderella, "a retelling of three classic Fairy Tales based on the French of Charles Perrault." Ill. by Eugene Karlin. Macmillan, 1963.
This delightful book includes a preface by the poet Marianne Moore on Charles Perrault and the three tales.

English Folk and Fairy Tales, ed. by Joseph Jacobs, ill. by John D. Batten. Putnam, n. d.

This edition of English folk tales is appealing to children. The tales are less somber than the German. For example, compare the English "Tom Tit Tot" with the German version, "Rumpelstiltskin."

East o' the Sun and West o' the Moon, ed. by Peter C. Asbjörnsen and Jörgen E. Moe, tr. by Sir George Webbe Dasent, ill. by Hedvig Collin. Macmillan, 1963.
A new edition of some of the stories which first appeared in 1859. These Norwegian tales are singularly absorbing either to read or to tell.

Look again at the illustrated editions of single tales listed on pages 98-99. These delight older as well as younger children and are apt to suggest the informal neighborhood dramatizations that sometimes take over for an entire summer. And don't be too uneasy about the violence in some of these old stories. Think what children are watching on television! Besides, in the folk tales, the violence is generally therapeutic: the wicked queen in "Snow White" and the cruel witch in "Hansel and Gretel" are exterminated—security measures, if you will, but their demise certainly makes a child feel safer. That is why such stories do not keep a normal, healthy child awake nights. In the folk tales, everything is in order at the conclusion, and so he goes peacefully to sleep.

FABLES

Fables are brief, single episodes that show dramatically in story form some human virtue or weakness. The story closes with a moral, and the characters are generally animals. For example, in the fable "The Crow and the Pitcher," a thirsty crow discovers a pitcher with a little water at the bottom, just beyond his reach. The crow then drops pebbles into the pitcher until the water is high enough so that he can drink it. The moral: "Necessity is the mother of invention." The fable sounds simple and easy to understand, but ask a child to put the moral into his own words, and you will discover that abstract ideas are difficult for children to grasp and still harder for them to explain. For these reasons and also because of the moralistic emphasis, a few fables at a time are more palatable than a large dose. In the primary years, expose children to perhaps a dozen fables until they know what they are like—not real stories but just little incidents that show wisdom or foolishness. By third grade, children should know the name *fable* and be able to identify a fable when they come across one in their reading. By ten or eleven or twelve, a child may enjoy a whole collection such as the ones listed below and should be able to see the fablelike quality of such a nonsense tale as Dr. Seuss' *Horton Hears a Who* or Hans Christian Andersen's "The Ugly Duckling," or some of the episodes in Hugh Lofting's *Dr. Dolittle* books. In Sunday School, children may notice the similarity between the parables and fables.[1]

Aesop's Fables, selected and adapted by Louis Untermeyer, ill. by A. and M. Provensen. Golden Press, 1965.
Here are forty of the fables well told and beautifully illustrated.

Fables from Aesop, retold by James Reeves, ill. by Maurice Wilson. Walck, 1962.
These fifty fables are told with dialogue that enlivens without destroying the character of the originals.

Fables from Aesop, retold by Ennis Rees, ill. by J. J. Grandville with wood engravings made for an 1838 ed. of La Fontaine's version of Aesop's fables. Oxford, 1967.
Ennis Rees, the translator of both the *Iliad* and the *Odyssey*, has retold one hundred eighty-seven of the traditional tales from Aesop.

Older as well as younger children will enjoy these editions of fables by Katherine Evans, Paul Galdone, and Marcia Brown:

A *Bundle of Sticks*, adapted and ill. by Katherine Evans. Whitman, 1962.
An amusing retelling of an Aesop fable. Miss Evans has also done *The Boy Who Cried Wolf* (1960) and *A Camel in the Tent* (1961).

The Hare and the Tortoise, ill. by Paul Galdone. McGraw, 1962.
The bright, action-packed illustrations delight children.

[1]See May Hill Arbuthnot, *Children and Books*, 1964, Scott, Foresman, pp. 298-300 for distinctions: Fables, Parables, Proverbs.

Once a Mouse . . . a fable cut in wood, by Marcia Brown. Scribner, 1961. Caldecott Medal.

The mouse turned by the hermit into a cat, then a dog, and finally into a tiger must, because of his arrogance, be turned back into a mouse.

MYTHS

The myths, particularly those of Greece and Rome, are an important and pervasive part of our heritage. Rarely does a day go by that we do not encounter some reference to the ancient myths. For example, think of only the most important gods of Greece and their Roman counterparts: Zeus (Jove or Jupiter), the king of the Olympian gods; Hera (Juno), wife of Zeus, goddess of women and marriage; Athena (Minerva), goddess of wisdom; Aphrodite (Venus), goddess of love and beauty; Eros (Cupid), god of love; Ar-

temis (Diana), the virgin huntress; Poseidon (Neptune), the god of the sea; Hades or Pluto (Dis), god of the underworld; Dionysus (Bacchus), god of wine and the harvest; Hermes (Mercury), messenger of the gods; Ares (Mars), god of war; Hephaestus (Vulcan), god of fire and metal working; Demeter (Ceres), goddess of agriculture; Persephone (Proserpina), goddess of the underworld, spring. How often are you reminded of one or more of these gods, their symbols, and their exploits? Hermes, or Mercury, and his winged sandals appear as a symbol for our modern air or ground transportation; Athena, or Minerva, is pictured in libraries along with her attendant owl; Aphrodite, or Venus, rising from the sea, advertises bath salts and other beauty aids. *Tantalize* comes from Tantalus, the son of Zeus and the nymph Pluto, who was punished for revealing the secrets of the gods to mortals—he suffered agonies of thirst and hunger with water and fruit just out of his reach. *Panic* comes from Pan, the god of pastures, forests, and flocks, who had the upper part of a man and the lower part of a goat. *Cereal* derives from Ceres, the patron goddess of grains. So it goes, ad infinitum.

The more complex tales and the intricate relationships of the gods to each other and to men are not, on the whole, for children, but it is a rare child who does not respond to single episodes or adventures of the gods. What child will ever forget the story of greedy King Midas, who was granted his foolish wish for a golden touch which turned palace, gardens, his food, and even his little daughter (in Nathaniel Hawthorne's version of the tale) into the golden metal. And how satisfying is the story of the hospitable old couple Philemon and Baucis, who entertained two gods in disguise and were rewarded for their kindness in godlike fashion. Children will also enjoy the many stories of transformations: of Clytie, who became the sunflower; of Arachne, who because of her foolish boasting about her weaving became a spider; of Echo, who because of her unrequited love for Narcissus pined away until she was only a voice; and of vain Narcissus, who was turned into a flower always gazing at his own image in the fountain. These and many others, the children should know—Demeter and Persephone, Bellerophon and Pegasus, Daedalus and Icarus, Pandora and her box of troubles, Jason and the Golden Fleece, Orpheus and Eurydice—because all carry something of the shining beauty of the bright and godly dwellers on Olympus.

To start children reading these myths for themselves, you may have to tell or read aloud a story or two with running commentaries about the nature of the gods involved in the myth. After that, give children a good collection of the myths and suggest some stories as particularly typical and interesting. Don't be disturbed if your offerings are rejected; it may simply mean that the children are not ready for the myths. But because of their importance in our language and literature, it is worth while to try to interest children in these timeless stories.

> *Stories of Gods and Heroes*, by Sally Benson, ill. by Steele Savage. Dial, 1940.
> Exceedingly well-told and illustrated, this is an outstanding edition.

> *The Heroes*, by Charles Kingsley, ill. by Vera Bock. Macmillan, 1954.
> Beautifully retold tales with a feeling for the grandeur and beauty of the myths.

> *The Gorgon's Head: The Story of Perseus*, by Ian Serraillier, ill. by William Stobbs. Walck, 1962. Also *The Way of Danger: The Story of Theseus* (1963).
> Children like the spirited pictures and fast-moving text of these tales.

> *A Book of Myths*, selected from Bulfinch's *Age of Fable*, and ill. by Helen Sewell. Macmillan, 1942.
> Striking, stylized illustrations make this selection from a standard source a distinguished edition.

> *The Golden Treasury of Myths and Legends*, adapted by Anne Terry White, ill. by Alice and Martin Provensen. Golden Press, 1959.
> Two distinguished artists and an equally distinguished author have collaborated in this fine edition of epics, myths, and legends.

EPICS

Epics are generally poetic compositions related to mythology but concerned chiefly with human heroes whose deeds have become so magnified that they make a whole cycle of tales. Sometimes the gods take a hand in the hero's activities, crowning him with success or thwarting him when he is out of line. Always the epic is a heroic narrative, filled with the courageous deeds and noble endeavors of a man, the central figure. This is their great value for young readers. It is good for children to follow Odysseus on his long journey struggling to return to his home and family after the Trojan War; to see him outwit Polyphemus, the giant Cyclops; to watch him tempted in the land of the Lotus Eaters and his men turned into swine by Circe, the enchantress; and to endure with him all the other vicissitudes of his perilous travels. Reading the *Odyssey*, children for days are steeped in examples of fortitude, self-discipline, singleness of purpose, and steadfast devotion to a cherished goal. When Odysseus finally reaches his home and finds the suitors besieging Penelope, his faithful but harassed wife, the hero, aided by his son Telemachus, triumphs in a tremendous fight with the miserable creatures. And every young reader is thrilled with a vicarious sense of satisfaction and righteous exultation. Here in the *Odyssey* you will find a noble substitute for the violence of television's Westerns. These are action-packed tales on a heroic scale.

The merriest epic, just right for the nines and tens, is, of course, *Robin Hood*, an English epic preserved in ballad form but rewritten

From *The Merry Adventures of Robin Hood of Great Renown in Nottinghamshire*, as written and illustrated by Howard Pyle. Charles Scribner's Sons, Publishers. Copyright, 1946, by Charles Scribner's Sons.

in spellbinding prose by Howard Pyle. *Robin Hood* has been the source of many moving pictures and television programs, and it also lends itself temptingly to home, school, or camp dramatizations. It is a diverting cycle of tales about the legendary outlaw from kingly injustice—Robin Hood, who gathered about his hiding place in Sherwood Forest a band of lively outlaws who preyed upon the rich to feed the poor. After a series of adventures, often very funny, they are joined by a stout fellow who listens patiently to their tales of wrongs and then reveals himself as their new king, Richard the Lion-Hearted. He rights their wrongs, they swear their loyalty to him, and all ends gaily. At least that is how the series of stories generally ends, but children may discover for themselves in Howard Pyle's version the death of Robin Hood at the hands of a false prioress. They will weep, of course, but it is well for them to know that treachery and death abound as well as heroism, and that nothing lasts in this world but the little legacy of character a man leaves behind.

Most of the epics belong to the elevens and twelves, and perhaps your children in the middle years will find even this pair, *Robin Hood* and the *Odyssey*, stiff reading. If so, see if you can discover a library where any one of the epics is being told serially. It will be worth your while to see that your child attends. And if there is no such storytelling treat available, why not read one of the epics aloud yourself over a series of days or weeks? That will be an exciting experience for you as well as for your child.

The *Iliad and the Odyssey of Homer*, retold by Alfred John Church, ill. by Eugene Karlin. Macmillan, 1964.
An excellent source (first published in two volumes in 1906, 1907) for children to read or for adults to tell. The stories in the *Odyssey* are arranged in chronological order, which is important.

The *Adventures of Odysseus*, retold by Andrew Lang, ill. by Joan Kiddell-Monroe. Dutton, 1962.
Both the *Iliad* and the *Odyssey* have been excellently retold by Andrew Lang. These versions are not, however, easy reading.

The *Odyssey of Homer*, retold by Barbara Leonie Picard, ill. by Joan Kiddell-Monroe. Walck, 1952.
A distinguished retelling of a favorite epic.

*The Merry Adventures of Robin Hood of Great Renown in Nottingham-
shire*, by Howard Pyle, ill. by author. Scribner, 1946. Also *Some
Merry Adventures of Robin Hood of Great Renown in Nottinghamshire* (1954).
  The Merry Adventures of Robin Hood (first published in 1883) is
the great prose edition of the Robin Hood tales, distinguished in text
and illustration. *Some Merry Adventures of Robin Hood* contains a
dozen stories adapted by Pyle from the longer work. It would serve
as an introduction to the tales for younger readers.

Robin Hood and His Merry Outlaws, retold by J. Walker McSpadden,
ill. by Louis Slobodkin. World, 1946.
  If the children cannot read Pyle, try this edition (first published in
1923), which is very good indeed and much easier.

Doesn't even this brief summary convince you that traditional
literature—folk tales, fables, myths, and epics—has much to offer
children? The folk tales say that even a poor lad, if he has a kind
and honest heart, courage and ingenuity, can rid the world of its
ogres, witches, and unjust laws. The fables deal out such sage advice as "Don't count your chickens before they are hatched." The
myths bring us man's first dreams of flying and of a bright world
called Olympus, while the epics take us back to earth with human
heroes who struggle mightily and leave the world a little better
because of their fortitude. Here, indeed, in these traditional tales
are the wit, dreams, and heroic deeds of the race.

MODERN FANCIFUL TALES

Andersen's Fairy Tales
  Out of poverty, loneliness, and heartbreak, Hans Christian
Andersen (1805-1875) created for children a world of magic and
beauty. He himself had dreamed of being a dancer, an actor, a
novelist, a playwright, but he failed at all four. He hungered for
love but won only sympathy. He encountered cruelty and kindness
in such extremes that in his stories they are personified as the great
combatants in life—the icy, heartless Snow Queen is pitted against
tender little Gerda, loving and therefore vulnerable. With chil-

dren, Andersen never failed. He told them stories, cut out for them lacy paper scenes of incredible intricacy, and, finally, wrote for them his poignant stories called simply *Andersen's Fairy Tales.* To his surprise, these brought him fame and fortune beyond anything he had ever dreamed of, with the acquaintance of and honors from royalty in his own country and abroad, and from famous men all over Europe. But it was the children who had first loved Hans Andersen and his creations, and for each generation of children "The Ugly Duckling," "The Real Princess," "The Emperor's New Clothes," and other stories weave their spells, and, incidentally, tempt other writers to try their hands at the creation of fanciful tales.

Andersen's stories belong in several categories. (1) Sometimes he retells folk tales—his beautiful "The Wild Swans," for example. (2) Sometimes he tells an original story in folk-tale style, as "Thumbelina." (3) Or he writes pure fantasy, as "The Little Match Girl" or his long novella "The Snow Queen," both so sad they may be

Illustration by Adrienne Adams and excerpt from R. P. Keigwin's translation of Hans Christian Andersen's *Thumbelina* (Copyright © 1961 Adrienne Adams) are reprinted with the permission of Charles Scribner's Sons and Adrienne Adams.

A nicely varnished walnut-shell did for her cradle, blue violet petals for her mattress, and a rose-leaf for her counterpane. That was where she slept at night; but in the daytime she played about on the table, where the woman had put a plate with a wreath of flowers. These dipped their stalks

saved for the twelves and thirteens. (4) His personifications of inanimate objects, as "The Constant Tin Soldier" or "The Fir Tree," are highly original but not so numerous nor so successful as his other types. (5) Among his talking-beast stories, "The Ugly Duckling" is a classic example. (6) Finally, although it must be admitted that the bulk of Andersen's tales has heavy overtones of melancholy, he does also have a sly sense of humor and has written some amusing tales. Children find "The Real Princess" and "The Emperor's New Clothes" genuinely funny, and adults, too, enjoy these satires on pretentiousness, false values, and pomposity. Children should not miss the gentleness and beauty of Andersen's tales (in collections and editions of single tales) and their great range of characters—fools, rogues, villains, along with a host of humble, decent, loving folk who seem to say to the reader, "Well, this is what the world is like. Which side are you on?" There are numerous collections of the tales. The following is one of the best:

> *It's Perfectly True, and Other Stories*, by Hans Christian Andersen, tr. by Paul Leyssac, ill. by Richard Bennett. Harcourt, 1938.
>
> This translation of twenty-eight of the stories has been a favorite collection for younger readers.

Other modern fanciful tales

After *Andersen's Fairy Tales*, the two great classics of modern fanciful tales are *Alice's Adventures in Wonderland* by Lewis Carroll and *The Wind in the Willows* by Kenneth Grahame. Since *Alice* is more often appreciated by the oldest children or even by high-school students, its discussion will be left to Chapter 9. But *The Wind in the Willows* is a must for the nines, tens, or elevens.

> *The Wind in the Willows*, by Kenneth Grahame, ill. by Arthur Rackham. Heritage, 1944. Also ill. by Ernest Shepard. Scribner, 1933 (first published in 1908). (9-12)
>
> Here is a story of friends who just happen to be talking beasts—Mole, Water Rat, Badger, and addle-headed, conceited Toad of Toad Hall. The friends "mess around in boats," enjoy picnics in the spring sunshine, dine elegantly at Toad Hall, only to find themselves involved in one of Toad's silliest misadventures, from which they rescue him with great difficulty. Once when the friends are lost in the wet and

cold of the Wild Woods, kind old Badger takes them in to enjoy the warmth and well-stocked larder of his home. Another time when Rat and Mole are searching for the lost Otter baby, they have a breathtaking encounter with "The Piper at the Gates of Dawn"—a chapter that should be read aloud for its sheer drama and beauty. Some of the adventures are hilarious, but in them all, the friends stand by each other and their neighbors. Each chapter is an episode. These were first told by the author to his little son who was ready to miss a vacation rather than miss one of the episodes. If you read the book aloud, you may skip judiciously some of the long descriptions. When the children reread the book for themselves and again reread it as adults, they will want to read it all for its warmth and beauty.

The Jungle Books, by Rudyard Kipling, ill. by Kurt Wiese. Doubleday, 1932 (first published in 1894). Also ill. by Fritz Eichenberg. Grosset, 1950. (10-14)

Kipling tells the story of Mowgli, a human baby, raised by a wolf pack, vouched for and then later repudiated by them because he is not a wolf. From that time on, he must hunt alone. In "Kaa's Hunting," a chapter no reader ever forgets, Mowgli is stolen by the irresponsible monkeys and rescued by his protectors, Bear and Panther, with the aid of Kaa, the snake. Kaa is only too glad to help, foreseeing a pleasant dinner for himself of monkey meat. After Kaa gets Mowgli safely away from the monkeys, he begins his spellbinding dance to charm the silly creatures right out of the trees. Then Mowgli rescues Bear and Panther, who, like the monkeys, are beginning to fall under Kaa's spell. This is a powerful story (not easy reading, by the way) that gives children, along with the exciting adventures, considerable insight into the curious likeness of animals and human beings and also the equally sharp lines of demarcation between them. See also *Just So Stories,* originally published in 1902. This is a delightful collection of humorous animal tall tales, including "How the Whale Got His Throat," "How the Leopard Got His Spots," and "The Elephant's Child," which no child should miss hearing read aloud. An attractive edition is *New Illustrated Just So Stories,* illustrated by Nicolas Mordvinoff (Doubleday, 1967). The picture book format appeals to younger children, six to ten.

The Children of Green Knowe, by Lucy M. Boston, ill. by Peter Boston. Harcourt, 1955. (9-12)

In this remarkably realistic fantasy, the story goes back and forth with convincing ease between the seventeenth century and today. Lonely young Toseland (Tolly) is sent to live with his great-grandmother, Mrs. Oldknow, in the family's ancient manor, Green Knowe. He is aware of other children but at first he does not see them, though he knows his great-grandmother does. She shows him a portrait of the three who died long ago in the year of the plague, but who still come back to their favorite play spots in and around the old house. Presently Tolly sees and plays with them but can never touch them. Their play eventually involves Tolly in terrifying peril from which he is strangely rescued. This might be but is not a somber, frightening tale. The character of the great-grandmother is unforgettable, the story is superbly told, and there is so much love and happiness for motherless Tolly in the old house that the scare is brief and the remembrance bright.

Mary Poppins, by P. L. Travers, ill. by Mary Shepard. Harcourt, 1934. (9-12)

Despite Disney's entertaining but largely irrelevant moving picture of *Mary Poppins*, the book is still avidly read by children and will probably continue to be so read long after the film has vanished. Mary Poppins is the airborne nursemaid carried neatly into the home of the Banks family by the east wind, and eventually carried off by the west wind. During her stay with the family, amazing things happen. She slides *up* the banisters with ease. She doses the children with medicine that tastes like strawberry ice. The children inhale laughing gas and have tea sitting comfortably on nothing at all around a table suspended in mid-air. Furthermore, the carrousel horses carry them right off for a cross-country ride. Mary never admits to any magic, but where she is, magic happens. The children, entranced, beg her never to leave them, but one day, when the wind changes to the west, off she goes, borne aloft by her faithful umbrella, leaving the disconsolate children down below. Fortunately for Poppins devotees, she returns in three more books—*Mary Poppins Comes Back, Mary Poppins in the Park*, and *Mary Poppins Opens the Door*.

Half Magic, by Edward Eager, ill. by N. M. Bodecker. Harcourt, 1954. Also *Magic or Not?* (1959) and *Seven-Day Magic* (1962). (8-12)

Mr. Eager may call his book *Half Magic*, but there is no question that his own magic as a writer of fantasy for children is full strength. He commands absorbed reading interest from the first page to the last.

In *Half Magic*, Jane, Mark, Katharine, and Martha are facing a dull summer in the city with their widowed mother hard at work. Then Jane finds what she thinks is an ordinary nickel, but it isn't. Jane discovers that it grants wishes, not entirely, only half way. However, the children soon learn to manage that by wishing twice as far or once again. So Mark got them all to the Sahara desert, Katherine took them back to the time of Sir Lancelot, and their mother, having borrowed what she thought was Jane's nickel, found a stranger who brought her safely home and eventually played an important and happy part in their lives. The magic in this story is so rooted in everyday life that it seems plausible enough to happen to any of us. The later books are equally popular.

The Borrowers, by Mary Norton, ill. by Joe and Beth Krush. Harcourt, 1953. (8-10)

Beloved by readers from seven to seventy, *The Borrowers* was an immediate success and remains a continuing favorite. Borrowers are not fairies but small people who live in old houses and take their names from the spots where they dwell, as the Overmantles, or the Harpsichords, or the Clocks—the entrance to their home is under a grandfather clock. This story is about the Clocks—Pod, Homily, and their little daughter Arrietty. Borrowers don't steal; they merely borrow from the wealth of objects the "human beans" scatter around, and what they do with these articles is fascinating. Pod is a brave, skilled Borrower, Homily is a fuss-budget, and Arrietty is far too adventurous to be safe. Surely enough, it is Arrietty's acquaintance with the boy that brings the terrible housekeeper down on them—with poison, traps, and ferrets. The Clocks have to flee their old home, and the boy does not know whether they are dead or alive. This ending so upset young readers that there had to be another book, and so there was—three more: *The Borrowers Afield*, *The Borrowers Afloat*, and *The Borrowers Aloft*, all as beloved as the first one.

The Gammage Cup, by Carol Kendall, ill. by Erik Blegvad. Harcourt, 1959. (9-12)

This is the story of the Minnipins or the Small Ones, who "dwelt along the banks of the Watercress River in the Land Between the Mountains," and it is particularly about the five nonconformists—Gummy, the rhymester; Curley Green, the artist; Mingy, the town treasurer; Walter the Earl, who spends his time in a thoroughly unorthodox way digging in his yard for "ancient scrolls and treasure"; and Muggles, the shy heroine of the story, who is keeper of the Museum and candymaker. Many years after Gammage had helped them escape from their enemies (the Mushrooms or Hairless Ones), the Minnipins in Slipper-in-the-Water have become pretty intolerant and smug— so much so that they drive the five nonconformists out of the village because they will not consent to green doors for everyone. How Muggles and the others set up housekeeping on the mountain, give advance warning of a new threat from the Mushrooms, and unite the villagers is an exciting tale. There is a harrowing battle, the villagers come to their senses and make amends, and they all decide they don't need the "famous vessel of wisdom—the Gammage Cup" to convince themselves that theirs is the "finest village in the Land Between the Mountains"—but they receive it anyway. *The Whisper of Glocken* (1965) is not quite so popular but is in similar vein.

Miss Happiness and Miss Flower, by Rumer Godden, ill. by Jean Primrose. Viking, 1961. Also *Little Plum* (1963). (8-11)

Doll-loving little girls should be forever grateful to the novelist Rumer Godden for her entrancing doll stories. *The Dolls' House* (1947, 1962) is one of the most dramatic, with a doll-sized tragedy and a tender conclusion. Two of Miss Godden's most charming doll stories, *Miss Happiness and Miss Flower* and *Little Plum*, are about some Japanese dolls and the influence they had on the children who owned them. Miss Happiness and Miss Flower help Nona Fell, a lonely, homesick child from India, to adjust to her new life in England with her uncle and aunt and cousins. The dolls also inspire a long and careful activity —the creation of a Japanese doll house. *Little Plum* is more child- than doll-centered and deals with the troubles between Belinda and the girl next door. Again, the gentle influence of the dolls brings about a happy conclusion. Miss Godden's dolls and children are convincingly real, but since the doll play is imaginative, these two delightful stories seem to belong naturally to a half-world of fantasy.

The Return of the Twelves, by Pauline Clarke, ill. by Bernarda Bryson. First American Edition, Coward-McCann, 1963. (9-14)

Winner of the 1962 Carnegie Medal for the outstanding juvenile book by an English author, *The Return of the Twelves* has as background the story Branwell Brontë made up about his twelve wooden soldiers. If an adult was reading this book to children, he could clarify some of the amusing references to the Brontë children. But even without such help, a child might still enjoy the fantasy about twelve very old toy soldiers who come to life, march, drill, and are determined to go back to their original home—the Haworth parsonage. It is eight-year-old Max who finds the soldiers in the attic of an old country house to which his family has just moved and also discovers their aliveness, that they had once belonged to the Brontë children, and that they are determined to return to their old home. Finally, Max has to enlist the aid of Jane and Philip, his older sister and brother, to help the Twelves with their perilous journey. And perilous it is. One of the funniest episodes occurs when, all aboard Max's roller skate, they go tearing pell-mell down the main highway, traffic and all. This superb fantasy has humor, everyday family conflicts, prying reporters, a hot-on-the-trail American collector, and, through it all, eight-year-old Max, who never gives up until the Twelves are safely installed in their beloved nursery at Haworth, where Branwell's *The History of the Young Men* also rests.

The Enormous Egg, by Oliver Butterworth, ill. by Louis Darling. Little, 1956. (9-11)
The village of Freedom, New Hampshire, is thrown into a twitter when young Nate Twitchell's hen hatches a dinosaur's egg. The growth of the creature makes it a national concern, and one hilarious episode leads to another. Very funny.

Pippi Longstocking, by Astrid Lindgren, tr. by Florence Lamborn, ill. by Louis S. Glanzman. Viking, 1950. (9-11)
For sheer, outrageous hilarity, Pippi the superchild takes all prizes. The continuations of Pippi's feats in two more books are not so successful. This one is fun.

Mr. Popper's Penguins, by Richard and Florence Atwater, ill. by Robert Lawson. Little, 1938. (9-11)
This wild yarn is a nonsense tale narrated with gravity and giving every indication of being a simple, realistic story. Strictly speaking, nothing in the book is impossible, but because the narrative carries improbability to its uttermost limits, it ends where Mr. Popper himself began—in the realm of the fanciful. It tells the story of Mr. Popper, an untidy paper hanger with a passion for the Antarctic. An explorer rewards his admiration with a penguin. That one becomes twelve, and

then the penguins revolutionize the lives of the entire Popper family. Eventually, the children return to school, Mrs. Popper gets to the meeting of the Ladies' Aid and Missionary Society, but Mr. Popper? Well, when last seen, Mr. Popper and his penguins were headed due north.

The Twenty-One Balloons, by William Pène du Bois, ill. by author. Newbery Medal. Viking, 1947. (10-14)

This delightful fantasy is as logical as the author's detailed and graceful drawings, and both text and pictures build up the conviction that the events are real. Professor William Waterman Sherman set off from San Francisco on August 15, 1883, in a marvelously equipped balloon, with the announced intention of flying over the Pacific Ocean. Three weeks later he was picked up in the Atlantic Ocean amid the wreckage of an elaborate platform and twenty deflated balloons. Despite the wild curiosity of the whole world, Professor Sherman insisted on telling his story first to the Western American Explorers' Club. And what a story he had to tell. As he explained, he longed to be alone, after forty years of teaching arithmetic to little boys. But the balloon trip he had planned did not go according to schedule. A seagull wrecked his balloon, and he barely managed to reach the Pacific island of Krakatoa. There he found twenty families living in secluded luxury, co-owners of the island's immense diamond mines. The island, unfortunately, was volcanic, and so the inhabitants had provided themselves with a means of escape. In Professor Sherman's report to the Explorers' Club, he gives a fascinating account of the daily life of the ingenious inhabitants of the amazing island of Krakatoa and also of their escape shortly before the explosion of the island.

As these examples show, some fine fantasies have come from writers in the United States as well as from British writers; nevertheless, the most distinguished fantasies and sustained, almost epic, fantasy cycles have emanated chiefly from Great Britain. There is no doubt that the English have a peculiar gift for this form of literature, and, until recently, no one in the United States had written sustained fantasy at the level of C. S. Lewis and J. R. R. Tolkien (see Chapter 9). But in 1964, Lloyd Alexander, a Philadelphian, delighted children with his *Book of Three,* which was the beginning of a heroic cycle that has five books and carries the hero, Taran, from boyhood to manhood.

The Book of Three, by Lloyd Alexander, maps and jacket by Evaline
Ness. Holt, 1964. Also *The Black Cauldron* (1965), *The Castle of
Llyr* (1966), *Taran Wanderer* (1967), and *The High King* (1968).
(10-14)

The Book of Three introduces the mythical Kingdom of Prydain,
right out of Welsh legends, the Middle Ages, and Lloyd Alexander's
inimitable imagination, and also presents Taran, a rebellious boy,
determined to find out who he is and to prove himself a hero. Instead,
as a first claim to renown, old Coll gives him the title of Assistant Pig-
Keeper, in charge of the pig Hen Wen. Fortunately, the "oracular pig"
runs away, with Taran after him, and when they are well lost in the
forest, adventures begin. In his quest for the pig, Taran acquires several
companions, including Princess Eilonwy, Fflewddur Fflam, and Gurgi.
Taran is determined to save their Kingdom of Prydain from "Evil that
is never far distant." They fight gloriously and well, sometimes by the
side of the legendary Welsh hero Prince Gwydion, sometimes alone.
If children enjoy the adventures in this first book, they will want them
all, and girls are going to love the pestiferous and beautiful Princess
Eilonwy. In spite of the allegory of Good and Evil and all the ordeals
of the Companions, the books are notable for their sly humor and growing significance.

Many more examples of well-written fanciful tales could be
listed, and many more distinguished fantasies are appearing yearly.
Children welcome them eagerly. Why is this? Why are these stories
being written in this scientific age, and why do the children keep
them in continual circulation? Perhaps because there is something
free and gay about these imaginative tales. For writers, they are
an escape from the anxieties and mechanization of our times. For
children, they provide thrills, chills, laughter, tears, beauty, fun,
and a brief excursion into make-believe that is so wonderful, so
real that maybe—perhaps—it could almost be true.

REALISM FOR ADOLESCENTS

FOR AGES TWELVE-THIRTEEN -FOURTEEN

8

Today's World in Books
Times Past, Historical Fiction
Animal Stories

In the years from eleven to fourteen, children vary so greatly in their physical, mental, and emotional growth that psychologists and psychiatrists have almost as much difficulty as parents do trying to describe these complex young human beings. In general, girls of twelve and thirteen are biologically a year older than boys of the same chronological age and so much taller that for a couple of years class dramatizations are painful, with the girls towering over the boys. But within each sex there will be an exception— a girl or two who look ten in a group of Amazons, and a boy who is a tall, thin beanpole in the midst of shorties. Such differences are sources of embarrassment to the exceptional child and all too often the cause of related social problems. Both boys and girls in these years are experiencing physical changes that may disconcert, worry, or obsess them. This preadolescent period, sometimes called "latency period," may be a time of depression, withdrawal, or continual anxiety; or it may be a time of exhilaration, tremendous increase in energy and initiative, and perhaps overassertiveness. In short, once more the child is insecure, uncertain of his competence and status, and struggling for his own niche in a baffling but alluring adult world.

In these latency years of early adolescence, children need parental reassurance of their place in the world as much as the four-year-olds also needed it. Again, because of their uncertainties they tend to downgrade themselves and to become obsessed with their limitations—too fat, too thin, bad skin, unsatisfactory figure development. These sound like and should be trivial worries, but they are of grave importance to the worrier. Parents need unlimited patience and sympathy in dealing with a child who is going through one of these turbulent periods of development, and should, of course, never laugh at him. He needs all the encouragement and faith you can give him. To be sure, some children make the transition from childhood to later adolescence so comfortably that there seem to be no problems, but these youngsters are exceptions. Most children show the strain of their growth in one area or another, and all of them need the reassuring warmth of family backing and understanding. It is of the greatest importance to these maturing children to develop feelings of self-esteem or worth, self-respect that derives from competence in some field. Parents can often help their groping child recognize his special abilities and build on those, rather than harping on his inadequacies.

Another phase of the child's struggle towards maturity, particularly disturbing to adults, is his sudden, critical reaction to his home and family. An adequate or delightful home is "a dump." Mother is "old-fashioned" and wears "horrible clothes." Father is "slow" or a "grouch," and both parents are hopelessly "behind the times." Fortunately, this painful state of affairs usually wears off by later adolescence as the young person goes into other homes and encounters other parents and discovers his own aren't so bad after all. The opposite extreme of this manifestation of growing up may be more unfortunate. It happens when a child accepts completely the values or standards his family lives by, but wishes to take them over at twelve or fourteen. The girls want the sophisticated clothes and make-up of women; boys demand latch keys, cigarettes, and the late hours of men. Although the boys' break for adult privileges may be more aggressive and seemingly more dangerous than the girls', both are symptoms of the same thing —the youngsters' desire and struggle to be accepted as responsible adults. The problem is how to satisfy this perfectly legitimate effort in acceptable ways.

These few examples of the preadolescent child's growing pains furnish clues to the fact that somewhere in that secret inner world of his mind and spirit, there is evolving an image of himself as he wants to be when he is an adult. To be sure, this image changes and grows in one direction or another as he matures. The little girl who saw herself as an exotic movie star may in adolescence yearn to be a nurse, and the lad who hoped to be a cowboy may as a youth become absorbed in the possibilities of space exploration and discipline himself accordingly. These are natural shifts in the child's growing image of himself, and are the result of the people, the ideas, and the ideals to which he has been exposed. But the child growing up in neighborhoods where brutality and crime are rife may begin to admire the bullies and gangsters who "get away with it" and achieve the flashy clothes and cars of under-world living. And these images of adult achievement may be rein-forced by the moving pictures and television programs he looks at. Where will that child find compelling pictures of wholesome living, of courage with gentleness, of achievement with decency, and family life that whether rich or poor is stable and warm?

For all these different children, books can play an important part, as teachers and librarians well know—provided, of course, there is the right book for the child at the right time. In books the child meets a vast variety of people. He sees them uncertain and afraid even as he has been. These book people make mistakes and taste failure, but pick themselves up again and go on. They overcome physical handicaps, poverty, lack of opportunity, and tragic disappointments, but they keep their self-respect and persist undismayed. Books can show children a wider, richer world than they ever dreamed existed. In books, they can share vicariously the experiences of varied people and places, different patterns of living, and, above all, the struggles and difficulties common to all peoples. When a young reader identifies himself with his book hero, he is really feeling, "I too might do this." And the sense of his own power and worth grows with the desirable image of competence the book hero has given him.

This means that the adult who guides children through the formative years of early adolescence needs two important areas of knowledge. First, he must know the child himself—his uncertainties, his needs, and his potentials; second, he must know a wide variety of books that will compel the child's interest, provide him with wholesome ideals, and strengthen his courage to fight the good fight as gallantly as he knows how.

Books to meet the needs of these growing, changing children are numerous. But for some of the children there is the plague of inadequate reading skills. There is also a vast range in social maturity. So with each child of twelve, thirteen, or fourteen, we must begin, just as we have begun at each previous age level, where the child *is*—in reading ability, in interests, and in social maturity. This means that for some children you will go back to bibliographies for the middle years (see Chapters 6 and 7) or even to the bibliographies for superior readers of eight and nine years (see Chapter 5). If your child has missed some of the major titles in these bibliographies, try them. Robert Lawson's *Rabbit Hill* or E. B. White's *Charlotte's Web*, for example, is popular at any age. But in the main, these children in early adolescence want books with considerable social significance—books that help them understand their social relationships in the family and with their peers and with people of social groups other than their own. These values must not be presented in the form of social tracts but must be embodied in first-rate stories in which the characters are modern, alive, and convincing. The bibliographies in this chapter begin with such examples. And remember that for every title mentioned, six or more could be added. But you and your children would then be swamped with numbers. A selective few are given, and if your child wants more, librarians will supply them gladly.

There is another interesting thing that is happening to children's reading from nine-years-old on. If a child likes a book by a certain author, he is likely to pursue all the books that author has written. Girls who liked Laura Ingalls Wilder's *Little House in the Big Woods* generally read through the entire eight books of the series. Boys race through William Steele's pioneer adventure tales and Marguerite Henry's horse stories. This means that the suggested readings are liable to stretch out beyond any one child's reading time.

TODAY'S WORLD IN BOOKS

Because the child of twelve, thirteen, or fourteen is full of social uncertainties and ever widening interests in the world around him, we'll begin with books about his modern world.

Two notable forerunners
Little Women, by Louisa May Alcott, 1868. Many editions. (11-14)
The Adventures of Tom Sawyer, by Mark Twain (pseud. for Samuel Clemens), 1876. Many editions. (10-14)

Realism in children's books about the United States was off to a brilliant start with these two classics. At some time every child should have a chance to read them both. *Little Women* seems more dated than *Tom*, but family warmth, fun, and struggles have a universal appeal. This is also a girl's story about the problems of growing from adolescence to maturity and encountering along the way heartbreak, even death, and romance, sometimes sweet and sometimes sad.

Tom Sawyer will never grow old. It is small-town adventure—funny, exciting, and often hair-raising. There is also in *Tom Sawyer* the emer-

Illustration by Rainey Bennett for "The Glorious Whitewasher," from *The Adventures of Tom Sawyer*, by Mark Twain, included in *Time for Stories of the Past and Present*, compiled by May Hill Arbuthnot and Dorothy M. Broderick. Copyright © 1968 by Scott, Foresman and Company.

gence of a boy's code—keeping one's word, seeing things through, protecting the weaker, and persisting even though one is scared half to death. Add, of course, the more difficult and mature *The Adventures of Huckleberry Finn*, by Mark Twain, 1885.

The United States

A Place for Peter, by Elizabeth Yates, ill. by Nora S. Unwin. Coward-McCann, 1952. (10-14)

This story is a sequel to *Mountain Born*, in which we encounter a younger Peter. Now at thirteen, Peter is struggling in vain to win his father's acceptance of him as a more mature and responsible person. With the mother called away because of her brother's serious illness, father and son have to see things through on their own. Peter's energy and practical good sense rise to the challenge, so that by spring he has proved himself in crucial situations, and father and son finally understand, trust, and enjoy each other. The story is enriched by Elizabeth Yates' ability to make real and beautiful the passing seasons and the closeness of these people to their woods, meadows, and, above all, to their animals.

The Year of the Raccoon, by Lee Kingman. Houghton, 1966. (11-14)

Joey is an ordinary boy, with two talented brothers and a successful father, and his limitations often make him feel inadequate. Then Bertie, the endearing pet raccoon, comes into his life, and Joey, loving and defending his mischievous, sometimes destructive pet, grows in compassion and self-realization, and in greater understanding of his relations with his family.

The Loner, by Ester Wier, ill. by Christine Price. McKay, 1963. (10-14)

"Boy" had no name and no family, and had been picking crops and turning over his earnings to whoever was keeping him, for as long as he could remember. One thing he had learned—to get along, a person looks out for himself and no one else. Then Raidy takes him into the circle of her love, only to be killed looking out for Boy. Heartbroken, sick, and half starved, he wanders off into the wilderness. There Boss, a big, competent sheep woman, finds him, carries him to her wagon house, and feeds and cares for him until he is on his feet once more. She names him David, and thinks he will be a shepherd like her dead son, but David's training is far too brief to permit him to move easily into his new role. He yearns to please Boss and stay with her, but he often fails her. It is his growing love for the helpless sheep, the wonderful dogs, and, above all, Boss herself that pulls the boy through. "David the shepherd boy" is a name worth living up to, and his work is worth doing. This powerful and absorbing story, with its remarkable characterizations and record of persisting after failures, is one of the most distinguished books of recent years.

My Side of the Mountain, by Jean George, ill. by author. Dutton, 1959.
(10-14)

Sam Gribley, a New York City fourteen-year-old, wants to prove that he can maintain life in the Catskill Mountains completely on his own for a year. He writes in his diary, "I am on my mountain in a tree home that people have passed without ever knowing I am here." Boys who love camping are fascinated with the details of Sam's homemade lamp, dishes, and clothes, and with his original menus and his self-sufficient survival. That he is glad of occasional companionship and ultimate reunion with his family is good too, but undoubtedly, the fascination of the book lies in the ingenious resourcefulness of this young Robinson Crusoe.

The Yearling, by Marjorie Kinnan Rawlings, ill. by N. C. Wyeth.
Scribner, 1939. (12 up)

This story, like Archie Binns' *Sea Pup,* turns upon the cruel demands growing up and meeting responsibilities can sometimes make on adolescents. Only the deep love of Jody Baxter for his father, Penny, carried the boy through his agony. Jody, growing up in the primitive wilds of Florida, was lonely until he found the little fawn he made a pet of and called Flag. Boy and fawn frolicked the summer days away and flourished. But by the next year the maturing deer had begun to eat the Baxter's scanty crops as soon as they came up. There would not be enough food for the family unless Flag was destroyed. Penny was bedridden and could not shoot the deer himself, but worse still, he had to make Jody face this cruel necessity. The boy was frantic, and after he had done what had to be done he ran away from home. When at last Jody returned, boy and father had a long talk, and Penny concluded, "You've takened a punishment. You ain't a yearlin' no longer." This poignant story of the pains of growing up is a woodland idyl, so beautifully written it will bear reading and rereading. It is also the story of obscure people, meeting bravely the harsh demands life makes upon them.

It's Like This, Cat, by Emily Neville, ill. by Emil Weiss. Harper, 1963. Newbery Medal. (10-14) Also *Berries Goodman*. Harper, 1965. (11-15)

It's Like This, Cat deals with the conflicts of a boy growing up in New York City and associating with the assorted types of young people to be found in a big city. Dave is concerned about his gentle, asthmatic mother but highly critical of his somewhat explosive lawyer father. As a matter of fact, Dave takes Cat as a pet partly to spite his Pop. The story, told by Dave himself, is a wryly amusing account of his hassles with his father; his friendship with "Crazy Kate the Cat Woman," as she is called by the neighborhood children; his adventures with various boy friends, including one older boy—shy, nineteen-year-old Tom Ransom, a New York University drop-out, who has real father troubles; and his growing affection for Mary, his first girl friend. One of the important developments is Dave's gradual realization that his Pop is a pretty good sort after all. Cat plays an important part in most of the adventures and is fittingly toasted at the end of the story—"Here's to Cat." The staccato style is as laconic as fourteen-year-old Dave and well suited to the content.

Berries Goodman begins with Berries' looking back on his family's experiment with living in a suburb fifty miles out of New York City, when Berries was nine, his older brother Hal, seventeen, and his sister Jennifer, two. There Berries was confronted with his first experience of anti-Semitism. When the girl next door commented superciliously on his friendship for a Jewish boy named Sidney Fine, Berries was outraged. His older brother backed him up and told Sandra that she talked like a Nazi. But bad feeling grew, and Sandra perpetrated a mean trick that led Sidney into a serious accident. Sidney's mother was so frightened and angry that she refused to let Berries see Sidney again. At the end of the book, six years after the main part of the story, the boys do catch up with each other, but meanwhile the Goodman family had moved back to New York City and had decided to let suburbia fend for itself, and the Fines, too, had moved away from the area. This story is told in the first person from Berries' point of view. Three highly contrasted "moms" enrich the story and add to Berries' confusions. A serious but amusing satire on snobbishness as well as anti-Semitism.

Irving and Me, by Syd Hoff. Harper, 1967. (10-14)

Thirteen-year-old Artie (Arthur) Granick hated to leave Brooklyn for Florida, but there wasn't anything he could do about it except grouse. As his father explained, "Your mother's got a touch of arthritis in her fingers and I've got an opportunity to go into business down there." Artie himself tells the story of his adventures and misadventures in Sunny Beach. He gets used to Florida and actually begins to like it, particularly after he meets Irving Winkelman. Artie isn't too fond of Irving's parents, though, particularly Irving's mother, who talks Yiddish to him. Of course, as Artie observes, "It isn't that Mom and Dad aren't good Jews. They just don't keep two sets of dishes—one for meat and one for dairy—and only go to temple for weddings and bar mitzvahs. But the first thing they did when we moved in here was hang up mezuzahs on the doorways." This is an amusing, bouncy story of Artie's and Irving's on-again-off-again friendship; of Artie's falling for dream-girl Arlene Morgan; of fighting with bad-guy Charlie Wolper; and, of all things, losing Arlene to Charlie, the "big baboon"; and, finally, joy of joys, finding a dog to replace his long-lost Labrador retriever, Pete. All in all, this is a delightful story about a very likeable boy in the throes of adolescence.

Mary Jane, by Dorothy Sterling, ill. by Ernest Crichlow. Doubleday, 1959. (11-14)

Mary Jane tells a story of newly integrated Wilson Junior High, and shows the tremendous courage it has taken for Negro children to serve as shock troops and for their parents to endure the cruel persecution of their children. Mary Jane's grandfather, Dr. Charles Douglas, is a retired college biology teacher and her father is a lawyer. Her older sister, Lou Ellen, is a nurse in a northern hospital and her older brother is in college studying to be a lawyer. Mary Jane herself is attractive and a good student. Yet on that first day when she and one Negro boy approach the all-white junior high school, they have to run the gauntlet of a howling, jeering mob, faces full of hate and voices uttering catcalls and threats. Yet those two young people walk with calm dignity through the mob to their classrooms. Their day by day experiences in school are often humiliating, sometimes terrifying, but gradually the situation begins to grow better. By the end of the school year, Mary Jane has discovered that she too can be prejudiced and grossly in the wrong, and that there are people ready to reach out friendly helping hands if she will meet them halfway.

Call Me Charley, by Jesse Jackson, ill. by Doris Spiegel. Harper, 1945. (10-12)

Charles Moss is the only Negro in an all-white school where he is tolerated but not really accepted. His white friend, Tom Hamilton, encourages him to stand up for himself, but Charley has had too many years of patiently accepting rejection and discrimination to do this easily. Finally, when Tom's mother and some other adults realize how deeply hurt and disappointed Charley is when he is excluded from the class play, they take a hand in his behalf, and Charley is made a part of the cast. The author is too realistic to imply that Charley's problems are over, but the story does end on a happy note.

Jazz Country, by Nat Hentoff. Harper, 1965. (12-16)
Sixteen-year-old Tom Curtis—white, musically gifted, and jazz crazy—is trying to decide whether to go to college or turn completely to his music. In order to discover how good his musicianship really is, he seeks out one of the great jazz band leaders to ask for an audition. He encounters rebuffs, but one of the men thinks he is good enough to profit by some lessons and takes him on. Through his close association with these great Negro artists, Tom discovers what a powerful compulsion the creation of this musical idiom has for the men. Reluctantly, he decides to go to college. But the friendship and good wishes of the men go with him, and Tom knows that not only his music but his life have been enriched by this association. In the last chapter, "Open End," Tom is at Amherst, liking it but still keeping up with his music and still, as he says, "not absolutely sure I'm going to stay here."

Up a Road Slowly, by Irene Hunt, ill. by Don Bolognese. Follett, 1966. Newbery Medal. (12 up)
This story of a stormy growing-up begins with seven-year-old Julie, hysterical over her mother's death and over being sent away from home to live in the country with her Aunt Cordelia, a teacher. Julie is filled with all the intolerant cruelties of youth. She loathes dirty, smelly Aggie, a retarded child in her school; she resents her sister's happy marriage and scorns her alcoholic liar of an uncle. Yet it is the watchful care of the irresponsible uncle and the prescient love of Aunt Cordelia that save Julie from the folly of a youthful infatuation. Aggie's death, her father's second marriage to a wise and delightful woman Julie admires, and their plans for her to return to her own home for her high-school years help Julie grow up and count her blessings. She realizes that she loves Aunt Cordelia and the big old house where they live

and that it has become her true home. The book ends with Julie's high-school graduation and with Julie a lovely young woman, understanding and appreciative of her friends and her family—above all, Aunt Cordelia —and radiantly in love with Danny, her friend since childhood. This story is sometimes overwritten, but it does not exaggerate the intoler-ance of self-centered youth and the pains and joys of growing up.

The Boy Next Door, by Betty Cavanna. Morrow, 1956. (12 up)

For Jane Howard, losing her long time friend Ken to her younger and more glamorous sister is truly crushing, and she responds with ill-concealed resentment. Her more worldly-wise friend Trudy encourages her to enter school activities and build a new life for herself, advice which proves wise for Jane, who discovers that she can even be good friends with Ken once more.

Betty Cavanna's talent for creating genuine characters in convincing settings of the teen-age home and school world gives her wide accept-ance. Among her other titles are *Accent on April* (1960) and *Angel on Skis* (1957).

Fifteen, by Beverly Cleary, ill. by Joe and Beth Krush. Morrow, 1956. (11-14)

Jane Purdy, at fifteen, is weary of her only admirer whose sole sub-ject of conversation is his rock collection. While she is baby-sitting with the most obnoxious child on her list, Stan Crandall, new in town and a part-time delivery boy, enters the kitchen, deftly puts the impish Sandra in her place, and quickly becomes the new hero in Jane's life.

This is an appealing and balanced story of two teen-agers in the throes of a mild first romance. Good family values and background of school life, and a humorous and sympathetic narrative of teen-age growing pains. *Jean and Johnny* (1959) and *The Luckiest Girl* (1958) are other favorites.

Seventeenth Summer, by Maureen Daly, ill. by Jay Robinson. Dodd, 1942. (12-16)

If the title of this book were changed to *Fifteenth Summer,* the en-tertaining story would seem as contemporary as the day it was pub-lished. Even so, it is still popular with youngsters and approved by adults. But because little girls are having their first encounters with dating and near-romance earlier these days, they need guidance sooner. Angie, the heroine, is a healthy, happy teen-ager, a member of a delightful family group, enjoying picnics, parties, and the usual fun of summer vacation. Apparently there are no problems, but suddenly finding herself popular with boys and even maybe beloved by a special boy make a heady combination. How and why Angie managed to weather these first encounters with romance and come through the summer a stable and wise girl makes a good story and presents a picture of growing up that younger girls can profit from.

The loner, the nonconformist, and the rebel have always been popular figures in children's reading. Examples are the amusing *Did You Carry the Flag Today, Charley?* for the youngest, and *Harriet the Spy* and *Queenie Peavy* for the middle years. These last two books along with such books as *The Egypt Game* and *How Many Miles to Babylon?* mark a trend that has been growing in stories for the children and young people, namely a frank treatment of the grave and often tragic social problems they are encountering and talking about today. Here are a few provocative examples of such books for older children:

Hank, by Dorothy M. Broderick. Harper, 1966. (12-16)
Hank and his father were unusually close. Both loved football, and Hank showed such promise for the game that his father coached him rigorously and would not let him play with a regular team until he was sufficiently trained to excel. Finally, in the sixth grade, Hank played with the Ramblers and was chiefly responsible for their winning the state championship. His father was overjoyed, as was Hank, and yet three months later, Hank's father walked out on the family and was never seen or heard from again. At first, Hank was sure his father would come back, and he played football for three years on the junior-high team. When hope died out and anger took its place, Hank became too bitter to try for anything—football, grades, or even friendship. From then on, Hank had a chip on his shoulder, and, as a high-school senior, sullen, rebellious, and reckless, he was an easy prey for a gang of young punks looking for the wrong sort of excitement. Hank's step by step descent into the cheap misdemeanors of the gang and, at last, his desperate attempt to extricate himself on the brink of a serious crime build up to a suspenseful and satisfying conclusion. This is a grim story, competently handled.

The Outsiders, by S. E. Hinton. Viking, 1967. (12-16)
Here is a powerful story, described as "about teen-agers, for teen-

agers, by a teen-ager." It deals with gang rivalry and rumbles, but also leaves the reader with incisive portraits of individual boys growing up in a hostile environment with their own standards of courage and loyalty. The story is told by fourteen-year-old Ponyboy.

The setting is an Oklahoma community with two rival gangs of boys. One, the Socs, drive Mustangs and wear right clothes. The others are the have-nots. They wear black leather jackets, have long, well-greased hair, and are known as the Greasers. One of the Soc girls makes friends with Ponyboy and tries to set him straight about the Mustang set, but it is too late. There has been a brutal beating of Johnny, a Greaser, and war is on. Ponyboy is attacked, Johnny defends his friend, and accidentally a Soc is killed. Ponyboy and Johnny flee. Eventually, they come to mountain country and find an empty church for refuge. Five days later, another Greaser takes them out to eat. When they return to the church, they find it in flames and learn that several young children have wandered into the building and have been trapped by the fire. Regardless of the danger to themselves, Ponyboy and Johnny rescue the children, but Johnny later dies of burns and of an injury he received from being struck by a falling timber. Eventually, Ponyboy is exonerated, partly because of the testimony of several members of the Socs.

The story shows boys of many varieties, still undecided which way they are going—on toward violence and crime or perhaps back to school, but then what? The characters are unforgettable, the action dramatic and moving.

Dorp Dead, by Julia Cunningham, ill. by James Spanfeller. Pantheon, 1965. (12-14)

In markedly different style from the unrelenting realism of both *Hank* and *The Outsiders, Dorp Dead* has the quality of a bad dream. Gilly Ground, an intelligent, withdrawn ten-year-old orphan, tells his own story. After an unpleasant stay in an orphanage, Gilly is placed in the home of Mr. Kobalt, a carpenter notorious for his excessive neatness and unreasoning emphasis on schedules. At first, the boy enjoys the order and the good food of the big house, but he begins to wonder about the man, particularly about his treatment of Mash, a cowed, starved, caged dog, which Gilly befriends. Gradually, the boy realizes that the man is bent on cowing him to the same doglike subservience. After some terrifying events, he finally runs away and, with Mash's help, eludes Mr. Kobalt. Boy and dog start out to join Gilly's mysterious friend the Hunter, apparently a symbol of kindness and nobility; but first Gilly scratches the words "Dorp Dead" on Mr. Kobalt's door —in defiance of Mr. Kobalt and all he stands for. The realism of the beginning of the story occasionally fades into fantasy, but the plight of the boy, helpless for a time in the hands of a psychotic man, is startlingly real. This haunting story suggests that children in the grasp of cruel older people must put up stiff resistance if they are to survive. It is a memorable scare story that will give children chills up their backbones.

Foreign lands

Children reading books about our racial and geographic minorities in the United States get a sense of differences in customs and attitudes as well as an awareness of the strangely universal nature of people's goals—material security, group approval, successful achievement, and love. However, by eleven and twelve, the child's world has expanded enormously, and he already knows more about how other people live in other countries than any geographies could possibly teach him. This is largely due to moving pictures and television. Travel programs and documentaries give viewers insight into the struggle for survival that different peoples have met heroically and are still meeting. Such programs not only enrich the child's background for reading, but should whet his appetite for some of the absorbing stories about the individuals in other countries who share his own longings but must of necessity solve their problems by means different from his. No longer are books about other countries dwelling unduly on picturesque, fiesta-type living. Instead, they give children pictures of the everyday struggles of everyday characters caught in and influenced by their peculiar environment. And if they are written with integrity, they will reflect modern changes in the tempo and problems of modern living. India today is not the India of several decades ago, as Shirley Arora's *"What Then, Raman?"* clearly shows. Here, then, are books about peoples in lands and circumstances different from our own, but with modern or universal problems—books rich in social significance as well as in story appeal.

Crystal Mountain, by Belle Dorman Rugh, ill. by Ernest H. Shepard. Houghton, 1955. (11-14)

One of the gayest books about other lands is *Crystal Mountain*.

It relates the adventures of three American boys—Gerald, Harry, and their five-year-old brother, Danny. There is also John, but he is too young to be a part of the adventures. They are living with their parents in Lebanon. The boys have learned the language, and they love the Lebanese people and the wild mountainous countryside that is their playground. A tomboy English girl, who has named herself Boadicea (Boadie for short), joins them and proves herself a worthy adventurer. Among the four of them, they rescue a mistreated pup from a brat of an American child, correct the boy's obnoxious disdain of the natives, make friends with a delightful Lebanese boy, and solve the mystery of a curiously deserted house. This is a rousing story, with excellent characterizations and dialogue and a provocative picture of the good and bad attitudes of Americans living in a foreign country. The grownups in the story are interesting, too, especially Boadie's governess, Miss Dunbar—one of the most sensible and amusing governesses in children's literature.

The Wheel on the School, by Meindert DeJong, ill. by Maurice Sendak.
  Harper, 1954. Newbery Medal. (10-12)
  This pleasantly detailed picture of life in a small Dutch fishing village is launched by a school composition on storks, written by Lina, the only girl among the six children of the school. The teacher praises Lina's composition and then asks the children to try to learn why there are no storks in Shora. This question leads to more questions and finally to the children's determination to bring the storks back to Shora. Here is a seemingly simple idea that gradually becomes more and more complicated and involves not only every person in the village but some from nearby towns as well. Before the seemingly impossible has been accomplished, there is danger and near tragedy, but the children never waver in their steadfast determination. This story illustrates Mr. De-Jong's respect for the inner life of children, their dreams that control their actions. He has the same reverence for the wordless hardships of animals, as in his *Dirk's Dog, Bello* and *Smoke Above the Lane.*

Banner in the Sky, by James Ramsey Ullman. Lippincott, 1954. (11-16)
  In spite of the action and scenery of the moving picture made from this story, the book itself is more gripping and will certainly outlive the moving picture for the reading child. Rudi's hero, his father Josef Matt, had lost his life trying to scale the famous Alpine Citadel, and so the mother was determined that her son should never become an Alpine

guide. Rudi was equally, though secretly, determined that he would do just that and would, moreover, some day place his father's red shirt on the peak of the Citadel. He practiced when he could but made little progress until an old guide took him in hand. This becomes, then, the story of Rudi's submission to the sternest kinds of self-discipline, learning not only the physical skills of the mountain climbers but their complete loyalty to the ethical code of the guides—your companions' safety before yours or anything else, a code that cost the life of Rudi's father. Finally, the boy's chance comes. He is chosen for a party trying the Citadel once more. But when success is just within his reach, he is faced with the choice of personal success or a man's safety. This is a tremendous story with an emphasis on self-discipline and human decency in dramatic and unforgettable terms.

If the children missed the stories of Australian ranch and family life by Joan Phipson (p. 128), they may enjoy them in these years. And here is another such story, a powerful one about a lone boy on an Australian ranch.

Boy Alone, by Reginald Ottley, ill. by Clyde Pearson. Harcourt, 1965. (11-13)

"Boy" is a "wood-and-water joey" on one of those huge cattle ranches that stretch for days of travel to the edge of that most terrible of all deserts, the Australian wilderness. His duties, as the author notes, are to "cut wood for the kitchen stove, clean watering troughs, and do many other odd jobs." The cook and the hard-working men are all good to the boy in a hurried, impersonal way, but he is alone nevertheless. When Kanga, who trains a pack of dogs to hunt predators, turns his finest bitch and her special pup over to Boy's care, he lavishes all his love on the two dogs, and they worship him. But time passes, and Kanga takes the mother dog back to the pack where she refuses to eat and dies heartbroken. To save his wonderful pup from what he expects to be the same fate, Boy takes the dog and sets out to cross the wilderness. Heat and thirst defeat them, and they curl up together to wait for death. Kanga finds them in time and carries them back to the ranch, but both the boy and the man have learned something. Boy realizes that the motherly cook and all those hard-working men have watched over him, and Kanga knows a boy must have something of his own to love. Sacrificing his own hopes for the dog, he gives Boy the pup. Storms, searing heat, snakes, and death make this an unusually impressive story about man's struggle for survival and his hunger for love.

This generation has lived through and is still involved in a series of wars. What do we want children of today to know about war? Certainly not details of carnage and atrocities, but rather the terrible waste of war—the waste of human lives; the disruption of families; the destruction of homes, farms, even cities; and the denial of the right to plan normally for the future—all these, children should know. Here are six books that will provide children in the United States, who have been mercifully spared many of these experiences but need to know about them, with pictures of the tragedy of war and of people with seemingly broken lives picking themselves up and beginning the heroic struggle back to normal living.

North to Freedom, by Anne Holm, tr. from the Danish by L. W. Kingsland. First American Edition, Harcourt, 1965. (12-14)

David has spent all of his twelve years in a prison camp; so when the man he hates offers him directions and provisions for escape, David is sure it is a trap. He tries it anyway, and does escape. The story concerns the boy's journey from Salonika to Denmark. In Italy he discovers color and hears the laughter of handsome, free people, all for the first time in his twelve gray years. Some people help him, some drive him away, others are suspicious, and there are episodes of heartbreaking disillusionment before his journey comes to a happy conclusion. If there is too much use made of felicitous coincidence, there still is strong characterization. Young readers invariably say of this book, "I could not put it down until I finished."

The Ark, by Margot Benary, tr. from the German by Clara and Richard Winston. Harcourt, 1953. (12-16)

The warm family story of the Lechows is in striking contrast to the story of the tragic, solitary boy in *North to Freedom*. *The Ark* takes place in a bombed-out West German city after the war. After nine months of moving from one refugee camp to another, what is left of the Lechow family is trying to find a place to live, and when they finally rent an unheated attic from an unwilling landlady, they consider themselves lucky. The doctor father is missing; Matthias, a born scholar, must go to work, no more school; Margret, the next oldest, is grieving over her twin, a war casualty; but the frail mother will not let them look back. Life must go on. The two youngest children furnish the comedy in their hard lives. The story centers on Margret, who gets herself a job in the country as kennel maid to a famous line of Great Danes, while Matthias becomes an apprentice gardener. On the farm they take over an old railroad car which the family and friends rehabilitate to the point where it shelters the whole family and wins the name "The Ark." At the end of the story, the father returns from prison camp, to the great joy of the family; and things, in general, are looking up for the Lechows. The sequel, *Rowan Farm*, continues their adventures. Somehow, throughout these stories, the frail little mother with her genius for homemaking radiates courage and warmth not only to her own children but to all the strays and lonely people their various lives happen to touch.

Darkness over the Land, by Martha Bennett Stiles. Dial, 1966. (12-16)
   This outstanding junior novel about Nazi Germany centers around the Elend family and the impact of their country's policies on their lives. The adults reluctantly endure, but young Mark at first is a dedicated patriot who only later becomes disillusioned. When he is finally told that he is of Polish birth and only a foster child of the Elends, he sacrifices his opportunity to escape the opprobrium of Nazi guilt and he remains behind to help in the rehabilitation of defeated Germany.

The Little Fishes, by Erik Christian Haugaard. Houghton, 1967. (12-14)
   A moving and mature tale of the "little fishes," the homeless child victims of World War II in Naples. Guido, at twelve, is the leader of a small group who beg and scrounge for food and coins to survive, and finally journey to Cassino in hope of aid. They arrive too late, but there is help for them in the end. Unforgettable characters, young and old, are portrayed in this story, which, though tragic in theme, always carries a note of hope.

His Enemy, His Friend, by John R. Tunis. Morrow, 1967. Also *Silence over Dunkerque* (1962) and *All-American* (1942). (12-14)
   His Enemy, His Friend is a far more mature and complex story than *Silence over Dunkerque*, with an ending so dramatic that it leaves the reader breathless. The story turns upon the age-old enmity between the French and the Germans, intensified to the breaking point during the German occupation of France. At that time, a young German ser-

geant, quartered in a small French town, makes real friends with the people, teaches the boys soccer, and becomes the hero of young Jean-Paul. Yet when a German soldier is shot, the sergeant is forced to command a firing squad that executes six hostages, among them Jean-Paul's father. So "my friend" becomes "my enemy." Several years after the execution, Hans, the German sergeant, is tried in Rouen and sentenced to ten years hard labor. Then, exactly twenty years after the deaths of the six French hostages, Jean-Paul and Hans meet again, this time as the principal antagonists in a championship soccer match between the great French and German teams. Finally, later that same day in Nogent-Plage, the little town where the story began, the tragedy is played out. If the conclusion seems somewhat contrived, it certainly underscores the theme that love is stronger than hate, and that love alone is the hope of the world.

Silence over Dunkerque is the story "of the terrible days in 1940 when the Battle of France ended and the British Expeditionary Force was pushed into the sea at Dunkerque"; it is the story of Operation Dynamo and of the part played in it by the twin sons of Sergeant Williams, but it is primarily the story of Sergeant Edward Henry George Williams himself.

From the earliest to the latest story, John Tunis' books are superbly written with a wonderful mixture of human mistakes and heroism and always with a strong emphasis on youthful idealism. *All-American* is one of his many sports stories. In it, young Ronnie encounters racial discrimination on the football team and puts up a courageous fight for his Negro teammate.

TIMES PAST, HISTORICAL FICTION

There is so much distinguished historical fiction for children and youth that it is difficult to choose a typical small sampling. First of all, to measure up to criteria for worth in this field, a story must be historically authentic. That is, it must be true not only to the major events of the period but true also in the re-creation of vivid details of everyday living. The story will have special values for the maturing youth when it shows conflicts or problems of the past that speak to him of conflicts and problems today. For instance, the theme of Esther Forbes' *Johnny Tremain* is "We give all that a man may stand up." Today, this speaks to us of the rights of little nations and of struggling minorities. Such parallels from the past, without being controversial or didactic, may help today's child understand something of the violence of our modern world and the biting frustrations of individuals, groups, and nations.

Not that historical fiction is bent on teaching moral lessons in social relationships, but unquestionably the greatest of these books are great partly because they are built around noble themes of timeless significance. Needless to say, from books with strong themes, action plots are likely to develop with plenty of excitement and well-drawn characters, unique and memorable. If such books live, you may be sure that part of their story appeal is because they are well written with a style that compels interest. Here are a few examples that will serve to carry children and young people into a fascinating area of reading.

Calico Bush, by Rachel Field, wood engravings by Allen Lewis. Macmillan, 1931, 1966. (12-14)

This distinguished story of pioneer America was reissued in 1966. The title comes from the settlers' name for the low-growing sheep laurel, with its pinkish blossoms, "springing out of every crack and crevice" on the rocky land. It is a poignant story of a thirteen-year-old French "bound-out girl," who travels with the family she serves, from Massachusetts to a new settlement in Maine, and who, like the calico bush, adapts herself bravely and beautifully to her new home. Marguerite Ledoux soon proves her worth to the Sargents but remains a servant and alien in their household. A remarkable old woman, Aunt Hepsa, befriends the lonely girl and teaches her some of the needful pioneer skills. This is an unvarnished picture of some of the hardships and dangers of pioneer life. There is the death of a baby who crawled too near the open fireplace; the threat of Indian raids; the toil, monotony, and isolation of life. After Marguerite has risked her life in vain to save the baby's life, averted an Indian attack, and proved her skill, courage, and devotion in a dozen ways, the Sargents take her to their hearts. So when they offer her freedom, she decides to stay with them. They are her family, and she feels she belongs with them.

Johnny Tremain, by Esther Forbes, ill. by Lynd Ward. Houghton, 1943. Newbery Medal. (12-16)

Esther Forbes, having won the Pulitzer Prize for her *Paul Revere and the World He Lived In,* decided to do a story about the Boston apprentices who were forever crossing the pages of her research on the American Revolution. Johnny Tremain, apprenticed to a silversmith in Boston, was such a boy. Because he was arrogant and vain about his skill, his fellow apprentices played a trick on him that turned out worse than they planned, crippling his hand so that he could no longer work at his craft. Bitter and brooding on revenge, Johnny was gradually caught up in the pre-Revolutionary plots of Boston's famous men. By the time Paul Revere, both silversmith and surgeon, had examined Johnny's maimed hand and told him it could have been saved, Johnny was past caring. Something bigger than himself, a dream of freedom from tyranny, a dream of a country where a man could stand up, had taken possession of Johnny, and he was ready to give his all in the struggle. Here is youth carried out of himself by an ideal. Here are famous

From *Johnny Tremain* by Esther Forbes. Illustrated by Lynd Ward. Published 1943 by Houghton Mifflin Company. Reprinted by permission of the publishers.

men risking hanging as traitors to the crown to win the nebulous freedom they have never known. There is plenty of action, and the story, based on a great theme, is beautifully told. See also *America's Paul Revere* (1946).

Tree of Freedom, by Rebecca Caudill, ill. by Dorothy Bayley Morse. Viking, 1949. Also *The Far Off Land*, ill. by Brinton Turkle, 1964. (11-14)

The events of this book, like those of *Johnny Tremain*, take place during the Revolutionary War, but the story is about the hardy settlers in faraway Kentucky. It begins in April 1780, when the Venables are starting out from North Carolina for their land claim in Kentucky. They endure many hardships on the journey and in settling their claim, and they also play a part in the war. Noel, the oldest son, joins George Rogers Clark in driving the British and their allies, the Indians, out of Kentucky; the father, Jonathan, sets off on a difficult journey to deliver a message to Jefferson; and resourceful thirteen-year-old Stephanie and the rest of the family bravely carry on the tasks of their new home. In the course of her various labors, Stephanie continues to care for the little tree she started from an apple seed brought from North Carolina—her "Tree of Freedom," which she finds needs careful nourishing if it is to survive in alien soil. Here again is a strong theme that speaks to our generation today. The richness of the story lies in the vivid re-creation of the everyday problems of living in a raw, new country. There is a father-son conflict, gradually resolved, and convincing characterizations of every member of the family. *The Far Off Land*, another frontier tale, tells of the hardships of young Ketty and her companions on the journey to the new settlements at French Lick.

The Witch of Blackbird Pond, by Elizabeth George Speare. Houghton, 1958. Newbery Medal. (12-16)

Set in an earlier period of American history than *Johnny Tremain* or *Tree of Freedom*, and more mature in content than either of those books, this novel deals with that brief, dreadful period when old women were hunted and hanged as witches. In April 1687, sixteen-year-old orphaned Kit Tyler leaves her home in tropical Barbados to live with Puritan relatives in colonial Connecticut. They try to be kind to Kit, but her finery and seeming frivolity shock them, and their sternness offends the young alien. She comes to love them, particularly her gentle Aunt Rachel and her brave, patient crippled cousin, Mercy, but she cannot curb her impulsive behavior. When she befriends Hannah Tupper, a lonely old Quaker outcast, who is already being watched as the "Witch of Blackbird Pond," Kit is really asking for trouble. Nat Eaton, son of the captain and second mate on the brigantine *Dolphin* which had brought Kit to Connecticut, carries Hannah off to safety, but Kit insists on staying to help take care of her relatives, particularly Mercy, who along with the others has been desperately sick with a strange fever. Because Hannah cannot be found, the villagers wreak their vengeance on Kit. She is arrested, jailed, and brought to trial as a witch, and is saved only by her stern old uncle's courageous defense, by Nat's quick thinking, and particularly by the artless testimony of a waif Kit had befriended. This romantic but frightening story is surprisingly popular even with the twelves, if they are good readers. Part of its strength lies in the contrasting characters—never all good or all bad, but complex mixtures like most of us.

Across Five Aprils, by Irene Hunt. Follett, 1964. (12-14)

The story of the Civil War, from April 1861 to April 1865, is seen through the eyes of young Jethro, a nine-year-old boy when the War began and only thirteen but a man in experience and responsibility when it ended. With his three brothers and his cousin Eb gone to war, three to fight on the Union side and his favorite brother, Bill, to fight on the side of the Confederates, Jethro and his fourteen-year-old sister, Jenny, had to take on more and more of the responsibilities of the farm. Even after the father had a debilitating heart attack and Jenny's sweetheart, the young schoolmaster, left for war, Jethro and Jenny never lost courage and met each day's challenge as best they could. The compelling power of this story lies in the vivid portrayal of all the characters, even comparatively minor ones like the town newspaper editor who kept heart and hope in young Jethro and pretty Jenny. This is a picture of how war can reach out and completely change the lives of remote and obscure people and how they survive with fortitude and sturdy persistence.

Rifles for Watie, by Harold Keith. Crowell, 1957. Newbery Medal. (12-16)

All too often children come out of their study of the Civil War strongly biased in their attitudes. It is important for them to know that neither nobility and selfless loyalty nor meanness and base disloyalty were the exclusive properties of either side. Such books as *Rifles for Watie* will help make this clear. Sixteen-year-old Jefferson Davis Bussey, despite his name, is a rabid Unionist from Kansas. But in the Union Army, along with brave men, he finds a villainous officer who persecutes Jeff unmercifully. Finally, to his horror, Jeff is chosen to go behind the Confederate lines as a spy. He is caught, but his alibi and his name save him and he lives fourteen months with these men—an Indian regiment with Watie, a full-blooded Cherokee officer—before he gets his information. Jeff comes to respect Watie thoroughly and to love some of the men who befriend him. His escape with his information back to Union territory is hair-raising, but in the end, Jeff knows that there are villains as well as honest, brave men and boys in both armies.

The Wonderful Winter, by Marchette Chute, ill. by Grace Golden. Dutton, 1954. (11-14)

In lighter vein and about another country and period in history is *The Wonderful Winter*, by the author of the Pulitzer Prize-winning *Shakespeare of London. The Wonderful Winter* gives children a good picture of Shakespeare, the theater, the plays, and the actors, and it is as authentic as it is amusing. Sir Robert Wakefield had run away from his castle because of what he considered an intolerable situation. But apparently his change to London was not a change for the better. Penniless, homeless, and starving, he was discovered hiding in the theater by Shakespeare and by one of the actors, the famous John Heminges, and was taken home to be fed. After the delightful Heminges family had accepted him as one of themselves, Robin felt in duty bound to repay their kindness somehow. He became one of the boy actors playing women's parts in the theater where he met Shakespeare and fell in love with his play *Romeo and Juliet*. The re-creation of the theater of Shakespeare, the people, and the plays is so lively, young readers will go into their study of the dramas with a rich and unforgettable background. They may even regret Robin's decision at the end to return to his castle and his duties. But both Robin and the reader are better for *The Wonderful Winter*.

The Lost Queen of Egypt, by Lucile Morrison, ill. by Franz Geritz and Winifred Brunton. Lippincott, 1937. (12-16)

With or without a social studies' unit on ancient Egypt, children are fascinated with mummies, pyramids, jewels, and all the accessories of Egyptian luxury shown in museums, in pictorial magazines, and on television. There are several absorbing stories about the ancient Egyptians but none better than *The Lost Queen of Egypt*, which is sometimes out of print, but invariably comes back. It demands a good reader who is not discouraged by the difficult names but hurries on with the story.

Already the reign of the enlightened but gravely ill Pharaoh, Akhenaten, and his queen, Nefertiti, is threatened. Consequently, at the insistence of the redoubtable Queen Mother Tiy, two of the older daughters are hastily betrothed in order to insure the succession, and one other daughter is betrothed to the son of the King of Babylon. The oldest daughter and her husband die of a fever; and so after the death of the Pharaoh, the lively and intelligent Ankhsenpaaten (later called Ankhsenamon) and her husband, Tutankhaten (later called Tutankhamon) ascend the throne. The young people are loved, guided, and guarded by Kenofer, an artist, but traitorous servants and villainous plots are too widespread. The young king is poisoned, and the queen becomes a prisoner in the hands of the arch plotter. Somehow, she is rescued by Kenofer, escapes by a river boat, and learns to live like humble fisher folk. For Ankhsenpaaten it means learning to live again, free of fear and happy in life and in love. With wonderful details of the court, the common people, religion, art, artists, slaves, courtiers, fishermen, the book gives a colorful cross section of life in ancient Egypt by way of a fine story.

The Faraway Lurs, by Harry Behn. World, 1963. (12 up)
Adults are as fascinated as young people are by this story of the conflict between Stone and Bronze Age peoples. The poet Harry Behn went to Denmark to visit his mother's farm. There he learned about an eighteen-year-old girl of the Forest People, a girl who had lived and died there nearly three thousand years ago. When the archaeologists opened her grave, "her face and her body were visible enough to show that she had been beautiful." Her blond hair was tied in a pony tail, her finger nails neatly manicured, and she was wearing a woolen blouse, a short fringed skirt, and bronze jewelry that had come from the Sun People, who made the lurs, the great brazen trumpets, they "used to speak to their god." From these fragments of information, the author has constructed a Romeo and Juliet story, heroic, sorrowful, and strangely moving.

Dawn Wind, by Rosemary Sutcliff, ill. by Charles Keeping. Walck, 1962. Also *The Eagle of the Ninth* (1954), *The Silver Branch* (1958), *The Lantern Bearers* (1959), and *Warrior Scarlet* (1958). (12 up)

Now we come to the greatest living writer of historical fiction for youth, on either side of the Atlantic, Rosemary Sutcliff. All of her books should be listed, but these have been chosen for special reasons and they should lead the mature reader to read all the others. They are records of England's earliest history with its continuous wars for occupation by Norsemen, Romans, Normans, Saxons, and others. But every book is built around a noble theme. Her heroes live and die for principles they held dearer than life, and which we still value. As one of her biographers points out, the conflict in her powerful stories is always between "the light and the dark." The light is all that is good and precious in life, and the dark is what threatens its destruction and return to barbarism. In *The Lantern Bearers*, a man sums up their defeats and their hopes, "We are the Lantern Bearers, my friend; for us to keep something burning, to carry what light we can forward into the darkness and the wind." Her heroes value courage and loyalty above all virtues; and a home hearth, children, and enough land for crops and a few animals are precious things that belong to the light and must not be destroyed. The beauty of that little island, England, haunts all the invaders and turns Romans into loyal Britons, loving and working for their "dear bought land." These books are no preachments but action stories about great-hearted men as real to young readers as heroes of today.

Most of the books are for children in their teens, but *Dawn Wind* is a little easier to follow and may be enjoyed by good readers of twelve, perhaps even eleven. The hero, fourteen-year-old Owain, is apparently the last survivor of a bloody battle between Saxons and Britons in which his people, the Britons, have been destroyed. In his travels, the boy is eventually joined by a noble dog and a waif of a girl. They unite in a gallant fight for survival until Regina is too sick to travel. Then Owain bears her straight into an enemy camp where she will be cared for, but as he expected, he himself is sold as a slave. His new master allows him to keep the dog, but they travel far away. After many years of loyal and effective service to his master, he is finally freed and seeks out Regina. "There is a dawn wind stirring," he tells her, and together they will "in-take a patch of hillside" and life—real life—will begin anew.

The author's great trilogy—*Eagle of the Ninth, The Silver Branch,* and *The Lantern Bearers*—carries the Roman Aquila family through three generations, until they have become a part of Britain and its early embattled history.

Warrior Scarlet occurs at a still earlier period in history and relates the struggles of a Bronze Age boy to achieve the right to wear the scarlet that marks a man. These books do not have to be read in order, because each one is complete in itself. Librarians say *Warrior Scarlet* is one of the great favorites, but whichever Sutcliff book children choose for their introduction to her writings it generally remains their favorite and is reread many times. These books build reading maturity and give youth a glimpse of the long, savage struggle by which men have kept barbarism at bay and moved painfully up the scale towards civilization.

Historical fiction, as these samplings should make clear, is an important area of reading for older children. Remember, though, that if these books seem too difficult for your child, the books described on pages 129-136 offer absorbing and easier reading for the early teens. Those by Howard Pyle, Laura Ingalls Wilder, and William Steele will also give children and youth a sense of time and of times past, with conflicts and problems that have meaning for us today.

ANIMAL STORIES

Animal stories for children and youth fall into three categories which do not concern children but help adults determine the maturity or immaturity of a story's appeal. The first category is, of course, the folk-tale or fable type in which the animal talks and is really not an animal but the prototype of human wisdom or folly. There is silly, credulous Henny Penny, who thought the sky was falling; the canny third Little Pig; the foxy foxes; and disobedient Peter Rabbit. Obviously, such stories are not reading material for twelve-year-olds. The second category includes stories about animals still talking but reasonably true to their species. For example, in *Bambi*, the deer lives the life of a forest deer, but he can warn other deer in words and persuade them that Man with his stick that shoots fire is the enemy of the forest creature. This is a difficult type of story to write and less and less popular with children. The third category, which captivates both older children and adults, is one in which the animal is realistically presented. That is, the animals are true to their own natures; they do not speak, and their thoughts are not interpreted except as indicated by their barks or purrs or cavortings. This is an enormously popular field of reading, because civilized peoples have long been interested in the variety of creatures that share with us this bright, brief period of activity we call life. How do birds find their way unerringly on their distant migrations? How do beavers build their dams or bees their hives? These are just a hint of the questions that have kept men observing the animals and writing about them as scientifically as they know how. Fine examples of such animal stories interest older children and indeed seem to be almost ageless in their appeal. For instance, any grownup who reads Marguerite Henry's *King of the Wind* aloud to a seven-year-old will enjoy it as much as the child, and in one family, three generations—six, nine, fifteen; the forties; and eighty-six—were equally spell-bound by Sheila Burnford's *The Incredible Journey*. This is a reminder that every one of the animal stories reviewed for the middle years, pages 137-140, will make acceptable reading for children growing into adolescence. No other area of reading has this range. The stories in this chapter are about animals realistically presented.

Smoky, the Cowhorse, by Will James, ill. by author. Scribner, 1926. Newbery Medal. (11-16)

The Newbery Award was never given to a finer story than *Smoky*. Told in cowboy vernacular, bad grammar and all, it is, nevertheless, one of the most poignant horse stories ever written. It is the life of a little range colt "fetched up by his mammy" and gently broken by Clint the cowboy. Horse and master understand each other so well that the spunky, handsome young cowhorse won't allow anyone but Clint to handle him. So when the young horse is stolen by vicious men, he has to be beaten and starved into submission. After that, his life is a grim sequence of underfeeding, overtaxing, and abuse by cruel owners. By the time Clint finds him, Smoky is a broken-down old nag with no room in his foggy horse brain for any memories of Clint. Only after months on the ranch with doctoring, good feeding, and kindness does memory return. Smoky nickers for Clint, and the book concludes, "The heart of Smoky had come to life again, and full size." If the cowboy dialect gives trouble to young readers, here is a book that can be read aloud to the enjoyment of the whole family. It is a classic in children's literature.

A *Stranger at Green Knowe*, by Lucy M. Boston, ill. by Peter Boston. Harcourt, 1961. (10-14)

Green Knowe is an old English manor house with green lawns running into a dense thicket. There this story ends, but for Hanno, the gorilla, it began in a tropical forest in the Belgian Congo, and for Ping, a little boy, it began in the Burmese borderland on the edge of a forest. Both were orphaned and displaced. After years of dreary gray cement, they met in a London zoo, Hanno behind the bars of his cage. The boy gave the gorilla his peach, and they stared at each other for a long time. Their next meeting, after both had escaped, was in the woods of Green Knowe. For the three days of Hanno's freedom, Ping brought him food, but they were too near civilization for Hanno to be safe, and the story moves inevitably to a tragic conclusion. Both Hanno and Ping meet it nobly, but for Hanno it is the end. For Ping there is promise of a new and better life, but always he will mourn for Hanno. No story has ever portrayed more movingly the nobility of wild creatures—Hanno's magnificent father defending his herd with his life and Hanno defending his young friend. These are scenes no reader will forget. See also *An Enemy at Green Knowe* (1964).

Gentle Ben, by Walt Morey, ill. by John Schoenherr. Dutton, 1965. (9 up)

Ben had been captured as a six-month-old bear cub by Fog Benson, a brutal man who kept him chained in a dark shed and half starved. Mark Andersen, the frail thirteen-year-old son of a salmon seiner, used to stop at the shed on his way home from school, feed and pet the neglected animal, and sometimes take a little nap with his head comfortably pillowed on Ben's rough coat. Mark's mother knew all about this (indeed, unknown to Mark, she had stood by with a gun until she was assured of the boy's safety), but she kept it from Mark's stern father until Mark himself gave it away. The father was of course horrified. However, when Mark heard that Ben's owner was going to sell the creature for some cowardly hunter to take out and shoot, the boy put up a passionate plea to his father to buy Ben and keep him as a pet. At first, Karl Andersen vehemently refused the boy, but after he had watched Mark lead the bear into the tundra, take off the chain, and set him free, with the bear coming back happily to Mark, the father consented. His decision was strongly influenced by both parents' deep concern for Mark's health and by the hope that the bear would give Mark new interests and get him out into the open more. The Andersens bought Ben, fed him, loved him, and he remained tame and gentle. Then a series of disasters began. The Andersens were forced to have Ben taken away to a bear island, Mr. Andersen's boat was shipwrecked, and his faithful helper Clearwater was lost. The Andersen family's livelihood lay in the Alaskan fisheries, and with their boat destroyed, their future was bleak indeed. How they survived and were reunited with Ben, now in full size and strength but still their gentle and devoted boarder, makes a warm and satisfying conclusion to this unique story of friendship between a boy and a wild animal. Incidentally, it provides a good account of Alaskan fishing activities and of the Alaskan country before statehood, where the oldtimers said, "If you really want to, you can get away with anything you're man enough to do."

Vulpes: The Red Fox, by John George and Jean George, ill. by Jean George. Dutton, 1948. (10-14)

John George and Jean George have produced some remarkable stories about wild animals and their struggles for survival. But the stories are not all struggle by any means. In each book the animals' joyful zest for life is also evident, even to the curious delight Vulpes takes in leading on the dogs and the hunters. However, the books are written with realistic integrity and never let the reader forget that death stalks wild creatures relentlessly. For Vulpes it comes swiftly, and that is good. Books like *Vulpes: The Red Fox; Bubo: The Great Horned Owl* (1954); and *Masked Prowler: The Story of a Raccoon* (1950) are for good readers with perhaps more than the ordinary interest in the wild creatures of woods and forests. *Bubo* is one of the most dramatic and *Masked Prowler* the most satisfactory, but all three are exceedingly well written and illustrated.

Big Red, by James Arthur Kjelgaard, ill. by Bob Kuhn. Holiday House, 1945, 1956. (11-15) Also *Irish Red, Son of Big Red* (1951), *Outlaw Red, Son of Big Red* (1953), and *Swamp Cat* (1957). (12-16)

Jim Kjelgaard's dog stories are as outstanding as Marguerite Henry's horse stories, but on the whole, they are at a more mature level. In the "Red" stories, Ross Pickett and his son Danny care for, train, and are completely devoted to the beautiful Irish setters, which are bred in the kennels of Mr. Haggin. In the first book, Danny and *Big Red* prove their training and their mettle in some exciting adventures that culminate in tracking down a big bear. In *Irish Red*, Mr. Haggin has imported some English setters to be bred and trained. But both father and son refuse to work with any breed except their "Irishmen," and so they leave. To their consternation, Mike, the "mutton-headed" son of Big Red, trails them to their forest camp and they have him on their hands. They start his training immediately, but men and dog have a rugged winter and some grim experiences in survival. When all three return to the kennels, Irish Red is a disciplined and worthy son of Big Red, well able to maintain the glory of the breed. *Outlaw Red* is in some ways the most moving of the three books. Another son of Big Red, Sean is lost in the forest, and through no fault of his own becomes an outlaw dog. He is suspected of sheep stealing and is hunted and shot at until he becomes a frightened and thoroughly bewildered dog. Yet somehow he manages to exist, find a mate of his own breed, and raise a litter of pups before he is finally rescued.

There are so few authentic cat stories, *Swamp Cat* is welcome. The hero is a sixteen-year-old boy, but the lost cat, independent and competent, is an equally important character. Indeed without Cat's astute adaptation to hard situations and problem solving, the hero might have been completely defeated. These are only a few of Jim Kjelgaard's absorbing stories, always true to the nature of whatever species of animal is described.

An Otter's Story, by Emil Liers, ill. by Tony Palazzo. Viking, 1953. (10-14)

An Otter's Story persuaded one skeptical man of the worth and fascination of well-written books for children. It is an authentic story of the life of an otter family—its ups and downs, hardships and satisfactions, dangers and frolics, hard work and lazy contentment. A more harmless and beguiling creature than these little river otters could hardly be imagined. Yet they are trapped, hunted, and all but exterminated as the farmers' enemies. Actually these gayest of creatures are important to the balance of nature if human beings could be so persuaded. A delightful story.

Old One-Toe, by Michel-Aimé Baudouy, trans. by Marie Ponsot, ill. by Johannes Troyer. Harcourt, 1959. (10-14)

Old One-Toe is an amusing variant of the Master Fox versus the Master Hunter, complicated by four city children, their clown of a dog, an earnest hunting dog, and sundry embattled farmer-huntsmen. The children, visiting an aunt on her chicken farm, are outraged when a fox massacres a whole brood of little chickens. They are all for the farmer-hunters, determined to get Old One-Toe, a famous and villainous fox. But one boy, Piet, decides to stalk the fox and learn all about his habits. He stalks so successfully that he becomes completely enthralled by his quarry, his beauty, resourcefulness, and courage. But Piet says nothing of this to the grownups. When the big hunt finally takes place, it is both deadly and hilarious, for Piet and the vixen are equally bent on helping One-Toe escape and on baffling hounds and hunters. The reversal of the children's attitudes should lead to some lively discussions, for Old One-Toe does get away.

The life of any wild animal means chiefly pursuit or being pursued, escape or death. Even the drama of a pet's life turns upon the uncertainty of its happy security with a tragic or triumphant outcome. So there is bound to be a certain similarity in the plots of realistic stories about animals, however dissimilar the details may be. Animal stories are also bound to involve considerable sadness and become more or less harrowing. Therefore, too many such books in succession are not desirable, but interspersed with other reading they have unique values.

First, for city children, they provide casually in the course of a good story the facts of life—sex, mating, birth, food getting, shelter, security, even death—all seen in perspective as parts of the cycle of life. Second, for farm children, they provide reminders of the cruel life animals, both tame and wild, must often endure. This is well, because farm children who must become accustomed to the seasonal slaughter of animals can become callous and indifferent to animal suffering. Some of the fine animal stories can open children's eyes to the vulnerability of all creatures at the mercy of men with their guns, traps, and ruthless power. For both groups of children, such books as Joan Phipson's *Birkin*, Marguerite Henry's *King of the Wind*, Sheila Burnford's *Incredible Journey*, John and Jean George's *Vulpes*, and Michel-Aimé Baudouy's *Old One-Toe* can call forth respect for animals' courage, resourcefulness, loyalty to mate or cubs or master, and for their gay zest for life, so like children's own. Animal stories also evoke a child's compassion, which is an aspect of love and one of the great civilizing forces in life.

In each of the preceding chapters, the books reviewed have shown considerable range in the maturity of their content, but none more strikingly than in this chapter. *Berries Goodman* and *Crystal*

Mountain, for example, look simple enough for younger children, while *The Outsiders, Jazz Country*, and the historical novels of Rosemary Sutcliff might be listed for young adults. This range reflects the wide variation in the social maturity of adolescent children, and so in suggesting choices from these books for a specific child or a group of children, you must exercise your best judgment. One quality that many of the books have in common, particularly those described under "Today's World in Books," is that they are provocative and cry out for discussion. The great value of such a book as *Berries Goodman* or *It's Like This, Cat* or *My Side of the Mountain* or *Dorp Dead* or *Mary Jane* lies in what the young reader has to say about it. When the child talks informally about a book he has read, an adult discovers what he is really thinking about the problems of growing up and of this modern world of ours. Personal guidance can often be slipped in casually in such discussions, but the books themselves, without any didacticism, provide their young readers with first aid to wholesome social attitudes and awareness, which the child greatly needs in these formative years.

MAGIC AND MAKE-BELIEVE FOR ADOLESCENTS
FOR AGES TWELVE-THIRTEEN -FOURTEEN

9

Folk Tales
Fables, Parables, Allegories, and Satires
Myths and Epics
Modern Fantasy

Parents sometimes feel that children growing into adolescence should be done with fairy tales and make-believe, that to keep reading such stories is a sign of immaturity. But when one comes to think of it, there were probably as many adults as children who watched and thoroughly enjoyed the moving-picture version of P. L. Travers' *Mary Poppins*, or Mary Martin's television performance of James Barrie's *Peter Pan*, or the televised version of "Cinderella." Indeed, fantasy seems to be something people never outgrow. It evokes the poetry and adventure of living, and jaded adults who know all too well that two and two won't add up to anything more glamorous than four chuckle delightedly when Mary Poppins' merry-go-round horse takes off for a bit of a canter across the meadow and ends up in a bona-fide race. Be thankful, then, and not worried if your children twelve, thirteen, and fourteen still enjoy make-believe, because under the impact of our modern mechanized world with its scientific explorations and terrifying wars, the poetry of make-believe is hard to come by. Both children and adults need, now and then, to turn away from their problems and relax joyfully in a world of happy, wish-fulfilling magic.

FOLK TALES

The familiar folk tales, such as "Hansel and Gretel," "Snow White," and "Cinderella," with their stereotyped characters and predictable plots, should be losing their appeal for children by the time they are twelve, thirteen, and fourteen. But a few of the twelves, usually girls, find it hard to relinquish them. If you find these children still poring over their old dog-eared copies of *East o' the Sun and West o' the Moon* or the *Grimm Fairy Tales,* then is the time to speed them on their way with some new or unfamiliar collection of traditional stories such as

Arabian Nights, collected and edited by Andrew Lang, ill. by Vera Bock. McKay, 1946. Also *The Arabian Nights*, retold by Amabel Williams-Ellis, ill. by Pauline Baynes. Phillips, S. G., 1958. (10-14)
These colorful, romantic tales from the Orient are lengthy, have complex plots, and are written at a more mature level than the familiar German or English folk tales. There are many beautiful editions to choose from, and no child should miss some of these familiar stories, which are a part of our language.

Heather and Broom: Tales of the Scottish Highlands, by Sorche Nic Leodhas, ill. by Consuelo Joerns. Holt, 1960. Also *Thistle and Thyme:*

Tales and Legends from Scotland, ill. by Evaline Ness. Holt, 1962.
(10-12)

The name of Sorche Nic Leodhas is no more unusual than the delightful tales she has collected. They are not so difficult to read as *Arabian Nights,* but the stories are subtler and wittier, and they call for a more mature level of appreciation. Wonderful to read aloud or tell, sometimes romantic, often droll, they have a freshness about them that stems both from good writing and from the unpredictable character of the Gaelic fairy folk.

FABLES, PARABLES, ALLEGORIES, SATIRES

Fables stand in startling contrast to the folk tales. Gone are romance, heroism, and all the dramatic conflicts between good and evil, replaced by abstractions as exact as a theorem. The animal characters are impersonal. It is no longer Third Little Pig, but Pig or Rabbit or Fox or Wolf, standing for such qualities as credulity or pride or greed or deceit. Always the animal illustrates some virtue or weakness, and a concluding line—"Pride goeth before a fall," "Do not count your chickens before they are hatched," "Plodding wins the race"—points the moral. At best, the fables never make absorbing stories, but they are clever intellectual exercises which acquaint children with the idea of double meanings and also supply them with some basic ethical understandings. Furthermore, the fables lead naturally into more mature uses of double meanings to be found in the parables of the Bible, old and modern allegories, and satires. For these reasons, every home library should include a basic collection of *Aesop's Fables.* If children have not encountered fables by now, they should have the edition adapted by Louis Untermeyer and illustrated by the Provensens, or the collection retold by James Reeves (see Chapter 7). Both editions are excellent, with lively adaptations.

By twelve or fourteen, children should know not only the fable form but the most familiar fabulist, Aesop, by name. Let's hope they can also recall a fable or two—perhaps "The Lion and the Mouse" or "The Boy Who Called Wolf" and make a guess at the morals. Perhaps in Sunday School they have encountered the parables of the New Testament or even the classic allegory *Pilgrim's Progress* by John Bunyan (see p. 321). However, lest they think the fable-type story is completely old-fashioned and done for, now is the time to expose them to one or two modern fables.

Horton Hears a Who! by Dr. Seuss (pseud. for Theodore Seuss Geisel), ill. by author. Random House, 1954. (5-7)

This book seems recent to children, while Andersen's "Ugly Duckling" seems long ago and faraway. Not that a twelve-year-old would be caught carrying this Seuss picture book unless he had the excuse of reading it to the small fry in the family. But if you happen to have it in your library, persuade him to look at it again to see if the story suggests anything current in our world today. In his usual light vein, Dr. Seuss has turned out a fable about the little people trying to be heard in a world-society where the huge ones make all the noise. Not only is this true of obscure peoples everywhere, but of the little nations today, trying to have a voice in world affairs. This light-hearted picture book, once the children catch its application, is an easy introduction to other more complex satires for our generation.

The Pushcart War, by Jean Merrill, ill. by Ronni Solbert. W. R. Scott, 1964. (10-14)

Illustration and text from *The Pushcart War* by Jean Merrill, illustrated by Ronni Solbert. Copyright © 1964 by Jean Merrill and Ronni Solbert. Reproduced by permission of William R. Scott, Inc., Publishers.

"But eighteen thousand—" said the astonished Commissioner.

"All of them," Frank said firmly. "I shot them all."

"*All* 18,991!" said the Police Commissioner.

Frank the Flower nodded. When the Police Commissioner mentioned the large number of flat tires that had been reported, Frank suddenly realized that if he confessed to shooting down only seventeen or eighteen, the police would go on looking for whoever had shot down the rest. If that happened, all his friends might be arrested, too, and that would be the end of the Pea Shooter Campaign.

Frank decided that as long as he had already been arrested,

The funniest of recent satires is *The Pushcart War*, which presumably takes place in New York City in 1976. It is, of course, at a more mature level than the Seuss picture book but well within the reading range of twelves and fourteens. Everyone knows the appalling traffic jams in our big cities, but no one suffered from them more than the pushcart peddlers. The thing of it was, the huge trucks were blocking the streets, running into cars, narrowly missing pedestrians, and ruthlessly running down pushcarts. But the owners of the carts refused to take these indignities lying down. They met, they organized, and they worked out a strategy of revenge guaranteed to stop the monsters in their tracks. The plan was so simple, so innocent, and so deadly that no one, not even the infuriated truck drivers, could figure out what was happening. Eventually it led to negotiations and the triumph of the pushcarts. The characters—General Anna, Frank the Flower, Morris the Florist, Maxie Hammerman the Pushcart King, and all the others—are hilariously pictured in both text and illustrations.

Animal Farm, by George Orwell. Harcourt, 1946.

A professional writer, George Orwell hated totalitarianism, deceit, greed, and cruelty, and fought them all his forty-seven years. He left behind this remarkable fable, "fairy story," allegory, satire—whatever you wish to call it. He cast it in the classic fable form, using animals that stand for frivolity, greed, heroic self-sacrifice, cunning, and just plain, stupid credulity. First, the farm animals revolt against their drunken, cruel master and, thanks to the strategies of the pigs, manage to drive him off his own farm. At first, the animals are happy when the farm is theirs. They work hard, peacefully, and with great success. Then, what Orwell calls in another book "the Jonah act" takes over, by which he means the act of allowing oneself to be swallowed. The hard-working, slow-witted beasts scarcely notice that the pigs are assuming more and more authority, to say nothing of food, money, leisure, and luxury. At last, the passive animal victims discover they are right back where they started from—the victims of cruel, greedy, drunken masters from their own society. The fable ends with the bewildered creatures staring through the window at these new lords. They "looked from pig to man and from man to pig and from pig to man again; but already it was impossible to say which was which."

Obviously this defeat of the decent animals at the hands of lazy liars and cheats is a bitter pill for children to accept, even at eighth-grade level. It is a scathing satirical fable on the totalitarian state and on corruption by power. It may well be too strong a dose for your child at this stage. If so, postpone it. It is worth waiting for.

MYTHS AND EPICS

The distinction between myths and epics was discussed in Chapter 7. In general, myths are stories about the gods of early peoples, their nature and activities. Epics are cycles of stories built around a human hero, sometimes with a background of mythology, of interfering gods, but sometimes with purely human adventures of human heroes. The two easier hero cycles—the *Odyssey* and *Robin Hood*—belong to the tens and elevens, and are thoroughly enjoyed in those years. But if the twelves and thirteens have missed this fascinating pair, they are not too old to enjoy the stories, especially the story of the heroic Odysseus.

Nowadays, it is difficult to interest adolescents in the old mythologies, and yet it is essential for them to bring to their social studies and history a background of Greek and Roman myths at least. These myths have entered our language and our literature. Children may also encounter the Norse and East Indian myths in their school history. For these reasons, some extraordinarily good editions of myths and epics are listed here, either to be taken from the public library at need, or in a few cases acquired as a part of your home reference library.

Mythology, by Edith Hamilton, ill. by Steele Savage. Little, 1942.
This authoritative retelling of Greek, Roman, and Norse myths is a fine reference for the home library. (12 up)

Beowulf, retold by Rosemary Sutcliff, ill. by Charles Keeping. Dutton, 1962.
The oldest English epic, derived largely from Scandinavian mythology and superbly retold by Rosemary Sutcliff.

Children of Odin, by Padraic Colum, ill. by Willy Pogany. Macmillan, 1920, 1962.
This edition carries the hero cycle of Sigurd with its background of Norse myth through to the death of Sigurd.

The Boy's King Arthur, by Sir Thomas Malory, ed. by Sidney Lanier, ill. by N. C. Wyeth. Scribner, 1917.
    This is the epic that introduces children to the Arthur stories they will meet in Tennyson's *Idylls of the King.* See also Mary MacLeod's *King Arthur and His Noble Knights.*

The Adventures of Rama, retold by Joseph Gaer, ill. by Randy Monk, Little, 1954.
    The ancient Hindu myth-epic, delightfully retold and illustrated.

MODERN FANTASY

Even though the ancient mythologies and epics may not be popular reading with children today, modern myth-making, oddly enough, is in high favor with youth. In this section on fanciful tales, two astonishing series of books are discussed. One of these is about a mythical land called Narnia, the setting for seven books, and the children read them all. The second series, involving the kingdom of Middle-earth, begins with a child's book *The Hobbit* and ends with three novel-sized books at adult level. College professors, young people, and even some children read all the books of this second series, and librarians complain that they cannot seem to stock enough copies. Why and how this Tolkien cult has developed in our age of bombs, battles, and machines is anyone's guess.
    But it should be reiterated by way of warning that there is no area in children's reading about which there are such violent differences in taste as in fantasy. Some children cannot abide it, while others revel in it and discuss it as seriously as they might discuss a Sutcliff historical novel. All you can do is to expose your children to fantasies that are examples of good storytelling and good writing. If you have a rabid anti-fantasy child in the family, it might do him good to get into one of these books even if you have to read it aloud to him. Go back, for instance, to *The Children of Green Knowe* by Lucy Boston (pp. 156-157). It begins so realistically and the magic builds up so gradually that the reader is a part of the fantasy before he is aware of it. Young Tolly is, of course, completely real to the last page.
    There are valid reasons for making an effort to induct young readers into this area of magic and make-believe. In the first place,

most of the books that follow are superlative examples of good writing. J. R. R. Tolkien said, "If fairy-story as a kind is worth reading at all it is worthy to be written for and read by adults."[1] And C. S. Lewis, a second distinguished writer in this field, said, ". . . a children's story which is enjoyed only by children, is a bad children's story." Two experts and Oxford scholars in complete agreement! Most of the books in the following list, to which you can add from the lists given for the middle years *The Wind in the Willows, Charlotte's Web, The Borrowers, The Book of Three,* and *The Children of Green Knowe,* were composed by good craftsmen whose writing skills are second only to their creative imaginations.

Is it a coincidence that three of the greatest fantasies we have ever had were written by Lewis Carroll, C. S. Lewis, and J. R. R. Tolkien—all scholarly dons at England's famous Oxford University?

Alice's Adventures in Wonderland and *Through the Looking Glass,* by Lewis Carroll (pseud. for Charles Lutwidge Dodgson), ill. by John Tenniel. Macmillan, 1923; Heritage, 1944. (First published in 1865 and 1871).

It is doubtful that the Alice books are really children's books, although they are usually listed for children ten to twelve, but in those years children are generally not amused by the books and are frequently bored or baffled. Whereas from twelve on, they begin to catch the tongue-in-cheek humor, the satire, and the wild fun. They even memorize and recite yards of those daft verses—"You are old, Father William," "The Jabberwocky," and other favorites. Experiment with them younger if you wish, but if they fall flat just wait and try later.

These books have no ancestor. They were a startling innovation and brought nonsense and hilarious satire to children's books. The first book became famous so quickly that Charles Lutwidge Dodgson, the professor of mathematics, was completely obscured by the flighty author Lewis Carroll, who made up this story to amuse three little girls he had taken on a picnic. Every adult should remember that inimitable beginning—Alice sitting by the river bank with nothing to do and then the White Rabbit, complete with waistcoat and watch, hurrying along muttering "Oh dear! Oh dear!" and going plop down a rabbit

[1]*Tree and Leaf.* Houghton Mifflin, 1965, p. 45.

hole with Alice just behind him. From then on, the most imaginative sort of lunacy takes over, with Alice growing an enormous neck or shrinking rapidly, queens who mutter casually "Off with her head," and a Mad Hatter's tea party that ends with the dormouse in the tea pot. Nowadays, adults are reading all sorts of Victorian political implications into the characters and episodes, but these need not trouble children and won't. On the whole, the atmosphere is utterly gay, and children, if they like it at all, accept it as good nonsense with a sort of reasonable quality that makes it convincing. The Tenniel illustrations are standard equipment, and as you grow familiar with them, the more effective these pen-and-ink interpretations will seem.

From *Alice's Adventures in Wonderland and Through the Looking Glass,* by Lewis Carroll, illustrated by Sir John Tenniel, with an afterword by Clifton Fadiman. *The Macmillan Classics,* 1963.

The Lobster-Quadrille   99

"Oh, *you* sing," said the Gryphon. "I've forgotten the words."

So they began solemnly dancing round and round Alice, every now and then treading on her toes when they passed too close, and waving their fore-paws to mark the time, while the Mock Turtle sang this, very slowly and sadly:—

"Will you walk a little faster?" said a whiting to a snail,
"There's a porpoise close behind us, and he's treading on
     my tail.
See how eagerly the lobsters and the turtles all advance!

The Chronicles of Narnia, by C. S. Lewis, ill. by Pauline Baynes. Macmillan. These tales consist of *The Lion, the Witch and the Wardrobe* (1950), *Prince Caspian* (1951), *The Voyage of the Dawn Treader* (1952), *The Silver Chair* (1953), *The Horse and His Boy* (1954), *The Magician's Nephew* (1955), and *The Last Battle* (1956).

C. S. Lewis, author of the famous *Screwtape Letters* (adult), was a theologian as well as a lecturer on English Literature; so adults who read these seven entrancing tales of mythical Narnia will discover that the allegories are full of Christian symbolism. Children may or may not sense this, for as magical adventure tales the books are completely satisfying. Each can be read separately, but the first is the best to begin with, and the last is the best to end with.

The Lion, the Witch and the Wardrobe introduces Peter, Susan, Edmund, and Lucy. They were staying in the very old house of a very old professor who left the children pretty much on their own. Lucy had the first adventure. She walked into an enormous wardrobe and out the other side and found herself in cold, snowy Narnia. From an amiable faun she learned that the wicked White Witch had put Narnia under a spell. It was always winter but never Christmas, a wonderful touch! Lucy returned to her own world and finally persuaded the other three children, only after they indulged in a great deal of skepticism and grumbling, to follow her to Narnia. Edmund turned traitor after he met the White Witch and was corrupted by unlimited Turkish Delight and bright promises. The other children encountered the beautiful, gentle, golden Lion Aslan and all the little talking beasts and talking trees that loved him. A terrible battle followed between the dwarfish forces of the White Witch and the Lion's followers. Because of Edmund's treachery, the Lion sacrificed himself for the others, and the Witch departed in triumph. But later, Aslan in turn was saved and he aided in the final violent fight and victory against the forces of evil. In the end, after a series of further adventures, the children, including the repentant and reformed Edmund, returned to their own world.

In each book there are battles between the forces of evil and Aslan's goodness and love. Other children and other characters succeed those in the first books, but all the human beings discover that a week on earth may mean thousands of years in Narnia, and that for a year or two in Narnia you are not missed on earth even momentarily. *The Last Battle* unites most of the characters and writes *finis* to the adventures. Once a child starts this series and likes it, he is apt to read through all seven books, but *The Last Battle* should be saved for the end.

Tom's Midnight Garden, by A. Philippa Pearce, ill. by Susan Einzig. Lippincott, 1958. (10-12)

Tom's Midnight Garden is a fantasy in time and space. Because his brother had the measles, Tom was packed off to stay with his aunt and uncle. Tom was outraged, especially because they lived in an apartment, a section of an old house, with no garden, only a dismal backyard with garbage cans. Lying awake one night, Tom heard an old grandfather clock in the downstairs hall strike thirteen. Wide awake and curious, he padded downstairs, caught a glimpse of a beautiful garden, and pushed his way through a bit of wall to explore. Soon he heard children's voices, and finally he saw young Hatty and her three boy cousins, all dressed in strange costumes—late Victorian, as Tom learned later. Hatty could see Tom, but none of the boys could. From then on, night after night Tom and the little girl played together, although gradually she grew older while Tom remained the same age. Finally, she was a young lady, and the last night before Tom was to return to his home, he found to his anguish that he could no longer get into the garden. The next day, Tom met old Mrs. Bartholomew, the owner of the house, and it was then that Tom learned the explanation for his dreamlike experiences. Beautifully written with a masterly blend of realism and fantasy, this story is a treasure of imaginative literature. Understandably, it was the winner of the Carnegie Medal as the outstanding English children's book of 1958.

A Wrinkle in Time, by Madeleine L'Engle. Farrar, 1962. Newbery Medal. (10-14)

This science-fiction fantasy begins realistically in the security of a warm, bright kitchen on a night of wild wind. Rebellious, stubborn Meg Murry, a high-school freshman, and her precocious five-year-old brother, Charles Wallace, are having hot cocoa with their mother. Suddenly, into the family group comes a strange old woman, Mrs. Whatsit, who explains that she had been "caught in a down draft and blown off course." But when she leaves, she has one final upsetting word for Mrs. Murry, that "there *is* such a thing as a tesseract," the concept Mr. Murry was working on for the government before he disappeared. The next afternoon, Meg, Charles Wallace, and a new acquaintance, brilliant Calvin O'Keefe, a high-school junior, meet a second old woman, Mrs. Who; and that very night the three children take off with Mrs. Who, Mrs. Whatsit, and a third old woman, Mrs. Which, on the first leg of their terrifying journey to rescue Mr. Murry. Their first stop is "Uriel, the third planet of the star Malak in the spiral nebula Messier 101," which they reach by tessering, or wrinkling—a process that takes no time at all and involves the "fact" that the shortest distance between two points is a fold or wrinkle. The tesseract is a solitary, painful experience of blackness and terrifying force, which finally lands them on Camazotz, a planet inhabited by robots controlled by an evil force called simply IT. Here the children are on their own. IT takes over the mind and body of Charles Wallace, who trusted too much to his own intelligence. Meg and Calvin free Mr. Murry, but Charles Wallace forces them to go to IT, a raw, horrible, pulsating brain that beats through all the inhabitants of this shadow land. There follows in the complex course of the rest of the book a battle between good and evil, love and hate, that in spite of the mixture of science, philosophy, religion, satire, and allegory, carries the story on at a horrifying pace. In the end, Meg's love triumphs and Charles is saved. All tesser back to earth, where they are greeted joyfully by Mrs. Murry and the ten-year-old Murry twins.

A Wrinkle in Time is written in terms of our modern world, in which youth knows about space travel, brainwashing, and the insidious, creeping corruption of evil. It is a grim and powerful story, terrifying in parts but avidly read and reread by children. If to an adult the symbolism is sometimes mixed, especially when the queer old women turn out to be guardian angels, the message is clear, the story absorbing and completely geared to our times.

This book may lead some children directly into the science fiction of Robert Heinlein and André Norton. Both are excellent writers with rare imaginative powers, scientific know-how, and story-telling appeal. But you wonder how long even the best of the science-fiction stories can hold their pseudo-validity for young readers who are experiencing the real thing—space exploration and all sorts of new scientific facts verified and audio-visualized for them daily. It remains to be seen.

Have Space Suit—Will Travel, by Robert Heinlein. Scribner, 1958. This will do as well as any of the other Heinlein books to start with. Either young readers want more or remain indifferent. Other titles include *Rocket Ship Galileo* (1947), *Red Planet* (1949), *Between Planets* (1951), *Time for the Stars* (1956), and *Citizen of the Galaxy* (1957).

The Time Traders, by André Norton. World, 1958.

Men from three different periods of life on earth clash in a time transfer. Other titles include *Star Man's Son* (1952), *Star Rangers* (1953), *Star Guard* (1955), *Star Born* (1957), *Sea Siege* (1957), *The Defiant Agents* (1962).

Modern science fiction got off to a spectacular start with Jules Verne's *Twenty Thousand Leagues Under the Sea* (1870), and *Around the World in Eighty Days* (1873). These old tales still have a spellbinding quality even if we do read or watch the *Eighty Days* smiling a bit because it is so dated. But even though Verne's books of miraculous travels have lasted a century, there is a still older world of fantasy—the world of nymphs, dryads, fauns, dwarves, giants, witches, ogres, elves, and the little people. This world has lasted for centuries and seems to be as firmly entrenched in modern imagination as ever. Recently, this ancient world has received re-inforcement from a new species, the hobbits. As. J. R. R. Tolkien says, they are "small people, smaller than dwarves (and they have no beards) but very much larger than lilliputians. There is little or no magic about them, except the ordinary everyday sort which helps them to disappear quietly and quickly when large stupid folk like you and me come blundering along making a noise like elephants which they can hear a mile off." In many ways, they are like men in speech, habits, tastes, and appearance except for their feet, which are handsomely furred and seldom shod. "Halflings," they are called, and Professor J. R. R. Tolkien has devoted four volumes to their history and adventures, and more absorbing books you have never read. Once you accept hobbits and hobbitry, you may find yourself a member of one of the Tolkien Clubs, which have taken over the colleges and the secondary schools and have even penetrated the inner circle of good readers at the elementary level.

The Hobbit, by J. R. R. Tolkien. Houghton, 1938. Also *Lord of the Rings,* in three volumes: Part I, *The Fellowship of the Ring;* Part II, *The Two Towers;* Part III, *The Return of the King.*

The hero of *The Hobbit* is Mr. Bilbo Baggins, an eminently respect-able hobbit, owner of a really splendid "Hole," beautifully paneled and carpeted and furnished with all the luxuries and comforts Hobbiton afforded. That is saying a lot, for the hobbits are a genial crew, fond of eating, drinking, and merry company. One morning "long ago in the quiet of the world, when there was less noise and more green," Gandalf the Wizard walked into Bilbo Baggins' serene life, and a series of the most outlandish adventures began. Poor Bilbo, without even a pocket-handkerchief to his name, was pressed into the service of the dwarves and quite against his better judgment started off to help them recover their dwarf-hoards held by the dragon Smaug. The only thing to account for Bilbo's lapse from conventional hobbit ways was that on his mother's side he had inherited some wild Took blood. Well, he certainly needed it now along with his sturdy Baggins variety. The adventures involved trolls, elves, horrible evil orcs, and noble eagles and resulted in battles and hardships of every kind. Eventually Bilbo and the dwarves re-captured the stolen wealth and slew the dragon. But once, Bilbo was lost for a while in an underground cavern with a slimy creature called Gollum. By accident, Bilbo found a magic ring and escaped with it. But he had won the enmity of Gollum and roused the curiosity of old Gandalf, who suspected that the ring had far more power than Bilbo realized. So obviously, even with Bilbo's triumphant return to his beautiful Hole with great wealth and honor, the tale is only half told.

This book is close, hard reading but completely enthralling. As Professor Tolkien says about a good fairy tale, adults "will, of course, put more in and get more out than children can." So all of his books make good adult reading, but children can and do enjoy thoroughly this first book, *The Hobbit*, and they are reading it earlier than they used to, perhaps because they hear older children and adults discussing seriously the trilogy that follows. By all means, expose your young readers to *The Hobbit*, and see if they care to go on from there.

The trilogy is a noble epic of the Ring. Frodo, Bilbo's nephew and heir, still has the Ring but has never used it. He learns from Gandalf that it is the Ring of Rings, wholly evil and there will be no peace in the world until it is thrown forever into the Crack of Doom. Frodo is a brave, dedicated soul, and his adventures carry him through many lands, some horribly evil, some of such innocent joy and beauty as neither man nor hobbits have known since the world began. The strug-gles are almost unbearable, but the evil Gollum and the Ring go down to Doom together. The final chapters of this great trilogy in *The Return of the King* are moving and masterful.

Why in this age of inventions, scientific research, and explora-tions of many kinds should children, youth, and even adults still enjoy the world of fairy? And what possible values can such reading have for a generation with a nuclear holocaust threatening?

First of all, with radio and television we have brought into our homes all the wars and disasters of the entire world. We get up in the morning, put on the coffee, and turn on the gloom—newscasters intoning their rituals of doom. A dismal way to greet the day! Children and youth go on their way, apparently unaffected, but are they? Isn't this continuous impact of the horrors and anxieties of the modern world one reason why they turn to fantasy? There they find a world full of laughter, courage, and beauty. There may be an epic struggle between Good and Evil—as between the noble Aslan and the wicked White Witch in Narnia or between little Bilbo Baggins or his nephew Frodo fighting the Dark Lord—Sauron of Mordor—and his evil cohorts. But in the end, Evil is worsted, the world is safe, and laughter and beauty are once more a part of life. Here in these books there are comfort and strength for the faint-hearted and a renewal of faith in decency and delight. These are a few of the values of such reading.

TRANSITIONS FROM JUVENILE TO ADULT READING

❖❖❖

10

Teen-age Books of Romance and Adventure
Popular Adult Fiction
Stranger Than Fiction
A Few Nineteenth-Century Classics

From several of the books recommended in the last two chapters, it is evident that some children of twelve, thirteen, and fourteen are moving rapidly in the direction of adult reading. In those chapters, there are reviews of such comparatively juvenile stories as *Big Red*, *A Place for Peter*, and *Crystal Mountain* along with reviews of more mature books such as *Johnny Tremain*, *Jazz Country*, the Sutcliff and Tolkien books, and the subtle satires *The Pushcart War* and *Animal Farm*. As has been said, these years—twelve, thirteen, and fourteen—are years of such baffling differences in children's reading abilities, social interests, and emotional stirrings that reading lists should be made only on an individual basis. One youngster in these years is a child, another an inquiring youth; one reads everything within reach—juvenile or adult; another stays with a few dog-eared favorites from earlier years or falls into reading ruts and stereotypes. Some children will be best served by choosing from the book lists for the middle years; but for a fourteen-year-old who has devoured *Gone with the Wind* and enjoyed every word of it, *The Wheel on the School* would be meager and unsatisfactory fare. So of necessity, a general book list for boys and girls in these transitional years will be a compromise between easy and hard books, between childlike and mature subject matter and treatment.

There is also a sex difference in the choice of books at these ages that is fairly marked. Most girls from eleven years on are deeply interested in stories of romance. Boys of the same age may be developing an interest in girls but decidedly not in stories of romance. Boys want stouter stuff—sports stories, adventure, maybe mystery, but action at all costs. None of this "mushy stuff," which boys resent as much in their moving pictures as in books. Fortunately, there are fine books to meet the divergent interests of both boys and girls.

There are other problems in book choice during these years. Physical changes and emotional stirrings are riding some children hard and are reflected in their activities, including their reading. Some children may lapse, temporarily it is to be hoped, into determined nonreaders. Others may reach out for the easy stereotyped fiction of the pulp magazines or, worse still, they may discover and pursue some of the prurient books that are circulating among adolescents today as always. It is a rare child who passes through these years without falling into one or another of these traps; so brace yourself, and try not to let your disapproval be too obvious or emphatic. A temporary lack of interest in books may be a healthy reaction for the avid reader. He is finding life more exciting than books; but be patient, he'll come back to his reading. The repetitious stereotypes of the slick magazine stories or teen-age novels or sports stories may be just the soporifics that for the time being, can lull a girl's anxieties and restless stirrings and a boy's need for excitement.

The "dirty book," prurient and pornographic, is harder to take, but remember it circulates in private and public schools and among children of suburbia as well as among urban children. If it comes your way, read it and try not to show your disgust. Give your child a chance to discuss it with you. After all, he may be as scornful of it as you are, but at least he should have a chance to talk it over with someone. In the conversation, you can let it be known that every generation has found such books and that they are also to be found among adult books. You can agree that they may satisfy curiosities, but you can also point out that there are a lot of adult books which meet the same problems forthrightly and far more thoroughly and honestly than these examples. Then help your youngster find some of these good adult books.

Robert Carlsen in his *Books and the Teen-age Reader* (Harper, 1967) gives this bit of advice: *"Keep the channels of communication between you and your teen-age child open."* And showing extreme revulsion or disapproval will immediately check all communication and dam up the questions he may so greatly need to ask and have answered. When you have had a frank, dispassionate talk with your child, then give a boy such a book as *The Catcher in the Rye* and a girl *Greengage Summer* and lead them both to *A Tree Grows in Brooklyn* or *To Kill a Mockingbird* or to *Gone with the Wind*. Such stout books touch on questions of sex, morality, growing up, and social problems of various sorts, all in the course of an absorbing and enlightening story. After any of these, the silly stereotypes or the slimy shockers will seem thin stuff indeed.

Concerning the romantic novel there is a strong difference of opinion among informed adults. Shall we give young persons the teen-age novel or adventure story, or discourage such reading and try to move them firmly into adult books? The answer depends upon the social maturity of the young reader and upon the content of the book. But whether it is a teen-age novel, an adult classic, a popular modern mystery, an adventure story, or an adult biography or autobiography, the book should widen a youth's horizons, give him a vicarious look at different areas of human experience, and leave him a more perceptive human being. His reading should deepen his sense of compassion and also his ability to laugh at some of life's absurdities and mock tragedies. Books that draw forth these responses will help him to become a part of the adult world, to know how intelligent grownups feel, and to experience a joyful sense of aliveness and awareness that he is himself moving toward adult stature. It is in these transition years that boys are often oppressed with the dullness of routines and with the frustrations of being young and not on their own. They need adventure, sports, mystery, and the idealism of the heroic. Girls need help in growing into the sometimes heartbreaking adult world where

Prince Charming does not always come riding to the door on schedule or, worse still, rides by to another door. Oh, what to do then?

TEEN-AGE BOOKS OF ROMANCE AND ADVENTURE

Regardless of the child's chronological age, his books should begin at his own level of interests and reading skills. In this respect, the years of later adolescence from fourteen on are no exception. And for the children who need them, teen-age stories of adventure and romance are to be found, so well written and with such absorbing story interest that they provide a good lead into more adult reading. So begin with a few of these.

Romance for the girls

If she has not already enjoyed them, give your young romantic Maureen Daly's *Seventeenth Summer* (pp. 173-174) or *The Witch of Blackbird Pond* (pp. 184-185) or the eighth book in the *Little House* series, *These Happy Golden Years* (p. 132). In addition to these, here are a few more teen-age novels of more than ordinary worth, beginning with a fascinating novel about ancient Egypt. These books tell absorbing stories, will certainly do young readers no harm, and may provide considerable guidance. Their only danger lies in the fact that young girls may settle contentedly into reading more and more of these youth books; and a lot of them, no matter how wholesome, are likely to prolong the reader's immaturity, both socially and intellectually. Meanwhile, be thankful for a few strong examples, but try without pressure to move girls into more adult reading.

> *Mara, Daughter of the Nile*, by Eloise Jarvis McGraw, drawings by Jack Myers. Coward-McCann, 1953. (12 up)
> Here are action-filled romance and exciting historical fiction to satisfy the most avid young lover of adventure. Mara is a seventeen-year-old slave in the days when Queen Hatshepsut ruled Egypt. The girl vaguely remembers better days and is determined to escape from her present enslavement, poverty, and brutal treatment. So when a mysterious man buys her and offers her an easy life of luxury if she will be a court spy for the queen, she readily consents. Later, she encounters

a virile, attractive young nobleman named Sheftu, who offers her pay to serve as a spy for Thutmose, the queen's half brother, who is practically a prisoner in his own palace. Mara thinks she is clever enough to play one group against the other. Unfortunately for her plans, she falls in love with Sheftu and is completely won over to the side of Thutmose. This new loyalty changes Mara from a liar, cheat, and self-seeking young woman to a single-hearted girl who endures torture rather than betray her loyalties. This is an enthralling novel, and it affords glimpses of ancient Egyptian life—everyday life as well as court life—of cities, villages, river traffic, and of the desperate struggle for power in high places.

Watch for a Tall White Sail, by Margaret Bell. Morrow, 1948. Also *Love Is Forever* (1954).

Although these books go back to the 1880's in Alaska territory, they are meaningful to young girls today, who, like Florence Monroe, are following their families or husbands into remote places all over the world, and finding that pioneer conditions are not limited to the past. The stories about Florence Monroe are timeless in their appeal. In the first book she is courageously adjusting to the hardships and strangeness of life in wild Nicols Bay, where her father and brothers are launching their salmon industry. The background of place, people, and work are part of the drama of this new life. The book ends with the rescue of sixteen-year-old Florence from drowning by the man she later marries. The second book begins with their unique wedding, which will delight girls. Then Florence and her husband leave for a still wilder and more remote part of the country. There in the wilderness, Florence, by her absurd standards of housekeeping and dress, antagonizes her native neighbors and her husband, who must work with these people. He is increasingly irked, and Florence is increasingly stubborn. The conflict grows to such alarming proportions that it begins to look as if this foolish young wilderness wife is going to fail completely. Only a near tragedy clears the air and helps the troubled young husband and wife work out their conflicts in love and mutual respect. These books exhibit a wholesome approach to human fallibility and contain vividly created characters.

Wait for Me, Michael, by Mary Stolz. Harper, 1961. Also *The Sea Gulls Woke Me* (1951) and *To Tell Your Love* (1950).

Mary Stolz, whether writing for six or sixteen, is first of all a competent writer. She has a sense of form, style, and outstanding story-telling appeal. Her approach to adolescent girls' problems in dealing with the opposite sex is sensitive and understanding. Although additional books for young girls could be described—*Who Wants Music on Monday?* (1963), *Second Nature* (1958), *Ready or Not* (1953), *Organdy Cupcakes* (1951)—these will provide samplings of subject matter and approach.

To Tell Your Love faces that overwhelming experience of failure in a first romance. Most girls feel no one else has ever suffered such humiliation, and a book like this helps them discover that it is a common experience.

The Sea Gulls Woke Me deals with another tragedy of youth—being a wallflower at a school dance. But Jean, working as a waitress in her uncle's resort hotel, has close, everyday companionship of other girl students and a look-in at their problems, and she develops a growing assurance that she too will be able to stand on her own two feet and get on with people.

Wait for Me, Michael tells of an immature girl who falls in love with an older boy. Fortunately, it is Michael who helps her grow up.

Giving just the gist of these stories may make them sound like books written to teach a lesson. Actually, they are free of didacticism, although they are built around some of the common problems that trouble adolescent girls and that need to be brought into the open. This Mary Stolz does admirably in the course of a good story.

The Rock and the Willow, by Mildred Lee. Lothrop, 1963.

A transition between the romanticism of teen-age stories and the adult novel, *The Rock and the Willow* is a starkly honest book. Earline Singleton, or Enie, as she was called, was thirteen when the story begins and going to college when it ends. Hers was the poverty-stricken, overcrowded home of a poor farmer. He was violently bad tempered and the victim of his own ignorance and prejudice. The mother was overworked; there were older brothers, younger children, and endless drudgery for all of them. Yet rebellious Enie had found a sanctuary, a rock under a willow tree, where she could steal precious moments to write and add to her list of beautiful words. But family troubles increased, and just as Enie was almost hopeless and broken with rebellion against her father's driving brutality, a new teacher came to the consolidated school. One day, she read one of Enie's compositions to the entire class, a class from which Enie's poverty had made her an outcast. As if this moment of glory were not enough, the teacher talked to Enie of her gift of words, of the necessity for her to go to college. Enie was reborn. The deprivations went on, but now Enie had a new image of herself, and there was a spark of hope. In the intervening years before college, Enie encountered birth and death, saw accidentally a sordid love affair, and suffered the first pangs of love and the temptations of the flesh, but her new image of herself saved her. She had developed not only self-respect but compassion for the piteous members of her family, victims like herself of poverty and ignorance, but struggling courageously, nevertheless. Well-drawn characters make this a memorable book.

Cress Delahanty, by Jessamyn West. Curtis, 1948. Harbrace Paperback Library. (12 up)

Five of the sixteen chapters of this book appeared originally in *The New Yorker*, in somewhat different form. Parents as well as teen-age girls should read this book about the growing pains of the years twelve through sixteen. Each of the chapters is a complete episode; many of them are hilarious, some are serious, and through them all, the tender relationship of Crescent Delahanty and her family gives warmth to the story and reassurance to the reader. If a modern growing girl can laugh at some of the earnest absurdities of young Cress, she will understand herself better and view the members of her family with greater tolerance.

Action for the boys

If your adventure-seeking boys missed some of the nonconformists and rebels in Chapter 8, now is the time for them to discover *My Side of the Mountain, Hank, The Outsiders, Banner in the Sky,* and *It's Like This, Cat.* Action stories for boys should include sports, pure adventure, mystery, and the kind of autobiographical accounts included in the list for "Stranger Than Fiction" (pp. 227-232). But with their absorption in action and, especially, sports, boys may fall into as deadly reading ruts as girls do with their saccharine love stories. There are a few strong sports stories and innumerable examples of mediocrity; so move boys into stouter fare with such autobiographical records, for example, as *Kon-Tiki* (p. 232). Meanwhile, here are some books that will provide helpful transitions into good adult literature.

Big Tiger and Christian, by Fritz Muhlenweg, ill. by Rafaello Busoni. Pantheon, 1952.

An English boy and a Chinese boy find themselves pressed into the service of a Chinese general. There is unrest between Mongolia and China, and the boys are to carry important messages across the Gobi desert. The Chinese boy has more know-how about the country and peoples, but Christian has other areas of competence, so that they complement each other admirably. Both have intelligence and resourcefulness, qualities they need, since they encounter various dangers in this thrilling tale of adventure and endurance. This is a well-written book which good readers will devour, but slow readers will find too long and difficult.

Guns in the Heather, by Lockhart Amerman. Harcourt, 1963. Also *Cape Cod Casket* (1964).

These Amerman books make a lively and sometimes weird introduction to mystery tales. Jonathan Flower's father is a famous and adroit secret agent; so when he sends a directive to his son, it is practically a command and invariably prevents Jonathan from confiding in anyone. In the first story, Jonathan is just leaving his Scottish boarding school expecting to join his father, when he finds himself involved in a complex international intrigue with no sign of his father. There are innumerable complications, including his besiegement in an old castle, with guns spitting fire from heather and copse. Jonathan should follow in his father's profession, for nothing stops him—knockout drops or dungeons. His resourcefulness and fight always pull him through.

Cape Cod Casket is less plausible because of the strange characters— a mad embalmer and a Parsi priest. But Jonathan and his father give a balanced sense of reality and inevitably solve the mystery. One of the interesting things about these books is the way the father expects competence from his son and is always certain that he will come through any difficulty—and Jonathan of course always does.

Storm over Skye, by Allan Campbell McLean, ill. by Shirley Hughes. Harcourt, 1957. Also *Master of Morgana* (1959).

No one can write better mystery tales than Allan McLean; and the wild haunting beauty of Skye, where the action takes place, enhances the overtones of dark foreboding. The plots of his stories usually center on sturdy village boys, sheepherders or fishermen, but a sister or a neighboring girl is apt to take a hand in the action. In *Storm over Skye*, the hero finds himself engaged in a dangerous battle of wits to discover who is stealing fine sheep from the village flocks. The second book involves an even more dangerous situation. The boy discovers that someone has tried and nearly succeeded in killing his older brother. But why, and who did it? He goes to sea on a fishing expedition and soon realizes that he, too, is in grave danger. But again the question, why? In both books, before the mystery is solved, the whole community is involved, the courage and resourcefulness of the heroes are taxed to the limit, and suspense rises to an exciting and satisfying conclusion.

Lord of the Flies, by William Golding. Coward-McCann, 1954, 1955. Capricorn Books (paperback), Putnam, 1959. (12 up)

A realistic parable and a gruesome story, this book relates what happened to a group of British schoolboys when their plane crashed and they found themselves marooned on an island with no adults. Leadership was established and law and order enforced. But presently, a rival leader with followers developed. This second group flouted all laws and rapidly reverted to savagery. Some appalling events followed, including two murders, before adult rescuers finally arrived. As E. E. Epstein points out in the notes to the paperback edition (p. 189): "*Lord of the Flies* is not, to say the least, a simple adventure story of boys on a desert island. In fact, the implications of the story go far beyond the degeneration of a few children." On pages 190-191, he summarizes some of the basic symbolism: "The emergence of this concealed, basic wildness is the theme of the book; the struggle between Ralph, the representative of civilization with his parliaments and his brain trust (Piggy, the intellectual whose shattering spectacles mark the progressive decay of rational influence as the story progresses), and Jack, in whom the spark of wildness burns hotter and closer to the surface than in Ralph and who is the leader of the forces of anarchy on the island, is also, of course, the struggle in modern society between those same forces translated onto a worldwide scale."

POPULAR ADULT FICTION

Teen-agers growing into adult reading rarely start with the classic novel. When some member of the family likes a book he has been reading well enough to talk about it, the young person in the family may pick it up, discover that he can read it, and become interested. The lists of books reviewed for teen-age girls and boys both concluded with a book originally published for adults but appropriated by youth, namely *Cress Delahanty* and *Lord of the Flies*. The following list of popular adult fiction contains some books teen-agers are enjoying, and among them are books of sound literary worth. Even the lightest of these novels—the Mary Stewart mysteries, for example—will introduce young readers to sophisticated backgrounds and characters. Several of the books involve grave social problems treated with contemporary frankness—for example, that vast panoramic historical novel *Gone with the Wind*.

To Kill a Mockingbird, by Harper Lee. Lippincott, 1960.

The events of this story, which take place in a small Southern town during the early nineteen thirties, are related by young Scout (Jean Louise) Finch, and they cover a period beginning with the summer before she entered first grade and ending with the Halloween night when Scout was eight. Here is a child's-eye view of a somewhat frightening adult world, a world which rambunctious Scout and her brother Jem, four years her senior, eagerly investigate, checked somewhat however by their wise and tolerant widowed father, Atticus, and by their stern, upright, colored housekeeper, Calpurnia. The climactic event of the story is the trial of an innocent Negro, whom Atticus stoutly and brilliantly defends, to the revulsion of many of the white community. The trial, the ugly disclosures, the obvious innocence of the Negro, the prejudiced verdict, the bitter aftermath, and the evil that reaches out even to the children are all forthrightly presented. When it is over, the children know, as they have always known, that their father's courage and integrity are unshakeable. And during the course of events, Jem and young Scout acquire new insights and understandings. Indeed, at the close of that fateful Halloween night, Scout is able to help her rigorously truthful father with a strange decision for him—to agree to a harmless deception to save a strange, shy recluse from added pain. As Scout reminds him, "It's a sin to kill a mockingbird."

Greengage Summer, by Rumer Godden. Viking, 1958.

Read this book before you offer it to your child. Most fourteen-year-olds should be ready for it, and a few children earlier. It falls somewhere between juvenilia and adult novels, and it is funny, tender, and startling. It is told in the first person by thirteen-year-old Cecil, an English child, who finds herself with an older sister, two younger sisters, and a little brother, in a not too respectable French pension. Their mother has been rushed to the hospital, critically ill. After the rigidly regulated confines of their British uncle's home, the children now find themselves completely on their own. This heady experience would have been too much for them if it had not been for a delightful young man named Eliot. He comes and goes mysteriously, turns up unexpectedly, but always manages to keep a protective watch over the children. Joss, the sixteen-year-old, is blossoming into rare beauty, which has a disturbing effect on everyone, from Eliot to Paul, the uncouth and terrifying boy-of-all-work. Cecil and the younger children encounter Paul in the kitchen, where the cook stuffs them amiably, and they gain considerable insight into some of the ways of adults which they might better have missed. But it is beautiful Joss, who unknowingly triggers the final explosion—an explosion that brings a new maturity for Cecil, terror for Joss, the final disappearance of Eliot, and a murder under the greengage plum trees. The whole episode might have gone badly with the children, but Eliot, before he took flight, had wired their English uncle to come for them. Back to England and home went mother and the five children—not much older but decidedly wiser. Here is a child's-eye view of a somewhat seamy adult world where the children are protected by their own innocence and canny intelligence.

A Tree Grows in Brooklyn, by Betty Smith. Harper, 1947.

The reader follows through sixteen years in the life of young Francie Nolan, growing up in a slum area of Brooklyn. Life for Francie was interesting and hopeful, because both Francie and her slender, beautiful mother had their eyes on a better future. Father was a handsome, charming young Irishman, a singing waiter with little or no earning ability and a weakness for drink. Mother was a scrub woman in the dreary wretched tenements where they lived. And there was a pretty aunt who broke all the rules but also loved young Francie. This is a sensitive picture of growing up under adverse circumstances, protected from the tragic, sordid reality by wondering innocence in the beginning, and as time goes on, by keen intelligence and a family love that somehow manages to erect its own shield against coarseness and despair. That Francie grows up to be a decent, ambitious young woman is a tribute to the indomitable quality of the human spirit.

This Rough Magic, by Mary Stewart. Morrow, 1964. Also *Airs Above the Ground* (1965) and other titles.

Whether Mary Stewart's mystery tale is set in a French chateau, an English manor house, a remote mountain convent, or a villa off the coast of Greece, the setting is always as intriguing as the plot. *Nine Coaches Waiting*, *The Ivy Tree*, and several others are as fascinating as the two examples chosen for this list. The action of *This Rough Magic* takes place on the island of Corfu, where rumor has it Shakespeare placed his *Tempest*. But visiting Lucy found that any surviving magic was rough indeed. On her first day, when she went swimming, she was joined by a playful dolphin, obviously friendly and tame. But a bullet whistled by, just missing them, and another followed. Thoroughly outraged, Lucy set out to find the culprit, but the discovery of a corpse did nothing to allay her fears. The solution of the mystery would have been easier if all the characters in and around her sister's beautiful villa had not been such urbane and delightful people. Romance further complicates Lucy's suspicions, but eventually it is the romance that saves Lucy and solves the mystery, a dangerous one indeed.

In some ways, *Airs Above the Ground* is not so satisfying, but children who loved Marguerite Henry's book about the Lipizzan horses will be delighted with this story about the mysterious disappearance of one of the famous Lipizzans from the Spanish Riding School of Vienna. The action centers on a small, insignificant traveling circus. The heroine, on her way to find her "missing " husband, has with her a youth who has made himself an authority on each one of the Lipizzan horses. To their amazement, he finds in this obscure little circus a clue to the famous missing horse. The two decide to rescue the horse, whose white coat has been dyed and who performs all by himself "the airs above the ground," to which he was trained. Murder, a deadly chase, near death for the heroine, mounting suspense—all rise to a magnificent conclusion. But the chase and the capture of the villain do not compare in interest to the Lipizzan horse-lore the story involves.

Rebecca, by Daphne du Maurier. Doubleday, 1948.

Almost a classic of mystery fiction, this adult novel is full of eerie overtones. It is the story of a second wife taking over a great English manor house. Both the house and its residents trouble the young wife, and her discovery that the first wife died under mysterious circumstances does nothing to lessen her anxieties. Spine-chilling situations,

2

3

growing suspense, a threat to an idyllic romance, and memorable characterizations bring this mystery story into the realm of literature. Some fourteen-year-olds can take it in their stride. For other youngsters, sixteen is a better age.

The Adventures of Sherlock Holmes, by Sir Arthur Conan Doyle. Originally published in 1891. Berkley Medallion Edition, 1963.
  Across the turn of the century, Sir Arthur Conan Doyle was writing stories involving his master detective, Sherlock Holmes, and his friend and foil, Dr. Watson. Before young people become obsessed with Mickey Spillane's creations and the pulp magazine detective stories, let's introduce them to some examples of this old spellbinder. For after all, Conan Doyle is the father of our modern whodunits and still unexcelled. Who ever forgets *The Sign of the Four* (1889) or *The Hound of the Baskervilles* (1902)? Here are twelve of his short stories, including "A Scandal in Bohemia," "The Red-Headed League," "The Five Orange Pips," "The Adventure of the Speckled Band," and "The Adventure of the Copper Beeches." "A Scandal" is one story in which the master mind was almost outwitted by a beautiful woman, and he never forgot her. With Conan Doyle's stories, the writing is smooth, the clues baffling, and the solutions logical with nothing unaccounted for. In short, these are teasers in the ungentle art of detecting, and they are enough to start teen-agers trying their luck at amateur detection or composing stories involving the art.

The Call of the Wild and Selected Stories, by Jack London. Originally published in 1903. A Signet Classic (paperback).
  This is one of the finest dog stories ever written and so poignant that to reread it is to be moved again to deep compassion. Buck, whose father was a St. Bernard and mother a Scotch shepherd dog, is a big powerful animal of some one hundred forty pounds. For the first four years of his life, he leads a pampered, happy existence on "Judge Miller's place," a large estate in the Santa Clara Valley in California. But with the coming of the Alaskan gold rush, dogs like Buck are selling at a premium, and so the gardener's helper, debt-ridden Manuel, leads Buck away and sells him to a stranger bound for San Francisco. After a series of brutalizing experiences, Buck winds up in Alaska, where he is pressed into service as a sled dog. "The law of club and fang," Buck learns fast, and as a working dog, he expects the worst of men and of his teammates. The story follows his life as he takes over by force

and cunning the leadership of the team but passes with the team from one master to another. Sometimes he is justly treated, sometimes cruelly. Buck not only adapts to this wild new country but begins to feel a growing kinship with the wolves, whose distant cries he often hears. After the tragic and brutal death of John Thornton, the only master he ever loved, there is nothing to hold Buck to so-called civilization. He has already established contact with a pack of wolves, and so now, in the full health and power of his maturity, he joins them and reverts completely to the wild. A strangely satisfying conclusion! In this small paperback, there are five more stories in London's powerful style.

How Green Was My Valley, by Richard Llewellyn. Macmillan, 1940.
Dell paperback, 1967.
A powerful and poignant story of Welsh coal miners—their glorious singing, the destruction of their valley by the creeping mountain of slag, their labor troubles and growing impoverishment—this book is for mature readers of any age capable of reading it. It is told by Huw Morgan, who was the youngest boy in the big Morgan family. While Huw was still a little fellow, his big brothers were marrying and bringing home pretty wives, but for Huw there would never be other women equal to Bronwen, his brother Ivor's wife, and his own beloved "Mama." They were both strong characters as was Huw's father, the head of the Morgan tribe and a leader in the community. And always the community played an important role in the lives of its people whether in tragedy or celebration or sometimes discipline. But the celebrations were glorious. Then all the choirs gathered from the different valleys to sing together, great thunderous melodies of song "until life and all living things are become a song," for tragedy never was able entirely to crush their courage and love of life. Finally, though, the Morgan clan was scattered—the mine claimed the lives of Ivor and the father; Owen and Gwilym went to the United States, Davy to New Zealand, Ianto to Germany, and one of the daughters, unhappy Angharad, to Cape Town. Huw, looking back as a grown man, remembers their beauty and their life and the greenness of the valley as it was then when they were all home together. Written with the cadence of Welsh speech, with a large gallery of vividly drawn characters, this is a story that will linger in the memory—a modern classic.

My Ántonia, by Willa Cather. Houghton, 1918. Sentry Edition (paperback).

The story is told by Jim Burden, who came to live on his grandfather's farm twenty miles out of Black Hawk, Nebraska, at the same
time that fourteen-year-old Ántonia Shimerda and her family arrived
to settle on a neighboring farm. The land was settled by people from
many different countries—Bohemians, Germans, Russians, Austrians,
Swedes, Norwegians. Of all of them, Ántonia's family seemed least
able to cope with the vast, lonely land. During their first bitter winter,
living in a wretched dugout, they nearly starved and froze, and tragedy
climaxed their year. Yet the child Ántonia grew up in this cruelly
poor family, learning the new language and ways fast and doing a
man's work joyously. Through every stage of her hard life, she lived
warmly and generously. This is a classic saga of prairie farm and village
life in early Nebraska. Willa Cather has told it with deceptive simplicity and has created a great-hearted heroine no reader is likely to
forget.

The Bridge of San Luis Rey, by Thornton Wilder. Originally published in 1927. A Washington Square Press paperback.

This novel, which received the Pulitzer Prize in 1928, asks the
question people have always asked when catastrophe strikes: "Why
did it happen to those particular people?" The story begins: "On Friday
noon, July the twentieth, 1714, the finest bridge in all Peru broke and
precipitated five travellers into the gulf below." The people of Lima
were shocked and sobered by the event, but Brother Juniper, a Francis-
can friar who witnessed the accident, decided to try to prove that it was
some divine plan that put those five people on the bridge at that particular time, and so he inquired into each of their lives—the Marquesa de
Montemayor; Pepita, her companion, an orphan of fourteen; Esteban,
a young man of twenty-two; and fifty-year-old Uncle Pio, traveling
with a frail little boy, Jaime. As it turns out, their stories and the people
themselves are as completely different as they could be, but equally
fascinating. Still, in the end, even after the stories have been told,
the question remains. This book is a small masterpiece, not to be
missed.

Gone with the Wind, by Margaret Mitchell. Macmillan, 1936, 1961.

This novel of the Civil War presents not only a picture of the progress
of that war as it was waged in the South but also a love story no reader
young or old ever forgets. Neither Scarlett, the heroine, nor Rhett,
the hero, are admirable characters, although Rhett is the better of

the two. Scarlett is a beautiful, spoiled, selfish deceiver but, under duress, amazingly competent and lion-hearted. Raised in pampered helplessness, before the story ends she has served as cook, farmer, nurse, midwife, and hard-as-nails money-getter for the people dependent on her. From the first day he saw her, Rhett loved her. He knew her for an unscrupulous cheat, but he admired her pluck, pitied her wrongheaded love for a married man and a weakling, but finally came to hate her. Yet their love story sings through all the horrors of that bloody strife, the poverty and ruin of the South, and the rebuilding of disrupted lives. This is an absorbing novel, but its thousand pages of action-packed details require competent readers.

Cry, the Beloved Country, by Alan Paton. Scribner, 1948.

It is to be hoped that apartheid will soon vanish from the earth, but the practice is sufficiently strong to make this poignant novel pertinent to our day. The story is told by a noble Old African, striving to perpetuate the old ways of life for his family and his people. He is fighting vainly the creeping evils of urbanization, racism, and dire poverty that are corrupting his flock and his own son. There are unforgettable pictures of "the beloved country" and the hardworking, deprived people, but suspicion, bitterness, and hatred grow. The story moves inevitably to its tragic conclusion, lifted and ennobled by the spirit of the grieving father.

The Catcher in the Rye, by J. D. Salinger. Little, 1951.

How and when did teen-agers discover this book? Not too long after publication it was in the process of becoming their special book regardless of adult disapproval. Written in the first person, the action covers only two days in the life of sixteen-year-old Holden Caulfield, who has been expelled from a private prep school and is afraid to go home and face an irate father. Holden is completely disillusioned with people, including himself, and is confused and aimless. He broods over all the "phony" grownups he has encountered. He is obsessed with sexual curiosity. He worries about his little sister for fear his homecoming will hurt her. Holden uses dirty words in his brooding, too many of them to be palatable to the reader.

He has an encounter with a prostitute and later with a homosexual and comes out of both experiences full of nauseated disgust. This book would be a real shocker if it were not written with such deep compassion for Holden's agonizing confusions and his genuine search for honest people and a decent world.

Other examples of popular adult fiction may be substituted for some of these books, but these few examples offer variety, substantial content, and good writing. If your teen-ager reads an adult novel, he is probably looking not for uplift or guidance or solutions to social problems, but for entertainment, and he may get a little of all three in the course of this reading. However, every one of these books is high in entertainment values, whether it is light hearted or serious. Moreover, these books should leave young readers a little easier and more knowledgeable in an adult world.

STRANGER THAN FICTION

These same desirable results may be accomplished by another type of reading, namely true records of real people or situations or happenings. Even though girls may prefer romance to all other types of reading, they will, like their brothers, enjoy factual accounts of other ways of life and of colorful adventures. Boys take to such reading with enthusiasm. But even in the following brief listing of factual records, there will be a sex difference in the choice of favorites. Take the two records of family life in the United States, for example. Both boys and girls chuckle over *Cheaper by the Dozen,* but few boys would be interested in Jade Wong's struggles to emancipate herself from old-world Chinese ways in San Francisco's Chinatown. Most of the books reviewed will be enjoyed by both boys and girls, with *Kon-Tiki* a breathtaking adventure that can hold the entire family spellbound. Incidentally, most of these books make delightful reading aloud for the whole family.

Cheaper by the Dozen, by Frank B. Gilbreth, Jr., and Ernestine Gilbreth Carey. Crowell, 1948. Bantam Pathfinder Edition (paperback).

Here is a very funny true story of a real family. It is also the love story of two brilliant and devoted intellectuals. As the authors say at the beginning of the story, "One reason he [their father] had so many children—there were twelve of us—was that he was convinced anything he and Mother teamed up on was sure to be a success." The father, an efficiency engineer, ran the family accordingly. The "assembly call," a tune he had composed, whistled loud and shrill, brought all twelve children on the gallop from wherever they were or whatever they were at. Tonsillectomies and excursions were en masse. Education assailed the children on all sides, not merely at school but in the bathroom and wherever a chart, a bulletin board, vocabulary lists, or mathematical problems could be posted. When this lively family group was broken by the sudden death of the beloved father, Mrs. Gilbreth took over. She gave the speeches in London and Prague that her husband was to have delivered and she carried on his work for the rest of her long life. A son and daughter wrote this account of a remarkable and hilarious family life, and someday there will have to be a biography of the distinguished woman, mother of a dozen, who, in her eighties and still at work, remarked, "Oddly enough at this age, I am still living in and planning for the future."

Fifth Chinese Daughter, by Jade Snow Wong, ill. by Kathryn Uhl. Harper, 1950.

When Jade Wong grew up in Chinatown, she had no idea that she was "ghettoized" in the modern sense of the word. Her parents were proud of their homogeneous neighborhood which enabled them to maintain many of their native traditions so precious to them. The children enjoyed it too, except for one deplorable drawback. At the end of their public school day, they had to proceed directly to the Chinese school, where they studied the Chinese language and its difficult calligraphy. Jade was gently and lovingly nurtured; and when she was a child, the old ways of her parents seemed good and proper. But by high school days, problems of dress and dates became acute. Only deep family affection and trust solved these. This is an enchanting record of Chinese customs and celebrations as well as the gradually unfolding talents of young Jade, who is now a well-known ceramist. Her happy adjustment to the dual demands of her Chinese-American life makes this an unusually significant book.

Dance to the Piper, by Agnes de Mille. Little, 1952. (12 up)

This autobiography of a ballet dancer and famous choreographer will delight girls whether or not they are interested in the dance. It is the story of Agnes de Mille's struggle to emerge from a pampered childhood into the grueling adult disciplines of the ballet. First, she

had to contend with her own plump body and with what she considered
to be an undistinguished appearance. Then, there was the killing
daily practice until every bone and muscle were under her control.
But her determination and complete devotion to the art of the dance
never wavered, despite bitter discouragements. Any young girl will
be better for reading this difficult pursuit of perfection, and will understand clearly that if good grooming, a fine body, and bodily skills are
to be achieved, indulgence must go.

Born Free: A Lioness of Two Worlds, by Joy Adamson, ill. with photographs. Pantheon, 1960. Also *Living Free: The Story of Elsa and
   Her Cubs.* Harcourt, 1961.
   The author of these books is married to George Adamson, Senior
Game Warden in a province of Kenya. His duties are to protect the
natives from prowling marauders outside the preserve, and to protect
the animals from poachers, who break into the preserve illegally. Joy
Adamson not only shares her husband's life but contributes her own
unique understanding and love of the wild creatures of the African
bush.
   On February 1, 1956, Adamson had to shoot an embattled lioness
to save his own life, but he brought home her three cubs for Joy to
raise. The two bigger cubs were eventually sent to a zoo, but Joy
kept Elsa, the smallest cub, and trained her much as you might train
an intelligent puppy. The first book is an account of Elsa's infancy,
cub days, and gradual maturing, during which she grew completely
into the lives and hearts of the Adamsons. She hunted with them,
fished, slept in their tents, adored Joy and loved George and his three
helpers. If her affection was often too athletic to be acceptable, she
was gradually trained to reasonably decorous behavior and obedience.
Her love for and dependence on her human family, even after she had
matured, was so complete the Adamsons began to question their own
success with this wild creature. Shouldn't she begin to live as a lion,
learn to hunt, kill, and guard her food? Shouldn't she learn lions,
instead of humans, mate, and raise her cubs? They decided in the
affirmative, and so the retraining of Elsa began. George watched over
her hunting, her first encounter with other lions, and her adaptation
to the demands of being on her own and not having her food provided.
She seemed happy enough, but always she would come tearing home
to the Adamsons' camp with the most violent demonstrations of affection and joy. Here was something everyone said could never happen

—an animal wild and natural in her native habitat but completely tame with the people who had raised her.

The second book tells of Elsa's mating, her cubs, and their lives in this unheard of balance between being wild predators and loving pets. Elsa never made a mistake. Her cubs were rougher and wilder, but to the end of her days Elsa remained gentle and vociferously affectionate. The splendid photographs and, of course, Walt Disney's moving picture enhance the fascination of these books.

The Ring of Bright Water, by Gavin Maxwell, ill. by photographs. Dutton, 1961.

Perhaps only the most dedicated young naturalists will read all this long record of a young man's life with two successive otters. But if they will start with Part II, "Living with Otters," they will get the gist of the book and can go back to Part I later if they wish. His first otter, Mijbil, came from the marshes of Arabia, and his second one, Edal, an entirely different species, came from West Africa. The photographs show strangely endearing animals, beautiful, funny, and indefatigably playful. So many studies are being made of porpoises, whales, and other water creatures that our respect for these animals has increased; Gavin Maxwell's accounts of his otters will reinforce that respect. How he ever managed to transport Mijbil from Basara and Cairo to London and later to Scotland is a hilarious story in itself. But once at home in a wild, remote part of the Scottish Highlands, with streams, waterfalls, and the sea, Mijbil really came into his own and was completely happy. There were no near neighbors, but a few remote ones he loved, and for miles around he was a well-known personality, friendly, amiable, and harmless. Yet a perfect environment did not give Mij security. He was killed by some unscrupulous man for his pelt. The second otter, Edal, was still alive at the end of the book, which also includes brief accounts of other wild creatures. The photographs of Mijbil and Edal would send any animal lover on a search for an otter; although as a housemate, he leaves some things to be desired.

Anne Frank: Diary of a Young Girl. Doubleday, 1952.
Introduction by Eleanor Roosevelt.

It is possible that this haunting diary of a little Jewish girl who lived from her thirteenth to fifteenth year in a wretched hide-out, and finally died in the Nazi camp at Bergen-Belsen, will be too poignant

for some young readers to endure. Yet it is also a gay, tolerant, humorous
record of one little girl who grew into maturity under the most adverse
circumstances without losing her sense of romance, her love of people
and nature, and her own unique wisdom. It happened during the
German occupation of Holland, when the Nazis began hunting down
and deporting the Jews to their infamous camps. Anne's father de-
vised a hide-out at the back and upper floors of his office building.
He made it shelter his family of four and four others. There they lived
with one toilet forever going out of order, little privacy, less and less
food, and constant fear of discovery. Anne's diary begins gaily with her
thirteenth birthday celebration with lots of presents, among them
this diary which she begins at once. The early entries are full of her
enjoyment of her school, her friends, especially boys, her difficulties
with her mother, her happy zest for living. During the years of hiding,
her vignettes of the occupants of the "annexe," their quarrels, weaknesses, and courage are acid and humorous. She herself has an early
romance about which she consults her father quite frankly and fully.
It never goes far, only two lonely, frightened young things finding
comfort in being together. Their discomforts and fears increase steadily
until that awful day when the Nazis find them and the diary ends.
Oddly enough, the Gestapo searched everything, but dumped the diary on the floor and left it. And that little book became not only a witness
to their inhumanity but a testimonial to the indomitable human spirit
that can rise above deprivation and suffering to rejoice in little glimpses
of sky, the sound of bird song, and an unshakeable belief in the essential goodness of man. This is one of the rare documents of this
century.

Anna and the King of Siam, by Margaret Landon, ill. by Margaret
   Ayer. Day, 1944.
   This is the record of an English widow, Anna Leonowens, who,
in 1862, journeyed with her little boy to Siam to become a governess
to the numerous children of the king. Anna found herself instructing
not merely the king's children but also his wives and concubines and
serving as his secretary. Because of Anna's interest in and sympathy
for these helpless women of the court, she became, in spite of herself,
deeply involved in their lives and the lives of their children. This
often brought her into violent conflict with the king and led to some
of the most dramatic and terrible episodes in the book. Sometimes
her pleas for justice and mercy prevailed, but not always, and some

of the king's decisions shocked her to the core of her being. The fact that she could sometimes help and that she was making a deep and lasting impression on the women and on the boy who was to be the next king, kept her at her post. Because of broken health, she finally went back to England but promised to return. With the king's death, however, it was unnecessary for her to keep her promise.

This record of Leonowens' five years of living in the court of Siam is as colorful as any novel, but for young readers who have seen either the play or the moving picture it must be said that the romantic overtones these productions accorded Anna's story are completely lacking in the book. The abridged version is very satisfactory, by the way.

Kon-Tiki, by Thor Heyerdahl, tr. by F. H. Lyon, ill. by photographs. Rand McNally, 1950.

A book for the whole family to enjoy either together in reading aloud or individually, *Kon-Tiki* is a universal favorite. Don't use the edition prepared for children; the whole book is not too long or too difficult. It relates the frustrating preparations for the trip and then the incredible journey of six young men, from Peru across the Pacific Ocean on a raft named *Kon-Tiki* in memory of the Peruvian sun-god, who "vanished westward across the sea." They had no engine, only a sail and the winds and the ocean currents to propel them. Whether or not their landing on a Tahitian island proves that the Polynesians came from South America by that route is still debated, but no one who reads the day-to-day record of their voyage can have any doubts about the daring of their experiment. For young people who have loved the book and have a chance to go to Oslo, Norway, it is a special thrill to visit the Kon-Tiki Museum. On the first floor is the raft from the deck up, with the funny little hut the men lived in, and all their scanty equipment. Then, down below is a reproduction of the underwater scene with fish and even a great killer whale swimming around and under the raft. One hump of the whale's back and it would have been all over with both raft and men. The photographs of their journey and experiences are preserved, and the whole exhibit seems entirely worthy of a museum close by the Viking Museum with all the early Viking ships. These look fairly seaworthy after that fragile bit of balsa wood—the Kon-Tiki raft.

See also *Aku-Aku* (1958), "an account of the 1955 Norwegian Archaeological Expedition to Easter Island and the East Pacific, organized and led by the author."

A FEW NINETEENTH-CENTURY CLASSICS

If the preceding lists of adult novels and factual records seem too casual an approach to serious adult reading, recall that many young people have ahead of them a highly organized and somewhat formidable curriculum of high-school English and American literature. Brilliant and gifted English teachers—and there are many of them—can help youngsters fall in love with at least a few of the so-called classics.

The home can help, too. Just as an early familiarity with picture stories can help prepare the six-year-old for his first encounters with reading, so a sampling of popular adult books and a few of the classics can ease the teen-age reader into the stiff dose of literature that lies ahead of him. These books may be bought in paperback editions or may be obtained from the public library. But whatever you do, don't try to institute a home course in English and American literature, and don't pressure your teen-ager to "read better books"! Instead, when his activities lag a bit (if ever), you might say, "Have you ever tried *Treasure Island?* It's a rousing story of a treasure hunt." Or "This nineteenth-century novel, *Jane Eyre*, is a chiller, and it moves along so fast that you can hardly put it down." Or "Did you know that Becky Sharp in *Vanity Fair* is a full-length portrait of a real gold digger?" Such casual remarks will sometimes induce a youngster to take a look at one of these novels, especially if it is a paperback.

This last remark must sound like heresy to adults brought up on fine editions of Charles Dickens', Jane Austen's, or Thackeray's novels. But to young people, there is something grim and forbidding about those long lines of well-bound, dull-looking books. Most youngsters wouldn't be caught dead carrying a hardback edition of one of those novels, but they will tuck a paperback into their pockets and read it unself-consciously. So be grateful for the paperbacks, because practically all of the classics and most of the adult books already mentioned are to be found in paperback editions. And when there is a moving picture based on *Gone with the Wind* or *Lord of the Flies* or *Wuthering Heights*, young people invariably flock to the stores to buy the paperback edition of the book, and so you will find them enjoying novels you would ordinarily not expect them to read except under duress.

Here are a few classics teen-agers have been known to read and enjoy on their own. Any one or all of these will promote their reading maturity and get them to the point where they can tackle long, detailed stories without quailing. However, it must be admitted that the length and the details of the earlier novels are sometimes stumbling blocks. Young people are so used to the journalistic, staccato style of many modern authors that they have no patience with the slower-paced novels of the past. Jane Austen's novels, for instance, with their "small canvas" infinitely embroidered, may discourage a young reader until he gets used to their unique style. And that is why *Jane Eyre* is more readily accepted than *Pride and Prejudice*. But once a young person accepts the leisurely pace of Jane Austen or George Eliot or William Thackeray, he is well on his way to becoming a discriminating reader. At least expose him to these books and hope for the best.

Pride and Prejudice (1813) and *Emma* (1816), by Jane Austen.

Pride and Prejudice and *Emma* are two of Jane Austen's most highly praised novels. The first is about a middle-class family, the Bennets, who have five grown-up daughters—Jane, Elizabeth, Mary, Catherine, and Lydia. The book is mostly concerned with Elizabeth and her suitor Darcy, who represent the prejudice and pride of the title. The heroine of the second book is wealthy Emma Woodhouse, who devotes her time to taking care of her invalid father and to meddling, with the best of intentions, in the love affairs of others. Jane Austen's effortless prose marches along with its own special rhythm and relates absorbing stories of quite unexceptional people of the various levels of the English gentry—scheming mammas, daughters ambitious or mousey, young men dashing or the reverse, but never stereotypes, just blundering human beings, sometimes stooping to villainy but generally erring through mistaken judgment, like the rest of us. Lest boys think these are girl stories, they should know that many men rank Jane Austen as a favorite author to be read and reread. For example, John Kenneth Galbraith, the well-known economist and author, reported that he rereads Jane Austen not only for pleasure but "to prime his own writing pump."[1]

Jane Eyre (1847) by Charlotte Brontë; and *Wuthering Heights* (1847) by Emily Brontë.

[1]*Time*, February 16, 1968, page 28.

For many a girl, *Jane Eyre* is the classic first novel, never to be forgotten. Unlike many heroines, Jane is small and plain, but she has great courage and integrity. An unloved and unlovely orphan, she spends the first ten years of her life with an aunt and cousins who despise her, the next eight at a boarding school for orphans, first as a student and then for two years as a teacher. At eighteen years of age she goes to live at Thornfield, a bleak English manor house, where she is governess to the young ward of the wealthy, saturnine owner— Edward Rochester. It is in this home that Jane finds a deep, passionate love, but on the day of her intended marriage to Rochester, she learns that he already has a wife, an insane creature hidden away in an upper wing of Thornfield. After a period of time and after many other events, including the suicide of the insane woman, the destruction of Thornfield, and the blinding of Edward, the lovers are reunited. Despite the stilted dialogue and the sometimes incredible plot, this is a stirring and dramatic tale, and Jane is a very real and human heroine.

Wuthering Heights is a somber story of the tragic love of Heathcliff, a strange, violent orphan, and Catherine Earnshaw, the daughter of his foster father. After Catherine's marriage to Edgar Linton, Heathcliff devotes himself to revenge on the Earnshaws and Lintons and on their children, including his own son, the child of his marriage to Isabella Linton.

Out of their unhappy childhood and youth and even more tragic maturity, Charlotte and Emily and their sister Ann wrote their stories and poems and watched their talented brother Branwell waste his life. It was he, with his wooden soldiers (see *The Return of the Twelves*, pp. 159-160), who started all of them living in a world of imagination and writing about it.

The Last of the Mohicans (1826), by James Fenimore Cooper.

The Last of the Mohicans is probably the most popular of Cooper's Leatherstocking tales: *The Pioneers* (1823), *The Last of the Mohicans* (1826), *The Prairie* (1827), *The Pathfinder* (1840), and *The Deerslayer* (1841). The five novels are held together loosely by the character of Natty Bumppo, variously known as Leatherstocking, Deerslayer, Pathfinder, and Hawkeye (as he is referred to in *The Last of the Mohicans*). The setting for the story is the lake and forest region of what is now upper New York State, "during the third year of the war which England and France last waged for the possession of a country that neither was destined to retain," and the climactic historical event is the massacre at Fort William Henry on August 9, 1757. The principal characters include Bumppo; brave young Uncas, "the last of the Mohicans"; his father, Chingachgook; Cora and Alice Munro, the beautiful daughters of the commander of Fort William Henry; Duncan Heyward, a young major; and Magua, their implacable enemy. The action is swift and bloody, with daring pursuits, captures, and escapes, and it ends tragically with the death of Cora and Uncas. The story communicates vividly Cooper's love for the unspoiled wilderness and the simpler life it fostered and his great respect for the Indian, whom he described as "daring, boastful, cunning, ruthless, self-denying, and self-devoted" in war and "just, generous, hospitable, revengeful, superstitious, modest, and commonly chaste" in peace.

The Mill on the Floss (1860), by George Eliot (born Mary Ann Evans).

Young people's first encounter with George Eliot is usually *Silas Marner.* A better introduction might be *The Mill on the Floss,* despite its length and complexity. It is primarily the story of Maggie Tulliver, a passionate, impulsive, and mischievous child and adolescent, a young woman torn between her "duties and desires, loyalties and loves." It is certainly not without humor, particularly in the first part of the story in the depiction of Maggie's aunts and uncles and their families. The story is also about Maggie's beloved older brother, Tom, almost her complete opposite in temperament. After a long estrangement, the two are finally reconciled in the last tragic episode, just before they are drowned together in the great flooding of the Floss.

Oliver Twist (book form 1838), *David Copperfield* (1850), and *A Tale of Two Cities* (1859), by Charles Dickens.

For Dickens' fans, every one of his novels is a must, offering as each does a vast and unforgettable gallery of characters. But of all his books, these three generally make an immediate appeal to young readers. *David Copperfield* is largely autobiographical, especially the picture of the young poverty-stricken David and of the famous Mr. Micawber, always "waiting for something to turn up," who is modeled after Dickens' own father. When young Oliver in *Oliver Twist* is taken out of the workhouse he runs away only to fall into the hands of the Artful Dodger and his master Fagin. With Fagin and his gang of thieves, Oliver is taught against his will to steal—a dramatic story heightened by the moving picture and the musical. These books as well as other Dickens novels give such revealing glimpses of the London of Dickens' day that that city and the author are forever associated. *A Tale of Two Cities* takes place in London and Paris during the time of the French Revolution and tells of the love of two men, who resemble each other strikingly, for Lucie Manette. Because of his love for Lucie, Sydney Carton goes to the guillotine in place of the man whom Lucie loves. For some readers, Dickens never becomes a favorite. Others read book after book and discuss them as if their events had just taken place. Young people should at least have a look at one or more of these novels.

Treasure Island (1883), *Kidnapped* (1886), and *The Strange Case of Dr. Jekyll and Mr. Hyde* (1886), by Robert Louis Stevenson.

Stevenson, whose life was as romantic as his stories, had great fun concocting the yarn told in *Treasure Island*. He tried it out on his step-

For all the world, I was led like a dancing bear (page 225)

This illustration is reprinted by permission of Charles Scribner's Sons: Illustration by N. C. Wyeth from *Treasure Island* by Robert Louis Stevenson.

son and they enjoyed it together. Stevenson himself was enthralled with the colorful villain he had created—Long John Silver, crutch under his arm and parrot on his shoulder, as smooth a pirate as ever trod the boards. The bumbling old Squire and the sagacious Doctor were of course no match for Silver, and their hunt for treasure was nearly fatal. Through all the excitement, young Jim Hawkins was in and out of tight places as only a boy could be. And although this is a pirate story and a tale of a treasure hunt, standards of decent or of devious behavior emerge, and the emphasis on the moral code by both Squire and Doctor impresses Jim as well as the reader.

Kidnapped is the exciting tale of the kidnapping and subsequent adventures of David Balfour in the year 1751.

The Strange Case of Dr. Jekyll and Mr. Hyde is a different matter. A kind of parable, on the simplest level it is a horror story about a man who is a mild and philanthropic doctor at times and a fiendish monster at others. The truth is that Dr. Jekyll has discovered potions by which he can change himself into Mr. Hyde and back again into Dr. Jekyll whenever he wishes to. He is finally revolted at a particular repulsive act of Mr. Hyde's, but he discovers that he no longer has complete control of the changes, can no longer at will shift back to Dr. Jekyll. In all three books, Stevenson tells an absorbing story in vigorous style.

Vanity Fair (1848), by William Makepeace Thackeray.

Thackeray's novels are indubitably lengthy, and *Vanity Fair* is no exception, but it is easier to read than his others partly because of the enthralling character of unscrupulous Becky Sharp. This is the drama of the rise and fall of a beguiling and completely amoral adventuress. Amelia Sedley, Becky's sweet, good, kindhearted school friend, is presumably the heroine, but Becky far overshadows the pallid Amelia. There is a magnificent account in this book of the Battle of Waterloo, but on the eve of this momentous event, it is beautiful Becky who steals the show.

The first sections of this chapter review a few well-written books for teen-agers, but later sections edge young people along into adult reading. Some children make this transition easily and as early as twelve years old, by picking up some book adults are discussing. Reading it gives the young person new stature in the family, and he is intrigued by glimpses of adult problems and

behavior. When this casual transition does not occur and a youngster continues to read more and more youth novels, there is danger
that these will prolong his immaturity and satisfaction with stereotypes. At this point, he needs to be introduced to some wholesome
adult fiction and to some factual records that give him an adult
viewpoint and expand his horizons by vicarious experiences with
a variety of people and backgrounds—some sordid or sophisticated,
or humorous, or cynical, or full of mystery and excitement. These
popular adult books, not too hard to read or understand, will help
him grow into the adult world and into the more mature reading
that lies ahead of him in his high-school and college courses.
Encountering the classics in the home will also assist him to ease
into this more difficult reading. Have some paperback editions of
these books around the house. They are less forbidding in appearance than the heavy hardbacks, and are actually an invitation to
read. Above all, don't urge certain books on your teen-ager, but
assist him unobtrusively to discover adult books he can read and
enjoy. They will in turn help him meet the next level of life with
more understanding and confidence.

PART THREE
READING IN SPECIAL AREAS

POETRY

11

The English language possesses one of the greatest bodies of lyric poetry in the world, and in earlier times, people read and spoke poetry because they loved it. Today, cultured British adults and youths still know quantities of noble verse, and speak it unselfconsciously when some association suggests it. This is generally not true of cultivated Americans today, perhaps because in their childhood they did not hear poetry read or spoken in the home. Yet here is this great body of English poetry waiting for children and young people to explore and absorb. Not to prepare them to enjoy some part of this special area of literature is to deprive them of one of their richest legacies.

"THE MUSIC AND THE DANCE OF WORDS"

Fortunately, small children invariably enjoy poetry as long as it is read to them by someone who likes it and reads it well. Their

enjoyment comes first from hearing the gay sounds of the words.
That is the way people long ago enjoyed the traditional ballads
and nursery jingles—from hearing bards or minstrels or scops or
troubadours chant or sing the old story poems for adults, and
nurses or grannies the jingles for children. The melodies made
both kinds of verses fun to hear and so easily remembered that
they were passed on by word of mouth for generations. The qualities of the verses that people enjoyed then are the same qualities
children first enjoy when they hear poetry today—melody and
movement, or "tune and runningness,"[1] or the "music and the
dance of words."[2] So, you see, children discover naturally through
their ears what some adults never find out until they read aloud,
that poetry, like music, is an aural art. The nursery jingles dance,
skip, run, hop, or swing gently. Other poems make a joyful noise
or have a solemn quietness. They may sound powerful or as
fluttery as a butterfly. Over and over again, the music and the
dance of words and lines reflect or reinforce the mood or the meaning of a poem from *Mother Goose* to Browning and Dylan Thomas.
Also this movement in words and lines makes little melodies
that are as ear-catching as a song. A child hears you speak the
hopping words of Christina Rossetti's

> And timid, funny, brisk little bunny,
> Winks his nose and sits all sunny.

and the tune makes him remember it, so that he begins to say the
poem with you. And the lovely, gentle melody in the refrain of
Stevenson's "The Wind"

> O wind a-blowing all day long,
> O wind that sings so loud a song.

is as haunting and as readily recalled as any song. And isn't it
better to have children unconsciously memorizing gay, beautiful
verse rather than the banal singing commercials, which also
utilize melody and movement to make people remember the
advertisements in spite of themselves?

Because poetry "will always exist as the music and the dance

[1]Walter de la Mare, *Come Hither.* Knopf, 1923 (first edition, many later ones),
p. xxxi.
[2]Elizabeth Drew, *Poetry: A Modern Guide to Its Understanding and Enjoyment.*
Dell, 1959, p. 26.

of words," it is important to treat it in the beginning as an aural art like music. Music can be read silently from a printed score, but its power cannot be fully enjoyed or understood until it is played or listened to. So poems may be read silently from the printed page, but their meaning and beauty cannot be fully savored until they are spoken aloud and listened to. As we said, children like poetry as long as someone who speaks it well, reads it to them with enjoyment. Then, hearing it spoken, children catch its melody and movement, and these in turn give them clues to its meaning. But if they are asked to read the queer-looking stuff from the printed page, when their reading skills are still faltering, they will probably derive neither enjoyment nor meaning from it. The lines, sometimes long and sometimes short; the delayed meanings; the rhyming words, which often lead them into faulty emphasis; and, above all, the compelling meter, which sends them galloping faster and faster—all these can turn a poem into a meaningless jumble. They begin to mutter about poetry assignments—"Oh, *not* poetry." And gradually such experiences may accumulate so that as adults they would never think of picking up a book of poems to read for enjoyment. If this is true for you, try reading poetry aloud or have someone in the family who really enjoys poetry read it to you. Explore a new anthology or the collected poems of a new poet with your family and see when you speak the poems or hear them spoken if they don't become alive and meaningful to an astonishing degree. This is not surprising, because poets use the sound, melody, and movement of their poems to clarify the meaning of the words, and over and over again when the meaning eludes readers, both old and young, it is because they do not *hear* the poems.

THE CONDENSATION OF POETRY

But often one reading is not enough. Sometimes several readings are required for us to fully understand and appreciate a poem. Why is this so? Why is poetry that is above the jingle or nonsense levels often difficult to understand? First, because of its extreme condensation. It packs into a few lines or stanzas an intense experience, often sensory—a keen response to seeing, hearing, smelling, touching, or tasting. Sometimes it is a response to an emotion—grief, joy, surprise, love, anger, longing; or to an idea— a sudden flash of understanding, a perception of meaning, of likeness or contrast that carries new significance. And great poetry communicates these experiences with a minimum of words, but *such* words—strong, vigorous words; delicate or passionate words; but always words chosen for their precise meaning or their emotional significance. And it is this concentration that forces us to read carefully and thoughtfully for the meanings the poet has only suggested. In poetry, in short, experience is so distilled and intensified that, except for the simplest little verses, poems must be read and reread for full meaning. This is why reading aloud helps. You speak a poem several times, and gradually additional meanings are revealed and your bewilderment vanishes. Suddenly the poem speaks to *you*, gives you an authentic chill up your backbone or a feeling of such complete oneness with the experience or emotion or idea the poem is about that it is forever *your* poem and you can read it so that others will share your understanding and enjoyment. This recalls a city boy who knew nothing about "lambkins frolicking with their mothers," but *did* know taxis. No one could speak Rachel Field's "Taxis"—"Ho, for taxis green or blue"—with the verve and enjoyment of this child. It was his poem by right of experience and pleasure. And eventually, it is to be hoped, he moved on to accepting and entering into new experiences by way of poetry. If he did, it probably was because some adult who knew and loved many kinds of poems shared her enjoyment with him, by reading them aloud again and again, answering his questions, leading him to an amplification of meanings—in short, beginning gently the process of reading poetry "in depth." But, someone may object, if poetry is as difficult as all that, why bother about it? What values has poetry over and beyond the immense values of prose in its many varieties?

QUALITIES OF POETRY

The words

In poetry, the choice of words is of first importance for the communication of an experience, an idea, or a mood, heightened and intensified by the very condensation of the expression. The precision of the words of poetry can not only enlarge the child's vocabulary but make him more sensitive to the music and cadence of our English language. The melody and the dance of words almost compel the recall of the poem. *Mother Goose*'s "One misty moisty morning" sings; Winifred Welles' "Skipping Along Alone" has a melody that is remembered even if the child has never been on an ocean beach; Mildred Plew Meigs' "The Pirate Don Durk of Dowdee" stamps along amusingly with piratical swagger; Christina Rossetti's "Oh, fair to see/Bloom-laden cherry tree" is both a picture and a melody that sings quietly; Robert Frost's "The woods are lovely, dark and deep,/But I have promises to keep" are strangely haunting words that you do not forget. And young people are comforted by that great ringing fugue of Dylan Thomas, "And Death Shall Have No Dominion." These are just a few fairly obvious examples of the way the words of poetry when they are chosen both for their meaning and their melody make the power and beauty of our language evident and memorable even to a young child.

The imagery

The imagery of poetry is another contribution to enlarging the child's perceptions, helping him to see contrasts and likenesses and to make unusual associations. Imagery begins as simply as *Mother Goose*'s personification of a flower as a fine lady all dressed up—"Daffadowndilly/ Has come up to town,/ In a yellow petticoat/ And a green gown." Carl Sandburg likens his baby in a bath tub, all soapy and slippery, to a "fish child." Stevenson hears a wild night wind as a mysterious rider galloping by "All night long in the dark and wet," and William D. Sargent hears this same wild night wind as a pack of "Wind-Wolves" hunting "the frightened bands of cloud-deer" across the sky. Images as they grow more complex and more subtle quicken the child's perceptions, stimulate his imagination, and presently begin to suggest fuller and deeper meanings. But to literal-minded children they may also be stumbling blocks to understanding. Only through reading and rereading with casual explanations can you be sure that your young listeners are not seeing a real man galloping up and down in "Windy Nights"; or visualizing real wolves hunting down real deer in "Wind-Wolves"; or confusing Cat with a real criminal in

T. S. Eliot's delightful nonsense poem "Macavity: The Mystery Cat." This sounds painfully elementary, but be warned that such misinterpretations do occur and that understanding is worth working for.

The insights

"Surprised by joy" may describe a poet's own joyful surprise when he gropes for and finds the precise words or image to express his meaning. So the reader of poetry may experience a flash of insight, a sudden illumination, when he catches the poet's meaning and shares his experience or emotion or mood. This entering into the poem is much like the identification of the reader with a character in a story. With a simple, readily understood poem, such intuitive insight may come immediately. For instance, a child who knows the seashore from long experience readily enters into the mood and sees himself, like Winifred Welles' child, "Skipping Along Alone" with the waves rolling in, shore birds skittering back and forth, and the sand under his feet; or he becomes the child in A. A. Milne's "Sand-Between-the-Toes" going to the beach with his father in a great gale of wind and coming home all sandy. But read these two poems to an inland child, and at first he may not be interested because he does not know sand, sea, shore birds, and ocean gales. But does that mean that children can read only about their personal experiences? Certainly not! Both these poems are so full of the fun of ocean shores, the mystery and the changing mood of the water, and the action of beachgoers that children can get a new experience vicariously and not only sense the fun but picture themselves exploring alone, or striding through the gale, full of sand but triumphant.

Elizabeth Drew speaks of two different responses to a poem as "recognition" and "revelation."[3] For the shore child, these poems would bring *recognition* of like experiences. For the landlocked child, they would give *revelation*, a flash of insight or understanding. Both responses are helped by rereading the poems aloud with reminiscence of other solitary strolls or family sorties to the beach or recollections of similar exciting outdoor activities— walking in the woods or walking city streets when a hard wind is blowing—any personal experiences that make the poems more

[3] *Poetry: A Modern Guide to Understanding and Enjoyment.* Dell, 1959, p. 31.

real. This is a first step in understanding, a *translation of the experience or scene or idea of the poem into our own experiences.*

LEVELS OF MEANING

Except for the simplest and most obvious verses, poetry often has deeper or secondary or symbolic meanings that lie well beyond the obvious meanings of the words. How far can we pursue these deeper levels of meaning with children without becoming heavy handed and spoiling their voluntary exploration of poetry? Again, reading aloud is the answer.

A small boy came to a children's librarian announcing that he must have a poem for "Clean-Up Week." The librarian was baffled but provided her client with two good anthologies. He came back triumphant with exactly the right poem, Robert Frost's "The Pasture," with its first line, "I'm going out to clean the pasture spring." The boy probably saw the children scurrying round cleaning up all the debris old Winter had left behind on the city streets. He had no spring to clean or young calf to watch, but he had made a translation, and Robert Frost would probably have been amused and pleased with this first level of appreciation. But suppose the teacher or some other adult had picked up the interpretation from there, asking the child what kind of chores he did that were more fun when a friend was along? Going to the store for mother or raking the leaves for father is not so interesting or so much fun if we are alone, but delightful when "You come too" and we can talk as we go along. These final words of both stanzas of "The Pasture"—"You come too"—are the heart of the poem and they are also the words which Frost chose as the title for a collection of his own poems for children and young people— a book that is a must for every home. "You come too" points up the universal hunger for companionship that at its best can heighten joy and soften sorrow. With a friend, a brother, a sister, or a beloved as a companion, life is always better and more satisfactory in every way.

Read aloud any of the poems in *Prayers from the Ark,* and you will find that children as young as seven or eight enjoy hearing them and catch at once the idea that the prayers tell a lot about the animals. That is, the Cock is cocky, the Cat is catty, the Giraffe is snooty, and the Old Horse is sad. But presently, as the children hear or speak these amusing or touching little verses, they begin to understand also how like themselves and other people these animals turn out to be. The Butterfly is a sort of fluttery, flighty Vera Vague. The Cock is a boaster. The Little Ducks are selfish, ridiculous snobs. This is a second level of perception for somewhat older children. Very likely only fairly mature children will also read into these gentle satires a rather biting condemnation of the kinds of prayers people sometimes pray. Perhaps "The Little Ducks" will remind them of their own childish prayers that it must not rain on the day of the school picnic. Or of prayers only for our kind of people—"all folk who quack." This is amplifying an idea at a fairly mature level.

Y O U   C O M E   T O O

FAVORITE POEMS FOR YOUNG READERS

R O B E R T   F R O S T

With wood engravings by T H O M A S W. N A S O N

HENRY HOLT AND COMPANY · NEW YORK

In *Children and Books*[4] there is a detailed description of a gifted teacher reading aloud to his class Robert Frost's "Stopping by Woods on a Snowy Evening," and carrying the children into deeper and deeper levels of meaning, chiefly by letting them hear the poem again and again. They discussed it first as a scene so vividly described they could draw or paint it from the words. Then they were reminded of times when the end of the day comes with a lot of work unfinished, sometimes even work they had promised to do but hadn't—"promises to keep." This seemed to complete the possible interpretations, but the teacher read the poem again, and one child, with one of those intuitive flashes of insight, "revelation," said hesitatingly, "Could the poet be talking about the end of life? Could he mean death?" The child of course had never heard of adult interpretations of this poem as a "death wish." But hearing those words "The woods are lovely, dark and deep," . . ."And miles to go before I sleep," she suddenly was caught by the idea of life ending with still so much to do, to see, to create, to finish—"And miles to go before I sleep."

If children can grow with one poem into these deeper levels of meaning, think of the riches that lie ahead of them as they explore poetry at more and more mature levels of meaning. Symbolism in poetry is perhaps most difficult for children and difficult even for youth, although the incident just described is a perfect example of what can be done, casually.

GOALS IN USING POETRY WITH CHILDREN

For the most part, the symbolism of poetry and the intricacies of its metrical forms seem well beyond the interests of children. Analysis of these qualities probably belongs to later adolescence or maturity. Our goals in exposing children to poetry are much simpler. What we want first and foremost is that *children will enjoy poems so whole-heartedly* that they will speak them, sometimes with us and sometimes alone, vigorously and unaffectedly for pure pleasure. Second, we hope that as a result of hearing and speaking poems *they will memorize* many of their favorites,

[4]May Hill Arbuthnot, *Children and Books,* Third Edition. Scott, Foresman and Company, 1964, p. 203.

not because they are forced to, but because they want to. (Unison speech, by the way, will aid memorization.) Third, we want to help them *explore all sorts of poems*—light verse, jingles, nonsense, story poems, dialogue, lyrics. Such exploration will be furthered by introducing children to a variety of poets, so that they will know at least some poems by author and book. Fourth, as part of this exploration, children should *learn what an anthology is and how to use it.* Show them the indexes—by author, title, first line, and even subject matter, so that they can find their patriotic poems or poems about travel or pets or whatever they need. And finally, very gently, very casually, help children *grow in poetry*—first, by encouraging them to translate unfamiliar experience into something familiar and understandable; second, by carrying them, without any nagging analysis, into the occasional larger or deeper meaning that lies beyond the literal sense of the words. To accomplish these goals, we must *start where children are*, with limited tastes perhaps only for humorous verse, or with a literal interpretation of any poem, and then we must carry them to the point where they can take poems of subtler meanings and better poetic qualities.

VALUES IN POETRY

Why so much emphasis on so special an area of literature as poetry? you may ask. One reason is that we are living in a period of unusual anxieties, discord, and violence, some of which are bound to affect children. In contrast, poetry is a highly ordered art, "a stay against confusion," as Robert Frost put it. To write or to read and enjoy a poem is to discover one little portion of life that is whole and meaningful. A poem takes a segment of life that is absurd or moving or tragic and sums it up, not as something trivial, but meaningful, whole, and significant. So a poem can literally open our eyes to the tragic and the absurd, and to the sheer beauty and excitement of life.

Moreover, the words of poetry have special values as language training. Because poetry is so disciplined an art, poets must use words with precision and with an ear for their sound. Poetry more than any other form of literature provides children with a rich use of words, words chosen with the utmost care for meaning, cadence, and aural effect. So the words of poetry are sparkling, dancing words; or strong, sonorous words; or words as quiet and peaceful as twilight. The child who has had rich experiences with poetry is bound to have an ear for the sounds and patterns of the English language and for other languages. Also because of the melodic patterns of the words and lines, poetry, like music, can comfort or arouse. It can lift young spirits or reassure them. Like music, it carries its own therapy.

Finally, poetry enjoyed and remembered is good armor against vulgarity and banality. It will help children to survive the oppressive anxieties of the adult world and it will immunize them against brutality. These are just a few reasons for giving children poetry.

ANTHOLOGIES FOR CHILDREN AND YOUNG PEOPLE

Time for Poetry, comp. by May Hill Arbuthnot and Shelton L. Root, Jr. Scott, 1968.
Over 770 poems, each section beginning with poems for very young children but including poetry that will carry a child through junior high school.

Sung Under the Silver Umbrella, comp. by The Association for Childhood Education International. Macmillan, 1935.
Around 250 choice selections for children 4-8.

The Golden Journey, comp. by Louise Bogan and William Jay Smith. Reilly & Lee, 1965. (10-14)
Compiled by two poets, this is a superb collection of authentic poetry for older children and youth.

The Birds and the Beasts Were There, comp. by William Cole. World, 1963. (6 up)
This is a popular collection of verse about all sorts of beasts. Mr. Cole's *Humorous Poetry for Children* is also a handy collection.

Roofs of Gold, comp. by Padraic Colum. Macmillan, 1964. (10 up)

Padraic Colum, Irish playwright, poet, and folklorist, has chosen his favorite poems from Shakespeare through Dylan Thomas.

Reflections on a Gift of Watermelon Pickle . . . and Other Modern Verse, comp. by Stephen Dunning, Edward Lueders, and Hugh Smith. Scott, 1966. Trade ed., Lothrop, 1967. (12 up)
A rich and varied collection of modern poems, most of them written during the lifetime of today's young people.

Lean Out of the Window, comp. by Sara Hannum and Gwendolyn E. Reed. Atheneum, 1965. (12 up)
Carefully selected modern poems for young people.

The Singing and the Gold: Poems Translated from World Literature, by Elinor Parker. Crowell, 1962. (12 up)

And they bought a pig, and some green jackdaws,
And a lovely monkey with lollipop paws,
And forty bottles of ring-bo-ree,
And no end of Stilton cheese.
 Far and few, far and few,
  Are the lands where the Jumblies live:
 Their heads are green, and their hands are blue;
  And they went to sea in a sieve.

And in twenty years they all came back,—
 In twenty years or more;
And every one said, "How tall they've grown!

For they've been to the Lakes, and the Torrible Zone,
And the hills of the Chankly Bore."
And they drank their health, and gave them a feast
Of dumplings made of beautiful yeast;
And every one said, "If we only live,
We, too, will go to sea in a sieve,
 To the hills of the Chankly Bore."
 Far and few, far and few,
  Are the lands where the Jumblies live:
 Their heads are green, and their hands are blue;
  And they went to sea in a sieve.

Illustration by Arthur Paul for "The Jumblies," by Edward Lear. From *Time for Poetry,* compiled by May Hill Arbuthnot and Shelton L. Root, Jr. Scott, Foresman and Company, 1968. Copyright © 1952, 1961, 1968 by Scott, Foresman and Company.

A book for children to grow into, for youth to grow with, and for poetry-loving adults to cherish.

The Earth Is the Lord's, comp. by Helen Plotz. Crowell, 1965. (12 up)
Inspirational poems of great variety, from the Psalms and the poetry of the classical writers to the poetry of Robert Frost and other moderns. It is mainly for adults and young adults, but there are a few choice bits for children too.
Another unusual collection of poems by Miss Plotz is *Imagination's Other Place*, with the poems about science and mathematics, ranging from atoms to relativity, Euclid to Einstein, and surgery to God. Of interest to teen-agers in general and to boys in particular.

A *Father Reads to His Children*, comp. by Orville Prescott. Dutton, 1965.
"An Anthology of Prose and Poetry" with an introduction by Mr. Prescott, the collection contains twenty-four poems and twenty-four stories that this father has enjoyed sharing with his children. They include old, familiar selections as well as recent, little-known ones, but all are of high literary quality. This book will enrich all children and adults who enjoy it together.

All the Silver Pennies, comp. by Blanche Jennings Thompson. Macmillan, 1967.
Silver Pennies, a children's favorite for forty years, and *More Silver Pennies* are reissued in an attractive single volume, illustrated by Ursula Arndt. Includes poems that even the youngest can enjoy along with many poems for older readers.

COLLECTIONS OF HAIKU AND OTHER ORIENTAL POEMS

The Japanese haiku has become popular with children as well as adults. These three books will inevitably lead to some creative experiments on the part of their readers.

Cricket Songs: Japanese Haiku, tr. by Harry Behn. Harcourt, 1964. (All ages)

For this volume, the poet Harry Behn has translated eighty-three delightful three-line poems.

The Moment of Wonder: A Collection of Chinese and Japanese Poetry,
   comp. by Richard Lewis. Dial, 1964. (All ages)
   Haiku and other choice selections illumine this little book. *In a Spring Garden* is another delightful collection by Mr. Lewis, also published by Dial, in 1965. The twenty-three haiku are exquisitely interpreted in color by Ezra Jack Keats.

COLLECTED VERSE OF INDIVIDUAL POETS

In Chapter 4, "Books Begin," adults were urged to use with young children a fine collection of the *Mother Goose* jingles and also Stevenson's *A Child's Garden of Verses* and A. A. Milne's *When We Were Very Young* and *Now We Are Six.* Here are some additional poets to whom children should be introduced during their preadolescent years.

Behn, Harry. *The Little Hill.* Harcourt, 1949. (5-9) *The Golden Hive.*
   Harcourt, 1966. (8 up)
   Harry Behn is one modern poet who is writing genuinely distinguished poetry for children and young people. His *Windy Morning* and *Wizard in the Well* are also for the 5's to 7's.

Benét, Rosemary Carr and Stephen Vincent. *Book of Americans.*
   Holt, 1933. (8-14)
   Patriots from Columbus to Woodrow Wilson are sketched with rare perception and considerable humor. This book should be in every school and home library.

Brooks, Gwendolyn. *Bronzeville Boys and Girls.* Harper, 1956. (7-11)
   The author is a Pulitzer Prize winner. These appealing poems are about the activities and problems of any of our children. Only the illustrations reveal them to be Negro children.

De la Mare, Walter. *Peacock Pie.* Knopf, 1961. First published in 1913.
   (5 up)
   This book for children and youth will never be outgrown. The poems are imaginative, provocative, and authentic.

Frost, Robert. *You Come Too*. Holt, 1959. (8 up)

This is Frost's own selection of his poetry to use with children and young people. Many of these poems he himself tried out with young audiences. Use with them records of the poet speaking his poems and follow this book with his last publication, *In the Clearing*, Holt, 1962.

Gasztold, Carmen Bernos de. *Prayers from the Ark*, tr. by Rumer Godden. Viking, 1962.

Tender, humorous, gently satirical, these prayers, supposedly uttered by all sorts of animals, are both amusing and moving.

McCord, David. *Far and Few*. Little, 1952. (8 up)

Deftly written light verses, these have unusual variety, charm, and occasionally a serious note.

McGinley, Phyllis. *All Around the Town*. Lippincott, 1948. (5-12)
The Year Without a Santa Claus. Lippincott, 1957. (5-6)

Noted for her witty adult writings, Phyllis McGinley is equally successful with her poems for children. The first book is an ABC of a big city, and each verse, with a picture by Helen Stone, is a gem. The second is a sparkling narrative poem about weary Santa's dreamed of but never achieved Christmas vacation, illustrated with Kurt Werth's gayest illustrations.

Innumerable little books of verses for children are appearing yearly. Some of them are worth examining, others are gay little nothings with pretty pictures. This small selection of light verse and lyrics, verses of the everyday and of the richly imaginative, will provide children and young people with a beginning in the experience of poetry.

BIOGRAPHY

12

When biography and historical fiction supplement each other richly, they should go side by side in children's reading. Children ordinarily make no distinction between the two. For instance, in the d'Aulaires' picture-biographies of *Leif the Lucky* or *Abraham Lincoln* young children find first-rate stories and have to be told that these men really lived and did the things the books say they did. On the other hand, even the older children find Johnny Tremain, the fictitious hero in the book by that title, every bit as real and authentic as Paul Revere, who appears in the same story. Children's and young people's confusion about or indifference to these distinctions is not surprising, because biography and fiction have some qualities in common, and biographies written for children lean even more heavily on the art of storytelling than adult biographies do.

The distinction between biography and historical fiction comes to children gradually. The child reads one of William Steele's rousing frontier stories and asks, "Did that really happen?" You have to answer in all honesty, "Perhaps not, but it could have happened just that way because the author knows a lot about those times, what was going on and how people lived." But when that same boy reads Nardi Campion's *Patrick Henry: Firebrand of the Revolution* and asks the same question, you may reply, "Yes, this *did* happen, because this is a biography, and in biographies the authors are supposed to tell you the facts as truthfully as possible. They look for the facts in all sorts of historical records —old letters, journals, records, and the like. A story is imagined, but a biography is as truthful as possible. What happens in a biography *did* happen."

Will he remember this distinction? Perhaps not, nor does it seem too important in these early years. But for adults, it is good to know that Daugherty's rousing biography of *Daniel Boone* will be even more convincing to the child who has read Steele's story *Tomahawks and Trouble* and that Freeman's biography *Lee of Virginia* will be enriched by Harold Keith's novel *Rifles for Watie*. And so we could go on pairing biography and fiction for almost any period of history to the enrichment of both areas of reading.

POPULARITY OF BIOGRAPHIES

Children's reading parallels adult reading

Biographies are growing more and more popular with children. The first reason is that trends in children's reading generally parallel trends in adult reading. Just at present, all sorts of informational books in general, including biography, are extremely popular with adults. And since adults choose books for children, it is not surprising to find biographies high on the preferred lists.

Improvement in biographies for children

A more compelling reason is that the lives of notable men and women have never before been so attractively presented to children and young people. The juvenile biographies of several decades ago often looked and were incredibly dull. Small print, crowded pages, dismal covers were bad enough. But when the heroes turned out to be stuffy paragons, always triumphant, never wrong, biographies were unendurable. Now the formats are as beguiling as the contents. The heroes and heroines are human beings with human weaknesses, because of which they suffer failures and humiliation but pick themselves up and win at least a partial triumph. If a young reader deeply admires a famous man and discovers that he too had a bad temper to contend with or was inclined to be lazy and irresponsible or was too poor to get the education he needed or was handicapped physically or by race or color, the young hero-worshiper is tremendously encouraged to find that his hero struggled through, failing sometimes, but persisting. It is the stark reality of such facts that makes a well-written biography fascinating reading and of the utmost importance to children and young people in shaping images of their own possible development.

The rise of the series
   Still another reason for the popularity of biography is the phenomenal production of biographical series, not an unmixed blessing. These have served a useful purpose in emphasizing the fact that the lives of notable men and women can make enthralling reading, and some of them have actually made avid readers of reluctant ones. Incidentally, they dovetail with and greatly enrich the school curriculum in history or social studies. Nevertheless, grownups who guide children's reading should be aware of the fact that books in a series should not be accepted en masse but should be judged individually like other books.

CRITERIA FOR BIOGRAPHIES

Historical authenticity
   Because the life of a notable man or woman is vouched for by history and some facts are well known, his biography must be historically authentic or it is worthless. But the accuracy of a juvenile biography is hard for the average person to assess. In a substantial adult biography, sources are listed—the books the author has consulted, as well as such first-hand sources as letters, diaries, and historical records of many sorts. In juvenile biographies, sources are rarely given and are greatly needed. Without

them, adults who choose biographies for young people must check them against articles in the encyclopedia perhaps, or against some reliable adult biography about the same person, or they must rely on the reputation of the author for careful research and honest writing. Let's say again, as we have said before, verifiable bases are as much needed for juvenile biographies as for adult biographies. Of course, children are not interested in lists of sources, but such verification of historical accuracy would be invaluable for teachers, librarians, and parents who must choose from among hosts of biographies for children and youth. Unless verification is provided, the average adult reader of biographies for children can only guess at historical authenticity on the basis of dates and facts in encyclopedia articles, his own wide reading, and the author's reputation.

The individual and the whole man

Another criterion by which to evaluate a biography is the author's ability to create a unique individual, not a hero stereotype, and to give his readers some measure of the whole man. For instance, even in the d'Aulaires' picture biography of Abraham Lincoln,

From *Abraham Lincoln*, by Ingri & Edgar Parin d'Aulaire. Copyright 1939 by Doubleday & Company, Inc. Reprinted by permission of the publisher.

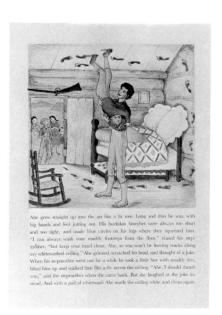

Abe grew straight up into the air like a fir tree. Long and thin he was, with big hands and feet jutting out. His buckskin breeches were always too short and too tight, and made blue circles on his legs where they squeezed him. "I can, always wash your muddy footsteps from the floor," teased his stepmother, "but keep your head clean. Abe, so you won't be leaving tracks along my whitewashed ceiling." Abe grinned, scratched his head, and thought of a joke. When his stepmother went out for a while he took a little boy with muddy feet, lifted him up and walked him like a fly across the ceiling. "Abe, I should thrash you," said the stepmother when she came back. But she laughed at the joke instead. And with a pail of whitewash Abe made the ceiling white and clean again.

children discover the hero's lifelong love of joking. In one account, the d'Aulaires tell that Abe held a youngster upside down so that he could leave his muddy footprints on the ceiling. But having had his fun with his dearly loved stepmother, Abe whitewashed the ceiling for her. The gravity and sorrows of Lincoln's later years are there too; even the fundamental differences between Lincoln and his wife, Mary Todd, are suggested in one revealing illustration.

In *Jules Verne: The Man Who Invented the Future,* Franz Born describes how Jules Verne's early passion for reading and for far-away travel set him apart even as a boy and made him a runaway from and a problem to his methodical lawyer father.

In *Emily Dickinson: Her Letter to the World,* Polly Longsworth makes clear that Emily Dickinson's shyness along with her gaiety made a unique combination even in early girlhood and that this same unquenchably blithe spirit marked the recluse and her poetry in later years.

The difficulty with presenting the whole man in a biography written for children and young people is the problem of completeness. Accounts of adult peccadilloes are not always fit reading for youngsters and may actually distort the picture of the whole man. For instance, frontiersmen often took Indian wives and left them behind when they moved on. One of our historical heroes did this, and the fact is related in the adult biography about him but omitted in the juvenile account of his life. Obviously, the d'Aulaires went into no details about the runaway reluctance of Abraham Lincoln to marry Mary Todd. But one full-page picture shows Lincoln sprawled on the floor of the disordered room with the children, and in the long mirror, the reflection of Mary Todd in the doorway, stiffly disapproving. This picture tells volumes about Abe's and Mary's differences. In both of these examples of biography for children and young people, the whole truth is not related; but what *is* told is true, and that truth reveals to children a unique individual whose lifelong achievements made him memorable.

Vivid details

The convincing reality of a biography also depends upon how vividly the author can re-create the homely everyday details of life. A biography of the famous ballerina Pavlova goes into every aspect of her rigorous training and daily routines in the School for the Russian Ballet. These details are of more absorbing interest to readers who are young would-be ballerinas than all the descriptions of Pavlova's triumphs. We are told that Daniel Boone traveled into the wilderness with his gun and some hard, saltless corn bread. This detail was illuminating to some school children who tried out saltless corn bread and wondered how Boone and the settlers ever got it down. To be told that William Penn dressed in sober brown is another dull fact, until we learn that even after he had turned Quaker and had to give up the velvets and brocades he had enjoyed, this handsome man still liked fine apparel. When he went to discuss a boundary dispute with the velvet-clad Lord Baltimore, Penn appeared in clothes of sober Quaker brown but made by the best tailor in London and from the finest material. Somehow that amusing detail makes Penn a human being, not just a historical personage. So the descriptions of those rough, interminable journeys by horseback or coach, endured by the colonials and early presidents, make their sturdy, uncomplaining spirit and their stamina clearly evident.

Revealing details are the very essence of effective biography. But what about the conversations which appear so frequently in juvenile books? Are they authentic? If so, who recorded them and where are they to be found? At the adult level, Irving Stone in *Lust for Life, The Agony and the Ecstasy,* and *Those Who Love* interprets his hero's thoughts and puts words into his mouth, thoughts and words sometimes based on letters or journals, but not actually recorded as such. As a result, Stone's books are classified as fiction or occasionally as fictionalized biography. Actually, he is a meticulous student of history, so that there is some basis for these liberties, but this concern for sources is not always characteristic of authors of biographies for young people. Of course, children don't care, just so the story interest is strong and the text readable. Librarians and a few historically-minded adults, however, wish there was not so much fictionalizing of facts in juvenile biographies and that there was more respect for authentic sources.

For instance, Sam Houston in his youth had run away from home and taken refuge with the Indians. Oo-loo-te-ka, the Cherokee chief, loved him and adopted him as his foster son. Again and again, when Houston was in trouble he retreated to his foster home with the Indians. Yet in his manhood, high in favor with President Jackson, Houston allowed himself to be used as a tool

of the President to drive the Cherokees off their long held lands
and on to a barren part of the West. In a readable but highly fictionalized life of Houston, we find this account:

> Sam's face burned. Had he been "very savage in the fight"
> because of his shame? His shame over what he was helping
> the government to do to these Indians.

It would be good to know that Sam could blush over his double
dealings with his devoted foster father, the Cherokee chief, but
is there any evidence that this was so?

On the whole, then, the fewer fictionalized conversations and
interpretations of thoughts, the more historically authentic a biography is apt to be. Writers sometimes help themselves by saying,
"Perhaps he thought. . . ." or "He might have been moved to
say. . . ." And this brings us to that perilous borderline between
true biography and historical fiction.

Biography as literature

Of necessity, biography and historical fiction have much in
common. Both should have historical authenticity, true and significant details of everyday living, and heroes with flesh-and-blood
qualities, who seem real individuals and not merely nebulous,
faraway figures or impossibly triumphant and ever-right paragons.
But fiction is free to create imaginary people, scenes, situations,
conversations, and even thoughts which have never been recorded
in any historical documents. Properly speaking, biography would
do none of these things. However, even in biography there is a
story to be told and it is the story of a hero, a star, a human luminary
who stands out nobly from the rest of his fellow men. His story
must take form, and much of that form belongs to literary storytelling; in short, biography is literature as well as history.

Theme and unity. In a biography, life itself provides the plot—
the obstacles to be overcome, the problems to be solved, the conflicts to be dealt with, and sometimes surprising climaxes or turning
points in a turbulent or confused action. But as the biographer
studies all these facts, studies more and more sources, and in the
process uncovers new facts and fresh evidence, he usually begins
to see in his hero's life a certain motive or theme running through
the confusing action. This emerging theme gives unity to the man's

whole life and to the strange conglomeration of incidents that beset him. An example of this at the adult level is Carl Van Doren's *Benjamin Franklin: A Biography*, in which the author shows the ambitious boy, the young printer, the secret writer, the philosopher, the wit, the civic innovator, the scientist, the politician, the ladies' man, the diplomat, the preacher of thrift but practicer of delightful extravagances, the patriot extraordinaire, and the creative genius in many fields. But not until the last sentence in this superb book does the author state his theme. Franklin, he says, "seems to have been more than any single man a harmonious human multitude." And that theme gives unity to the amazing diversity of Franklin's life.

Another example is the biography of Sam Houston adapted from Marquis James' adult biography called *The Raven*. This briefer, simpler edition for young people by the author and his wife is called *Six Feet Six: The Heroic Story of Sam Houston*, a title that suggests the theme of the book. For Sam Houston was a big man in both height and deeds. Sometimes what he did was tragic, often flamboyant, but never petty. He made dire mistakes, but lived them down grandly, and invariably came up after a fall, triumphant and bigger than ever. He was a very human big man worth knowing.

Like *Six Feet Six*, many biographies for children and young people indicate a theme in their titles. *Jules Verne: The Man Who Invented the Future* is the title and the striking theme around which Franz Born built his life of the inventor of science fiction. The title *Patrick Henry: Firebrand of the Revolution*, by Nardi Campion, gives an immediate clue to the temperament and the achievement of the hero. *Dancing Star: The Story of Anna Pavlova*, by Gladys Malvern, indicates the dedication of the great ballerina to her art; and *Ishi, Last of His Tribe*, by Theodora Kroeber, is a summary of the tragic events that give unity to this biography. To be sure, not every biography adheres as closely to theme and unity as these examples would seem to indicate. But many of the authors of the most readable and historically reliable lives of great men, after studying their sources, have used theme and unity to give motive and a sense of wholeness to the narratives and to the lives.

Style. Another quality of good biography is style, a compelling way of writing that keeps the reader absorbed, curious, and charmed. It is probably this special gift of a good storyteller that tempts so many writers of juvenile biographies to lapse into unauthenticated dialogue and interpretations of thoughts. Any grownup who has ever tried to tell a child about his own grandfather or about George Washington or Abraham Lincoln finds himself saying, "So George Washington's father said to his son, 'George, . . .'" or "Abraham Lincoln thought to himself. . . ." This is quite natural and sometimes legitimate if the action involved is recorded in reliable sources. But on the whole, dialogue is not desirable as a main style of recording the life of a famous man. It is interesting to see how the best writers avoid these pitfalls but still maintain an enthralling storytelling style.

A gripping biography for children and young people is Margaret Coit's *Andrew Jackson*. The style is terse, fast-paced, and revealing, and the book is adroitly documented. The first chapter, with three illustrations and only a scant nine pages, manages to sum up Jackson's family background of poverty, his premature manhood, and his stubborn, fiery character. When he was still only a prankish, rather frail, red-headed lad, neighbors remembered that

> A strong boy could throw him down easily, but "he never would stay throwed." Once some boys teased him by giving him a big gun to fire. The recoil knocked him flat. He sprang up, his brilliant blue eyes blazing. "If one of you laughs," he shouted, "I'll kill him!" No one did. No one was ever to laugh at Andrew Jackson. (p. 2)

His brutal treatment at the hands of a British officer and a taste of imprisonment obviously fostered his lifelong anti-British feeling and his appalling ruthlessness in waging war on "Redcoats or Redskins." Yet with childhood ended at fifteen, this high-spirited youth set himself to work, and that brief first chapter ends

> But, for all his frolics, Jackson went at the study of law with the intensity with which he did everything else. "I was but a raw lad then," he said afterward, "but I did my best." And it was as a full-fledged attorney-at-law that young Andrew Jackson finally left Salisbury to resume its interrupted peace, and crossed over the mountains into Tennessee.

About his unfortunate courtship and his devoted love for his wife, Rachel, the author presents a dispassionate record. Later, when Andy was beginning to be more and more away from home, already possessed by political ambitions, Dr. Coit writes

> He loved her, of course, devotedly: the man who was the terror of the Army camp and later of official Washington was never impatient with his wife or children. . . . Yet after viewing one of Jackson's partings from his emotional wife, a friend wrote a strange paragraph, . . . "History will never record how many men have performed great deeds because they were driven out of their homes by some unbearable trait of their wives. . . ." (p. 67)

The author neither expresses her own opinions about this nor imputes these words or thoughts to Jackson. She lets the record stand, and the reader can make his own judgment. Describing a tribute to Jackson during the inauguration of Van Buren, Dr. Coit quotes Benton:

> As if in one gesture, all hats came off. . . . "For once, the rising was eclipsed by the setting sun." Then, as Benton noted, a great shout arose that "power never commanded." This was love, gratitude, adoration, and looking on, Benton felt the surge of an emotion he had never known before. (pp. 132-133)

Again, turning to the record, the author uses it for a final comment on Jackson, the President.

In striking contrast to the fast-moving style of *Andrew Jackson* is Theodora Kroeber's slow-paced but nonetheless absorbing story, based on history, of the boy Ishi and the last years of his tribe, the peaceful Yahi Indians of California. Ruthlessly hunted and massacred by the invading miners and gold seekers, Ishi's people had learned to survive in concealment, but the opening paragraphs tell volumes:

> Morning mists, white and still, filled Yuma Canyon, clinging to boulders and bushes, and to the round, earth-covered houses in the village of Tuliyani. The fires in the houses were banked; no smoke came out the smokeholes.

In the men's house, three men and a boy lay sleeping. Each was rolled up in a rabbitskin blanket; only the brush of long black hair at one end of the roll made them look different from four bundles of alder tree logs. Nearby, in the family house, two women and a young girl were also sleeping, wrapped head to foot in rabbitskin.

The boy, Ishi, wakened. (*Ishi, Last of His Tribe,* p. 1)

As Ishi climbs noiselessly out of the smokehole and makes his way to Black Rock, you learn something of the customs of the tribe and the startling fact that there are only seven survivors. And as the narrative continues, the reader begins to fall into the style pattern of this book. Straight narrative carries the action forward or in flashbacks describes something of the tribe's past. But in italics are Ishi's thoughts. For instance, when his little cousin Tushi questions him about the white men, the "saldu," whom she knows he has been secretly watching, he answers,

"Little Cousin, I cannot say."

and then, in italics,

Mother does not wish me to say much about the saldu to Tushi. She says Tushi is too young to hear such talk. (p. 2)

Ishi, the last surviving member of his tribe, lived to discover that there were "good saldu," and to communicate with them. They honored and loved him and to these white men he himself told his whole story and the tragic story of the extermination of his people at the beginning of this, the twentieth century. Something of the quiet nobility, the deep reverence for all that lives, the wonderful gentleness and uncomplaining endurance of these people comes through in the narrative style of this remarkable book.

It is interesting to see how Polly Longsworth makes that shy recluse Emily Dickinson, the poet, into a fascinating heroine and her life into an absorbing book, *Emily Dickinson: Her Letter to the World.* Emily's life was a strange series of negations, yet it is revealed in these pages in light touches, revealing flashes, all suggested in recorded sources, and showing her strange progress from a gay, sparkling girl to a timid recluse who fled from people but expressed her joys and agonies in a rare outpouring of poems which she hid away in her bureau drawer. Fortunately, Emily was a tremendous writer of letters and little notes that her family, friends, and neighbors preserved, sensing their uniqueness, and so Mrs. Longsworth had no lack of sources.

> "Infinite March is here, and I 'hered' a bluebird. Of course I am standing on my head!" (p. 95) "Mother went rambling, and came in with a burdock on her shawl, so we know that the snow has perished from the earth. Noah would have liked mother." (pp. 131-132)

Her bubbling, gay-spirited letters show a happy girlhood. She delighted in her studies—Latin, mathematics, history, sciences, philosophy. She read prodigiously and worried over religion but more than compensated for these worries with her joy in nature, especially in her garden. However, the mature Emily began to shun people and to see only her family and a few close friends. She never went anywhere, but even in her isolation she kept a radiant joy, "ecstasy," she called it (p. 160).

> Take all away from me, but leave me Ecstasy
> And I am richer then than all my Fellow Men—
> Ill it becometh me to dwell so wealthily
> When at my very Door are those possessing more,
> In abject poverty.

Through perceptive flashes from letters, records, and poems, Emily Dickinson comes through the pages of this book, alive and fascinating.

Finally, there never will be a better example of the perfect compatibility of style and subject matter than James Daugherty's robustious *Daniel Boone:*

> When Daniel came back to the Boone's farm in the Yadkin valley, he up and married his Irish sweetheart, Rebecca Bryan, whose family had settled in the valley near them. There was a hilarious shindig with the Carolina fiddles shaking down the moon. When the logs were all cut for the house-raising, the neighbors for miles around took a hand. By sundown they stuck a pine tree on the ridgepole of a brand new cabin in the clearing and ate and danced till morning. (p. 21)

So, obviously, no one style is good style, but different styles
are good when they suit the subject matter, command interest, and
read agreeably.

BIOGRAPHIES FOR YOUNG CHILDREN

It has been generally assumed that biography is not for young
children, four to eight or nine years old. Yet when a child says
"Daddy, tell me about when you were a little boy," he is asking
for biography. Or when he hears his older brothers and sisters
talking about Washington's or Lincoln's birthday, he wants to know
who these men were and why we celebrate their birthdays. If some
grownup tries to tell a child or write for him an understandable
account of either patriot, the biography will, of necessity, be highly
simplified and probably told largely in terms of what the patriot
did. For children in these early years are interested in action and
achievement and in heroes who are doers rather than saints or
scientists in the making. So although biography makes a start in
these early years, it is generally an action narrative, but it need
not be stereotyped. It is understandable that the offering is small,
but it includes some fine books. However, there are very few recent titles among them.

Abraham Lincoln, by Ingri and Edgar Parin d'Aulaire. Caldecott Medal.
  Doubleday, 1939. Also Benjamin Franklin (1950). (6-10)
  These artist-writers made a fine contribution to children's books
  when they began their series of picture-book biographies, in which
  the pictures not only illustrate but add to the text. The biographies of
  Lincoln and Franklin are particularly rich in content and Leif the Lucky,
  Pocahontas, and Buffalo Bill are the most colorful. Columbus tells more
  of the explorer's life and achievements than the biography of Columbus
  by Alice Dalgliesh, but both books are good introductions to the man.

The Columbus Story, by Alice Dalgliesh. Scribner, 1955. (7-10)
  Brilliant illustrations in full color, among the finest Leo Politi has
  done, add much to this well-told account of Columbus' first voyage.
  None of the later tragedy is included. Miss Dalgliesh has a way of
  making the past come alive for children. They enjoy this book as young
  as five and can read it for themselves by the time they are eight or nine.

Squanto, Friend of the White Men, by Clyde Bulla. Crowell, 1954. (7-12)

Strictly speaking, this is fiction rather than biography, but it tells movingly the incredible adventures of this kindly Indian. In 1605 he was taken to England where he lived for eight years. Back in this country, he was captured and sold into slavery in Spain. Rescued by some friars, he returned once more to his native land. What must he have felt and thought? As in all of his books, Clyde Bulla tells this story in easy-to-read style that is never commonplace. The illustrations by Peter Burchard enhance the text.

Benjamin West and His Cat Grimalkin, by Marguerite Henry. Bobbs, 1947. (7-12)

This illustration is reprinted by permission of Charles Scribner's Sons: Illustration by Leo Politi from *The Columbus Story* by Alice Dalgliesh. Copyright 1955 by Alice Dalgliesh and Leo Politi.

This humorous and delightful account of the childhood beginnings of America's first notable artist, called "the father of American painting," is impossible to confine to any age bracket. It is fun to read aloud, and children as young as six thoroughly enjoy it, but it is easy and amusing reading for the elevens and twelves who are slow in attaining their reading skills. How the young Quaker began to draw, learned about colors from the Indians, used hairs from his cat's tail for his brushes, and finally won the reluctant consent of his family and the Quaker community to study art makes a fascinating story and the beginning of a biography. Wesley Dennis' illustrations greatly enhance the text.

Children need more such books. They mark the beginnings of and introductions to the bona-fide biographies for older children. If these beginnings are not pure biography, we need not worry as long as they are substantially true, have some distinction in style and characterizations, and leave children wanting to read more books about "real people."

BIOGRAPHIES FOR OLDER CHILDREN

George Washington, Leader of the People, by Clara Ingram Judson. Follett, 1951. Also *Abraham Lincoln, Friend of the People* (1950). (10-14)

Clara Ingram Judson has made a real contribution to biography for children and youth. Her style is pedestrian but holds the reader's interest, and every one of her books was written only after careful research into sources. She believed there was no excuse for retelling the lives of such well-known men as Washington or Lincoln unless she could give children some new slant on the hero's life or character. So she rescued Washington from the usual stereotype and introduced a fresh view of each of her heroes.

Penn, by Elizabeth Janet Gray (Mrs. Vining). Viking, 1938. (12 up)

You may find this author catalogued under Gray or Vining. Her *Penn* not only is one of the most distinguished biographies in the juvenile field, but will take its place beside any adult biography yet written about William Penn. One father read his son's copy of this book and remarked that it had told him more about Penn in England and in this country, than all his college history had ever done. It is a full-length portrait of the man who gave our country ideas of religious and racial tolerance and brought to our courts the right of their juries to have their decisions sustained.

Daniel Boone, by James Daugherty. Viking, 1939. Also *Poor Richard* (1941), *Abraham Lincoln* (1943), *Of Courage Undaunted* (1951), and *Marcus and Narcissa Whitman, Pioneers of Oregon* (1953). (10-14)
It is a question which is more vigorous—James Daugherty's style of writing or his rhythmic, powerful illustrations. Both tell a lively story, whoever the hero may be. *Daniel Boone* is particularly successful in capturing the personality of the man against colorful glimpses of the times. *Poor Richard* is a full-length portrait of this "first civilized American." Lewis and Clark, the heroes of *Of Courage Undaunted,* are amusingly contrasted; whereas the story of Marcus and Narcissa Whitman is hauntingly tragic. No single biography of Lincoln can give the full stature of that complex man, but Daugherty's *Abraham Lincoln* is

From *Abraham Lincoln* by James Daugherty. Copyright 1943 by James Daugherty. Reprinted by permission of The Viking Press, Inc.

remarkably satisfying. Any one of these Daugherty biographies would be a valuable and lasting addition to a child's home library.

Patrick Henry: Firebrand of the Revolution, by Nardi Reeder Campion. Little, 1961. (10 up)
This is an absorbing and well-documented narrative, and makes use of letters and other records. That Patrick Henry began as an irresponsible, half-educated youngster and became "spokesman for the Revolution" and respected first Governor of the State of Virginia is a remarkable record. This book is good for family reading aloud.

Amos Fortune, Free Man, by Elizabeth Yates. Dutton, 1950. (10-14)
With distinguished illustrations by Nora Unwin, this Newbery Medal winner tells the remarkable story of an African prince, cruelly kidnapped and brought to Boston in a slave ship under dreadful conditions, and sold into slavery. He was, relatively speaking, well treated by his masters, learned the tanner's trade, and became a competent and highly respected man. He eventually won his freedom. But after that, Amos devoted his whole life to buying freedom for other slaves including the woman he married. He died an honored citizen of the little New Hampshire town of Jaffrey, where he had lived so many years. A remarkable life, beautifully told.

Andrew Jackson, by Margaret L. Coit. Houghton, 1965. (11-14)
There have been other lives of Jackson for children and youth. This is outstanding.

Six Feet Six: The Heroic Story of Sam Houston, by Marquis and Bessie James. Bobbs, 1931. (11-14)
There is still no other life of Sam Houston comparable to this retelling of Marquis James' adult biography, *The Raven*, by his wife, Bessie James. Sam was a complex and contradictory character, and his record can lead to some heated discussions as to the right or wrong of his behavior. That in the end his contribution to his country was on the plus side is evident, even though his path was sometimes dubious.

Abe Lincoln Grows Up, by Carl Sandburg. Harcourt, 1928. (11-16)
There are more complete biographies of Lincoln than this cutting from Sandburg's *Abraham Lincoln: The Prairie Years*, but no child or young person should miss this poignant story of Lincoln's background

and of his childhood and boyhood. The style is sometimes pure poetry, the parts about young Nancy Hanks for example. The pictures of Lincoln's father; the beloved second wife, Abe's wise, compassionate stepmother; the blab school; the struggle for books and education are all here. Splendid to read aloud if a child can't swing it for himself. Since it covers only Lincoln's youth, use with it either Clara Ingram Judson's *Abraham Lincoln, Friend of the People* (Follett, 1950) or James Daugherty's *Abraham Lincoln* (Viking, 1943). All three books have notable illustrations—Sandburg's and Daugherty's, both by Daugherty; the Judson by Frankenberg with photographs of dioramas.

Lee of Virginia, by Douglas Southall Freeman. Scribner, 1958. (12 up)
  This eminent historian did not make a cutting or adaptation of his four-volume adult life of Robert Lee, but wrote this book especially for young people. He brings out strongly the sacrifice Lee made when he espoused the Southern side in the Civil War, and Lee's early triumphs and tragic ultimate defeat which he bore with equally calm acceptance. There are the bitter days for the South and this leader after the surrender, and the quiet obscurity of his later days. Through it all shines the selfless nobility of a dedicated man. With this book, children should read MacKinlay Kantor's *Lee and Grant at Appomattox* (Random, 1950), a thrilling account of both Lee and Grant in the last two weeks before the surrender.

America's Robert E. Lee, by Henry Steele Commager, ill. by Lynd Ward. Houghton, 1951. (11-14)
  This book is particularly significant, emphasizing as it does the fact that Robert E. Lee is a hero all America is proud of. Northern children should certainly read a good biography of this man, who was held in high regard as a strategist and as a man by his contemporaries on both sides of the tragic struggle. Children will close this quiet biography with a deeper understanding for that sorrowful war.

Jules Verne: The Man Who Invented the Future, by Franz Born, tr. from the German by Juliana Biro, ill. by Peter P. Plasencia. Prentice, 1964. (10-14)
  This is not precisely a biography but a fascinating introduction to a writer and his books, books that live today and brought the writer the well-deserved title "inventor of science fiction." The story of his strict upbringing as a child, and of his continual escape into reading and

daydreams of fabulous journeys, is well told. So is the account of his early manhood in Paris, where he kicked up his youthful heels, spent tuition money for high living, brought down the wrath of his father on his unrepentant head and the withdrawal of all financial support. How he made out, spending hours in the libraries reading everything he could find on science and tucking the facts away in his prodigious memory, and the almost accidental way in which a publisher started him writing his books make an absorbing story. The details of his mature life are skimpy, but each of his books is briefed in considerable detail. Moreover, the author is at pains to show how much modern inventors owe to their youthful reading of Jules Verne.

Jules Verne: Portrait of a Prophet, by Russell Freedman. Holiday House, 1965. (12 up)

While the Born biography of Verne is a good introduction for younger readers, *Jules Verne: Portrait of a Prophet* is a superbly analytical and absorbing life of this man of many talents, who did incredible research in the preparation of his books. The author gives an impressive introductory summary of the many scientific fields in which Verne was almost prophetic of future developments. There is also a complete list of Verne's writings, ranging from his plays to his "extraordinary journeys," and his output was truly prolific. Sources used by Freedman in the writing of this book are included, and many illustrations from Verne's original tales are used throughout.

Ishi, Last of His Tribe, by Theodora Kroeber. Parnassus, 1964. (10-14)

This moving story should be required reading for all young Americans. The massacre of a tribe of peaceful California Indians was completed early in 1900, but one man, Ishi, survived to tell the story of the slow extermination of his people and to discover for himself that some white men are honorable and kind. Ruth Robbins' illustrations add their authenticity to a tragic story that has great warmth and beauty.

Emily Dickinson: Her Letter to the World, by Polly Longsworth. Crowell, 1965. (12 up)

Girls and a few boys discover the brief, cryptic poems of Emily Dickinson as young as twelve and are curious about the poet's life. However, it is probable that it will be teen-age girls rather than boys who will enjoy this sensitively written story about the gay, witty New England girl who turned gradually into a gentle recluse and saw only the members of her family, a few close friends, and children. The author of this perceptive biography had no lack of documentation, because Emily wrote hundreds of letters and still more notes—wise, witty, gay, and full of both the agonies and the ecstasies of living.

Paderewski, by Charlotte Kellogg. Viking, 1956. (12 up)
This is not a great biography, but it is a biography of a great man whose gifts were many and whose life was as complex as it was distinguished. Musically gifted from early childhood, the boy was determined to be a pianist despite every discouragement. He was told his hands were not right for the piano, but nothing lessened his determination. Twice suspended from the conservatory for rebellion, he finally graduated with highest honors. More study and more work were crowned with spectacular success in concerts from Paris to San Francisco. Then came World War I. Paderewski poured out a fortune for Polish relief. After the war, he was made premiere and later president of Poland. His contribution to the Paris Peace Conference was as notable as his speeches. After his presidency, he had to recoup his lost fortune, and began again grueling practice and concerts. When he died, he was buried in Arlington Cemetery by the decision of the President of the United States. During his life, Justice Harlan Stone rated him as "the world's greatest pianist . . . . and perhaps the greatest living man."

Dancing Star: The Story of Anna Pavlova, by Gladys Malvern, ill. by Susanne Suba. Messner, 1942. (12-15)
For children interested in ballet, *Dancing Star* presents not only the story of a great ballerina but a fascinating picture of ballet training.

HISTORICAL FICTION

In Chapters 6 and 8, notable examples of historical fiction are reviewed in detail. They begin with the simpler examples—*Otto of the Silver Hand* and *The Door in the Wall*—but move on in maturity of content to *Johnny Tremain* and to the magnificent historical novels of Rosemary Sutcliff. In both chapters, there are books no reading child should miss; so turn back to those chapters, and if you find books your child has not encountered, supply the lack. Over and over again, such books bring alive the historical periods or movements children are meeting in their social studies.

At the beginning of this chapter, the nebulous distinction (for children) between biography and historical fiction is discussed, and in the bibliography some borderline books are listed. To further emphasize this narrow borderline between the two types of writing, here is one more example, a distinguished book that is catalogued sometimes as biography and sometimes as fiction. In either case, it is a decidedly worth-while book for children and young people.

Carry On, Mr. Bowditch, by Jean Lee Latham, ill. by John O'Hara Cosgrave II. Newbery Medal. Houghton, 1955.

Born in Salem, Massachusetts, in 1773, Nathaniel Bowditch early showed a mathematical precocity that made the learned men of the town say he must prepare for Harvard. But there was no money for his education, and so at ten he had to stop school and at twelve he was apprenticed to a ship's chandlery for nine years. That was the end of his schooling but not the end of his education. An old man told him, "Only a weakling gives up when he's becalmed! A strong man sails by ash breeze!"—on his oars. So Nat sailed. The men of the town lent him books. He taught himself mathematics, astronomy, navigation, Latin, French, Spanish. When his indenture ended, he was ready to face the world. On a series of voyages, he served as clerk and second mate, interpreted for the captain, corrected some 8000 mistakes in the accepted book on navigation, and conducted regular classes in navigation for the crews, making the subject understandable and comparatively simple. Eventually, he wrote the definitive book, *The New American Practical Navigator.* And Harvard, which he had never had a chance to attend, gave him the degree he had missed. There is romance in Nat's story, and some tragic as well as some extremely humorous episodes. All in all, it is a thrilling story of New England fortitude and love of learning. Miss Latham has told it splendidly, and Mr. Cosgrave's illustrations add to the distinction of this Newbery Medal book.

Biography is a special area of reading which children do not always discover for themselves. When they do, it is sufficiently different from the fiction they have been reading that they may or may not like it. Some children are immediately impressed with the fact that what they are reading is really true, that the man or woman described in the book actually lived, and that the events recounted took place at specified times in the past. Here we get the first stirrings of a time sense, a feeling for and curiosity about the past that we call history.

Writers, librarians, and teachers have all fostered this feeling by providing children with biographies so well written and absorbing that they bridge the gap between fiction and history. Parents with a liking for both biography and history can assist even more effectively. Perhaps if a child has never read a biography, he might acquire an interest if he hears a lively example read aloud in the home. Or an easy example might start him reading on his own. Even if it is fictionalized a bit more than it should be, it might be the very book to excite his curiosity about heroes who actually lived, and about times past. Once such an interest is launched, provide him with sound biographies and encourage such reading by discussing the heroes with him and adding any facts you may know from your adult reading. These will add prestige to his own reading.

The biographies reviewed in this chapter are only a sampling of this rich and varied area of reading. They should arouse and nourish a child's interest, and his taste for biography should grow as he grows. Biography more than any other type of reading stirs emulation, because it provides children with hero images of real men struggling with a great variety of obstacles and disappointments but achieving mightily.

INFORMATIONAL BOOKS

❖❦❧❖

13

Book Lists
Criteria for Informational Books
Dictionaries, Encyclopedias, Atlases
Building a Child's Reference Library
Science Books
Social Studies Books

Children are great interrogators. First they ask, "What's that?" As soon as they know the names of things, their "Why's" begin, and these cover life and death, man and God, the stars above, the earth beneath, the waters under the earth, and everything that creeps, crawls, flies, swims, walks upright or on all fours—in short, the universe. Adults are apt to get bored with children's incessant questioning when they should feel profoundly thankful that these young minds are stirring. It is the absence of curiosity that is frightening. However, when questions go beyond a grownup's range of information, then the only honest answer is, "I am not sure. . . ." or "I don't know, but I think we can find out about it from a book. We'll look it up." And so you and your child embark on a fascinating and limitless search for facts, for accurate information in place of guesswork. This is a wonderful attitude of mind and a fine habit to establish with children, the younger the better.

It soon becomes evident to families that some children gravitate to fact books more readily than to stories. If they want books about stones or stars, dinosaurs or grasshoppers, don't be surprised. This age fosters all sorts of curiosities by way of what we call mass media—newspapers, pictorial magazines, radio, television, and moving pictures. Through these media, children travel around the globe, see stone-age men in their villages and astronauts walking in space, life in the depths of the ocean or a flower unfolding or a baby being born, and scientific research reported by scientists. It would be a dull mind indeed that would not respond to such vicarious experiences with interest and probably with more questions. Sometimes the mass media presentations satisfy the child's curiosities, but sometimes, by their very speed and brevity, they only whet his curiosity to know more about some area of knowledge that has caught his interest. Happily, this is not an infrequent result of television viewing and is an outcome devoutly to be hoped for, because it sends a child to his books. Good reference books supply more details; reading is a slower process that allows time to reread, to pore over the details, and to digest elusive facts. This curiosity of young minds to find out more about this wide, wonderful world of ours is worth encouraging, and fortunately we have today informational books for children and youth, in many areas of human knowledge and written for varying levels of reading skills—more pictures and less text for the beginning readers, solid texts but with strong child appeal for older readers, and both types giving reliable information. Every home should accumulate some of these standard references both for adults and children. And children in the home should acquire the reference habit, not from enforced dictionary work in schools, but from a family that turns eagerly to reliable books to prove a point, verify a fact, widen knowledge, answer questions, and launch new questions. These are the goals of all first-rate books of information in any field.

BOOK LISTS

The first questions the lay person asks—parents, uncles and aunts, camp counselors, any adult interested in children's reading —are where can such books be found and how can their reliability be judged? There are innumerable books, but only experts can judge their validity, and fortunately, lists in the fields of the sciences and social studies have been prepared by such experts. Of these the most reliable and well organized are:

> *The AAAS Science Book List for Children,* Second Edition, 1963. (Paperback and hardback). Compiled under the direction of Hilary J. Deason with Nora A. Beust, Consultant. American Association for the Advancement of Science. Washington, D.C.
>
> The 1291 books on this list were checked both for scientific accuracy and for values in teaching children basic scientific concepts. The arrangement is topical. Books are marked *P* for primary, *I* for intermediate, and *A* for advanced, with sometimes a combination *PI* or *IA,* where a book has range of appeal. The group responsible for this list recommends that 25 per cent of the titles in a school library should be in the field of pure and applied science, a suggestion which adults might follow for home libraries. Eighty-one titles carry a double asterisk denoting "first priority." This is a list with which to check books and also from which to glimpse this vast field. Another good source is *The AAAS Science Book List for Young Adults* (1964), also compiled under the direction of Hilary J. Deason. This list contains over 1300 titles for readers of junior-high age and above.
>
> Since April 1965, these titles have been kept up to date with *Science Books: A Quarterly Review,* which appraises current science publications for all ages, even adult and professional books. Many titles are included for younger readers.

> *Children's Books to Enrich the Social Studies,* Revised Edition, 1966. Prepared by Helen Huus. National Council for the Social Studies.
>
> The books in this list are arranged under these general topics: Our World, Times Past, People Today, The World's Work, Living Together, with many subheads under each. Grade levels follow the annotation for each book. Textbooks are not included, only so-called trade or library books. Informational books are listed along with a great deal of fiction, but there are no folk tales or poetry. One person only prepared this list, and so the evaluations are necessarily personal and subjective. Nevertheless, it is a helpful list and well indexed.

> *History in Children's Books: An Annotated Bibliography for Schools and Libraries,* by Zena Sutherland. McKinley, 1967.
>
> An excellent bibliography, worldwide in scope, the list includes fiction, biography, and informational books, 1370 in all.

Children and Books, Third Edition, by May Hill Arbuthnot, Scott, 1964. See Chapter 18 and the bibliography. Also the supplementary bibliography prepared by Margaret M. Clark, called *Keeping Up with Children and Books*. These include titles of some of the best books in the fields of the sciences and social studies.

CRITERIA FOR INFORMATIONAL BOOKS

Accuracy

Obviously, if a child is eager to find out about something, "for sure," as he says, then you want him to have a good reference book, with authenticated information. For instance, a book purportedly about American Indians in general, but with illustrations showing as Indian dwelling places only wigwams or tepees on the edge of a lake, would be of no use to a child who is studying the Pueblo Indians and their deserted cliff dwellings, or the Navahoes in their hogans, or the Indians living on a modern reservation learning a building trade, or trying to adjust to life in a big city. Informational books need to be specific and up to date on such knowledge as is available, and, above all, accurate. So the modern child who has watched a televised "soft landing" on the moon by a machine that takes and sends back to earth photographs of the moon's surface and even of its own shadow is going to ask about other matters: "But how did they find that out?" or "How do they know that for certain?" And these are the same questions that every scientist and investigator in any field must ask and answer satisfactorily if his statements are to be respected. Actually, this present-day child is so habituated to the visible and audible documentation by the mass media and by visual aids in the schools that he is acquiring unconsciously a basic concept of scientific research—detailed documentation. Because of this, the foremost requisite of informational books today is *scrupulous accuracy*.

Clarity

Clarity in the presentation of facts is another requisite. But what is clear to a twelve-year-old may not be to a seven-year-old. Looking up a word in an adult dictionary may leave the younger child baffled and annoyed because he can neither read nor understand the words in the definition. Yet he does not want babyish answers to his questions. Children detect and resent patronage immediately. They need reference books that they can read, understand, and respect, which means that the information must be clearly and forthrightly presented, with consideration for the reader's intelligent curiosity.

Adequate treatment

Adequate treatment is more difficult to achieve for children than for adults. What is adequate for a child of eight to twelve may be too meager for older children and overwhelming for the younger ones. This means that some adult will have to scan each book with a particular child or group of children in mind. Usually the level of a child's questions will help determine the details with which the questions should be answered. The old storytelling clichés of Jackie Frost or Mother South Wind are irrelevant, confusing, and odious. The real facts of the universe are fascinating enough, whether it is the red-legged grasshopper's brief life span or the curious activities of the little sea horse or of the huge whales. In every case, the child deserves accurate, clear, adequate pictures of such marvels as come his way or excite his curiosity.

Style

Style may seem an irrelevant requirement for an informational book. Certainly a dictionary can hardly be expected to exude charm, but a science book in any field or a study of a people may and should. A child who finds a history textbook full of lively facts appealingly presented is apt to approach all of his other textbooks more hopefully and to look for information more eagerly. For instance, why is Isaac Asimov's title *The Kingdom of the Sun* more appealing than the title *The Solar System?* Both books explore the same subject matter, but the second title is bald fact, whereas the curious magic of words in Mr. Asimov's title piques the imagination and starts the wondering. And read this sampling of his introduction:

In these days of rockets and satellites, we all know that the Earth is a planet. We all know it circles about the sun, along with eight other sizable planets and many thousands of smaller objects.

Yet how do you suppose we came to know that? If we look at the universe about us, and trust our eyes, what we see is nothing like what we are told is so. The Earth does not seem to be moving; it seems absolutely motionless. The sun is a glowing patch of fire that seems quite small, much smaller than the vast world we live on. The planets are merely dots of light in the night sky and are in the company of thousands of other dots we call stars. Then there is the moon, which seems as large as the sun, but which changes shape constantly.

All these objects seem to move steadily about the Earth.

It took thousands of years for mankind to decide that our eyes could not be trusted; that what seemed to be so was not so. The story of how that decision was reached and of what happened afterward is an interesting one, and I would like to tell it in this book.

It's only fair to begin by simply looking at the sky. That is all primitive man did to begin with, when he started wondering about the heavens, so that is where the story starts.[1]

Biochemist Dr. Asimov's scientific facts never cripple his style. His books for all their carefully authenticated information are as spellbinding as fiction and so are the books of Margaret Mead, Gerald Johnson, the inimitable Van Loon, and at a younger level, Jeanne Bendick. As the illustration and text (see p. 285) from *How Much and How Many* suggest, Mrs. Bendick can make weights and measures less weighty than they might otherwise be.

Adults may take their information from books written with pedestrian dullness and lack of charm, but children are not so docile. They shy away from boredom and betake themselves to a livelier world. So the writer of informational books for the young had better look to his style of writing. Are his descriptions brief, vivid, and memorable, and can he explain and develop an idea so that it holds interest and compels further reading? Such writing is good expository style at any level, and is essential in children's books.

DICTIONARIES, ENCYCLOPEDIAS, AND ATLASES

Emily Dickinson, a poet noted for her fresh and sometimes electrifying use of words, "read" her dictionary all her days. It was

[1] Isaac Asimov, *The Kingdom of the Sun.* Abelard, 1963.

a volume worn with use, and the feeling she had for words could only come after such years of study and wide reading in various fields. Furthermore, she had the privilege of hearing language employed to express thought precisely and beautifully, for she listened to the Bible read aloud daily. Few children today have that privilege, but substantial books read aloud will help, and good language usage in the family is an unmitigated if not a universal blessing, alas!

Dictionaries

As soon as a child can read for himself, he should have his own dictionary. Then, when a word question arises, you can say to him, "You look that up in your book and I'll look it up in mine, and we'll see whether our dictionaries agree." Checking one reference

142   **Science**

A very important measurement of area is an *acre*. An acre was originally the amount of land a yoke of oxen could plow in one day. You can see how in the beginning it varied a great deal, depending on whether the farmer and his oxen were lazy or ambitious. At last Henry VIII of England limited an acre to an exact size. It was the

area of a piece of land 40 measuring rods long by 4 rods broad. (These rods were 5½ yards long.) During the middle ages, the length of a rod was determined by lining up 16 men outside of church on Sunday morning, and measuring the combined length of all their left feet.

So the area of an acre was, and still is, 160 square rods, or 4,840 square yards. A piece of ground 200 feet by 200 feet is nearly an acre.

From *How Much and How Many*, written and illustrated by Jeanne Bendick. Copyright 1960 by McGraw-Hill Book Company. Reprinted by permission of the publishers.

against another is a wonderful habit to acquire young, and the adult source that agrees with the child's adds prestige to the latter. Juvenile dictionaries for children, beginning with picture dictionaries for the youngest, are a fine investment because their definitions are geared to the child's understanding, the words to his reading level, and their print to his young eyes. Annis Duff writes delightfully of her family's dictionary habits. The dictionary was considered standard equipment for the dining room—a condiment or "something to add relish to food." So mealtimes were made even more satisfying because someone's vague guess about a word could be checked immediately: spelling, meaning, and use all neatly settled on the spot. Incidentally, for young children, the alphabetized arrangement of words falls naturally into place if the children have encountered some of the matchless *ABC* books listed on pages 60-61. No child should miss the fine woodcuts of Wanda Gág's *ABC Bunny* and the big-city verses of Phyllis McGinley's choice *All Around the Town*. Children are entertained by these books and learn their alphabet painlessly. Fortunately, there are dictionaries for very young children as well as for older children. Here is a sampling of what is available:

My Little Pictionary, rev. ed., by Marion Monroe and W. Cabell Greet. Scott, 1964. (6-7)

Words that young children often wish to spell and write are grouped according to meaning and function under such headings as "Words for Things," "Words for People," "Words That Tell What Kind." There are over 1300 words of which more than 260 are illustrated with four-color pictures for youngsters who may not be able to recognize in print the words they wish to write. An index is included.

My Second Pictionary, by Marion Monroe and W. Cabell Greet. Scott, 1964. (7-8)

To solve a word problem, children may turn to the section "Words and Pictures," where 3600 words are grouped and illustrated much as they are in *My Little Pictionary;* or they may consult "Words and Meanings," where the same words are listed alphabetically, with definitions and illustrative sentences at the second-grade level.

Thorndike-Barnhart Beginning Dictionary. Doubleday. (8-10)
Thorndike-Barnhart Junior Dictionary. Doubleday. (9-12)

Thorndike-Barnhart Advanced Junior Dictionary. Doubleday. (11-14)
Definitions that are easy to comprehend, an abundance of illustrative material, simple pronunciation system, and clear print distinguish these dictionaries for children.

American College Dictionary. Random House.
Although this is an adult dictionary, it can be used profitably by children who are advanced readers. It employs a modern, simplified pronunciation key and bases pronunciations on current usage. The most common meaning of each word is given first. Frequently revised.

Webster's Seventh New Collegiate Dictionary. G. & C. Merriam.
A standard desk-size dictionary for adults and children who are mature readers.

Webster's New World Dictionary of the American Language, College Edition. World.
Another desk-size adult dictionary that is exceedingly popular with adolescents.

Encyclopedias

Most grownups see the usefulness of a child's dictionary, but are not so willing to concede the desirability of investing in a juvenile encyclopedia. If budget and space are both limited and a family can barely squeeze in an adult encyclopedia, then two are out of the question. When these conditions exist, it is indeed better to buy an adult encyclopedia which the grownups in the family can use with the child, until he is able to use it on his own. Besides, this is a good way to teach the child to use an encyclopedia, if you make sure also that he understands the importance of these reference sources. By the time the child is ten or eleven, referring to the encyclopedia should be an established habit—a habit which he will start as a small child in the home and will carry on to college and into his own home, when he establishes one. A fine adult encyclopedia is an investment for a lifetime. Some aspects of its information will become dated, but the bulk of it will have lifetime values. So if a choice must be made between an adult encyclopedia and a child's, obviously the family should buy an adult encyclopedia. However, if there are space and money for both, a child's encyclopedia is a precious investment, and fortunately there are several fine ones available. All are well illustrated and kept up to date. Certainly, a well-worn encyclopedia on a child's bookshelves is a cheerful sight. It seems to guarantee a human being who is going to enjoy ideas, everything his mind can explore.

Britannica Junior Encyclopaedia. 15 volumes.
Prepared under the supervision of the editors of the adult *Encyclopaedia Britannica.* The content is directed to children of elementary-school level. The articles are readable, well illustrated, and authentic. (9-14)

Compton's Pictured Encyclopedia and Fact-Index. 15 volumes, F. E. Compton, a division of Encyclopaedia Britannica, Inc.
A competent survey of knowledge, with good indexing, illustrations, and reliable articles. (9-16)

The World Book Encyclopedia, 20 volumes. Field Enterprises.
Comprehensive articles that may be used by adults as well as children. Well illustrated and bound. (9 up)

Columbia-Viking Desk Encyclopedia, Columbia University.
If a family has no room or money for an adult encyclopedia, then, by all means, invest in this amazing one-volume compendium of human knowledge. The information it contains never ceases to surprise its devotees.

Atlases

Maps of cities and countries have always been fascinating and are almost as essential to a home's reference sources as the dictionary. But today they are more than ordinarily necessary when the map of the world's countries and even the names of countries sometimes change overnight. Who can tell in what country or countries the next international crisis is going to break forth? And wherever it is, a good atlas can show both the kind of country it is and its relation to other countries. The family who keeps its atlas on the top of the television set is, after all, just being properly prepared. But this sort of flux in national affairs makes the selection of an atlas more than ordinarily complicated. What holds this year may be gone or changed the next. So all you can do is to be in-

formed about a few standard examples, and then, before buying,
find out the date of the latest revision.

Rand McNally World Atlas. Rand McNally.
This publisher is, of course, the standard source for maps and atlases
at the adult level. Since children cannot follow or absorb all the intricacies of a modern atlas, it might be well to purchase the *Rand
McNally World Atlas* in its most recent revision for the use of the
whole family.

The World Book Atlas. Field Enterprises.
Published in connection with *The World Book Encyclopedia*, this
atlas is kept up to date, is recommended by librarians, and is well
liked by children. In addition to the usual variety of maps, there are
clear descriptions of population, climate, political and religious conditions, languages, etc. There are also such useful guides as how to gauge
distances on maps and how to use star charts. Indeed this fine reference
will serve the whole family.

Please remember that children are fascinated with maps once
they know what they are all about. Do you remember the fun of
drawing and coloring maps, especially the topographical kind, not
as a school assignment but just for the fun of it? Cross-country
drives by the whole family keep this interest alive and make an
atlas a necessity.

After choosing these prime requisites of a family library—a
dictionary, an encyclopedia, and an up-to-date atlas—there is the
problem of selecting a small group of informational books for the
home. One family is interested in birds and another in stars. One
child is fascinated by snakes, and his sister is an active rock hound.
Their neighbors take a trip to Mexico, and the children return wanting all the information available about the Mayans and the Aztecs.
There are reliable informative books for children in every one of
these fields and many more. The challenge is to make a good
selection.

BUILDING A CHILD'S REFERENCE LIBRARY

In building a child's reference library, one must consider two
factors: the age range of the book and the breadth of the informa-

tion. For instance, the eye appeal of a book is of first importance for children under seven. Even for children seven to ten, illustrations are still important, and so is a text that is easy to read, not too solid looking, but still reliable and satisfying to young curiosities. For beginning but not too experienced readers, such books as Olive Earle's *Crickets* or Alice Goudey's *Houses from the Sea*, with its exquisite illustrations by Adrienne Adams, or Franklyn Branley's *A Book of Planets for You* are admirable examples of how appealing and rich these informative books can be even for young children.

In addition to such delightful books as W. Maxwell Reed's *The Stars for Sam* and Rachel Carson's matchless *The Sea Around Us*, adapted by Anne Terry White, good readers of ten to fourteen also need more advanced books. They may not be able to absorb completely Franklyn Branley's *Experiments in Sky Watching* or Anne Terry White's *Lost Worlds: The Romance of Archaeology* or Russel Hamilton's *Science, Science, Science* or Isaac Asimov's fine *The Kingdom of the Sun*, but they may at least dip into these books, ask their older brothers and sisters or their parents about them, and know what lies ahead. Easy-to-read books may be essential for some children, but others need the challenge of fuller, more advanced books to satisfy their eager curiosities. So while you supply some of the books for each age or reading level, invest chiefly in reliable reference books that are full in treatment and of lasting value.

SCIENCE BOOKS

In the field of science you are immediately confronted with the interminable series such as *First Books, All About Books*, and *True Books*. As in biography series, the values of individual books vary both in the richness of the content and the quality of the writing. Look first for the books outside the series. However, distinguished writers have contributed to the various series, and individual books within the series are excellent. Just consult librarians or look before you buy, and never take a whole series of anything. Look until you find what you think your child or children need.

Isaac Asimov, writing chiefly for advanced readers, is a scientist. Besides writing his own books, he reviews science books for *The Horn Book,* a page or more well worth following in each issue. Born in Russia but educated in this country, he received his Ph.D. in 1948, and by 1955 was Associate Professor of Biochemistry in the Medical School of Boston University. He speaks with authority in the science field, writes with clarity and compelling interest, and with refreshing flashes of humor. His own books or his recommendations of other books can be relied upon. His *Realm of Numbers* and *Realm of Measure* are fascinating accounts of the history and advancement of these sciences and of man's gradual development of tools and theories. These are so well written they would interest the most science-resistant readers. *The Kingdom of the Sun* tells of the development of knowledge of the solar system, from earliest records to modern times. This book is superbly written. *The Human Body: Its Structure and Operation* is an authoritative treatment of man's place in the scale of living creatures, his bodily structure, and his various systems such as circulatory, digestive, and reproductive. The AAAS recommends this book not only for adolescents but for elementary-school libraries and for a teacher's reference, which means that it is also an exceedingly valuable book for the whole family.

Professor Herbert Zim of the University of Illinois has himself written almost as many books for children in the science fields as those included in one of the long series. The data in his books are carefully checked by specialists. He writes simply and clearly but never talks down to his readers who enjoy his books even as they absorb a really impressive amount of information by way of them. Although he has a number of books for the younger children and a few for adolescents, most of his writing is directed to the middle years, children eight to twelve. For the primary children, five to eight, *Snakes* and *Frogs and Toads* are of special interest, and any of the *What's Inside* books—*What's Inside of Engines? What's Inside of Plants? What's Inside of Animals? What's Inside of Me?*—are also well liked and well illustrated. For the middle years, one of his most popular and useful books is *Rocks and Minerals* (coauthor, Paul R. Shaffer), a handbook to carry into the field for rock and mineral identification. Good pictures in color assist the young rock hounds, and there are helpful hints on what specimens to collect and how to collect them. This book is highly recommended. His *Dinosaurs* and *Stars* (coauthor Robert H. Baker) are also well organized and helpful. *The Sun* is excellent, but be warned: It looks simple, but is not. Both the vocabulary and concepts are demanding. Choose from his some forty books according to your child's age and interests.

Franklyn M. Branley is almost as prolific a writer as Herbert Zim. Dr. Branley is Director of Educational Services, Astronomer, and Assistant Chairman at the American Museum-Hayden Planetarium. His simplest book is *Mickey's Magnet* (coauthor, Eleanor K. Vaughan), which explains the characteristics of the magnet, a perennially fascinating object for young children. *A Book of Planets for You, A Book of the Milky Way Galaxy for You,* and *The Big Dipper* are also for children six to seven or eight. All of his books are copiously illustrated and remarkably informative. *A Book of the Milky Way Galaxy for You* gives a fascinating and understandable explanation of how vast distances are measured. *The Sun: Star Number One* and *The Earth: Planet Number Three* are fuller and more advanced than books on similar subjects by Zim, but the style and striking pictures by Helmut K. Wimmer make them comprehensible and fascinating. *Experiments in Sky Watching,* which won the Edison Foundation Award for the best science book for children in 1959, is also for advanced readers. Clear directions are given for locating and observing the stars and planets and even for performing simple experiments. The Branley books are well written and have made a brilliant contribution to children's science interests, especially in the field of astronomy.

Jeanne Bendick came into the science field by way of art, and her own illustrations have added clarity and humor to her lively writing. Even the AAAS lavishes high praise on her books which are checked for accuracy by scientists and for interest by approving children. Mrs. Bendick's books have made a valuable addition to the *First Books.* Of *The First Book of Fishes,* for example, it would be hard to believe that any ichthyologist could have prepared a more skillful introduction to the field. *The First Book of Time* is a remarkably full treatment of time in relation to space and motion. Even relativity is discussed in understandable terms. One of her most popular books is *How Much and How Many: The Story of Weights and Measures.* It is delightful from the first picture to the last word, and the humor does not lessen or detract from the emphasis on scientific exactness. In fact, no child can read this book without an added respect for accuracy. These books are all for the middle years, eight to twelve. In *All Around You*, for the fives to sevens, she has made a science picture book that answers the young child's casual questions about the world he sees in his own neighborhood.

The science picture books are a real contribution to children's books for the early years. They may be read aloud to the fours, fives, and sixes or read by the sevens. Popular in this group are Robert M. McClung's old favorite *Bufo: The Story of a Toad*, which will be enjoyed by children up to ten, and his more recent *Sphinx: The Story of a Caterpillar*. Children encounter both of these creatures in their yards and gardens and find them odd and fascinating. *Bufo* carries the toad from the polliwog stage through three years to maturity. During this span of time Bufo has found shelter and food, has escaped enemies, and has shed his skin.

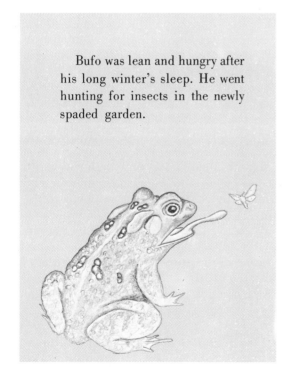

Bufo was lean and hungry after his long winter's sleep. He went hunting for insects in the newly spaded garden.

From *Bufo, The Story of a Toad*, written and illustrated by Robert M. McClung. Copyright 1954 by Robert M. McClung. Permission to reprint granted by the Publisher, William Morrow and Company, Inc.

When the book leaves him, he is on his way back to the pond and ready to mate. The caterpillar narrative discusses the phases of the life cycle and the natural enemies of the caterpillar. The illustrations in both books help to clarify and extend the information.

Olive Earle does her own delicate, delightful illustrations. *Robins in the Garden* provides the youngest children (5-8) with a close view and fuller knowledge of what is usually their first familiar bird. *Crickets* is equally informative, with a well-told story of the species and charming illustrations. These science picture books are really little introductions to nature study, but *Birds and Their Nests* goes beyond this introductory narrative to give older children (9-12) an account of some forty-two birds and their unique nest building.

Alice Goudey is also contributing richly to the area of the science picture book. Two distinguished examples are her *Houses from the Sea* and *Butterfly Time,* both exquisitely illustrated by Adrienne Adams. The last section of *Houses from the Sea* has a clear, definite chart of shells for identification. *Red Legs,* illustrated by Marie Nonnast, is an equally charming account of the brief life span of the red-legged grasshopper, one of the more familiar of its species and a creature no small child can resist.

For every science book mentioned in these brief samplings, some ten more books, equally valuable and appealing, could be named, in the same or in a completely different area of science. Follow your child's dominant interest if he has one; if not, introduce him to a few choice selections to start him reading in this science field. Use library books to begin with, but when your child finds one book or one special area of science that interests him deeply, encourage this interest by adding at least one book to the family library.

The science books described in this discussion are listed below along with several others. Also check the list that follows the discussion of books in the social studies field in the next section of this chapter. Several of the books to be found there will appeal to children with interests in such sciences as archaeology, anthropology, and geology.

Asimov, Isaac. *The Human Body: Its Structure and Operation.* Houghton, 1963. (12 up)

The Kingdom of the Sun. Abelard, 1963. (12 up)
Realm of Measure. Houghton, 1960. (12 up)
Realm of Numbers. Houghton, 1959. (12 up)

Barnett, Lincoln. *The World We Live In.* Time, 1955. (12 up)
Here is a book for the whole family. It was originally published in *Life* with magnificent full-page illustrations in color, covering every aspect of the earth's development, structure, and history. There is a special edition for young people, but the original is not hard reading and is completely fascinating.

Beeler, Nelson F., and Franklyn M. Branley. *Experiments with Light.* Crowell, 1958. (12 up)
Recommended by the AAAS, which says of it, "Achieves a very successful balance between explaining outright and encouraging the reader to see and prove for himself."

Bell, Thelma. *Snow.* Viking, 1954. (8-12)
Thunderstorm. Viking, 1960. (9-12)
Informative and beautiful books, especially *Snow*, which give adequate explanations of the formation of these weather phenomena, their helpful and destructive aspects.

Bendick, Jeanne. *All Around You.* McGraw, 1951. (5-8)
Electronics for Young People. McGraw, 1960. (8-12)
The First Book of Fishes. Watts, 1965. (8-12)
The First Book of Space Travel. Watts, 1963. (9-12)
The First Book of Time. Watts, 1963. (8-12)
How Much and How Many: The Story of Weights and Measures. McGraw, 1960. (8-12)

Berrill, Jacquelyn. *Wonders of the Arctic.* Dodd, 1959. (7-12)
This is an account of such animals of the arctic as the arctic fox, lemming, musk ox, and polar bear. It will fascinate children as young as five, but the reading level is older. *Wonders of the Antarctic* (1958) is equally absorbing.

Branley, Franklyn M. *The Big Dipper.* Crowell, 1962. (6-8)
A Book of Planets for You. Crowell, 1961. (6-8)
A Book of the Milky Way Galaxy for You. Crowell, 1965. (6-8)

The Earth: Planet Number Three. Crowell, 1966. (12 up)
Experiments in Sky Watching. Crowell, 1959. (12 up)
The Sun: Star Number One. Crowell, 1964. (12 up)

Branley, Franklyn M., and Eleanor K. Vaughan. *Mickey's Magnet.* Crowell, 1956. (5-8)

Carson, Rachel. *The Sea Around Us,* rev. ed. Adult edition. Oxford, 1961. Adapted for children and young people by Anne Terry White, Golden Press, 1958. (8-12)
While the adaptation lacks the style and beauty of the original work, it is well done and retains the fascinating aspects of the story of the sea, its origin, tides, currents, and marine life. Sections of the adult book are wonderful for family reading aloud.

Earle, Olive. *Birds and Their Nests.* Morrow, 1952. (9-12)
Crickets. Morrow, 1956. (5-8)
Robins in the Garden. Morrow, 1953. (5-8)

Forbush, Edward H., and John B. May. *A Natural History of the Birds of Eastern and Central North America.* Houghton, 1939.
Small bird guides for identification in the field are useful, but nothing equals a comprehensive and authoritative source of information such as this fat volume with its 97 color plates. For the whole family.

Goudey, Alice E. *Butterfly Time.* Scribner, 1964. (5-8)
Houses from the Sea. Scribner, 1959. (5-8)
Red Legs. Scribner, 1966. (5-8)

Hamilton, Russel, ed. *Science, Science, Science.* Watts, 1960. (12 up)
This is a collection of writings about science and scientists that is definitely for advanced readers. They will find it both interesting and informative.

Hess, Lilo. *Sea Horses.* Scribner, 1966. (8-12)
Remarkable photographs extend the clearly written information about the feeding, habits, and curious reversal of roles of these fascinating creatures, the male carrying the eggs and giving birth to the young. The second half of the book describes the incredible difficulties of having these ethereal creatures as pets.

Knight, David C. *The Science Book of Meteorology*. Watts, 1965. (11-14)
   Reviewing this book for *The Horn Book*, April 1965, Isaac Asimov rates it as "the best children's book in its field." It covers all the various aspects of weather, the part played by the sun, the invention of the barometer, and even includes a discussion of our modern weather satellites.

McClung, Robert M. *Bufo: The Story of a Toad*. Morrow, 1954. (4-9)
   Sphinx: The Story of a Caterpillar. Morrow, 1949. (4-9)

Reed, W. Maxwell. *The Earth for Sam*. Harcourt, 1960. (10-14)
   The Sea for Sam (W. Maxwell Reed and Wilfrid S. Bronson) Harcourt, 1960. (10-14)
   The Stars for Sam. Harcourt, 1960. (10-14)
   These classics, written in the thirties, were revised and reissued by Harcourt in 1960. They are exceptionally well written, illustrated with pictures, photographs, and diagrams. *Earth* gives the history of our planet and the thirteen periods in its development. *Stars* covers basic astronomy, and *Sea* the usual marine life, currents, tides, icebergs, etc. Paul Brandwein's revisions have added to the content but left intact the lucid, appealing style of the late Maxwell Reed.

Scheele, William E. *The First Mammals*. World, 1955. (10 or 12 up)
   Prehistoric Animals. World, 1954. (10 or 12 up)
   These two books by William Scheele, Director of the Cleveland Museum of Natural History and an artist, are fine references for a home library. Charts of geologic time, comparative sizes, skeletal drawings, and superb pictures of these monsters make the books fascinating to look at and read.

Zim, Herbert S. *Comets*. Morrow, 1957. (9-12)
   Dinosaurs. Morrow, 1954. (9-12)
   Frogs and Toads. Morrow, 1950. (8-11)
   Snakes. Morrow, 1949. (8-11)
   The Sun. Morrow, 1953. (9-12)
   What's Inside of Animals? Morrow, 1953. (7-10)
   What's Inside of Engines? Morrow, 1953. (8-11)
   What's Inside of Me? Morrow, 1952. (5-9)
   What's Inside of Plants? Morrow, 1952. (7-9)

Zim, Herbert S., and Robert H. Baker. *Stars.* Golden Press, 1956. (9-12)

Zim, Herbert S., and Paul R. Shaffer. *Rocks and Minerals.* Golden Press, 1957. (9-12)
Like other "Golden Nature Guides," *Stars* and *Rocks and Minerals* are handbooks rich in conveniently organized information.

SOCIAL STUDIES BOOKS

There are almost as many books for children in the social studies as there are in the sciences. Man is eternally curious about other men, past and present. Even very young children will stare at strange people or other children with fascinated attention. As they mature and their experiences increase, so should their curiosities. Where do those strange people come from? What do they do? Do they live the way we live? Do they have autos and airplanes and TV? What do they eat? How did people live long ago? Such questions are only the beginning of wonderment about other peoples, places, times, and ways of living and working that should grow as the mentally normal child grows. Fortunately, there is today such a plenitude of substantial books about man's past and present, his ways of living and working, his inventions and his arts, that the problem is to select from this abundance the particular area of the child's interest and the books suitable for his age and understanding.

For children under eight

For the prereading child and the child just beginning to read, turn back to some of the earlier chapters to the picture stories which induct children so pleasantly into various aspects of social studies. There are, for instance, Ethel Collier's *I Know a Farm* (pp. 84-85); Virginia Burton's man with a machine—*Mike Mulligan and His Steam Shovel* (p. 63)—and her evolution of a city—*The Little House* (pp. 63-64). In addition to these, there is no better example of two cultures mingling happily than in Leo Politi's *Little Leo* (p. 66). The hero travels to Italy and there inducts Italian children into the joys of playing Indians, complete with feathers, war dances, and whoops. Five-year-old togetherness! Norman

Bate's *Who Built the Bridge?* with beautiful pictures and an almost poetic text, introduces children to some of the huge modern machines, driven by powerful and skillful men, that can tear up the landscape and build bridges over great rivers. Geography begins with beauty in Herman and Nina Schneider's *Follow the Sunset*, in which children discover the reason for night and day, and with a brief easy-to-read text, follow the effect of the earth's rotation through different countries, from sunset to sunset.

Moving toward more information, there is Frances Cavanah's *Our Country's Story*. With gay, colorful pictures and a clear, appealing text, it tells the story of the United States from 1492 through colonization; the first Thanksgiving; our wars for independence, for the Union, and for other causes; expansion; and inventions—in short, it is a brief introduction to our history and growth. Miriam Schlein's *It's About Time* and Feenie Ziner and Elizabeth Thompson's *The True Book of Time* capitalize on the child's early preoccupation with learning to tell time and with watches and clocks. The first book deals with time itself, from seconds to years. The Ziner and Thompson book surprises the modern child by telling him all the ways men told time before clocks or watches were invented.

If children of the Southwest or other children who may travel westward become interested in the Indian cliff dwellers and the remains of their habitations, they will enjoy *Cliff Dwellers of Walnut Canyon* by Carroll Lane Fenton and Alice Epstein. These Arizona cliff dwellers who lived over eight hundred years ago are vividly described and pictured together with their tribal customs. The text is unnecessarily primerish, but the pictures are unusually clear in revealing the cliff dwellings and the activities of the people. Easy reading with the maximum information for slow readers.

For these youngest children there are also innumerable picture books about fire engines and firemen, airplanes and airports, trains, machines, boats, etc. These sometimes satisfy or rouse interest, but are for the most part too ephemeral to warrant purchase. Rather borrow them from our generous and well-stocked public libraries.

For the middle years—eight to twelve
During these years, eight, nine, ten, and eleven, there is aston-

ishing growth in many directions, including intellectual curiosities along many lines. Prehistoric man; the ancient civilizations of Egypt, Greece, and Rome; the growth of our own United States; the different tribes of American Indians; man's inventions, explorations, and arts are all to be found discussed for children and youth in well-written, well-illustrated books. Obviously, no family should acquire books in all of these fields, but here is a brief sampling of outstanding authors and choice books to buy or to borrow from the public library. Remember also that biographies and historical fiction belong in this category of social studies; so reconsider some of the books listed in the bibliographies for those areas.

Anne Terry White has written remarkably fine books in the field of anthropology and the prehistoric world. Fairly simple to start with are *The First Men in the World* and *Prehistoric America.* The latter describes geological findings that reveal how this continent was formed and how it has changed over the millions of years of its existence. It also shows how the bones of prehistoric reptiles, mammals, and men fit into the geological time table. *The First Men in the World* is a more general approach to archaeological studies all over the world. The writer tells about Stone Age Man, Neanderthal Man, Java Man, Swiss Lake Dwellers, and others, showing how the findings from excavations have contributed to modern theories of man's slow evolution. Both books are well illustrated. *All About Archaeology* contains brief and fascinating accounts of the early civilizations of the Egyptians, Etruscans, Aztecs, and many others. It is fascinating reading, but you may prefer to have the fuller, more advanced book on similar lines called *Lost Worlds: The Romance of Archaeology.* This is harder reading but a fine book to grow into and to read aloud for general family enjoyment.

Mary Renault, distinguished author of those popular historical novels *The King Must Die* and *Bull from the Sea*, has written for children an unforgettable account of one of the most heroic pages in history—the Greek-Persian wars. She calls her book *The Lion in the Gateway.* It gives an appealing account of Greek civilization in all its richness and then records the magnificent resistance of the Greeks to Persian invasion under King Darius in the fifth century B.C. Here are descriptions of the famous battles of Marathon, Salamis, and Thermopylae, which were fought against seemingly unsurmountable odds, but with the Greeks so gloriously triumphant the victories are a satisfaction to readers of any age. This is authentic history so dramatically presented it lives.

Holling C. Holling has given children books of rare pictorial beauty and of unusual content. Child after child who has owned these books has cherished them and kept them into his adult years. They are, every one of them, books the whole family can enjoy. *Paddle-to-the-Sea* is a colorful introduction to the geography of the Great Lakes with the connecting rivers that move eastward to the sea. It tells the dramatic story of a small carved canoe with a little figure, the "Paddle Person," made by an Indian boy. This canoe with a message carved on it, he launched on a spring freshet which emptied into Lake Superior. After many an adventure and some human first aid now and then, Paddle Person, still erect in his small canoe, came at last to the ocean and was carried on eastward to France. *Seabird* is an equally dramatic account of the development of our shipping vessels and industry, from sailing boats and clipper ships to our huge modern steamships. Different from both of these is *Tree in the Trail,* which begins with Indian tribes hunting buffalo. Then come the white men, moving westward with long wagon trains crawling painfully over prairies and mountains, seemingly impassable country, and stalked by hunger and hostile Indians. Yet the same tree in the trail sees the white men weather every obstacle and settle the new country. The West was theirs. In these and all of Holling C. Holling's books there are anthropology, geography, science, history, and imagination making beautiful books of timeless interest and values.

Gerald Johnson, a well-known writer of adult history, has written for his grandson Peter a three-part history of the United States. The books are called *America Is Born, America Grows Up,* and *America Moves Forward.* In the first book, he introduces what is to children an unfamiliar idea, namely that for a long time our colonists thought of themselves as loyal Englishmen. Meanwhile, their new country was at work turning them into quite different people—Americans. Robert Frost's poem "The Gift Outright" develops the same idea. The first book carries our history from 1492 to 1787 and the achievement of our independence. The two later books carry our development forward to modern days and succeed in giving children a glimpse of the roles played by European powers not only in our history but in world history as well.

These are provocative books, clearly written for children ten to thirteen and well worth owning and reading aloud.

For advanced readers, twelve and up
    Hendrick Willem Van Loon's book *The Story of Mankind,* which was the first book to receive the Newbery Medal, has become a classic in the field, and is beginning to pay the usual penalty of classics—neglect. Yet it is a book the whole family can enjoy and use as a reference over the years. Van Loon brought to informational writing rare insight; gay, lively style; a new approach to history and biography for young people; and an inexhaustible richness of information. He traces man from his beginnings through all the major stages of development through World War I. For example, the wanderings of the Jews, Caesar's western conquests, the periods of exploration, the rise of towns, the invention of machinery, and the coming of factories are all described. Into the account of periods and movements are inserted brilliant character studies or "profiles" of men who proved to be "world shakers" and changed the direction of civilization. There are also illuminating glimpses of momentous development in the arts during different periods and countries. The 1951 edition of the book includes six additional chapters written by the author's son. These cover World War II and the formation of the United Nations.
    Although this book belongs to the fourteens upwards, there are single chapters which can be used with younger children. The first ten are good to read aloud, as are chapters on Greek and Roman life or the Greek theater or the chapter "At the End of the Eighteenth Century, Europe Heard Strange Reports of Something Which Had Happened in the Wilderness of the North American Continent." This is a rich book indeed, not to be read through as a chore, from cover to cover, but to be dipped into, used as a reference, and enjoyed for its sound scholarship presented with a light touch. If only Van Loon might have lived to bring to bear on modern space exploration his imaginative wonder and rich scholarship. Van Loon's scratchy-looking sketches are amazingly interpretative. Look, for example, at that contrasting pair "Man Power and Machine Power."
    For mature readers of thirteen upwards, Isaac Asimov's two books on *The Roman Republic* and *The Roman Empire* are good reading for the whole family. The two books record the history

of Roman life from its early days to the onset of the Middle Ages. The story in both books is told with such clarity that centuries, movements, laws, emperors, philosophies are made understandable and fall into logical sequence. The scholarship is sound and the otherwise oppressive weight of facts is enlivened with characteristic flashes of humor, homely details, and a superb sense of the dramatic pageant of events and human beings that make history. But it must be admitted that political and military exploits over centuries, especially in the second book, make heavy reading. These are fine reference books for the family library to be supplemented at the adult and young adult levels with Edith Hamilton's *The Greek Way* and *The Roman Way*.

Another notable writer-artist with an original approach to history is Genevieve Foster with her books *George Washington's World, Abraham Lincoln's World, The World of Captain John Smith, Augustus Caesar's World, The World of Columbus and Sons*. In each of these five books, the author takes a horizontal look across and around the world to tell what was happening of importance when the hero was born, during his childhood, in his youth and early manhood, and so throughout his life. In this world's-eye view of countries, periods, and people, young readers see movements rise and culminate or disappear, men who turn the tide of history in one direction or another leaving the world markedly better or worse for their presence. The effect is curiously impressive and gives children a rounded sense of history that their textbooks rarely suggest. Only an author-artist with a remarkable sense of design could integrate her text and illustrations as Mrs. Foster does. One or more of these books is fascinating to own as a reference. What was China doing in those days? What impact did Napoleon make on world history? The answers to these and similar questions may be found in these books.

Margaret Mead is a distinguished anthropologist. Her book *People and Places*, for children and young people, is an authoritative introduction to the methods and findings of modern anthropologists and is handsomely illustrated as well. She presents five cultural groups—Eskimo, Plains Indian, Balinese, Ashanti, and Minoan, describing their family life; group organization; clothing in relation to environment; and artistic, religious, and economic development. She concludes these studies with a section called "Man Asks About Man," in which she talks about similarities and differences between peoples, with some suggestions for solving the major problems in the world and moving toward a more orderly world. Dr. Mead, whether writing or lecturing, is unfailingly provocative, and this book has a scope that will challenge the thinking of young minds and old ones too.

The Caves of the Great Hunters, by Hans Baumann, reads like a story. In Lascaux, France, September 12, 1940, four boys were poking around cave country, when Simon's dog suddenly disappeared down a hole. Of course, the boys went after him and found themselves in an imposing cave whose walls were covered with huge drawings of animals. These were so lifelike they seemed to move. Frightened and awed by what they had discovered, the boys brought their teacher to the cave. He realized the great importance of their find and sent for Abbé Henri Breuil, a famous authority, to come down from Paris. Breuil pronounced their find a relic of the ice age. In learning about the significance of the Lascaux cave, the boys (and the reader) also learn of other similar discoveries. The book is both anthropology and art, for these powerful cave drawings are the living testimonial to life and civilization in prehistoric days.

The list below includes the books for the social studies that have been discussed, as well as some additional titles that you may find helpful. If these books, or those in the earlier list of science books, do not include your child's special hobby, go to the lists mentioned on pages 281-282 and to your children's librarian, and you will probably find precisely what you need.

Ames, Gerald, and Rose Wyler. *The First People in the World.* Harper, 1958. (8-10)

Asimov, Isaac. *The Roman Empire.* Houghton, 1967. (13 up)
   The Roman Republic. Houghton, 1966. (13 up)

Bate, Norman. *Who Built the Bridge?* Scribner, 1954. (4-8)

Baumann, Hans. *The Caves of the Great Hunters,* rev. ed., tr. by Isabel and Florence McHugh. Illustrated with pictures of the cave drawings and with drawings by Hans Peter Renner. Pantheon, 1954, 1962. (12 up)

Cavanah, Frances. *Our Country's Story*, rev. ed. Rand McNally, 1962. (6-10)
This revised edition includes Alaska and Hawaii.

Clark, Ann Nolan. *In My Mother's House*. Viking, 1941, 1951. (5-8)
This pictorial narrative is already a classic, giving children pictures of the homes, food, festivals, farming, and sheep herding of the Pueblo Indians. Poetic, cadenced prose and sensitive pictures make this a rarely beautiful book.

Duvoisin, Roger. *And There Was America*. Knopf, 1938. (7-11)
Stylized, colorful pictures by the author and a simple text tell the dramatic story of the discovery, exploration, and colonization of our country. It is told around the theme that Columbus set sail for China "and there was America." The narrative first tells of the discovery and exploration of America. Then, it covers the colonization by the Spanish, Dutch, French, and English. A clear chronology would help, but it is a fascinating beginning of American history.

Evans, Eva Knox. *All About Us*. Golden Press, 1947. (8-12)
People Are Important. Golden Press, 1951. (8-12)
Both books develop the idea that regardless of the differences of peoples in race, skin colors, foods, dress, homes, and customs, all human beings have an innate dignity that makes them worthy of respect.

Fenton, Carroll Lane, and Alice Epstein. *Cliff Dwellers of Walnut Canyon*. Day, 1960. (7-10)

Foster, Genevieve. *Abraham Lincoln's World*. Scribner, 1949. (11-14)
Augustus Caesar's World. Scribner, 1947. (11-14)
George Washington's World. Scribner, 1941. (11-14)
The World of Captain John Smith. Scribner, 1959. (11-14)
The World of Columbus and Sons. Scribner, 1965. (11-14)

Hamilton, Edith. *The Greek Way*. Norton, 1930, 1942.
The Roman Way. Norton, 1932.

Holling, Holling C. *Paddle-to-the-Sea*. Houghton, 1941. (8-12)
Seabird. Houghton, 1948. (8-12)
Tree in the Trail. Houghton, 1942. (8-14)

Johnson, Gerald W. *America Is Born*. Morrow, 1959. (10-13)
America Grows Up. Morrow, 1960. (10-13)
America Moves Forward. Morrow, 1960. (10-13)

Mead, Margaret. *People and Places*. World, 1959. (12 up)

Myron, Robert. *Shadow of the Hawk*. Putnam, 1964. (12 up)
   This is a powerful creation of the Mound Builders of the Ohio River
Valley, the Hopewell and Adena Indians, from 500 B.C. to 500 A.D.
Their artifacts, carvings, and drawings show a surprisingly sophisticated civilization, and the illustrations for this fascinating record,
made by John F. Hopkins, add much to the interest of the book. Adults
as well as young people will enjoy it.

Perkins, Carol Morse and Marlin. *"I Saw You from Afar."* Atheneum,
   1965. (8-12)
   The title is an ancient Bushman's greeting to make small people feel
tall. The authors have told an appealing story of these gentle, friendly
folk who live in the Kalahari desert with little food, less water, and
extreme heat and cold. With only grass shelters, if any, these Bushmen
have both dignity and grace in their way of living. Fine photographs
and a well-told story make this a delightful book.

Renault, Mary. *The Lion in the Gateway*. Harper, 1964. (10-14)

Robinson, Charles A. *The First Book of Ancient Egypt*. Watts, 1961.
   (9-12)
   The First Book of Ancient Mesopotamia and Persia. Watts, 1962.
   (10-13)
   A member of the Commission for Excavation of the Athenian Agora,
Professor Robinson writes of these civilizations, also Greece and Rome,
with authority and appeal.

Scheele, William E. *The Earliest Americans*. World, 1963. (11 up)
   The Mound Builders. World, 1960. (11 up)

Schlein, Miriam. *It's About Time*. W. R. Scott, 1955. (5-8)

Schneider, Nina and Herman. *Follow the Sunset*. Doubleday, 1952.
   (4-8)

Spencer, Cornelia (pseud. of Grace S. Yaukey). *Made in Japan*. Knopf, 1963. (12 up)
A brief history of the Japanese people is followed by delightful chapters on their houses, "clay to porcelain," their crafts, gardens, paintings, woodcuts, and festivals. An appealing reference book.

Tunis, Edwin. *Colonial Living*. World, 1957. (10 up)
Frontier Living. World, 1961. (10 up)
Copious illustrations help to re-create the everyday life of people of the seventeenth through the nineteenth centuries in this country. Fine reference books for children to know and use.

White, Anne Terry. *All About Archaeology*. Random House, 1959. (8-12)
The First Men in the World. Random House, 1953. (8-12)
Lost Worlds: The Romance of Archaeology. Random House, 1941. (11 up)
Prehistoric America. Random House, 1951. (8-12)

Van Loon, Hendrick Willem. *The Story of Mankind*. Liveright, 1921, 1951. (12 up)

Ziner, Feenie, and Elizabeth Thompson. *The True Book of Time*. Childrens Press, 1956. (6-8)

It is worth noting at this point that in the fields of the sciences and the social studies there is an enormous multiplicity of titles. This occurs not only in the series—*First Books, True Books, All About Books*, and *Landmark Books*—but in the books by individual authors as well, and who but a specialist can say which book is best? Librarians remark that when a group of children gets started on dinosaurs or on Greek and Roman life, they gratefully assemble every book available, and the children choose according to their reading abilities. If you can't obtain one of the Anne Terry White books, *The First Men in the World*, for instance, look for *The First People in the World*, by Gerald Ames and Rose Wyler, with stunning illustrations by Leonard Weisgard. It is simpler, and while it won't satisfy advanced readers, it is a good beginning. Or try for William Scheele's *The Earliest Americans*, in which he describes archaeological discoveries on this continent and explains their significance. Or if your children are fascinated with the Mound Builders, try either Robert Myron's *Shadow of the Hawk* or William Scheele's *The Mound Builders,* both well-illustrated and absorbing books for good readers of eleven on. Such multiplicity of titles, by the way, makes possible comparisons in handling of data, etc., an excellent training for young people.

Probably the informational books will not have so wide an appeal as other sorts of reading. They are books for the special child with a special interest, who demands facts and answers. Some are so well written and so beautiful to look at that they will satisfy the reader aesthetically as well as factually. Among such books are Mary and Conrad Buff's *Big Tree* (pp. 96-97), Mary Renault's *The Lion in the Gateway,* and Margaret Mead's *People and Places.* Best of all, the entire family can profit by a look into these books. Even those for the youngest readers are amazingly informative, and those for the advanced readers will prove adequate and fascinating for most adults who are not specialists. So let your young interrogators question as they will. There are books to answer their questions and keep their curiosities growing.

RELIGION, ETHICS, AND THE ARTS

✦❧❦✦

14

Religion, Ethics, and Books
Music
The Graphic Arts
Religious Education in the Home
Conclusion

It seems natural to consider books on the arts and religion in the same chapter, because they have been associated so often. From earliest times, poetry, music, and painting often grew out of religious ceremonial or out of the welling up in human beings of the need to express joy or grief, thanksgiving, praise and supplication. And so there were primitive ceremonials and cave drawings, and later the moving chants of the Jewish liturgy, the magnificent masses of the Catholic Church, the great hymnology of the Protestants, and the incomparable Psalms for all three faiths. Religion has always inspired people to poetic expression, from simple little verses like Christina Rossetti's charming night blessing:

> Angels at the foot,
> And angels at the head,
> And like a curly little lamb
> My pretty babe in bed.

to Gerard Manley Hopkins' poem of praise "Pied Beauty" (see *Poems of Gerard Manley Hopkins*, Oxford, 1918).

In the history and development of various religious groups, the graphic arts, too, have contributed a magnificent inheritance. Christianity, for example, inspired a great treasury of European art. Indeed, there is hardly a story from the Old or New Testaments that has not been represented in some famous painting. Thus, time and time again, we find religion and the arts supplementing each other richly.

Another reason for considering books about religion and the various arts together is that although there is no prohibition for teaching the arts in the public schools as there is for religion, considerable responsibility for both will always remain with the family. Tolerance or intolerance toward differing religious groups stems from the family. Home experiences with the arts or the lack of them will send children into the schools keenly interested or the reverse. Arts programs in the public schools differ widely throughout the length and breadth of this huge country of ours. Many of the big city public schools have rich offerings in music, literature, and art, but in rural areas or in remote towns and villages programs may be meager or nonexistent. More is the pity, because in this age of discord and violence both children and adults need the humanizing influence that the arts and religion have traditionally provided. An understanding and appreciation of religious literature and the various arts are not only civilizing forces but an essential part of an educated person's background. And no matter how rich the school programs in the arts may be, the strongest impetus toward both the arts and religion will always come most naturally from the home.

RELIGION, ETHICS, AND BOOKS

This seems to be an age of controversy in many fields with no area developing greater diversities and extremes than religion. The press has printed articles about individuals claiming "God is dead," sometimes on the same page with reports of the success of a famous revivalist. The fasts, feasts, and meetings of Catholic and Jewish groups are constantly in the news, as are the conferences of various Protestant groups—Presbyterians, Episcopalians, Quakers, Mormons, and sundry others. Yet simultaneously with these religious activities sympathetically reported, the anti-religious groups have been sufficiently zealous to have hymns, prayers, and religious literature legislated out of the public schools.

Fortunately, in the United States each family not only has the right to decide on its own religion or on no religion at all but also is entitled to have its decision respected. The family may be Jewish or Catholic or may belong to one or another of the many Protestant faiths or it may believe in Hinduism, Islamism, Buddhism, Confucianism, or Shintoism, or it may be agnostic or atheistic. But whatever the family's faith or lack of faith, it would seem only fair and decent to establish in the home, attitudes of amiable, even sympathetic, acceptance of religious differences and a courteous respect for other people's points of view. If the adults in a family feel this respect and show this courtesy, so will the children, and right here is one foundation stone in social understanding among peoples.

It is well for all of us to realize and to help our children realize the fact that from every major religion, great moral and ethical standards of behavior have developed. The classical world of ancient Rome, for example, had its great Stoic philosopher Marcus Aurelius, whose *Meditations* embody an ethical code that in spite of his limited vision in some areas the world could profit from today. Furthermore, as the African and Asian nations become more important in the world scene, we will do well to acquaint ourselves and our children with their dominant religious beliefs and practices. However, it is particularly important that children be familiar with the Judaeo-Christian traditions, since those principles of moral behavior predominate in our modern Western civilization even if they do not always prevail. And writers for newspapers and magazines and authors of both fiction and nonfiction assume that their readers are familiar with the Bible stories that exemplify those principles. For example, an article deploring the indifference of onlookers to a crime and its victim was headed: "Good Samaritan Not Afraid of Involvement." And when a famous man fell from grace, the comment in another article was: "He sold his birthright for a mess of pottage." Do your children know the stories that dramatize these sayings? They should know them and dozens more from the Old and New Testaments, if they are to be decently literate and aware of the traditional code of ethics of their civilization.

Furthermore, all religious folk must remember that many people apply the ethical codes of religion without believing in any church or organized religious faith. These agnostics or nonbelievers are frequently leaders in civic welfare and world charities and are often people with deep personal compassion and general helpfulness. This is so often true that church members can never afford to be censorious of their unchurched neighbors. Rather, their wide charities and broad sympathies should be a challenge to the religious. If the Judaeo-Christian ethics are truly a part of our lives, it behooves all of us to pull together to see that our children know this code of ethics and that they grow up with adults—in or out of churches—who love their neighbors as themselves and make themselves their brothers' keepers. Ethics at work in the world!

To sum up. Regardless of our belief or lack of belief in some specific religion, it would seem desirable for all adults to help children (1) develop tolerance and sympathetic understanding for the religious beliefs of others, (2) learn about other religious beliefs and practices, perhaps with emphasis on the Judaeo-Christian traditions and literature, since they are predominant in our Western civilization, and (3) understand that nonreligious peoples can— and often do—have just as high ethical standards as those who follow some specific organized religion. How can we accomplish these goals? One of the first and easiest ways is through children's books.

Religion should never be a lugubrious or belligerent matter, and happily in children's books it is presented cheerfully and often casually in the development of good stories. In the course of their reading, it is possible for children to encounter quite a sampling of different religious beliefs and practices and also to achieve some understanding of the part faith and prayer have played in the lives of many people. In the following books, for example, children meet attractive young heroes and heroines, and in reading about their adventures are introduced in some detail to various religious beliefs and customs:

All-of-a-Kind Family, by Sydney Taylor, ill. by Helen John. Follett, 1951. (8-12)
This book about an orthodox Jewish family, living on the Lower

East Side of New York in the early twentieth century, presents amusing everyday adventures against a background of piously kept Jewish feasts and fasts. Naturally, the five little girls prefer the feasts and Mama's mouth-watering foods. Delightful for all children. (See review, p. 125).

. . . *And Now Miguel*, by Joseph Krumgold, ill. by Jean Charlot. Crowell, 1953. Newbery Medal. (9-14)
   This is a notable story about growing up, with a Catholic background and a unique discussion of prayer between Miguel and his brother. (See review, p. 117).

The Bronze Bow, by Elizabeth Speare. Houghton, 1961. Newbery Medal. (12-16)
   An exciting historical novel about the Jewish people during the life of Christ. Eighteen-year-old Daniel, confused and wrong headed, is fighting desperately to free the Jewish people from the yoke of the alien and arrogant Romans. When he encounters Jesus and his gospel of love, Daniel's whole life is changed.

Daughter of the Mountains, by Louise Rankin, ill. by Kurt Wiese. Viking, 1948. (9-12)
   When a little Tibetan girl discovers that her beloved dog has been stolen, she sets off on a long and dangerous journey to recover it. No matter what difficulties she encounters, she feels secure in the love and protection of Buddha.

Henner's Lydia, by Marguerite de Angeli, ill. by author. Doubleday, 1936. Also *Thee, Hannah!* Doubleday, 1949. (8-12)
   Marguerite de Angeli was a pioneer in writing perceptive stories about minority groups in an often insensitive world. The first story is about a little Amish girl on a Pennsylvania farm. The second story is about a small rebellious Quaker in Philadelphia, who discovered unexpectedly the worth of her sect and was proud to be counted a Quaker.

In My Mother's House, by Ann Nolan Clark, ill. by Velino Herrera. Viking, 1941, 1951. (9-11) Also *The Desert People*, ill. by Allan Houser. Viking, 1962. (7-9)
   The first story tells of a Navaho child's feeling about her home, family, ways of living, and the beauty of her world. The illustrations

by an Indian artist add beauty to the cadenced text. In the second story a Papago Indian boy tells about the life of his people. The illustrations for this book are also by an Indian artist.

Mrs. Clark is able to interpret the Indians' ways of life so that modern children respect them. *Secret of the Andes* (1952) is the story of a dedicated Peruvian Indian boy. It was a Newbery Medal winner. *Santiago* (1955) is about a Guatemalan youth, raised in a Spanish home but determined to find his place in the world as an Indian. Both of these perceptive stories are for children eleven to fourteen.

Juanita, by Leo Politi, ill. by the author. Scribner, 1948. Also *Moy Moy* (1960) and *Pedro, the Angel of Olvera Street* (1946). (4-8)
   Juanita and *Pedro* are both laid in the Mexican quarter of Los Angeles. In *Juanita*, young readers see the Catholic custom of Blessing the Animals the day before Easter. In *Pedro*, a small boy is chosen to play a part in the traditional Christmas festival. The Chinese section of Los Angeles is the setting for the story of *Moy Moy*, which means "little sister." It tells of Moy Moy's participation in the celebration of the Chinese New Year.

Little House in the Big Woods, by Laura Ingalls Wilder, ill. by Garth Williams. Harper, 1932, 1953. (9-12)
   A Protestant background but not markedly so except for occasional church festivals and the missionary barrel! (See review on p. 132).

Meeting with a Stranger, by Duane Bradley, ill. by E. Harper Johnson. Lippincott, 1964. (10-12)
   To a proud African tribe comes an American, Sam Jones, to teach the people how to raise more and better sheep. The boy Teffera, like the rest of his tribe, is suspicious that the American may try to poison the sheep and take the people captives. It is the story of breaking down one suspicion and one superstition after another, with intelligent young Teffera holding out to the last. Finally, tribal men and boys come to trust the good will of these strange Americans who have a way of proving their point and also infinite patience and kindness.

Orange-Robed Boy, by Patricia Wallace Garlan and Maryjane Dunstan, ill. by Pau Oo Thet. Viking, 1967. (9-12)
   A delightful and detailed introduction to Buddhism from the standpoint of a lively twelve-year-old boy. At that age, Burmese boys put on

the orange robes of Buddhist priesthood and follow the priests into the monastery. There they are prepared in the ways of Buddhist manhood or for the priesthood itself. The choice is theirs. Of the six active game-playing boys in this story, Aung Khin is the only one who feels strongly drawn to the priesthood, so strongly that he remains after all the others have returned to their families. But in the end, through the patient counseling of a wise old priest, Aung Khin also returns to his family and the everyday world. This is a charming picture of Burmese village and family life, and both the hero and his five companions, with their frequent falls from grace and continual hunger for family foods, are amusing and real. Yet the eight-fold ways of the Buddha are seriously presented and considered by these same boys.

Plain Girl, by Virginia Sorensen, ill. by Charles Geer. Harcourt, 1955. (9-11)
Like Marguerite de Angeli's *Henner's Lydia*, this is the story of a little Amish girl. In a perceptive narrative, young readers learn how Esther grows in understanding of the basic faith of her people.

Waterless Mountain, by Laura Armer, ill. by the author and Sidney Armer. McKay, 1931. Newbery Medal. (12-14)
Like Ann Nolan Clark's *In My Mother's House*, this is a story about the Navahos. Here we have a rather detailed account of the Indians' religious beliefs and practices, because the hero is preparing to become a Medicine Man.

Wee Joseph, by William MacKellar, ill. by Ezra Jack Keats. McGraw, 1957. (7-10)
A delightful Scotch Protestant story about the way Davie's prayers for his runt of a dog, "Wee Joseph," combined with a rare scientific event worked a "wee miracle" in his behalf.

Young Fu of the Upper Yangtze, by Elizabeth Lewis, ill. by Kurt Wiese. Winston, 1932. Newbery Medal. (10-14)
Although this is an older book, it is about China in conflict and the young hero running into more perils and excitement than he has been prepared for by the Confucian precepts he has been taught. The book is full of Confucian proverbs used by adults to teach Fu the error of his ways.

After a few such easy introductions to other faiths and customs, one or more nonfictional books like the following might be read and discussed together in the family group:

One God: The Ways We Worship Him, by Florence M. Fitch, ill. with photographs. Lothrop, 1944. (8-12)
Here is a side by side report of Jewish, Catholic, and Protestant ways of worshipping God, with detailed pictures inside the churches and temples. It is a beautiful and sympathetic presentation of each group.

The Story of World Religions, by Katharine Savage. Walck, 1967. (12 up)
The development of the main religions of today—Judaism, Hinduism, Buddhism, Confucianism, Christianity, and Islam—is described in this book without comparisons but adequately. A good reference.

The Tree of Life: Selections from the Literature of the World's Religions, ed. by Ruth Smith, ill. by Boris Artzybasheff. Viking, 1942. (12 up)
Verse and prose translations selected from the sacred writings of thirteen religions—American Indian, Babylonian, Buddhist, Christian, Confucianist, Egyptian, Greek, Hebrew, Hindu, Mohammedan, Norse, Taoist, and Zoroastrian. There is a brief introduction to each group of selections in this handsome book. It is a good source for the literature of a religion, perhaps more useful in the school library than in the home library.

World Faiths: A Story of Religion, by Liva Baker, ill. with photographs. Abelard, 1965. (12 up)
A fascinating account of the major religions of the world. In a comparative study of the world faiths, Liva Baker discusses the principal beliefs of each religion and at the same time points out the similarities and contrasts in the holy places and the observance of holy days, etc., of the various religions. A highly readable and enlightening book.

The World's Great Religions, by the Editorial Staff of *Life*. Special Edition for Young Readers, adapted by Jane W. Watson. Illustrated. Golden Press, 1958. (10 up)
The illustrations in this juvenile edition of the adult publication by *Life* have lost something of the glowing richness of the originals. So

look at both editions before you buy. The adaptation is well handled, and children and young people will never miss the details of the theological beliefs of the major world religions taken up in the adult edition. The book discusses Hinduism, Buddhism, Islam, Judaism, Christianity, and the various Chinese philosophies. This is a deservedly popular reference both for children and young people, and either version— adult or juvenile—is a fine book for the home library.

Add also the biographies of some of our great religious men such as St. Francis of Assisi, Father Damien, George Washington Carver, and Ben Gurion, to name a few. Such reading is bound to expand the child's understanding of the fact that a sense of security rising from a belief in and practice of prayer as communion with God has been and still is a source of strength to many people. Sometimes, reading the lives of the Christian saints and heroes has the effect of revealing more vividly Christ's own life and ministry. Certainly, when we see young people today volunteering for the Peace Corps in remote and unappealing parts of the globe, or for service in the most turbulent trouble spots of our big cities, it renews our faith in Christ's gospel of love that can forget the comfort and security of one's self and reach out to help fellow beings wherever that help is needed and at whatever cost. Up until now, we have had very few stories of the great leaders of religions outside the Judaeo-Christian traditions, but one such (*The Prince Who Gave Up a Throne: A Story of the Buddha*) is included in the following list of books arranged alphabetically by title:

Ben Gurion's Israel, by Benjamin Appel, ill. with photographs. Grosset, 1965. (12 up)
As the title implies, this book is about the country of Israel, its beginnings and development, as well as the life of the man who did so much to make it what it is today. See also *Ben Gurion: The Biography of an Extraordinary Man*, by Robert St. John. Doubleday, 1959.

Doctor Tom Dooley: My Story, by Dr. Thomas Dooley. New and revised edition, Ariel Books, 1962. (11-15)
This personal account of a young physician's arduous and selfless work with people in the Far East is a moving record of service. Even after he knew he had incurable cancer, he came to the United States

to raise money for his mission and then returned to his work. This little book has something of the electrifying effect that Dr. Dooley's gallant personality also had.

Girl in White Armor: The True Story of Joan of Arc, by Albert Bigelow Paine. Macmillan, 1927, 1964. (12-15)
Abridged from the author's adult biography, this book is nevertheless a full-sized account of the good Joan, from her simple peasant beginnings to her martyrdom. It is a story no reader ever forgets.

God's Troubadour: The Story of St. Francis of Assisi, by Sophie Jewett, ill. with reproductions of frescoes by Giotto. Revised edition. Crowell, 1957. (8-12)
There have been other lives of St. Francis for children, but this still remains the choice version. It is lovely to look at, to read aloud, and to reread. Leo Politi's *St. Francis and the Animals* (Scribner, 1959), with its tender, colorful illustrations, is a small child's introduction to the much loved saint. (5-8)

John Wesley, by May Yonge McNeer, ill. by Lynd Ward. Abingdon, 1951. Also *Martin Luther* (1953). (12-14)
The powerful illustrations by Lynd Ward add much to the effectiveness of these two biographies. If the life of John Wesley seems simpler and easier to understand, the fighting spirit of Martin Luther adds zest to the record of his turbulent life.

The Life of St. Paul, by Harry Emerson Fosdick, ill. by Leonard Everett Fisher. Random House, 1962.
A magnificent re-creation of the life and times of St. Paul, a militant early Christian who endured dangers and hardships to establish the early Christians as a church. His journeys through Europe to Ephesus, Jerusalem, and, finally, the fatal last journey to Rome and his death are vividly described. How that little band of early Christians, scattered over the vast Roman Empire, could have had the impact on civilization that it has had is due largely to this gallant fighter who wrote his own epitaph with the words: "I have fought the good fight, I have finished the race, I have kept the faith."

Man of Molokai: The Life of Father Damien, by Ann Roos, ill. by Raymond Lufkin. Lippincott, 1943. (12 up)

Long before there were modern leprosariums for the care and cure of lepers, Father Damien, a young Catholic priest, went out to the leper colony of Molokai and spent the rest of his life ministering to these neglected and pitiful people. This is a stirring record of his work and his life, which did much to publicize the plight of these unfortunates and to bring about modern treatment.

Moses, by Katherine Shippen. Harper, 1949. (12-15)
This story of the great leader of the Israelites is told with emphasis on his complete dedication to his God and his people. It will make the Bible narrative more alive and more understandable.

Pope John XXIII, by Roy MacGregor-Hastie, ill. with photographs. Criterion, 1962. (11 up)
This biography of the universally beloved Pope John makes the "Pope of Peace" a very real and lovable human being as well as a great man and Christian. *Pope Paul VI* (1965) is an excellent introduction to today's papal leader.

The Prince Who Gave Up a Throne: A Story of the Buddha, by Nancy Serage, ill. by Kazue Mizumura. Crowell, 1966. (9-12)
Like the story of St. Francis of Assisi, this moving record of a saint's progress is a story of renunciation, dedication, and fulfillment. Born a prince around 563 B.C., Siddhartha Gautama was raised in the rich splendor of an Oriental court. At twenty-nine, he renounced his family and luxurious way of life to seek God. It was six years later before he attained union with God and became Buddha the Enlightened One. After that, he returned to people and the world, preaching his eight-fold way of life, first to his father's court and then throughout the Eastern world. Beautifully told and illustrated, this small book is a fine introduction to Buddhism.

The Story of George Washington Carver, by Arna Bontemps, ill. by E. Harper Johnson. Grosset, 1954. (10-12)
For somewhat older children, see also *Dr. George Washington Carver: Scientist*, by Shirley Graham and George D. Lipscomb, ill. by Elton C. Fax. Messner, 1944. (11-15) A great and original scientist and a humble saintly man, the Negro George Washington Carver surmounted almost incredible obstacles to obtain his education and achieve the eminence that brought him honors from fellow scientists and the world. Both books are excellent biographies.

The Story of Saul the King, by Helen Waddell, ed. by Elaine Moss, ill. by Doreen Roberts. Constable, 1966. (10-14)

Here is a dramatic retelling of the whole story of that complex hero Saul. The narrative carries him from boyhood to his anointing as Israel's first king, his mighty deeds on behalf of his people, his growing hunger for personal power, consuming jealousy of young David, and finally his downfall and death. The colorful and dramatic illustrations make this look like a picture book for young children, but both the text and the hero are complex and subtle. See also Meindert DeJong's *The Mighty Ones: Great Men and Women of Early Bible Days* (p. 344).

Ten Saints, by Eleanor Farjeon, ill. by Helen Sewell. Walck, 1936. (8-12)

SAINT PATRICK

Such well-known saints as St. Francis and St. Christopher are here along with some who are less familiar, at least to Protestant children. Their lives are beautifully told by the poet Eleanor Farjeon, and the pictures are unusual.

Perhaps as a guide to these real flesh-and-blood saints and heroes, children should first encounter seventeenth-century John Bunyan's fictional hero, the timeless "Christian" of *Pilgrim's Progress*. This great allegory, written while Bunyan languished in jail for nonconformity, is the story of a troubled soul on his long pilgrimage through life, beset by the Giant Despair, almost lost in the Slough of Despond, but struggling on. He is any one of us, the Everyman of each generation, and no adult who read this book as a child can fail to identify his battle with the Giant Despair and smile at himself when he finds he is slipping into self-pity, a real "slough" if ever there was one. The following edition, which has been trimmed of moralizing and illumined by some of Robert Lawson's finest drawings, is a treasure:

> Bunyan, John. *Pilgrim's Progress*, ed. by Mary Godolphin, ill. by Robert Lawson. Lippincott, 1939. (9-12)

More books with religious backgrounds and themes and more biographies of saints and heroes are available. But remember that great literature—with or without a religious background or theme— can often broaden a child's religious and ethical concepts, and it will most certainly give him a deeper sensitivity to the terror, the wonder, and the beauty of life.

MUSIC

Poetry and music seem to move along almost interchangeably. Poetry inspires songs, and songs are often as good to speak as to sing. Certainly it is a lucky child who is born into a book-loving and music-loving family—a family that likes to sing and to make music as well as to listen to it. There may not be any professional musicians in the group, but to sing together or to play instruments together can be sources of the keenest enjoyment as long as a person lives. Listening to hi-fi, radio, or television may provide a noble education in music or a demoralizing lapse into frenetic noise. But even at their best, these listening experiences are passive as compared with making music oneself and with others.

Musical experiences

For a child, musical experience often begins with someone in the family singing to him as a baby and develops as he begins to join in on his favorites. Eleanor Farjeon remembered her mother singing the songs of the South to her British-born children. A neighbor's son remembered his father's lusty baritone singing the rollicking songs from the old Gilbert and Sullivan operas, as modern fathers might sing the lyrics of Irving Berlin or Rodgers and Hammerstein. In earlier days, families used to gather around the piano to sing favorite hymns, but that custom has largely disappeared and the ubiquitous television has taken over. However, there is some indication that a revival of interest in playing and singing together is under way. Teen-agers, adults, and even children are earnestly taking guitar lessons, and wherever a proficient performer turns up he is sure of an enthusiastic group to sing along with him. Folk music, the most popular, is more romantic than religious, but all the old human problems are there to mull over melodically and sadly and to remind the singers of the strange ways of life and love. The beauty of this renewed interest in making music together is that it unites all ages in common enjoyment. In a family with three boys, one is the pianist and the other two are guitarists and singers. In that family, it is not unusual to find mother, father, and their guests all joining in the singing, lustily and unself-consciously. This is not the highest level of musical expression, but it is a move in the right direction and may well lead on to better music.

All through the ages, music has been used in the service of religion. As already noted, there are the melancholy and magnificent chants of Judaism, the great masses of the Catholic church, and the hymnology of the Protestants. These are wonderful traditions for the child to grow up in. To be sure, in the beginning your children will probably know only your traditions, but there is some common ground. The Psalms belong to everyone, and there is for all Catholics and Protestants the joyous singing together of the Christmas carols in churches and homes. These traditional songs are gay, melancholy, triumphant, tender, and altogether moving. And how the body of carols has grown! Not through the addition of modern carols but by a delightful infiltration of traditional carols from other countries, all over the world. When you hear our choirs and singing throngs of carolers at Christmas time, it is always a question who enjoys singing them more, the grownups or the children. Both are carrying their songs to nursing homes and hospitals to the joy of the residents. And what child grown to manhood, who came from a carol-singing family, can hear the familiar songs without emotion? For those who want to begin or to perpetuate the carol-singing tradition, here is a list of songs and carols for families to enjoy together:

Boni, Margaret Bradford, ed. *Fireside Book of Folk Songs*, arranged for piano by Norman Lloyd, ill. by Alice and Martin Provensen. Revised Edition. Simon & Schuster, 1947, 1958.
A good collection of folk songs with pictures in the beautiful tradition of the Provensens, many in full color.

Carmer, Carl. *America Sings: Stories and Songs of Our Country's Growing*, ill. by Elizabeth B. Carmer. Knopf, 1942, 1950.
Some thirty tall tales with related folk songs arranged according to geographic origin.

Engvick, William, ed. *Lullabies and Night Songs*, music by Alec Wilder, ill. by Maurice Sendak. Harper, 1965.
In many ways, *Lullabies and Night Songs* is the most unusual collection in this list. Forty-eight selections include folk songs, an arrangement of "Brahms' Lullaby," and modern verses by De la Mare, Farjeon, and Alec Wilder, set to music. Maurice Sendak has never done lovelier or more appropriate illustrations.

Seeger, Ruth Crawford, comp. *American Folk Songs for Christmas*, ill. by Barbara Cooney. Doubleday, 1953.
This is a beautiful book in format and content. Over fifty well-chosen holiday songs have made it a great favorite.

Simon, Henry William, ed. *A Treasury of Christmas Songs and Carols*, ill. by Rafaello Busoni. Houghton, 1955.
A comprehensive collection from many lands with historical notes for each song and delightful illustrations in color.

Look Away to Bethlehem

Wasner, Franz, ed. *The Trapp-Family Book of Christmas Songs*, ill. by Agathe Trapp. Pantheon, 1950.

Here are songs from many lands. For bilingual or trilingual families, the book has the added attraction that foreign songs are printed in the original language as well as in English.

Books on music and musicians

The best of all musical experiences is actual music making— singing and playing instruments, alone and with others—and listening to good music. But with music as with many other areas, books can be useful. The following list suggests some of the kinds of books that may lead to or enhance experiences with music:

Briggs, John. *Leonard Bernstein: The Man, His Work, and His World.* World, 1961. (15 up)

Critic and author John Briggs presents a fascinating and enjoyable tale of one of America's favorite contemporary musicians. Many excellent photographs are included.

Britten, Benjamin, and Imogen Holst. *The Wonderful World of Music*, ill. with reproductions from masterpieces of art and black-and-white photographs. Doubleday, 1958. (12 up)

This beautifully and lavishly illustrated volume offers a simple and readable introduction to the field of music. The text is factually sound for all its brevity, and the illustrations are a delight to the eye.

Bulla, Clyde Robert. *Stories of Favorite Operas*, ill. by Robert Galster. Crowell, 1959. See also *More Stories of Favorite Operas*, ill. by Joseph Low. Crowell, 1965. (11-15)

For young fans interested in knowing the stories of the great operas, these two volumes should provide most enjoyable reading. Twenty-three of the best known, and then another twenty-two are offered here in large print and straightforward style. Brief background materials, as well as the synopses, are provided.

Commins, Dorothy B. *All About the Symphony Orchestra and What It Plays*, ill. by Warren Chappell. Random House, 1961. (10-14)

Many line drawings and good photographs (Boston Symphony musicians) illustrate this interesting text whose title is self-explanatory. Capsule accounts of the instruments, the art of conducting, various types of concert music, and nearly fifty of the more famous composers are presented in most appealing fashion.

Davis, Marilyn K., and Arnold Broido. *Music Dictionary*. Doubleday, 1956. (9 up)

The more than 800 definitions and descriptions in this music dictionary present brief and accurate information on the child's level. Many line drawings are included, and pronunciations also, where needed. This will serve well as a handy basic reference book.

Eaton, Jeanette. *Trumpeter's Tale: The Story of Young Louis Armstrong*, ill. by Elton C. Fax. Morrow, 1955. (12 up)

The fourteenth biography for young people by this author, the story of Louis Armstrong presents the young readers with a bright and spritely account of the famous jazz trumpeter's—and singer's—life. From minstrel quartet days in New Orleans to the toast of America and Europe, "Satchmo" has won his place in the hearts of jazz lovers the world over.

Ewen, David. *Leonard Bernstein*. Chilton, 1960. See also *The Story of George Gershwin* (Holt, 1943), *With a Song in His Heart: The Story of Richard Rodgers* (Holt, 1963), *Tales from the Vienna Woods: The Story of Johann Strauss* (Holt, 1944), and *The Story of Arturo Toscanini* (Holt, 1960). (12-14)

The prolific Mr. Ewen has written more popular books on the musical scene than any other author. His texts offer entertaining and informative tales about favorite musicians from Strauss to Toscanini, Gershwin to Rodgers and Bernstein. Full of interesting anecdotes, they tell of trials and adversities as well as success and accomplishment.

Holst, Imogen. *Britten*. Crowell, 1966. (12-16)

One of a series of attractive books on the Great Composers, this slim volume is full of photographs, line drawings, and musical scores. Imogen Holst has worked closely with Britain's Britten and presents a clear account of his life and works up to 1966.

Hughes, Langston. *Famous Negro Music Makers*. Dodd, 1955. (12 up)

Biographies of sixteen notable Negro musicians make up the greater part of this collection for young people. Mostly popular artists are included, but a few conductors and composers appear as well. The sketches are not long but are informative and well written, with photographic illustrations.

See also Hughes, *The First Book of Jazz* (Watts, 1955), for children 12-14, and his *The First Book of Rhythms* (Watts, 1954), for children 7-9. In the first book, Blues, Ragtime, Boogie, Bebop—all part and parcel of the jazz scene—are briefly traced and described, from African Drums to Swing. Louis Armstrong pops up frequently, hand in hand with the other jazz history makers. Discographies are immediately obsolete, and the manuscript score lines are a bit fuzzy, but never mind—it swings!

As the author makes clear in the second book, rhythm in its broadest sense is all inclusive. The rhythm of music and dance is but a small part—the author speaks of words, athletics, machines, nature, architecture, work—all of life itself! Copiously illustrated with line drawings by Robin King.

Kaufmann, Helen L. *History's 100 Greatest Composers*, ill. by Samuel Nisenson. Grosset, 1957. (12-15)

The 100 brief biographies chosen for inclusion here are based on the majority opinions of sixty-two American music critics, which should certainly give some measure of validity for their appearance. Each sketch is just a page or two in length, with a litho picture of the composer. The information offered is factual, concise, and well written.

Norman, Gertrude. *The First Book of Music*, ill. by Richard Gackenbach. Watts, 1954. (8-10)

Fanciful drawings and illustrations appear on every page of this little book, which presents a very brief and simplified account of various aspects of music. History, instruments, notation, songs, types, composers, even acoustics are each touched upon ever so lightly—a good appetite whetter.

Posell, Elsa Z. *American Composers*, ill. with photographs. Houghton, 1963. (12-14)

Cleveland authoress Elsa Posell has chosen twenty-nine well-known American composers for her book. To each she devotes a half dozen pages or so of easy reading material, as well as a full-page photograph.

See also Posell's *This Is an Orchestra* (Houghton, 1950). (10-14) For a child attending symphony concerts, this is an invaluable guide to the identification of musical instruments.

Seligmann, Jean, and Juliet Danziger. *The Meaning of Music: A Young Listener's Guide*, ill. with drawings by Donald Leake and with photographs. World, 1966. (9 up)

This delightful book begins with the chapter "What Is Music?" It then considers various forms of music, each in connection with a particular composer associated with it—for instance, "The Fugue and Bach," "The Concerto and Mozart," "Beethoven and the Symphony," "The Song and Shubert," and comes finally to piano music, opera, and modern trends. The book makes exciting reading, not too exhaustive or difficult for older children and young people, and good for adults as well.

Siegmeister, Elie. *Invitation to Music*, ill. by Beatrice Schwartz. Harvey House, 1961. (12-16)

A variety of types of illustrations and musical examples appears in this excellent volume, which is indeed an invitation to music. Mr. Siegmeister presents his material so clearly and concisely that the reader will have a good groundwork for the many phases of music—and should want to delve further into the subject.

Streatfeild, Noel. *The First Book of the Opera*, ill. by Hilary Abrahams. Watts, 1966. (10-15)

The enjoyment of opera is an acquired taste for the most part. This eminently readable text on the subject traces history, writers, producers, and the like in a manner well calculated to strike the initial spark of interest. Useful line-drawing illustrations are included.

THE GRAPHIC ARTS

While man was gradually learning better ways of feeding, clothing, and sheltering himself and more skillful ways of protecting himself and his family against his various enemies, he was also developing skills in crafts and various arts. The prehistoric cave paintings in France and Spain, and Denmark's "lurs" or brazen trumpets, said to be the first musical instruments in Europe, all bear testimony to the parallel development of work-a-day skills and art skills. Therefore, most books that present the history and development of a people will take account of their painting, carving, dancing, music, and literature, insofar as these have been recorded. This is especially true of books for children. For instance, a book about an Indian tribe will probably show pictures of the Indians' weaving, basketry, pottery, jewelry, and perhaps their ceremonial dances also. So, in general, children do not need books devoted, say, to the arts of the early Egyptians or Vikings or Romans, because the social-studies books about these and other peoples generally include such information and illustrations. However, detailed books about any one of these special areas, perhaps borrowed from the art museum or public library, will add richly to the child's understanding and enjoyment.

As we have already noted, there is scarcely a story from the Old or New Testaments that has not been represented in a famous painting. This is a glorious inheritance to grow up to. But before the child is old enough for either the stories or the paintings, he is already learning to look at pictures, to look again, and to pore over them until he not only sees but understands. In short, he is learning to "read" pictures.

Experiences with art

Experience with art begins simply and casually, with young children enjoying their pictorial *Mother Goose* books or their picture stories. When a child flips over the pictures, he does not really see them, and so you call his attention to some amusing details. For instance, in Leslie Brooke's "This Little Pig," the delightful illustration shows pig portraits on the walls and a carrot design in the curtains at the windows. In the pictures for Bemelmans' *Madeline* books, children generally count the little girls to see that all twelve are there, but they might be led to look more closely at the charming background details—the houses, churches, bridges, so different from our own. In Arthur Rackham's pictures, they learn to look for elves and gnomes hidden in the woods, or for trees that reach out long arms and look scarily human. If a child has been looking at the delicate pastel colors of Tasha Tudor and Adrienne Adams, will he see the startling differences between their pictures and those of Lynd Ward and Robert McCloskey, with their strong contrasts and their bold lines? Maybe not, and certainly you won't make much of a point of such differences, but casually talking about the pictures helps children become more aware. A child may discover in Marcia Brown's inimitable *Once a*

Mouse that he can tell just how mean the mouse, turned cat, turned lion, is really getting by looking at his face, his strut, or his crouch. When that happens, the child is learning to read pictures. And he may also discover that this Marcia Brown, who illustrates so many of his favorite stories, does each one differently. Why are the pictures for *Dick Whittington* in black and brown, very solid, while those in *Puss in Boots* are in deep blues and yellows with dashes of shocking pinks, and those in *Cinderella* are in beautiful pastel shades, as delicate as a dream? These observations should be happy, informal enjoyment of different types of pictures that will pave the way for a vastly more mature appreciation of various styles in art. And if the art of the picture book ranges from the traditional to the modern, from the representational to the abstract and even nonobjective, think what lies ahead of the child in the rich tradition of European art and in the startling variety of modern adult art expression!

In the middle years, eight through twelve, and continuing into adolescence, a child sometimes develops a strong and special interest in one of the arts. If so, he should be supplied with books that will clarify and extend his interest. You may borrow such books from the library or you may decide they have family values and so purchase them. Some of the books in the graphic arts certainly are worthy of a place in the family bookshelves.

Art books for children and young people
The books listed here are designed for the most part with children in mind, but it is hard to imagine an art-minded adult who would not be charmed with them also. Actually almost every book on the list is an exercise in looking, a fascinating lure into the world of pictures and a lead toward the traditional masterpieces as well as modern art. So choose a favorite or two from the library or the bookstore. Your family shelves will be richer for their presence, and the family itself will be guided painlessly into art enjoyment.

> Chase, Alice Elizabeth. *Looking at Art*, ill. in color and black and white. Crowell, 1966. (12 up)
> Written by an art historian and illustrated with over one hundred reproductions, this book will help children and adults look at pictures with greater understanding and enjoyment. Miss Chase shows the many

ways in which artists have handled landscapes, interiors, and the human figure, changing and manipulating their subjects to express their unique ideas. Children will be fascinated with her fourteen pictures of lions, ranging from a 650 B.C. representation to a modern photograph, each one different but each unmistakably lion. You may also want to study Miss Chase's *Famous Paintings: An Introduction to Art for Young People* (Platt & Munk, 1951, 1962.) and *Famous Artists of the Past* (Platt & Munk, 1964).

Craven, Thomas. *The Rainbow Book of Art*, ill. with reproductions in color and black and white. World, 1956. (12 up)

The Rainbow adaptation of the adult collection has almost 400 pictures, of which 32 are in color. This is not too overwhelming as an introduction to the great tradition of masterpieces. On the other hand, you may prefer to invest in the adult *Treasury of Art Masterpieces from the Renaissance to the Present Day* to use *with* the younger children and to open the eyes of adolescents to the matchless wealth of beauty to be found in the European galleries. This is a heavy book and should be used on a table or in a chair where the reader is well propped. The color reproductions are superb and the treasures inexhaustible. If the child who pores over these pictures goes to Europe, he will feel curiously at home in the art galleries there. And if he never gets there, he can still know the works of many artists from many schools of painting in different periods and countries.

Denny, Norman, and Josephine Filmer-Sankey. *The Bayeux Tapestry: The Story of the Norman Conquest: 1066*, ill. with reproductions. Atheneum, 1966. (9 up)

This immense strip of embroidered linen cloth, 230 feet long and 20 inches wide, tells the events that culminated in the battle of Hastings, the death of King Harold, and the victory of William, the new Norman master of England. The fascinating introduction tells the history of the tapestry, and the text relates the pictured events in large type and adds detailed commentaries in smaller type. The glowing colors of the reproductions and the astonishing action make this book a choice addition to art books for young people and adults.

Downer, Marion. *The Story of Design*, ill. with museum photos. Lothrop, 1963. (12 up)

The Story of Design is for older children and adults, and yet for the delight that comes from looking at objects of beauty, it belongs to all ages. Even a young child will like some of the pictures, animal figures especially, and his eyes will see more as he lingers with such a book. The pictures, all black and white, emphasize line and form without the distraction of color. Beginning with prehistoric art, text and pictures move through the arts of Egypt, Greece, China, Japan, India, Persia, Turkey, to our western countries, Colonial America and her Indians, and finally to modern design for our modern world. This book presents an impressive record of man's eternal search for adequate expression in rhythmic lines, form, order, and a patterned relation of the parts to the whole. A companion book to *The Story of Design* is *Discovering Design* (Lothrop, 1947). According to *The New York Times Book Review* "it helps those without benefit of technical training or criticism to see the element of design which makes a picture or which turns the most commonplace object into a minor work of art."

Emberley, Ed. *The Wing on a Flea.* Little, 1961. (5-8)

This is an amusing transition between the picture story and the instructional art book. The subtitle, "A Book About Shapes," accurately describes the content; it presents the youngest children with the triangle, the rectangle, and the circle, found in the most unexpected places, as: "A triangle is/ The wing on a flea,/ And the beak on a bird,/ If you just look and see." That last line should be the motto for all art education: "If you just look and see."

Freund, Miriam, *Jewels for a Crown: The Story of the Chagall Windows*, ill. with reproductions in color. McGraw, 1963. (9-13)

For children who are beginning the stories of the Old Testament, especially Jewish children, here is a book they will not soon become tired of. It is the story of Chagall's making of the twelve windows for the synagogue of the Medical Center in Jerusalem. The windows represent the twelve sons of Jacob as the Old Testament describes them. From the deep blues of the Reuben and Simeon windows, through the fiery reds of the Judah and Zebulon, the greens of Issachar and Gad to the golden yellows of Benjamin and Joseph, even the photographs of these windows sparkle with every color of the spectrum. To pore over them with a child is to keep discovering new delights—figures, flowers, fishes, little crooked houses, such birds and beasts as never were. The symbolism of these glass pictures, their touches of humor, and their beauty are all on a grand scale. The text interprets the symbolism and relates the history of the windows' creation by Chagall.

Grigson, Jane and Geoffrey. *Shapes and Stories: A Book About Pictures,* ill. with reproductions in color and in black and white. Vanguard, 1965. (12-14)

The absurdly prancing green dragon on the cover of this book would tempt any beholder to a further look. Inside the cover are still more delights. Selections of art from the Renaissance to modern times, including William Blake's "Adam Naming the Beasts" as well as Paul Klee's witty fantasy in the abstract, "The Revolution of the Viaduct." Although the comments about the pictures are geared to the older children, they are often extremely interesting "stories" and add to the appeal of the pictures. No one lucky enough to encounter this book will leave it without a deepening awareness of the variety and charms of many different sorts of pictures.

Holme, Bryan. *Drawings to Live With,* ill. with 140 reproductions in black and white. Viking, 1966. (12 up)

This companion volume to the author's *Pictures to Live With* is a fascinating presentation of various types of drawings, including classic, impressionistic, and modern or abstract. The greatest exponents of the intimate and exciting art of drawing are represented, old masters as well as modern experimenters such as Picasso and Paul Klee. Since drawing is generally a basic discipline for painting and is something most people attempt now and then, this is a particularly stimulating book for children, youth, and adults to own and study. The chapters are provocative—"No Two Alike," "Three Ways of Drawing," "Sketches," "Pen, Pencil and Chalk," and the concluding ninth chapter, "A Time to Laugh," where we find such old friends as Charles Addams, Walt Disney, Bemelmans, Steinberg, Thurber, and others.

MacAgy, Douglas and Elizabeth. *Going for a Walk with a Line . . .* a step into the world of modern art. Ill. with reproductions in color and in black and white. Doubleday, 1959. (7-12)

Here indeed is a bold and delightful first step into the world of modern art. And since the modern world is the world the child is born into, he had better take a look at it and see what is happening. In a lively and poetic text that scampers and skips just as lines do, the authors show a variety of modern masterpieces. Each picture is accompanied by a line of text that illumines the intention of the artist but does not analyze. For instance, with two highly contrasted pictures facing each other, the text says: "Lines may make moonlight that shines on a bird/ or skitter and bounce like bugs flying among flowers." This is a beginning book for young beholders, but the pictures and the provocative text are enlightening for any age.

Ripley, Elizabeth. *Rodin*, ill. with photographs of the sculptor's work. Lippincott, 1966. (11-14)
One in a remarkable series of excellent biographies of great artists. In each book, the life and work of the artist are simply and attractively presented through a brief, clear text and reproductions of some of the artist's greatest works. See also *Velázquez* (1965); *Raphael* (1961); *Botticelli* (1960); *Goya* (1956); *Titian* (1962), and others.

Rockwell, Anne. *Filippo's Dome*, ill. by author. Atheneum, 1967. (9 up)
A story of the life, work, and ideals of Filippo Brunelleschi and of his great masterpiece, the dome for the cathedral of Maria del Fiore in Florence. Brunelleschi lost to Lorenzo Ghiberti in a contest to design the bronze doors for the old Baptistery, but his plan for the dome of the Cathedral was accepted and worked out in a period of over sixteen years.

Ruskin, Ariane. *The Pantheon Story of Art for Young People*. Pantheon, 1964. (10 up)
Here is a chronological approach to art development written with enthusiasm and sound scholarship. It is a handsome book with splendid reproductions in color and black and white, and it moves through periods and art from the cave paintings to present days.

RELIGIOUS EDUCATION IN THE HOME

Most of the books discussed in "Religion, Ethics, and Books" (pp. 310-321) can be used with all children regardless of the family's religious or nonreligious convictions. Such books can contribute to a child's general education and help him develop courteous respect and kindly tolerance for religious and nonreligious beliefs and practices that differ from his own. Some parents— perhaps many—will stop there. For other parents, such attitudes, while desirable and important, are not enough. In addition, they hope to inculcate in their children strong religious convictions that will guide and sustain them throughout their lives. The following suggestions, then, have been provided for those parents who are concerned about the religious education of their children and have wondered how they can foster such education in the home.

How you will begin the religious education of your child depends upon your conviction, your church, and chiefly upon you. Love is a foundation stone in most religions. The child's induction into the gospel of love begins in the security of his parents' arms and in their tender, cherishing care. Actually, the birth of a child is the first great miracle of love beside which all other miracles seem relatively simple. A young Rabbi told a group of parents that every night from the time his baby came home with his wife from the hospital he took the child in his arms and, holding him warm and close, said a Psalm or verses from the Psalms or some other portions of Scriptural thanksgiving. The twenty-third Psalm was a favorite, but so were the first five verses of Psalm 103:

Bless the Lord, O my soul: and all that is within me, bless his holy name.
Bless the Lord, O my soul, and forget not all his benefits:
Who forgiveth all thine iniquities; who healeth all thy diseases;
Who redeemeth thy life from destruction; who crowneth thee with lovingkindness and tender mercies;
Who satisfieth thy mouth with good things; so that thy youth is renewed like the eagle's.
Bless the Lord, O my soul: and all that is within me, bless his holy name.

Favorites, too, were verses from the ninety-first or the one hundred ninth or the one hundred forty-seventh—there are so many full of thanksgiving and praise, and all of them would help to introduce young children to the cadence and beauty of their native language and to the accompanying feeling of warmth, security, and love.

A young mother who had grown up in a hymn-singing family used to sing hymns to her baby—her favorites for the quiet times were John Greenleaf Whittier's "Dear Lord and Father of mankind,/ Forgive our foolish ways!" and Isaac Watts' "O God, our help in ages past/ Our hope in years to come," but for the times when she felt hard pressed, her favorites were that lusty old fighting hymn of John Bunyan's, "He who would valiant be/ 'Gainst all disaster," and those still more up-and-at-'em verses, "Fight the good fight with all thy might." Singing these quiet or these rousing old hymns, this mother said, relieved pressures and made her feel better. As for the baby, he gurgled with satisfaction.

Some parents begin when their child is still a baby to kneel by his crib or bed and say a goodnight prayer. Presently, the baby, grown a little older, may listen and be comforted, even when he does not understand the words completely, by that tenderest of all blessings: "The Lord bless you and keep you. The Lord make his face to shine upon you, and be gracious unto you. The Lord lift up his countenance upon you and give you peace, this night and evermore."

Such induction into the language and thought of faith makes no demand upon the child at first but will probably pique his curiosity, so that presently he will begin to ask questions—"Who are you talking to?" or "Who is the Lord? Who is God?" and you will answer according to your belief—"God is Spirit" or "God is the creator of people and the universe we live in" or "He is Spirit, and a spark of his spirit is in each of us." Give whatever answer satisfies you, but don't run away from answering the child to the best of your ability. And when the questions persist, be honest. Say, "I am not sure, but it seems to me it is like this. . . ." or "We'll find books and see what other people think." And meanwhile, there are books for this very young child, no longer an infant but still a prereader or just beginning to read and thus dependent on pictures, that will continue this informal induction into what we can only call first steps in the language and basic beliefs of religious faith.

Books to use with the youngest children

    David and Goliath, by Beatrice Schenk de Regniers, ill. by Richard M. Powers. Viking, 1965. (5-8)

    This tells the dramatic story of the boy David, who killed the giant Goliath, and tells it in fine Biblical style. The illustrations seem somewhat lurid, but the story will always be a favorite with or without pictures.

    The First Seven Days: The Story of Creation from Genesis, ill. by Paul

Galdone. Crowell, 1962. (5-8) See also *Shadrach, Meshach and Abednego: From the Book of Daniel*, ill. by Paul Galdone. McGraw, 1965. (5-8)
Both of these colorful and imaginative picture books use the Biblical language and interpret the text dramatically and unforgettably. Even older children will be caught by these pictures, and the language will have more meaning for them because of the illustrations.

The Shepherd Psalm, ill. by Maud Petersham. Macmillan, 1962. (4-8)
It would be difficult to find a lovelier introduction to the twenty-third Psalm than this pictorial text by Maud Petersham. It begins with a brief introduction about King David and how he happened to sing this song of thanksgiving. Then each verse is illustrated by a sensitive and imaginative illustration, never too literal, but illuminating the idea of the verse.

Small Rain: Verses from the Bible, chosen by Jessie Orton Jones, ill. by Elizabeth Orton Jones. Viking, 1943. (4-8)
This older book will never lose its significance either in text or illustrations. It contains a choice selection of Bible verses interpreted in terms of today's children and their activities. An obvious example is a picture of children of different races and color playing happily together and the single line, "All of you are children of the most high." These same differing children are to be found in other pictures, as well as a pair of pigtailed, bespectacled twins who appear cheerfully throughout the book and are certainly "making a joyful noise unto the Lord" in a rhythm band. A small pajama-clad figure gazing at the stars illustrates "And the firmament showeth his handiwork." The book closes with the picture of a child tucked cozily in bed while myriads of stars are swirling about overhead; the verse says, reassuringly, "And underneath are the everlasting arms." Basic and wonderful concepts to build into a young child's consciousness, the earlier the better.

There are so many beautiful and unique pictorial editions of the Christmas story and so many books with the Nativity theme that you must look them over and choose for yourself. Here are a few from many:

The Nativity
    The Christ Child. As told by Matthew and Luke, ill. by Maud and Miska Petersham. Doubleday, 1931. (4-9)

For all of their illustrations for Biblical stories, the Petershams did painstaking research in the country where the stories took place. But authenticity is only one of their virtues as illustrators. They catch the spirit of these matchless tales and picture them with grace and understanding. This will always be a favorite edition of the Nativity. The text has never been surpassed, and the pictures have tenderness and beauty.

Lindgren, Astrid. *Christmas in the Stable,* ill. by Harald Wiberg. Coward, 1962. (5-8)

In contrast to traditional Biblical tellings of the Nativity is this delightful modern version with illustrations by the inimitable Mr. Wiberg,

From *The Christ Child,* illustrated by Maud & Miska Petersham. Copyright 1931 by Maud and Miska Petersham. Reprinted by permission of Doubleday & Company, Inc.

And there were in the same country shepherds abiding in the field, keeping watch over their flock by night.

21

who did pictures for *The Tomten*. The story is tenderly told in terms of the Swedish farm child's own familiar barn and stable. The wintry Swedish landscape, the weary travelers, the gentle animals, and the Mother and Babe are all there in wonderful pictures, dramatic and moving.

Menotti, Gian-Carlo. *Gian-Carlo Menotti's Amahl and the Night Visitors*, adapted by Frances Frost, ill. by Roger Duvoisin. McGraw, 1952. (All ages)
   This opera has become almost as much of a Christmas classic on radio and television as Dickens' *Christmas Carol*. Retold from the opera, the story reads well, and Roger Duvoisin has never made more striking illustrations than for this book, all in dark jewel tones as befit the story. It is about the Three Kings stopping at a poor hut to inquire the way to find the Child. Their brief stay marks a turning point in the humble lives of a lame boy and his mother, with new hope for both. It will be easier for children to follow the opera if they have read the book.

Nussbaumer, Mares. *Away in a Manger: A Story of the Nativity*, ill. by Paul Nussbaumer. Harcourt, 1965. (6-8)
   And here is a modern Swiss version of the Christmas story, retold with simplicity and reverence and illustrated with great beauty by the Swiss artist Paul Nussbaumer. This is a large book; so the Swiss landscape and the stable scenes are colorful and impressive. No retelling quite satisfies, but perhaps these different versions and strikingly different pictures will make the story more real, more clothed in homely details, for the modern child.

Jewish holidays and religious observances
   It seems a pity that there are not comparable books with the same aesthetic values for the great Jewish festivals and fasts. However, one publishing house is issuing a series of books on holidays, and here are the first three on the Jewish calendar. Two are primarily for younger children, six to nine, and one is for the seven- to ten-year-olds. Easy-to-read, well-illustrated, they present Jewish ceremonial observances beautifully.

Cone, Molly. *The Jewish New Year*, ill. by Jerome Snyder. Crowell, 1966. (6-9)

Rosh Hashonah welcomes in the Jewish New Year with a blast from the traditional shofar or ram's horn. This and the following days are times for righting wrongs, starting over again, and, above all, it is a season of hope. These high holy days begin as a harvest festival and end with Yom Kippur, a solemn day of atonement. The history and customs of these days are movingly described.

Cone, Molly. *The Jewish Sabbath*, ill. by Ellen Raskin. Crowell, 1966. (6-9)
This is the oldest religious holiday of the Jewish people. It begins Friday evening and ends at sundown Saturday. Again, the author describes with great warmth the history and customs of the day.

Simon, Norma. *Hanukkah*, ill. by Symeon Shimin. Crowell, 1966. (7-10)
The origins of Hanukkah are grimmer than those of other holidays,

Illustration by Symeon Shimin in
Hanukkah, by Norma Simon.
Copyright © 1966 by Symeon Shimin.
Thomas Y. Crowell Company,
New York, publishers.

but the observances are warm and beautiful in family traditions. For
an orthodox Jewish family, it is a time of pride in their Jewish origins
going back to the heroic fight for religious freedom by the Maccabees.
The lighting of the first candle on the family Menorah recalls the original Menorah, which burned miraculously for eight nights. After the
lighting of the lights and the blessings, there are games and fun for the
children and usually gifts. Fine illustrations enhance the dignity of
the observances described.

Prayers

Beautiful and significant picture books and simple explanations
of religious holidays make first steps in the religious education
of children easy for all of us, but where do we go from there? Again
we try to follow the lead of children's questions, answer them as
adequately as we know how, and try to carry them beyond their
often primitive interpretations. We are often astonished and puzzled by children's early conceptions of God and prayer. For instance, according to an article in the *Cleveland Plain Dealer* (August 7, 1965), two University of Denver professors of psychology
and one of their former students asked some children these questions: "What is prayer? Where does it go? And how should one
feel if it is not answered?" A five-year-old thought prayer was
"about God, rabbits, people, and fairies and deer, and Santa Claus
. . . and Jesus and Mary. . . ." A seven-year-old thought it was
"asking God for water, food, rain and snow." By nine, some children had developed an idea of prayer as communication with God,
a spiritual being, of asking Him for forgiveness or help. The
younger children thought prayer flew up to God, or floated, or that
God used magic, or that angels picked up the prayers. From nine
to twelve, the researchers said, children were able to think of prayer
as communicating with a spiritual being who "always hears." By
twelve, let us hope that their "gimme" prayers had ceased or had
been modified as Miguel's[1] were with the concept of "Thy will be
done." It is well for children to learn that some prayers may be
praise and thanksgiving, or prayers for help in our weakness, or
help against danger to loved ones or to nations—just so that these
prayers of petition are more frequently for other people than for
ourselves. As children grow older, help them understand that

[1]Joseph Krumgold, . . . *And Now Miguel*, Crowell, 1953.

prayer is not to tell God what He ought to do for us but rather to ask God to guide us, His children, to know what we should do, in order to be instruments of His Grace. These are a few of the principles to think about in teaching children to pray and to use in finding them prayers that will train them to a commitment to God that will stand up to the question, "How should we feel when our prayers are not answered?" Two beautiful and inspirational books dealing with prayers are Elfrida Vipont's *Bless This Day* and Elizabeth Yates' *Your Prayers and Mine:*

Bless This Day, comp. by Elfrida Vipont, ill. by Harold Jones. Harcourt, 1958. (All ages)
This is a preferred collection of prayers for every member of the family from the youngest to the oldest. There are prayers, Bible verses, and devotional hymns that are as effective to speak as to sing. Harold Jones' beautiful, colorful illustrations have the strength and dignity the text merits.

Your Prayers and Mine, comp. by Elizabeth Yates, ill. by Nora Unwin. Houghton, 1954. (11-15)
This also is a beautiful book, which uses—in addition to Bible sources —some of the aspirational literature from other religions. Nora Unwin's beautiful decorations give this book the appearance of an old manuscript.

Here are two books of prayers to use with the younger children:

A Prayer for Little Things, by Eleanor Farjeon, ill. by Elizabeth Orton Jones. Houghton, 1945. (5-8)
From rain drops to fledglings, colts, and children, this is a book of tender awareness, compassion, and thanksgiving. The lovely illustrations expand the imagination and deepen perceptiveness.

Song of the Sun: From the Canticle of the Sun, by Francis of Assisi, ill. by Elizabeth Orton Jones. Macmillan, 1952. (5-10)
A person who owned this book when he was little is apt to cherish it all his days. It is, of course, a wonderful Gloria that sharpens awareness and lifts the spirit. The pictures catch the exultation of the words and have rare beauty.

Because the sense of wonder has given rise to scientific exploration and also to speculations about God, man, the universe, and the meaning of life, it seems only appropriate to follow St. Francis' *Canticle of the Sun*, a hymn of praise if ever there was one, with Rachel Carson's *Sense of Wonder*. This book expresses the author's reverence for the mystery and beauty of all life and belongs both to books of science and to religion.

> *The Sense of Wonder*, by Rachel Carson, photographs by Charles Pratt and others. Harper, 1965. (4-10)
> A young child is the central figure in these beautiful pictures, many in color, and that child is being shown the marvels of his everyday world of nature. The book is a testimonial to Rachel Carson's love of nature and her keen desire to help children see what lies underfoot, within reach, and close by. While intended for the young child, all ages will rejoice in its beauty.

Regardless of your religious affiliation, it is wise to give children experience in two types of prayers: the written prayers, which they memorize, and the spontaneous prayers, which they make up themselves. Memorized prayers should be changed from time to time, lest children, like some adults, get so that they rattle them off mechanically. Prayers the child makes up himself may begin as simply as "Thanks, God, for our new puppy," or "Oh God, Peter has the measles. Please make him well quick." These, at least, represent a child's first efforts to praise or seek help for others at the source, and as he uses different prayers, his own will grow in maturity, and those "Don't-let-it-rain-tomorrow-on-our-picnic" sorts of prayers will begin to drop out.

The Bible

The Bible and Bible instruction can begin delightfully for young children with the picture-book editions, but as the child matures, he should have a Bible of his own. He has heard the Psalms spoken by his father or mother and in church, but he needs to know the Book of Psalms for himself. When a third-year college student can write "And those Psalms you were talking about—what are they and where do you find them?" apparently we take too much for granted. The particular Bible you choose for your child will depend upon his maturity or immaturity, and your religious group —for the Jewish child, the torah; for the Catholic child, the Douay translation; and for the Protestant child, the King James translation. But shall they have these texts in full or in a cut or somewhat modified version to start with? If the modified version refrains from talking down to the child, cuts but does not greatly change, and retains much or all of the Biblical language, then it is probably justified. The following books are notable examples for you to examine, and many are splendid for reading aloud, with the assurance that you won't run into a page of "begats" or into some episode that is too adult:

Andrés, Stefan. *The Bible Story*, trans. from the German by Michael Bullock, ill. by Gerhard Oberlander. McGraw, 1966. (12 up)
A fairly mature retelling of the continuous stories of the Old and New Testaments as a developing whole by a German novelist, Stefan Andrés. In this powerful narrative, the author shows a growing, changing concept of God, first in relation to the Jewish people and later to all peoples. Over one hundred fine illustrations add to the effectiveness of the book, which would be especially useful in connection with a standard Bible. Certainly the action and import of the Old Testament stories are clarified, and thoughtful young readers will find them absorbing and understandable. There is a sweep and grandeur to this narrative that is compelling. While this book in no way supplants the Bible itself —no retelling ever can—it might interest young people and lead back to the original.

Barnhart, Nancy. *The Lord Is My Shepherd*, ill. by editor. Scribner, 1949. (10-14)
This large, handsome book does not cover the whole Bible but tells the major stories with strength and considerable use of Biblical language. The illustrations were made in the Holy Land.

DeJong, Meindert. *The Mighty Ones: Great Men and Women of Early Bible Days*, ill. by Harvey Schmidt. Harper, 1959. (11 up)
These retold stories of the Old Testament are fascinating to read but illustrate the problem of all retellings. Inevitably, they involve the personal interpretation of the author which may or may not agree with yours. In this book, Mr. DeJong introduces each story with an excerpt from the Bible. Then he takes over, fills in the details, and interprets the significance or motivation of the story. Anything Meindert DeJong writes is sensitively and beautifully handled. These Old Tes-

tament hero tales are no exception. If you like them, you will like them tremendously, and so will your child. The narrative carries the stories through David, crowned King of Israel.

Goodspeed, Edgar J., ed. *The Junior Bible; An American Translation,* ill. by Frank Dobias. Macmillan, 1936. (9-13)
This book is taken from Goodspeed's adult translation and is printed with modern paragraph and sentence structure. The modernization makes reading easier and more comprehensible, but for such books as the Psalms leaves much to be desired.

Gwynne, John Harold. *The Rainbow Book of Bible Stories,* ill. by Steele Savage. World, 1956. (10 up)
A scholarly clergyman has retold in dignified Biblical style the major stories of both the Old and New Testaments. Steele Savage has provided excellent black-and-white and color illustrations.

Petersham, Maud and Miska, ill. *Story of Jesus.* Macmillan, 1967. (7-12)
At a much simpler, younger level than the other Bible stories listed, this is a beautiful book for younger children. Text is the Revised Standard Version of the New Testament.

There are many retellings of Bible stories, but these examples are especially strong for different age levels. The matter of interpretation must be for each home or religious group to decide individually. There are also other translations of the Bible, notably the *Revised Standard Bible,* which you may prefer to the King James translation, also The New English Bible, New Testament, which many like best of all. However, even the enthusiasts for modern editions admit that nothing equals the majesty and beauty of language that makes passage after passage in the King James Version remembered for a lifetime.

Some families worry about giving the whole Bible to children because of adult episodes described in adult fashion. What people should really worry about is whether children discover the Bible, learn how to read it, and begin to explore its richness. Whatever you believe theologically or disbelieve about this remarkable book, it will give your child the most civilized code of morality we have, couched in memorable language. Of course, you can't hand your child this tremendous book and leave him to flounder through the "begats" on his own. Use it with him until he knows the great hero tales of the Old Testament. These are the heritage of both Jewish and Christian children. They are different from all other hero tales because those men walked with a sense of God and therefore of good and evil. Gradually, your child should know also the great Psalms of thanksgiving and supplication. He should hear some of the wise and witty words from Proverbs and Ecclesiastes and eventually the great and moving sequence of action in the New Testament. Then he will be able to find his way around in the books of that tremendous compilation we know as the Bible and find in it sources of help and strength.

Books for adults

For general help in fostering religious education in the home, adults may be interested in the first two books described below. And for a more specialized approach to religious education, they may enjoy the third book, *Let the Children Paint.*

> Chaplin, Dora P. *Children and Religion.* Revised Edition. Scribner, 1951.
>
> This is an extraordinarily helpful book for parents. It considers religious ideas for the periods of early childhood and various stages of adolescence. Major topics include prayer, death, disbelief, and an approach to religion through the Bible and through pictures, music, poetry, and books. Probably no one will agree with all of any other person's pronouncements in these fields, but to read such a book is to clarify problems and provoke thinking.

> Jones, Jessie Orton. *The Spiritual Education of Our Children.* Viking, 1960.
>
> This small, inspirational book presents the premise that "Silence creates the impression in the minds of the young that religion is unimportant." So since the public schools must be silent, more responsibility than ever rests with the family. Indeed, the role of the home is the chief concern of this book, and some wonderful examples illumine the principles. There are good bibliographies for further reading.

Wright, Kathryn S. *Let the Children Paint: Art in Religious Education.*
Seabury, 1966.
This is a record of, and a tremendous plea for, the use of creative art
expression in church schools for children of elementary-school ages.
Painting for joy, for acceptance, for growth and understanding, for fellowship and appreciation are discussed with many brief case-study
examples. If this is a somewhat exaggerated emphasis on one media
of expression, it is an interesting one.

CONCLUSION

So now we come to the conclusion of this book about *Children's
Reading in the Home.* Before your children will have read even a
small number of books described in these chapters, they will have
grown up, and you will be saying, "Where have the children gone?"
Then some of their books, still on your bookshelves, will show you
where they were once upon a time. And perhaps some of those
left-behind books eventually will travel to new bookshelves where
your children of yesterday are starting libraries for their children
of today. That is the way it happens, as life moves on.

The books in these brief lists have been chosen out of many for
a variety of reasons—some for the advanced and some for the delayed readers, some for the children with special interests, others
to wake young minds to new interests and wider curiosities. For
almost every book in these lists other books could be substituted
and many more could be added—from the older books as well as
from the new ones coming out each year. These are just samplings.

Don't feel that your child should read every book in a list, and
don't expect him to enjoy every book he does read. He won't. Always remember that reading in the home should be a joyous affair,
and that pressure to read can turn children—as well as adults—
against a particular book and against reading in general. As one
little girl said sadly, "I know it's a classic, but I just don't like it."
If your child has such a reaction to one of your favorites, accept
his honest admission and say, "Well, that's all right. Not all of us

like the same music or the same pictures or the same books. Sometimes we like them later on, and sometimes we never care for them. But there are lots of books, and so let's get on to something else."

One thing is certain. No matter how much we ourselves may like a book, it is fatal to force a child into reading it against his inclination. Leave books around the house, talk about them casually and briefly. Then, give the child plenty of leeway to explore on his own.

When your little girl reads a favorite book four or five times, or your thirteen- and fourteen-year-olds begin to reach into your shelves for adult books or ask you to bring adult books from the library, or your eighteen-year-old carries his dog-eared copy of a childhood favorite off to college with him, then you know the home and school exposure to good reading has taken effect. Your child is a reader. So blessings on the books, the home, and the schools that have made him so.

Long may he read!

May Hill Arbuthnot

THE NEWBERY MEDAL BOOKS

The Newbery Medal is awarded annually to the author of the year's "most distinguished contribution to American literature for children." The winning book is selected by a committee of the Children's Services Division of the American Library Association. The Newbery Medal, sponsored in 1922 by Frederic G. Melcher, an American publisher, was named in honor of John Newbery (1713-1767), an English publisher who first believed in children as discriminating patrons of books.

1922 Van Loon, Hendrik Willem. *The Story of Mankind.* Liveright.

1923 Lofting, Hugh. *The Voyages of Dr. Dolittle.* Stokes (Lippincott).

1924 Hawes, Charles Boardman. *The Dark Frigate.* Little.

1925 Finger, Charles J. *Tales from Silver Lands.* Doubleday.

1926 Chrisman, Arthur Bowie. *Shen of the Sea.* Dutton.

1927 James, Will. *Smoky, the Cowhorse.* Scribner.

1928 Mukerji, Dhan Gopal. *Gay-Neck.* Dutton.

1929 Kelly, Eric P. *The Trumpeter of Krakow.* Macmillan.

1930 Field, Rachel. *Hitty, Her First Hundred Years.* Macmillan.

1931 Coatsworth, Elizabeth. *The Cat Who Went to Heaven.* Macmillan.

1932 Armer, Laura Adams. *Waterless Mountain.* Longmans (McKay).

1933 Lewis, Elizabeth Foreman. *Young Fu of the Upper Yangtze.* Winston (Holt).

1934 Meigs, Cornelia. *Invincible Louisa.* Little.

1935 Shannon, Monica. *Dobry.* Viking.

1936 Brink, Carol Ryrie. *Caddie Woodlawn.* Macmillan.

1937 Sawyer, Ruth. *Roller Skates.* Viking.

1938 Seredy, Kate. *The White Stag.* Viking.

1939 Enright, Elizabeth. *Thimble Summer.* Rinehart (Holt).

1940 Daugherty, James. *Daniel Boone.* Viking.

1941 Sperry, Armstrong. *Call It Courage.* Macmillan.

1942 Edmonds, Walter D. *The Matchlock Gun.* Dodd.

1943 Gray, Elizabeth Janet. *Adam of the Road.* Viking.

1944 Forbes, Esther. *Johnny Tremain.* Houghton.

1945 Lawson, Robert. *Rabbit Hill*. Viking.

1946 Lenski, Lois. *Strawberry Girl*. Lippincott.

1947 Bailey, Carolyn Sherwin. *Miss Hickory*. Viking.

1948 Du Bois, William Pène. *The Twenty-One Balloons*. Viking.

1949 Henry, Marguerite. *King of the Wind*. Rand McNally.

1950 De Angeli, Marguerite. *The Door in the Wall*. Doubleday.

1951 Yates, Elizabeth. *Amos Fortune, Free Man*. Aladdin (Dutton).

1952 Estes, Eleanor. *Ginger Pye*. Harcourt.

1953 Clark, Ann Nolan. *Secret of the Andes*. Viking.

1954 Krumgold, Joseph. *. . . And Now Miguel*. Crowell.

1955 DeJong, Meindert. *The Wheel on the School*. Harper.

1956 Latham, Jean Lee. *Carry On, Mr. Bowditch*. Houghton.

1957 Sorensen, Virginia. *Miracles on Maple Hill*. Harcourt.

1958 Keith, Harold. *Rifles for Watie*. Crowell.

1959 Speare, Elizabeth George. *The Witch of Blackbird Pond*. Houghton.

1960 Krumgold, Joseph. *Onion John*. Crowell.

1961 O'Dell, Scott. *Island of the Blue Dolphins*. Houghton.

1962 Speare, Elizabeth George. *The Bronze Bow*. Houghton.

1963 L'Engle, Madeline. *A Wrinkle in Time*. Farrar, Straus.

1964 Neville, Emily. *It's Like This, Cat*. Harper.

1965 Wojciechowska, Maia. *Shadow of a Bull*. Atheneum.

1966 De Treviño, Elizabeth Borten. *I, Juan de Pareja*. Farrar, Straus.

1967 Hunt, Irene. *Up a Road Slowly*. Follett.

1968 Konigsburg, E. L. *From the Mixed-Up Files of Mrs. Basil E. Frankweiler*. Atheneum.

THE CALDECOTT MEDAL BOOKS

In 1938, Frederic G. Melcher established the Caldecott Medal—an award given annually to the illustrator of the "most distinguished American picture book for children." The winning book is selected by a committee of the Children's Services Division of the American Library Association. The medal is named in honor of Randolph Caldecott (1846-1886), an English artist whose illustrated books still delight today's children. See the two-volume *Caldecott's Collection of Pictures and Songs*, published by Frederick Warne & Company, Inc.

1938 Lathrop, Dorothy P. *Animals of the Bible*. Stokes (Lippincott).

1939 Handforth, Thomas. *Mei Li*. Doubleday.

1940 Aulaire, Ingri and Edgar Parin d'. *Abraham Lincoln*. Doubleday.

1941 Lawson, Robert. *They Were Strong and Good*. Viking.

1942 McCloskey, Robert. *Make Way for Ducklings*. Viking.

1943 Burton, Virginia Lee. *The Little House*. Houghton.

1944 Slobodkin, Louis, ill. *Many Moons*, by James Thurber. Harcourt.

1945 Jones, Elizabeth Orton, ill. *Prayer for a Child*, by Rachel Field. Macmillan.

1946 Petersham, Maud and Miska. *The Rooster Crows*. Macmillan.

1947 Weisgard, Leonard, ill. *The Little Island*, by Golden McDonald. Doubleday.

1948 Duvoisin, Roger, ill. *White Snow, Bright Snow*, by Alvin Tresselt. Lothrop.

1949 Hader, Berta and Elmer. *The Big Snow*. Macmillan.

1950 Politi, Leo. *Song of the Swallows*. Scribner.

1951 Milhous, Katherine. *The Egg Tree*. Scribner.

1952 Mordvinoff, Nicolas, ill. [Nicolas, pseud.]. *Finders Keepers*, by William Lipkind [Will, pseud.]. Harcourt.

1953 Ward, Lynd. *The Biggest Bear*. Houghton.

1954 Bemelmans, Ludwig. *Madeline's Rescue*. Viking.

1955 Brown, Marcia, ill. *Cinderella*, by Charles Perrault. Scribner.

1956 Rojankovsky, Feodor, ill. *Frog Went a-Courtin'*, retold by John Langstaff. Harcourt.

1957 Simont, Marc, ill. *A Tree Is Nice*, by Janice May Udry. Harper.

1958 McCloskey, Robert. *Time of Wonder*. Viking.

1959 Cooney, Barbara, ill. and adapter. *Chanticleer and the Fox*, by Geoffrey Chaucer. Crowell.

1960 Ets, Marie Hall. *Nine Days to Christmas*, by Marie Hall Ets and Aurora Labastida. Viking.

1961 Sidjakov, Nicolas, ill. *Baboushka and the Three Kings*, adapted from a Russian tale by Ruth Robbins. Parnassus.

1962 Brown, Marcia. *Once a Mouse*. Scribner.

1963 Keats, Ezra Jack. *The Snowy Day*. Viking.

1964 Sendak, Maurice. *Where the Wild Things Are*. Harper.

1965 Montresor, Beni, ill. *May I Bring a Friend?* by Beatrice Schenk de Regniers. Atheneum.

1966 Hogrogian, Nonny, ill. *Always Room for One More*, by Sorche Nic Leodhas. Holt.

1967 Ness, Evaline. *Sam, Bangs & Moonshine*. Holt.

1968 Emberley, Ed, ill. *Drummer Hoff*, by Barbara Emberley. Prentice-Hall.

PUBLISHERS AND PUBLISHERS' ADDRESSES

ABELARD. Abelard-Schuman Limited, 6 W. 57th St., New York, N.Y. 10019

ABINGDON. Abingdon Press, 201 8th Ave., S., Nashville, Tenn. 37202

AMERICAN ASSOCIATION FOR THE ADVANCEMENT OF SCI-ENCE. 1515 Massachusetts Ave., N.W., Washington, D.C. 20005

ARIEL BOOKS. (See Farrar.)

ASSOCIATION FOR CHILDHOOD EDUCATION. Association for Childhood Education International, 3615 Wisconsin Ave., N.W., Washington, D.C. 20016

ATHENEUM. Atheneum Publishers, 122 E. 42nd St., New York, N. Y. 10017

BANTAM BOOKS. Bantam Books, Inc., 271 Madison Ave., New York, N. Y. 10016

BERKLEY MEDALLION EDITION. Berkley Publishing Corporation, 200 Madison Ave., New York, N. Y. 10016

BOBBS. The Bobbs-Merrill Company, Inc., 4300 W. 62nd St., Indianapolis, Ind. 46206

R. R. BOWKER COMPANY. The R. R. Bowker Company, 1180 Ave. of the Americas, New York, N. Y. 10036

CASE WESTERN RESERVE UNIVERSITY PRESS. Press of Case Western Reserve Univ., 11000 Cedar Rd., Cleveland, Ohio 44106

CHILDRENS PRESS. Childrens Press, Inc., 1224 W. Van Buren St., Chicago, Ill. 60607

F. E. COMPTON. F. E. Compton & Company, 1000 N. Dearborn St., Chicago, Ill. 60610

CONSTABLE. (See Longmans Young Books.)

COWARD-MCCANN. Coward-McCann, Inc., 200 Madison Ave., New York, N. Y. 10016

CRITERION. Criterion Books, Inc., 6 W. 57th St., New York, N. Y. 10019

CROWELL. Thomas Y. Crowell Company, 201 Park Ave., S., New York, N. Y. 10003

CURTIS. Curtis Books, Div. of The Curtis Publishing Co., 641 Lexington Ave., New York, N. Y. 10022

DAY. The John Day Company, 62 W. 45th St., New York, N. Y. 10036

DELL. Dell Publishing Co., Inc., 750 3rd Ave., New York, N. Y. 10017

DIAL. The Dial Press, Inc., 750 3rd Ave., New York, N. Y. 10017

DODD. Dodd, Mead & Co., 79 Madison Ave., New York, N. Y. 10016

DOUBLEDAY. Doubleday & Company, Inc., 277 Park Ave., New York, N. Y. 10017

DOVER. Dover Publications, Inc., 180 Varick St., New York, N. Y. 10014

DUELL. Duell, Sloan & Pearce, 250 Park Ave., New York, N. Y. 10017

DUTTON. E. P. Dutton & Co., Inc., 201 Park Ave., S., New York, N. Y. 10003

ENCYCLOPAEDIA BRITANNICA. Encyclopaedia Britannica, Inc., 425 N. Michigan Ave., Chicago, Ill. 60611

FARRAR. Farrar, Straus & Giroux, Inc., 19 Union Sq., W., New York, N. Y. 10003

FIELD ENTERPRISES. Field Enterprises Educational Corporation, 510 Merchandise Mart Plaza, Chicago, Ill. 60654

FOLLETT. Follett Publishing Company, 1010 W. Washington Blvd., Chicago, Ill. 60607

GOLDEN PRESS. Golden Press, 850 3rd Ave., New York, N. Y. 10022

GROSSET. Grosset & Dunlap, Inc., 51 Madison Ave., New York, N. Y. 10010

HARCOURT. Harcourt, Brace & World, Inc., 757 3rd Ave., New York, N. Y. 10017

HARPER. Harper & Row, Publishers, 49 E. 33rd St., New York, N. Y. 10016

HARVEY HOUSE. Harvey House, Inc., Publishers, 5 S. Buckhout St., Irvington-on-Hudson, N. Y. 10533

HERITAGE. Heritage Press, 595 Madison Ave., New York, N. Y. 10022

HILL & WANG. Hill & Wang, Inc., 141 5th Ave., New York, N. Y. 10010

HOLIDAY. Holiday House, Inc., 18 E. 56th St., New York, N. Y. 10022

HOLT. Holt, Rinehart & Winston, Inc., 383 Madison Ave., New York, N. Y. 10017

HORN BOOK. Horn Book, Inc., 585 Boylston St., Boston, Mass. 02116

HOUGHTON. Houghton Mifflin Company, 2 Park St., Boston, Mass. 02107

KNOPF. Alfred A. Knopf, Inc., 501 Madison Ave., New York, N. Y. 10022

LIPPINCOTT. J. B. Lippincott Co., E. Washington Sq., Philadelphia, Pa. 19105

LITTLE. Little, Brown and Company, 34 Beacon St., Boston, Mass. 02106

LIVERIGHT. Liveright Publishing Corp., 386 Park Ave., S., New York, N. Y. 10016

LONGMANS. (See McKay.)

LONGMANS YOUNG BOOKS. Longmans Young Books Ltd., 48 Grosvenor Street, London W.1., England

LOTHROP. Lothrop, Lee & Shepard Co., Inc., 381 Park Ave., S., New York, N. Y. 10016

MCGRAW. McGraw-Hill Book Company, 330 W. 42nd St., New York, N. Y. 10036

MCKAY. David McKay Co., Inc., 750 3rd Ave., New York, N. Y. 10017

MACMILLAN. The Macmillan Company, Publishers, 866 3rd Ave., New York, N. Y. 10022

G. & C. MERRIAM. G. & C. Merriam Co., 47 Federal St., Springfield, Mass. 01101

MORROW. William Morrow & Company, Inc., 425 Park Ave., S., New York, N. Y. 10016

NATIONAL COUNCIL FOR THE SOCIAL STUDIES. The National Council for the Social Studies, National Education Association, 1201 16th St., N.W., Washington, D.C. 20036

NATIONAL COUNCIL OF TEACHERS OF ENGLISH. National Council of Teachers of English, 508 S. 6th St., Champaign, Ill. 61820

NEW YORK LIBRARY ASSOCIATION. Children's and Young Adults' Services Section, New York Public Library, Public Relations Office, 5th Ave. & 42nd St., New York, N. Y. 10018

NORTON. W. W. Norton & Company, Inc., 55 5th Ave., New York, N. Y. 10003

OHIO STATE UNIVERSITY. Ohio State University Press, Hitchcock Hall, Rm. 316, 2070 Neil Ave., Columbus, Ohio 43210

OXFORD. Oxford University Press, Inc., 200 Madison Ave., New York, N. Y. 10016

PANTHEON. Pantheon Books, Inc., 437 Madison Ave., New York, N. Y. 10022

PARNASSUS. Parnassus Press, 2422 Ashby Ave., Berkeley, Calif. 94705

PHILLIPS, S. G. (See Hill & Wang.)

PHOENIX BOOKS. The University of Chicago Press, 5750 Ellis Ave., Chicago, Ill. 60637

POCKET BOOKS. 630 5th Ave., New York, N. Y. 10020

PRENTICE. Prentice-Hall, Inc., Englewood Cliffs, N. J. 07632

PUTNAM. G. P. Putnam's Sons, 200 Madison Ave., New York, N. Y. 10016

RAND MCNALLY. Rand McNally & Co., 8255 Central Park Ave., Skokie, Ill. Address mail to Box 7600, Chicago, Ill. 60680

RANDOM HOUSE. Random House, Inc., 457 Madison Ave., New York, N. Y. 10022

REILLY & LEE. The Reilly & Lee Co., 114 W. Illinois St., Chicago, Ill. 60610

SCOTT. Scott, Foresman and Company, 1900 E. Lake Ave., Glenview, Ill. 60025

W. R. SCOTT. William R. Scott, Inc., 333 Ave. of the Americas, New York, N. Y. 10014

SCRIBNER. Charles Scribner's Sons, 597 5th Ave., New York, N. Y. 10017

SEABURY. The Seabury Press, Inc., 815 Second Ave., New York, N. Y. 10017

SENTRY EDITIONS. (Imprint of Houghton Mifflin Co.)

SIGNET CLASSICS. The New American Library, Inc., 1301 Ave. of the Americas, New York, N. Y. 10019

SIMON & SCHUSTER. Simon & Schuster, Inc., 630 5th Ave., New York, N. Y. 10020

TIME. Time Incorporated, Book Division, Time & Life Building, Rockefeller Center, New York, N. Y. 10020

VANGUARD. Vanguard Press, Inc., 424 Madison Ave., New York, N. Y. 10017

VIKING. The Viking Press, Inc., 625 Madison Ave., New York, N. Y. 10022

WALCK. Henry Z. Walck, Inc., 19 Union Sq., W., New York, N. Y. 10003

WARNE. Frederick Warne & Company, Inc., 101 5th Ave., New York, N. Y. 10003

WASHINGTON SQUARE PRESS. Washington Square Press, 630 5th Ave., New York, N. Y. 10020

WATTS. Franklin Watts, Inc., 575 Lexington Ave., New York, N. Y. 10022

DAVID WHITE. David White Company, 60 E. 55th St., New York, N. Y. 10022

WHITMAN. Albert Whitman & Co., 560 W. Lake St., Chicago, Ill. 60606

WHITTLESEY HOUSE. (See McGraw.)

WINSTON. (See Holt.)

WORLD. The World Publishing Company, 2231 W. 110th St., Cleveland, Ohio 44102

INDEX

The entries in this index have been alphabetized letter-by-letter (dictionary style).

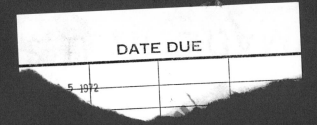